BARBAROSSA

Полный текст документа о подготовке Германии к нападению на СССР

("План Барбаросса")

НЮРНБЕРГ, 25 ноября. (ТАСС). На нюрнбергском процессе в распоряжении обвинения имеется документ о подготовке Германии к войне против СССР, называемый «планом Барбаросса». Документ гласит:

«Германские вооруженные силы должны быть готовы победить Советскую Россию в результате быстрой кампании, даже до окончания войны против Англии (план Барбаросса). Армия должна использовать для этой цели все находящиеся в ее распоряжении силы, за исключением тех, которые необходимы для защиты оккупированных территорий от неожиданностей. Главная задача воздушных сил заключается в том, чтобы использовать в восточной кампании такие большие силы для помощи наземным войскам, чтобы было обеспечено быстрое развитие наземных операций. Повреждения, наносимые вражеской авиацией восточно-немецкой территории, должны быть наименьшими. Эта концентрация войск на Востоке может быть лимитирована только необходимостью достаточной защиты территорий для боевых операций и производства вооружений, находящихся под нашим контролем, от рейда врага. Атаки против Великобритании, и особенно ее линий снабжения, не должны совершенно прекратиться. Главные операции военно-морского флота должны оставаться направленными против Англии, даже во время восточной кампании. Я прикажу начать наступление на Советскую Россию, если это необходимо, за 8 недель до соответствующей даты начала операций. Приготовления для операций, которые потребуют более длительной подготовки, если они уже не сделаны, должны начаться теперь же и должны быть завершены не позже, чем к 15 мая 1941 года. Решающее значение должно быть придано тому, чтобы наши намерения наступления не были распознаны. Приготовления верховного командования должны быть сделаны на следующем базисе:

I. Общие намерения

Масса русской армии, собранная в Западной России, должна быть уничтожена смелыми операциями: танковые клинья должны быть вбиты глубоко вперед. Отступление боеспособных войск на широкие просторы русской территории должно быть предотвращено. Быстрым преследованием должна быть достигнута линия, от которой русские воздушные силы не будут в состоянии совершать налеты на имперскую территорию Германии. Конечной целью операций является создание защитительного барьера против Азиатской России на линии река Волга—Архангельск. Таким образом, если необходимо, последний индустриальный район в Уральских горах может быть уничтожен воздушными силами. Балтийский флот в ходе этих операций быстро потеряет свои базы, становясь, таким образом, не способным продолжать борьбу. Эффективное выступление русских воздушных сил должно быть предотвращено мощными ударами в самом начале операций.

II. Возможные союзники и их задачи

1) На флангах наших операций можно рассчитывать на активное участие в войне против Советской России Румынии и Финляндии. В соответствии с этим время верховное командование вооруженных сил поведет переговоры и установит порядок, в котором вооруженные силы обеих стран будут подчинены германским приказам в соответствии с этими операциями.

2) Задачей Румынии в сотрудничестве с немецкими войсками будет сковать стоящие против нее силы противника. Позже она должна оказать помощь в тыловых районах.

3) Финляндия должна прикрывать наступление немецкой группы «Север» (группа 19-я), идущей из Норвегии. Финляндия будет сотрудничать с этими войсками. Кроме того, Финляндия будет ответственна за уничтожение Ханко.

4) Можно рассчитывать на использование шведских железных и шоссейных дорог для наступления немецкой группы «Север», во всяком случае с начала боевых операций.

III. Оперативные планы

Армия. (Утверждение намерений, представленных мне). Оперативное пространство разделяется Припятьскими болотами на северную и южную части. Центр наступления должен быть подготовлен в северной части этого пространства. Для этого сектора должны быть предоставлены две армейские группы. Южная из этих групп — центр всей линии фронта — должна наступать с особенно сильными танковыми и механизированными соединениями из района вокруг и севернее Варшавы и разгромить силы врага в Белоруссии. Этим должен быть создан базис для поворота сильнейших частей механизированных соединений на север. Их задачей должно быть в сотрудничестве с северной армейской группой, оперирующей из Восточной Пруссии в общем направлении на Ленинград, уничтожить силы врага, дерущиеся в Прибалтике. Эта задача исключительной важности и срочности; за ней должен последовать захват Ленинграда и Кронштадта; только после захвата этих об'ектов наступление должно быть направлено на Москву — важный центр коммуникаций и военной промышленности. Только неожиданно быстрое крушение русской силы сопротивления может оправдать наше нацеливание на об'екта одновременно.

Охрана Норвегии есть и остается наиважнейшей задачей группы 19 даже в течение восточной кампании. Излишние войска должны быть использованы на севере (горный корпус); прежде всего для захвата района Петсамо с его железорудными копями и для овладения дорогой к Ледовитому океану. Затем вместе с финскими войсками они могут нажимать в направлении мурманской железной дороги и пересечь линию снабжения в районе Мурманска. Будет ли такая операция осуществлена более сильными немецкими войсками (2—3 дивизии) из района Рованиеми и южнее его, зависит от того, согласится ли Швеция предоставить свои железные дороги в наше распоряжение для этого наступления. Основной массе финской армии будет дана задача сковать наибольшие русские силы, атакуя западнее или по обе стороны озера Ладога, и захватить Ханко. Это должно быть сделано в соответствии с продвижением германского северного фланга.

Армейская группа, оперирующая южнее Припятьских болот, должна сконцентрировать свои главные усилия в районе Люблин в общем направлении на Киев с целью нанести быстрый удар сильными бронетанковыми силами в глубокий фланг и тыл русских войск и повернуть их фланг на линии реки Днепр. Немецко-румынская армейская группа должна иметь задачи:

а) прикрыть румынскую территорию и южный фланг всей операции;

б) приковать войска противника в течение наступления северного крыла армейской группы «Юг» и быстрым преследованием предотвратить организованный отход русских войск через Днестр в соответствии с развитием ситуации.

При выполнении этой задачи эти войска получат помощь от авиации. На севере — быстрое достижение Москвы. Захват этого города означает решающий политический и экономический успех и, кроме того, уничтожение наиболее важного узла дорог.

Воздушные силы. Их задачей будет затруднить и уничтожить эффективность русских воздушных сил в такой степени, как только будет возможно, и оказать помощь армии в ее операциях на участках ее главных усилий: это будет, прежде всего, необходимо на фронте центральной армейской группы и на фланге армейской группы, которая выполняет задачу главного наступления. Русские железные дороги должны перерезаться в соответствии с их важностью для операций. Наиболее важные железнодорожные сооружения (речные переправы) должны быть захвачены смелым использованием парашютных и воздушных войск. Военная промышленность не должна подвергаться атакам в течение главной операции, дабы все силы были собраны против вражеских воздушных сил и для помощи армии. Только после окончания оперативных передвижений такие операции могут быть сконцентрированы главным образом против Уральского горного района.

Военно-морские силы. В течение операции против Советской России морской флот будет иметь задачу защищать наш собственный берег и предотвратить прорыв вражеского морского флота из Балтики. Когда русский достигнут Ленинград, русский Балтийский флот будет лишен его последней базы и окажется в беспомощном положении. До тех пор надо избегать крупных операций на море. После уничтожения русского флота будет важно обеспечить морское сообщение в Балтийском море, особенно снабжение через море северного крыла армии (очищение от мин).

IV. Все приказы, которые будут изданы главнокомандующим в соответствии с этой инструкцией, должны быть составлены в таких выражениях, чтобы они могли быть приняты, как меры предосторожности на случай, если Россия изменит свою теперешнюю позицию в отношении нас. Число офицеров, привлеченных для первоначальных приготовлений, должно быть низвозможно ограничено. Новые люди, привлечение которых необходимо, должны быть привлечены как можно позже и должны быть проинструктированы только в рамках их ограниченных задач. Иначе имеется опасность возникновения серьезных политических и военных неудобств в результате раскрытия наших приготовлений, время исполнения которых еще не назначено.

V. Я ожидаю устных докладов главнокомандующих об их намерениях, основанных на этих инструкциях. О приготовлениях, планируемых всеми родами войск, а также о ходе их должно докладываться мне через верховное командование.

Документ подписан Гитлером. Кроме того, поставлены инициалы Иодля, Кейтеля, Варлимонта и еще одного офицера.

Text of Directive No. 21, 'Operation Barbarossa', 18 December 1941.

BARBAROSSA

The Axis and the Allies

Edited by
John Erickson and David Dilks

EDINBURGH UNIVERSITY PRESS

© The Contributors, 1994
© Translations of Chapters 4, 7, and 11, Ljubica Erickson

Edinburgh University Press Ltd
22 George Square, Edinburgh

Typeset in Monotype Sabon
by BPC-AUP Glasgow Ltd, and
printed and bound in Great Britain by
The University Press, Cambridge

A CIP record for this book is available from the British Library

ISBN 0 7486 0504 5

Contents

Preface   John Erickson and David Dilks   vii
Acknowledgements   x
Foreword   Rhodri Jeffreys-Jones   xi

Part 1: Germany Turns East, 1939–1941
              Introduction   3
Chapter 1   Ribbentrop and The Soviet Union, 1937–1941   7
              Geoffrey T. Waddington
Chapter 2   The Yugoslav *Coup d'État*, 27 March 1941   34
              Dušan Biber
Chapter 3   British Intelligence and Barbarossa   43
              H. F. Hinsley
Chapter 4   The German Attack, the Soviet Response,   76
              Sunday, 22 June 1941
              Dmitri Volkogonov

Part 2: Strained Alliances, Flawed Strategies
              Introduction   97
Chapter 5   An Alliance of Sorts   101
              Allied Strategy in the Wake of Barbarossa
              Gabriel Gorodetsky
Chapter 6   Barbarossa and the Soviet Leadership   123
              A Recollection
              Stepan A. Mikoyan
Chapter 7   The Collapse of Stalin's Diplomacy and Strategy   134
              Andreï Mertsalov
Chapter 8   The Imperial Japanese Navy and the North–South   150
              Dilemma
              John Chapman
Chapter 9   Moscow 1941   207
              The Turning-Point
              Klaus Reinhardt

Part 3: Conflict, Compromise, Cost

Introduction   227

Chapter 10   The Brutalisation of Warfare, Nazi Crimes   229
              and the *Wehrmacht*
              Klaus-Jürgen Müller

Chapter 11   The Hidden Dimension   238
              Wartime Collaboration in the Soviet Union
              Sergei Kudryashov

Chapter 12   Soviet War Losses   255
              Calculations and Controversies
              John Erickson

Notes on the Contributors   278
Index   280

Preface

This book is not unlike Topsy, since in many respects 'it just grow'd'. It had its distant origins in a conference held in Leeds in June 1991, organised by the Institute for International Studies in the University of Leeds in conjunction with the British National Committee for the Second World War. The theme was Operation *Barbarossa*, the Soviet Union, Germany and World War; the occasion the presentation of some nineteen papers on the military, diplomatic, intelligence and even the 'psycho-political' aspects of the German invasion of the Soviet Union. The conference also examined the Soviet response – or the lack of it – and the crisis which speedily beset alliances and strategies. In what became the greatest land campaign in the history of the world, with all its strategic complexities and military variations, it was imperative to take account of the calamity which this gigantic encounter produced in human terms, the scale of the losses, the unimaginable excesses generated by the barbarisation of the warfare in the east, the deviousness and dilemmas of collaboration, not to mention the quest for slave labour.

To bring this assembly of scholars, specialists, diplomats and senior soldiers from the United Kingdom, the Federal Republic of Germany, the Soviet Union, Belgium, Israel and Yugoslavia together would have been impossible without help on a substantial scale. Such assistance was generously forthcoming from individuals – including Mr J. Paul Getty jun., Prince Vassiltchikov and Mr H. H. Nathaniel – and from organisations – the Foreign and Commonwealth Office, the British Council, Anglo-Soviet Shipping, Barclays Bank, British Petroleum, the Koeppler Trust, the British Academy, the Economic and Social Research Council and the University of Leeds itself.

While this present work grew largely out of the 1991 conference, it should not be construed as a 'conference report'. It is, as a sub-title might suggest, a work combining retrospect with recollection, not least on the part of those whose lives were scorched by the grim realities of the war itself. Not that this excludes an element of revision; indeed that is the express purpose of most of these chapters but without any excess of ideological rigour or commitment.

A number of chapters printed here were presented in a rather different form at the conference itself, and have been revised as new source material became available or as recollection took precedence. Others have been specially written as this inquiry widened, and dialogue, discussion and debate continued for many months. There is also the thread of the difference in generations, ranging from the impassioned view of a battle-hardened veteran of the fearsome encounters of Moscow, Stalingrad and Kursk – more than ever painfully aware of what calamity Stalin and Stalinism brought down on the heads of the Soviet people – to the researches of younger Russians, able to peer into hitherto inaccessible archives, uncovering the minutiae of wartime collaboration – some commitments to the enemy side plainly sordid, self-seeking; others simply an inescapable response to the exigencies of day-to-day life under enemy occupation. What in wartime and in the post-war period was damned as heinous treason is now being hailed in some of its manifestations by certain quarters as laudable rebellion, transfigured from dereliction of duty or abandonment of obligation into a political crusade abhorring the norms and the abnormalities of the Stalinist state. Yet all is submerged in the endless bestial killings and the vast premeditated degradation from which there is no escape even at a distance of half a century, to account for which continues to torment scholars and ignite political passions – whether out of shame, condemnation or exculpation.

The compilation of losses continues, a doleful task which has lost none of its power to shock and disturb with its findings. Even now the whole enterprise is not free of political manipulation, as if some grotesque bargain might be struck with the mountains of the dead over the forms and terms of their annihilation, all to heap yet further blame on the leaders and their systems or else to evade responsibility.

Strategies all too soon became tattered, torn apart and trampled down by battlefield realities, by time, distance and inconsistencies. Behind the wartime screen of diplomatic formulae and propagandistic flourishes, 'Big Three' alliance politics were strained affairs barely concealing fundamental antipathies and animosities, at best momentarily smothering them in the interests of bargaining for or buying the immediate prospect of survival and possibly nurturing hopes for a better post-war world. As the German army's *Blitzkrieg* first slithered in autumnal mud and was then gripped in a Muscovite winter, Japan played its national cards cannily enough, widening the war at a time and place of its own choosing, playing havoc with pretensions to global strategic co-ordination on the part of the Axis powers, adding only to the holocaust.

Of revision there is much which is largely subliminal. This is no attempt to overturn history outright. Adolf Hitler was bent on the destruction of

Russia. Stalin, in attempting to outmanoeuvre Hitler, was catastrophically outplayed, for which the people of the Soviet Union paid an appalling price in blood and treasure. A war of extermination was begun, to be continued almost mindlessly. Human misery grew to apocalyptic proportions, the bitter memories and harsh consequences of which have to this day been neither eased nor fully erased.

The young and the old have combined here to present research, recollection and reflection on this tempest in world affairs.

John Erickson   David Dilks
Defence Studies   Vice-Chancellor
The University of Edinburgh   The University of Hull

Acknowledgements

The preparation of this book owes everything in its essentials to the prodigious efforts of three people. Rita Winter's speedy and deft copy-editing considerably enhanced the value and the appearance of the chapters. Ljubica Erickson, in addition to sustaining an intensive international correspondence, undertook the formidable task of translating and elucidating complex Russian texts. Penny Clarke of Edinburgh University Press organised its collation and passage to the presses. The contributors all worked unstintingly to provide additional material and clarification, but a special acknowledgement is due to Professor John Chapman for making available his research derived from Japanese materials, and to Lieutenant-General Dr Klaus Reinhardt, commander of the *Bundeswehr* III Corps, who amidst most onerous duties generously agreed to prepare a special study of the battle of Moscow, combining his military expertise with his extensive archival research. Dr Stane Mrvič of the Museum of Contemporary History in Ljubljana very kindly located and supplied rare photographs dealing with the demonstrations in Belgrade in March 1941.

Foreword

RHODRI JEFFREYS-JONES

Series Editor: Perspectives in Intelligence History

Two surprise attacks, Germany's on Russia in June 1941 and Japan's at Pearl Harbor just over five months later, transformed an essentially European war into a worldwide conflict. It turned out that the aggressors had over-stretched themselves, and the attacks eventually contributed to the defeat of the Axis powers. In 1941, however, they appeared to be disasters for the defending nations. Critics then and since have asked how the Soviet Union and the United States could have been caught off guard, given the known aggressive proclivities of their attackers. According to one interpretation, Stalin and Roosevelt were ill-prepared because they were ill-informed. For this reason, the intelligence dimensions of the two attacks have prompted discussion, controversy, and, all too often, speculation of a sensational character.

Over the last two decades, a dedicated group of historians has introduced more scholarly standards to the study of intelligence. One of the initiators of this volume, David Dilks, encouraged this development in 1984, when he co-edited, with Christopher Andrew, *The Missing Dimension: Governments and Intelligence Communities in the Twentieth Century*, a book that gave the new discourse a widely-used catch-phrase. Other historians, notably Donald Cameron Watt, pushed forward the frontiers of intelligence history, while stressing the axiom that 'the missing dimension' should be studied in a wide context. With the publication of *Barbarossa*, its editors signal their implicit agreement with the proposition that such episodes demand a broad contextual approach. In the following pages, while Harry Hinsley and Dmitri Volkogonev do focus on its intelligence dimension, the assault on Russia is placed in a wide military and strategic framework.

The guiding hand of the great historian of the Red Army, co-editor John Erickson, is evident in this book's emphasis on multi-lingual primary evidence. This is important, for the opening of the Soviet archives is potentially perilous, with many pitfalls awaiting the credulous and/or linguistically handicapped historian. In *Barbarossa*, we are protected from such pitfalls not only by the erudition of John Erickson and Ljubica Erickson, but also by two further factors – the distinction and seniority of most of the contributors, and their diversity of perspective and opinion.

Yet, while the viewpoint in this book is not monolithic, it is still in some respects loosely unified by an approach that was also evident in two earlier volumes in 'Perspectives in Intelligence History', the series in which *Barbarossa* appears. Rhodri Jeffreys-Jones and Andrew Lownie, eds, *North American Spies* (1992) and Sallie Pisani, *The CIA and the Marshall Plan* (1992) both challenged prevailing interpretations of *American* history. The reader will find in *Barbarossa* a refreshingly revisionist approach to contemporary *European* history.

Part 1
Germany Turns East, 1939–1941

Introduction

After fifty years and more, the rolling thunder which Adolf Hitler unleashed with his massive attack on the Soviet Union on 22 June 1941 continues to reverberate throughout the world. Though both warring regimes are now extinct, the Nazi and Stalinist state systems alike, the political and social after-shocks of this collision endure and continue to make themselves felt. During the Cold War historical analysis was transformed into an ideological duel, triggering off a sustained Soviet campaign against Western 'falsifiers'. While there have been major – some might say insuperable – problems in dealing with Soviet history, immured in secrecy and guarded by the praetorian sentries of the Communist Party, recent access to the archives and the easing of the ideological grip have changed perception and understanding. Two prime examples, furnished by Colonel-General Dmitri Volkogonov and Dr Sergei Kudryashov, are included in this book.

The ghost of Frederick Barbarossa is abroad once more, though not in the fiery form with which his name was associated in June 1941. But his is not the only ghost which haunts the battlefield. An accompanying wraith has emerged, showing remarkable resilience: the avowal that the German attack on the Soviet Union was a justifiable 'preventive war', a theme which first made its appearance at the time of the German attack and which might well have been understood as an inevitable part of wartime propaganda and the buttressing of morale, steeling the will of the German soldier for what was to come. What this does not dispose of – either at the time or in retrospect – is Hitler's unqualified decision to attack, taken well before the Soviet build-up on the western frontiers attracted the attention of the German military commander. For operational purposes, to be able to profit from falling on an unsuspecting enemy, the analysis that Soviet dispositions were *'rein defensiv'* was more than a comforting thought; for propaganda purposes, to portray the Bolshevik military monster as about to strike was another matter. Here was the 'threat' which grew greater the longer it matured retrospectively and experienced substantial elaboration.

The approach which has been adopted here is less concerned with troop movements, deployments and operational plans than with the implications

of the cycle of decision, information and ambiguity (or indeed any per-
mutation of these constituents). The decision aspect – decision-making and
decision-taking – appears to be relatively amenable to careful analysis.
Equally, the information dimension (both by volume and by type) is increasingly identifiable. The real problem is posed by ambiguity, whether inherent
or perceived. Indeed, there is some difficulty in distinguishing between those
two categories, where perceived ambiguity – even when little or none
existed – was politically or personally convenient. It is not that Stalin lacked
information of German intentions and preparations: his desk was heaped
with reports, many of them highly detailed. A certain German generosity
with information was designed to serve a major deception plan. None,
however, told Stalin what he really wished to know: would Hitler choose
not to attack, out of faithful adherence to the Nazi – Soviet non-aggression
Pact; would sheer self-interest inhibit Hitler from attacking Russia; or would
Hitler, who was a rational actor, be calculating enough to avoid a war on
two fronts? Of Stalin's convictions none was stronger than his belief that to
declare a general mobilisation was the equivalent of an act of war. On the
other hand, there was sufficient ambiguity in much of this information for
Stalin to be reasonably convinced that the attack might not materialise and
could be 'negotiated away'. Europe, the Far East and the United States were
awash with 'information'. If later in the war Prime Minister Churchill,
seeking to cloak preparations for the Second Front, proposed a 'bodyguard'
of lies (deception) to hide the truth, in 1941 Hitler reversed that process,
using the screen of truth to protect an invaluable mass of lies. The truth was
uttered, selectively, precisely, with such exactitude that it could only be
construed ambiguously, as it was designed to be! Only the lies remained
plausible and credible.

   The disaster, for such it was, was manufactured out of mismanaged information. Little credence was paid to the evidence of Hitler's unqualified
decision to attack, long in its political and emotional gestation. In the tor-
tuous debate over German intentions few British officials in the Foreign
Office were of a mind to turn up *Mein Kampf*. Stalin culled the ambiguities,
brooded on them and from them invented a certainty all of his own. One of
these was a British *provokatsiya* designed to embroil him in a war with
Germany, a war which he believed he could at least defer and at best unleash
at a time of his own choosing. One aspect of this miasmic business which
would bear yet more intensive examination is the British handling of the
flight of Rudolf Hess – the Führer's deputy – to Scotland in May 1941, the
Hess affair and its exploitation – or its 'explanation', specially concocted
for consumption in Moscow. Much remains to be clarified about this

circumstance and the degree to which it might have been of decisive importance in working on Stalin's preconceptions. The 'Hess affair' troubled Stalin
for many a year.

Part One opens with an examination of the 'decision – information ambiguity' matrix of Germany's turn to the east, first in a diplomatic mode and
latterly in the phase leading to the military attack. It closes with the monstrous situation depicted by Colonel-General Volkogonov of the price which
had to be paid for Stalin's 'certainty'; of a warfare state without a functioning
war machine, caught up in an unimaginable catastrophe, where Stalin clung
obsessively, criminally to the ambiguity that this was not war, could not be
war, only arguably yet one more snaking tendril of a 'provocation'.

Chapter 1

Ribbentrop and the Soviet Union, 1937–1941

GEOFFREY T. WADDINGTON

In August 1965 Valentin Berezhkov, the interpreter in the Soviet embassy in Berlin at the time of the German attack on the USSR, added an illuminating footnote to the circumstances surrounding the launching of *Unternehmen Barbarossa*. Berezhkov had accompanied his ambassador, Vladimir Dekanozov, to the Wilhelmstrasse in the early hours of 22 June 1941 and had witnessed the interview during which the foreign minister of the Third Reich, Joachim von Ribbentrop, had announced that in view of Soviet hostility and provocations, Germany had been forced to respond with military countermeasures. In short, after almost two years of fruitful collaboration with the USSR, Germany had declared war. According to Berezhkov, just as the Soviet diplomats were leaving the room Ribbentrop hurried after them, protesting that he personally was opposed to the Führer's decision, that he had argued against it and that he considered it an act of madness (*Wahnsinn*). However, he had been unable to make any impression; Hitler's determination was unshakeable. 'Make it known in Moscow', pleaded the German Foreign Minister, 'that I was against this invasion.'[1] Writing in his cell at Nuremberg some five years later, Ribbentrop himself recalled the events of that fateful summer. In one of the few credible passages of his otherwise desultory memoirs, Ribbentrop declared that the German attack on the USSR represented the breakdown of a policy which had been pursued at his suggestion since 1939, the aim of which was to have been a 'lasting settlement between the two great empires'.[2]

The Nazi–Soviet Pact of August 1939 was without doubt Ribbentrop's greatest diplomatic triumph. It was intended to be the crowning feature of an anti-British political *Konzeption* which he had been developing since the winter of 1937.[3] During his disastrous term as German ambassador in London, Ribbentrop had become convinced that no basis existed for the kind of Anglo-German agreement envisaged by Hitler. The British, he believed, were not only opposed to the Führer's schemes for the German domination of the Continent, but would fight to prevent it, if they felt strong enough to do so. By December 1937 Great Britain was, in Ribbentrop's view, Germany's 'most dangerous enemy', and the most pressing requirement of German foreign policy was the transformation of the Anti-Comintern Pact into a tripartite military alliance in order to confront the British with a stark choice: acquiesce over Germany's territorial expansion, or risk the very existence of the British empire, should they attempt to oppose it.[4] Ribbentrop then began to urge upon Hitler an alternative political strategy which by implication counted upon at least Soviet neutrality in what the embittered Ambassador considered 'the inevitable conflict with the western powers'.[5]

The views put forward by Ribbentrop at the close of his ambassadorship in London differed markedly from those held by Hitler at the time, although even the Chancellor himself had gradually come to despair of the chances of an alliance between Britain and Germany.[6] At the Hossbach Conference the Führer had expatiated upon British weakness and had discounted the possibility of British intervention if Germany moved against Czechoslovakia. Moreover, he had emphasised once again the *idée fixe* which had dominated his thoughts since the mid-1920s and around which all other calculations in the field of foreign policy essentially revolved: the conquest of *Lebensraum* in the East.[7] Certainly there had been differences between Hitler and Ribbentrop before – over policy towards France in 1933,[8] over the colonial question,[9] and evidently over the initial stages of the Italo-German *rapprochement*[10] – but these had generally been resolved as Ribbentrop allowed himself to be convinced of the Führer's 'genius' and adapted his own views accordingly. However, the divergence of opinion over Britain and Russia was more fundamental, and was to last at least until the launching of *Barbarossa*, if not beyond. The root cause was essentially a difference of *Weltanschauungen*, for although Ribbentrop shared Hitler's antipathy towards Bolshevism, he was not the prisoner of an inflexible ideological framework of the kind which fuelled the Führer's drive to attack the USSR, exterminate or enslave the indigenous population and colonise European Russia for future generations of Germans. Indeed, several eminent West German scholars have noted that Ribbentrop's foreign policy objectives corresponded far more to traditional German goals – hegemony in central Europe, political and economic penetration of south-eastern Europe and the acquisition of colonies overseas – than to Hitler's dream of a continental empire stretching from Alsace-Lorraine to the Urals.[11] Thus, whereas for the Führer the Soviet Union was nothing more than a target for German expansion, for Ribbentrop it remained a power factor which could be conspired against, ignored or courted according to the dictates of *Realpolitik*.

It is not suggested here that Ribbentrop was an enthusiastic advocate of Russo-German collaboration at any time before 1937; only that, unlike Hitler, his lack of ideological constraints meant that he could easily *become* one.

The first indication that Ribbentrop was considering some form of co-operation with the Soviet Union against Great Britain reached Group-Captain Malcolm Christie in the spring of 1937. Christie had formerly been British Air Attaché in Berlin and disposed of excellent contacts in German military and diplomatic circles. According to Fritz Hesse, a London correspondent of the *Deutsches Nachrichten Büro*, Ribbentrop had developed an elaborate plan which envisaged German mediation in the Sino-Japanese conflict, a settlement of differences between Tokyo and Moscow, the elimination of Jewish influence in the USSR and the abolition of the Comintern. These were the necessary conditions under which the four 'fascist states'– Germany, Russia, Japan and China – could then collaborate together at the expense of the British empire. By this arrangement Germany would acquire a free hand in Africa; Japan would concentrate upon Malaya and Australia; India would fall to Russia; and China would receive Hong Kong.[12] As fantastic as this scheme appears, it may well be that Ribbentrop's disillusionment with his mission in London was already beginning to lead him down a path radically different to that of Hitler's projected Anglo-German *Idealbündnis*. Significantly, the desire for German expansion in Africa, foreshadowed in this unlikely constellation of powers, reflected Ribbentrop's own preference for the acquisition of a colonial empire. Moreover, the spheres of influence and the general direction of anti-British activity envisaged for Japan and the USSR corresponded in all essentials to those proposed by Ribbentrop to Molotov in November 1940.[13]

Although Ribbentrop had been careful not to make any concrete suggestions on future policy towards Russia in his final reports from London, his very silence on the subject is significant in itself. For years he had attempted to convince the British that Bolshevism was the greatest danger to civilisation, a cancer in the heart of Europe which made imperative the closest possible degree of Anglo-German collaboration. Indeed, such were Ribbentrop's exertions in the cause of anti-Bolshevism that Sir Nevile Henderson was later to reflect that he might have been able to see some humour in the German–Soviet non-aggression pact, 'with Ribbentrop, the anti-Comintern prophet going to sign it at Moscow', if it were not so 'potentially and terribly dangerous'.[14] However, away from what he himself described as the overwhelming influence of the Führer,[15] Ribbentrop appears to have been rather more candid in his assessments of the possible role of the USSR in German foreign policy calculations. For example, Fritz Wiedemann recalled that even before his appointment as Reich Foreign Minister, Ribbentrop had been heard to express ideas on German–Soviet relations which were far more reasonable than those espoused by Hitler.[16] Similarly, in December 1939 Ribbentrop claimed to have discussed with Japanese diplomats the possibility of an adjustment of relations between Germany, Japan and Russia during his term as ambassador in London, while the following November he told Molotov that he had advocated a Soviet–Japanese reconciliation since the early 1930s.[17] While at least the latter of these claims must be assessed with due scepticism, there were certainly indications during 1938 that Ribbentrop was seriously contemplating an adjustment of German–Soviet relations. Shortly after his appointment as Foreign Minister, Ribbentrop outlined in greater detail how his thoughts were developing. During conversations in the early spring of 1938 with the new state secretary at the Wilhelmstrasse, Ernst von Weizsäcker, the Nazi Foreign Minister betrayed his unyielding hostility towards the British and argued that whereas Russia should continue to be regarded as the official enemy, in reality everything was to be directed against Great Britain.[18] Moreover, the failure of attempts to transform the Anti-Comintern pact into a tripartite military alliance led to the Soviet Union assuming more importance in Ribbentrop's calculations as the summer of 1938 progressed.

Alarmed by General von Brauchitsch's sobering revelations about the true state of German military preparations at the height of the 'May crisis',[19] and frustrated by the continuing vacillation at Rome and Tokyo in the alliance negotiations,[20] Ribbentrop became convinced that Germany required additional security if it were to run the risk of war with the western powers over the mounting crisis in Czech–German relations. With little prospect of creating even an appearance of solidarity between Germany, Italy and Japan in an ever deteriorating international situation, that security could only be provided by an assurance of Russian neutrality in the event of war. For if hostilities broke out and France came to the aid of her Czechoslovak ally, the USSR would also be bound to assist Czechoslovakia under the terms of their 1935 treaty. This eventuality would confront German military planners with the nightmare scenario of a two-front war and would create the very contingency which Ribbentrop, as he had told Weizsäcker on 17 April 1938, was anxious to avoid: a war with the western powers *and* with Russia.[21] The following June, information from secret sources in Germany reached Sir Robert Vansittart, indicating that Ribbentrop was seeking to align himself with pro-Russian circles in the General Staff and, 'in an attempt to find the way out of a rather hopeless situation', was seeking means of approaching Moscow. The report continued:

> In these circles it is being stated (of course with suitable respect to the incalculable moodiness of Hitler) that Russian Bolshevism up to date,

which has always been branded as a Jewish institution by the Nazi
Party, is being changed more and more into a Russian type of fascism
(Faschismus russischer Prägung) by the large scale removal of jewish
functionaries by Stalin, and that therefore soon no politico-philosophic
obstacles will any longer stand in the way of a revival of good relations
with Russia.[22]

Although this advice appears, at least outwardly, to have had no impact
upon Hitler during the Czechoslovak crisis, the very fact that it was proffered
as early as the summer of 1938 makes more credible Ribbentrop's claim that
the inspiration for a normalisation of Soviet–German relations the following
year came largely from himself.[23]

The German Foreign Minister was not alone in desiring an improvement
in relations with the USSR. Despite the radical deterioration of those relations
after Hitler's assumption of power, there remained considerable enthusiasm
for a return to the Rapallo policy of collaboration with Russia in the traditional national-conservative élites of the *Wehrmacht*, the Wilhelmstrasse
and in some German industrial circles.[24] Here it was felt that Russia was
Germany's natural partner in view of their common hostility towards Poland
and, not least, because of the vast possibilities for Soviet–German trade;
indeed, this was maintained at a relatively high level even under the Nazi
régime. As far as Ribbentrop was concerned, however, trade agreements and
the isolation of Poland were only secondary considerations in his own
support of a Soviet–German *Ausgleich*. As the negotiations with Japan
dragged on without positive issue over the spring and summer of 1939,
Ribbentrop became increasingly attracted by the prospect of an agreement
with Moscow. For although Germany and Italy had signed the 'Pact of Steel'
on 22 May 1939, the mission of Count Cavallero only eight days later
indicated the degree of military support which Germany could expect from
its ally in the event of a general conflagration in the near future.[25] In effect,
to those who were aware of Italy's position as outlined in the famous
Cavallero memorandum, the 'Pact of Steel' was only of use to Germany in
creating an *image* of Axis solidarity which would be exposed as soon as the
first shot was fired in a conflict between the European great powers. Moreover, by June 1939, procrastination in Tokyo had led Ribbentrop to warn
Japanese diplomats that if agreement to a military pact were not forthcoming, Germany would ultimately be forced to turn to the USSR.[26] In
Ribbentrop's view, a Soviet–German alignment would not only enable Germany to proceed against Poland without having to fear western intervention,
but would also form the basis for long-term collaboration between Germany
and Russia against the British empire. For the Nazi Foreign Minister, therefore, agreement with Russia was not intended as a temporary expedient to

solve the Polish problem but as a fundamental shift in German foreign policy. Having failed to extract any commitment from the Japanese, and with a virtually worthless treaty with the Italians should it come to war, Ribbentrop intended to bind Russia to Germany as the first component of a Euro-Asiatic *Kontinentalblock* in the hope and expectation that Germany's Anti-Comintern partners might adapt their policies to this system at a later date. The French ambassador in Berlin, Robert Coulondre, was among the first western diplomats to realise the real thrust of Ribbentrop's Russian policy. Commenting upon the possibility of a fourth partition of Poland, he wrote to Bonnet on 22 May 1939:

> In Herr von Ribbentrop's mind the idea of such a partition was closely linked with that of a *rapprochement* between Berlin and Moscow. To him such a reconciliation seemed, in the long run, both indispensable and inevitable. It would be in accordance with reality, and with a tradition still very much alive in Germany and would be the only way of bringing about a permanent settlement of the German – Polish dispute ... But above all it would give the rulers of the Reich the means of destroying the power of Great Britain. That was the chief objective which Herr von Ribbentrop had set himself, the *idée fixe*, which, with fanatical determination, he was unceasingly striving to achieve.[27]

The authorities in London were acutely aware of the dangers of a Russo-German combination. Indeed, papers had been circulated within the Foreign Office since at least 1936 which discussed that very contingency and its probable repercussions for the already vulnerable position of the British empire. Some comfort was taken in these surveys that Hitler's hatred of Bolshevism was so deep rooted as to render a *rapprochement* between Germany and the Soviet Union exceedingly unlikely, although it was admitted that the idea had its supporters in the German army, in industrial circles and even in some sections of the NSDAP.[28] However, in early 1938, an important and hitherto overlooked point was registered in a Foreign Office memorandum on the strength of the Franco-Soviet Pact and the possibility of a *rapprochement* between Germany and the USSR. Having noted that the possibility of some form of Soviet–German accommodation was often mentioned by leading Germans – notably Goering – as an inducement to the British to be more forthcoming *vis-à-vis* German ambitions in central Europe, the authors continued in prophetic vein:

> It must be appreciated that both Germany and Soviet Russia, being modern totalitarian states, are able to produce by sheer propaganda an impression of mutual hostility which cannot be accepted entirely at

its face value. Each country finds the other a convenient target for abuse, which serves primarily to impress its own public at home. Both Governments could, if they wished, discontinue this propaganda at fairly short notice and come to an understanding, without experiencing any really serious reactions from their own public, since their citizens have for so long been deprived of the faculty of independent thought.[29]

Just over a year later, following the seizure of Prague and the British guarantee to Poland, the question of British and German relations with the USSR had assumed far greater importance than it had occupied in the past. This was particularly so in view of a report which had reached the Foreign Office in January 1939, which indicated that Ribbentrop was already seriously considering an approach to Moscow.[30] Such indications increased as the year progressed. In April, Ribbentrop was reported to have told the Commander-in-Chief of the Lithuanian armed forces that Great Britain was about to suffer a diplomatic and political defeat 'such as she had never before experienced in her history';[31] the following month, as a result of further rumours of Soviet–German contacts, Kirkpatrick suggested that the defeat predicted by the Nazi Foreign Minister might well be some form of Russo-German agreement;[32] in June the story was doing the rounds that Ribbentrop already had a secret 'reinsurance treaty' with Stalin.[33] Although it was exceedingly difficult to verify information of this nature, its very existence gave both ministers and officials cause *furieusement à penser*. Nobody was more acutely aware of the dangers of a Russo-German alliance than the Permanent Under-Secretary of State for Foreign Affairs, Sir Robert Vansittart, who set his thoughts to paper on 16 May. The whole Russian problem, he wrote, was of such vital importance that only issues of real weight should be allowed into the scales when considering it. He posed the question as to which was the greater of the two evils, an alliance between Germany, Japan and Italy or a Russo-German *rapprochement*, and came down decidedly on the side of the latter. Worse still was the prospect of an understanding between the USSR, on the one hand, and Germany, Italy and Japan, on the other. His reasoning was as sound as it was terrifying:

> Japan is already in the Anti-Comintern triangle, and she is already partially exhausted by an endless war in China. Her accession to the Italo-German alliance would therefore not be nearly so formidable as it would have been without this long and exhausting war. Further, and this seems an important point, if the Russian negotiations were to end in deadlock and Russia were then to drift from isolation into rapproachement with Germany, it is unlikely that this would end German relations with Japan. There is enough boodle in the British

Empire for all, and we might then have a fourfold combination to face – which would be quite impossible.[34]

Three days later, the First Lord of the Admiralty submitted his views to the Foreign Secretary. On balance he believed that the political disadvantages of an Anglo-Russian agreement outweighed any military benefits which might accrue from one. However, like Vansittart, Stanhope was extremely nervous at the thought of an alignment between the Axis and the Soviet Union. He concluded:

> Having said all the above, there is one qualification that I feel I must make, and that is in connection with the suggestion that if we do not make an alliance with Russia, Germany and Russia will themselves come to terms and we may find Russia lined up with the Axis. For myself I find this possibility very difficult to accept so long, at any rate, as Hitler retains his power. If, however, it were a real possibility, then I feel it would be an overriding consideration. An alliance between Germany and Russia is the greatest thing we have to fear.[35]

Between them, Vansittart and Stanhope had correctly divined the ultimate aim of Ribbentrop's diplomacy during the summer of 1939 – the conclusion of a Soviet–German alliance and its eventual harmonisation with the Anti-Comintern Pact – and had equally correctly identified the British empire as the intended victim of this seemingly awkward coalition.

This latter point could not have been lost upon Stalin during Ribbentrop's first visit to Moscow in August 1939. According to the Reich Foreign Minister, neither the Anti-Comintern Pact nor Germany's friendship with Japan was aimed at the Soviet Union. Indeed, Britain was the real enemy and had always attempted to poison relations between Germany and Russia. Even in its present state of weakness, its policy aimed at allowing others to fight for its 'presumptuous claim to world domination'. Stalin appeared to agree, adding that it was ridiculous that India should be held by 'a few hundred Englishmen'.[36] Ribbentrop also mooted the possibility of German mediation between Russia and Japan, and here too Stalin's response was not altogether discouraging. All things considered, and provided provocation ceased, the USSR was prepared to live in peace with Japan; and any help which Germany could offer towards this goal would be considered 'useful'.[37] At this first meeting, Stalin made an extremely favourable impression upon the German Foreign Minister, not least, perhaps, because of his evident hostility towards Britain and his remarks about a possible Soviet–Japanese arrangement. Upon returning to Germany, Ribbentrop spoke to all who would listen of his admiration for Stalin and the other 'men with strong faces' in the Kremlin.[38]

Although to many an *alter Kämpfer* his likening of the atmosphere in Moscow to that at meetings between old Nazi Party comrades must have seemed an outrageous blasphemy, Ribbentrop was convinced that Stalin was 'a personality of major calibre, gifted with a revolutionary sense of the highest order'.[39]

A further meeting the following month certainly did nothing to detract from this impression. Stalin was full of sincerity about his desire for a lasting collaboration with the Reich and ridiculed the idea that Russia had any interest in exporting its ideology to Germany with the remark that communism was about as suited to Germany as was a 'saddle to a cow'.[40] However, the Soviet leader refused to be drawn on the possibility of a further strengthening of German–Soviet relations for, as Ribbentrop later put it, 'the coming battles with the Western Powers',[41] and on this occasion he reacted in a markedly lukewarm fashion to Ribbentrop's suggestion for the inclusion of a favourable reference to Japan and to the idea of a Russo-Japanese settlement in the final communiqué.[42] It seems reasonable to assume that by the time this conversation took place, Stalin and Molotov, having secured their immediate objectives under the terms of the non-aggression pact, fully appreciated the thrust of Ribbentrop's proposals, and had concluded that there was little to be gained from an even closer alignment with the Nazis, which could only bring the increased odium of the western powers and the USA upon the Soviet regime. Moreover, having secured greater freedom of action in the Far East as a result of his treaty with the Germans, Stalin was clearly in no mood to concede anything to the Japanese. At the very least, the reserve of the Soviet leader suggested that he believed that a German – Russian–Japanese–Italian combination would be far more difficult to bring into being than his German guest seemed to imagine – and well he might.

The Nazi–Soviet Pact had had a disastrous effect on German–Japanese relations.[43] Not only was it instrumental in precipitating the fall of the Hiranuma Cabinet, but it also led to an immediate deterioration in the position of pro-German circles in Tokyo. Moreover, it soon became clear that the new Japanese Government had neither the intention nor the inclination to co-operate with the Soviet Union on anything like the scale envisaged by the German Foreign Minister. Subsequent events, including the systematic removal of pro-German elements from the Gaimushō, the General Staff and the War Ministry, served only to confirm that this sudden and unwelcome departure in German policy was widely perceived in Japan as a diabolical act of treachery.[44] In these circumstances Ribbentrop was forced, for the time being, to rely upon the efforts of Hiroshi Oshima, the fanatically pro-Nazi Japanese ambassador in Berlin, and his equally zealous counterpart in Rome, Toshio Shiratori, to explain to their superiors the benefits for Japan of the new Soviet–German arrangement and the desirability of a Russo-Japanese settlement.

It was perhaps as a means of furnishing his Japanese friends with suitable arguments that Ribbentrop received Oshima within days of the outbreak of the European war in order to explain the future possibilities for German and Japanese policy. The fate of Japan, he told the Ambassador, was closely bound to that of Germany, and only in the event of a German victory over the west could Japan's position in East Asia be secured. Contrary to the prevailing mood in Japan, the German–Soviet agreement was entirely con-sistent with Japanese interests, as not only did it represent a strengthening of Germany's position, which Japan would surely welcome, but it also opened up the prospect of a settlement between Moscow and Tokyo. Germ-any, he stressed, would be happy to act as mediator towards such an end. Such a settlement would enable Japan to extend its influence towards the south where, in Germany's view, its real interests lay. Moreover, the idea of co-operation between Germany, Italy and Japan was 'by no means dead'. On the contrary, such co-operation could now be directed 'exclusively' against Great Britain and would thus 'bring the policy of the three Powers as well as of Russia into a uniform line corresponding to the real interests of all concerned'. Ribbentrop intended to work vigorously towards this goal and hoped that his ideas might find an echo in Tokyo in order that 'the impact of the said combination of powers might still be felt during our present struggle with England'.[45]

However, despite the accommodating attitudes of Oshima and Shiratori and, not least, Ribbentrop's untiring attempts to convince Japanese diplo-mats, soldiers and industrialists of the usefulness of Soviet–German and Soviet–Japanese friendship,[46] there was little chance at this stage of a fun-damental change in Japan's attitude towards the USSR. Much to Ribbentrop's displeasure, Oshima, whose position had become untenable as a direct result of the new Russo-German alignment, was replaced in late 1939 by the more moderate Kurusu, who described himself as standing halfway between the supporters of collaboration with the Axis and those who favoured a settle-ment with the British.[47] Indeed, by mid-October 1939 it was clear that the Nomonhan armistice, signed on 16 September, represented the very limit to which Japan was prepared to go in adjusting its relations with the Soviet Union. The ascendancy of pro-western influence in Tokyo was a decisive setback for Ribbentrop's aims, and it clearly rankled with the German Foreign Minister. On 1 October, he was moved to comment to Ciano that at present Japan had the 'misfortune to be governed by a clique of not very intelligent and very backward militarists'.[48] Clearly no progress could be expected with the Japanese in the foreseeable future, but, Ribbentrop continued, 'in the event of German victories, the spirit of the Japanese army would come to the fore and establish a new government which, with the backing of the Japanese navy, would enable Japan to take advantage of the greatest opportunity of her political existence'.[49] And so, to an extent, it would prove with the signature in September 1940 of the Tripartite Pact.

There were similar problems with the Italians. Although the repercussions of the German – Russian agreement had not been so dramatically felt in Rome as in Tokyo, there was nevertheless great concern and suspicion within the Italian leadership at this latest volte-face in German policy. Ciano, who viewed the pact as yet another example of German duplicity, considered it a 'monstrous union' which contradicted both the letter and the spirit of the 'Pact of Steel'.[50] For his part, Mussolini felt that Hitler would rue the day that he had 'brought the Bolsheviks into the heart of Europe',[51] and at the turn of the year was moved to address a letter to the Führer in which he sharply criticised Russia while simultaneously reminding his ally where Germany's *Lebensraum* was to be won.[52] Reports from Rome indicated that although the Italians professed to appreciate the logic underlying the Soviet–German agreement, they were profoundly disturbed by the prospect of any further strengthening of relations.[53]

Thus, in much the same way as he attempted to convince the Japanese of the benefits of the German–Soviet *rapprochement*, Ribbentrop was frequently at pains to demonstrate to the Italians the wisdom of friendship between Russia and the Axis. On numerous occasions he sought to persuade Mussolini, Ciano and Bernardo Attolico, the Italian ambassador in Berlin, that the normalisation of German – Russian relations was of great advantage to both Italy and Germany, and that the USSR posed no threat to the interests of either power. The sentiments expressed in Mussolini's letter of 3 January 1940 to Hitler were especially displeasing as they clearly stressed as the main priority the destruction of Bolshevism as opposed to the vigorous prosecution of the war against Great Britain and France. On 10 January, therefore, Ribbentrop expressed his 'astonishment' to the Italian Ambassador at the 'extreme anti-Soviet' thrust of Italian policy. Giving expression to his own innermost convictions, Ribbentrop asserted, somewhat disingenuously, that Hitler and Mussolini had always agreed that the western powers were the principal enemies of the Axis, a fact which made Italy's attitude towards the Soviet Union even more puzzling.[54] These arguments, however, cut no ice with the Italian leadership during the winter of 1939–40. Ciano, who found Ribbentrop's new-found infatuation with the Bolsheviks imprudent, vulgar and perplexing,[55] not only opposed any softening of the Italian position over Russia, but was, in fact, actively working to sabotage Ribbentrop's efforts to bring about a *rapprochement* between Japan and the USSR;[56] and at the end of December 1939 Italo-Soviet relations hit a new low when both governments withdrew their ambassadors following a series of acrimonious disputes arising from the Russian attack on Finland. As far as Ciano was concerned, this was also a development which was at least partially designed to pose further obstacles to Ribbentrop's plans.[57]

By the following March, however, there were some signs of progress. During a visit to Rome, Ribbentrop took great pains to explain to the Duce the fundamental changes which he believed were taking place in the Soviet Union. Stalin, he averred, had abandoned the idea of world revolution, and Russia was 'not only in the process of becoming a normal national state, but had even progressed quite far in that direction'.[58] A systematic purge of jewish elements from all important areas of government had been carried out, the Politburo now consisted of '100 percent Muscovites' and even Kaganovich, who was thought to be of Jewish extraction, 'looked more like a Georgian'. To be sure, there was a fundamental difference between fascism and communism, but with Russia engaged in a transformation of 'global proportions' it no longer constituted a threat to Italy or Germany in terms of either domestic or international policy.[59] Mussolini appeared to be impressed by these arguments, not least, perhaps, because they mirrored those developed by the Führer in the letter which Ribbentrop had brought with him to Italy.[60] Although the Duce declared himself to be an avowed opponent of communism, he seemed prepared to consider an improvement in Italo-Soviet relations and did not exclude the possibility of Italian support for German efforts to mediate between Russia and Japan. Moreover, without any prompting from Ribbentrop, Mussolini himself referred to the idea of a possible German–Italian–Japanese–Soviet bloc, thus reflecting perfectly the ultimate goal of Ribbentrop's policy.[61] Following the Brenner meeting – during which Hitler spoke in similar fashion about internal Russian developments, though with notably more reserve than his Foreign Minister had done eight days earlier[62] – Ribbentrop began to work in earnest for an improvement in Italo–Russian relations and was eventually to see his efforts rewarded with a limited success later in the summer when both governments agreed to restore their ambassadors.[63] But it ultimately proved impossible to persuade the Italians to consider any form of active co-operation with the USSR. As Ciano told Mackensen in August, Italy had in mind 'only an improvement of relations on a very general basis without envisioning any concrete agreements'.[64] Mussolini said much the same, to Ribbentrop himself during their meeting in Rome the following month.[65]

By that time, however, there were increasing signs of deterioration in German–Russian relations which threatened to ruin Ribbentrop's schemes.

Alarmed by the speed and magnitude of the German victory in the western campaign, Stalin had proceeded in June 1940 to occupy the Baltic States and Bessarabia. Although the Soviet leader was acting entirely within his rights under the terms of the German–Russian treaties of 23 August and 28 September 1939, his actions greatly irritated Hitler, who was loathe to see any increase in Russian power and who appears to have questioned Ribbentrop about the legality of Moscow's actions.[66] Moreover, the Soviet claim to Bukovina was not covered by the secret protocols of the German–Russian treaties, and Soviet action in this area precipitated what one commentator has identified as the 'first serious wranglings between the two partners'.[67] Stalin's decision to force the issue in Bessarabia opened up a hornets' nest in the Balkans and threatened to plunge that region into conflict, a development which Hitler, owing to his dependence upon Yugoslavian and especially Romanian raw materials, had sought to avoid since the outbreak of the war. In their turn, Hungary and Bulgaria could not resist the opportunity created by the Russians to press their own revisionist demands upon the Romanians, which eventually forced a reluctant Hitler to impose a solution of the Hungarian demands upon the hapless Bucharest Government by the Second Vienna Award of 30 August 1940.[68] The Bulgarian claims were finally settled by the Treaty of Craiova, negotiated under German pressure, on 7 September 1940.

Moreover, it was not only in the Balkans that German–Soviet relations were subject to increasing strains. The Germans had also been alarmed by the infringement of their rights in Lithuania and by the complete Russian occupation of the Baltic States in mid-June, while Stalin and Molotov viewed with concern the conclusion in mid-September of the first Finnish–German Transit Agreement providing for the transport of German troops and supplies through Finland to bases in Norway. The German guarantee to what remained of the truncated Romanian state equally perturbed the Soviet leadership as, following the satisfaction of the Hungarian and Bulgarian claims, it was difficult to see against what Romania was being guaranteed other than Soviet aggression. Equally, the guarantee implied that by accepting German protection Romania was firmly established in an as yet undefined but seemingly increasing German sphere of influence in the Balkans. The dispatch of German units to Romania in October 1940 certainly did nothing to detract from this impression.[69]

A further factor making for Soviet–German estrangement was the signature of the Tripartite Pact between Germany, Italy and Japan on 27 September 1940. Although Ribbentrop evidently hoped to soften the blow by informing Molotov in advance of the pact's impending conclusion, and despite his fulsome assurances that it was aimed exclusively against the 'democratic warmongers',[70] the further consolidation of relations between the Anti-Comintern powers could hardly have been a comforting development for the Soviet Government. Not even Ribbentrop's assurance that a special clause had been inserted into the new agreement affirming that it 'in no way' altered the relationship of Germany, Italy and Japan to the USSR could assuage Molotov's suspicions that there was perhaps more to the pact than met the eye.[71]

In these circumstances it seemed advisable to clarify Soviet–German relations before mutual misunderstandings and suspicions developed into something more serious; and the late autumn of 1940 appeared to be a propitious moment for such a clarification. For although Hitler had spoken of moving against the USSR even before the close of the western campaign[72] – and, indeed, had announced his intention to attack Russia in the spring of 1941 during a conference at the Berghof on 31 July 1940[73] – he seemed for the time being to have been won over to Ribbentrop's *Konzeption* of collaboration with Russia as part of a *Kontinentalblock*,[74] and on the advice of his military leaders to pursue a strategy which, by attacking Britain at the 'periphery', would succeed where *Unternehmen Seelöwe* – itself never a popular option as far as Hitler was concerned – had failed.[75]

In mid-October, therefore, Ribbentrop wrote to Stalin with a formal invitation for the Soviet Foreign Minister to come to Germany for conversations with himself and the Führer.[76] Ribbentrop's aim remained the same as it had been since the initiation of the Soviet–German *rapprochement* in 1939. As he later wrote, an attempt would have to be made to

> convert the Three Power Pact into a Four Power Pact including Russia. If we succeeded in this our position would be favourable, for such a combination would neutralise the USA, isolate Britain and threaten her position in the Near East. Such a strong system of alliances might make it possible to end the war with Britain by diplomatic means; without it this was impossible.[77]

The basis of Ribbentrop's scheme was to induce the USSR to join the Tripartite Pact and, as he recognised, for this 'something would have to be sacrificed to Russia',[78] which meant a settlement of the differences which had caused the gradual deterioration in Soviet–German relations since June 1940. With these ideas in mind Ribbentrop assured Stalin of Germany's desire for continued collaboration, declaring that the war against Great Britain was already won and that the only remaining question was how long it would take the British finally to admit defeat. Germany's policy in the Balkans and in Scandinavia had been aimed not at the Soviet Union but solely against England; similarly, the Tripartite Pact was directed exclusively

against the British empire and the USA; it was designed to prevent an extension of the war and was entirely compatible with Russo-German friendship
and, indeed, with friendship between the Axis, Japan and the Soviet Union.
The German Foreign Minister expanded at length upon this latter point,
declaring that Soviet–German friendship, 'neighbourly relations' between
Russia and Japan and the close association of Berlin, Rome and Tokyo were
'logical elements of a natural political constellation which, if intelligently
managed, will work out to the best advantage of all the participating powers'.
Reminding Stalin that he had mooted similar ideas during the Moscow
negotiations in 1939, Ribbentrop once more urged the Soviets to work
towards a readjustment of their relations with Japan – an essential prerequisite for the construction of the proposed *Kontinentalblock*. In conclusion he wrote:

> I should like to state that, in the opinion of the Führer, also, it appears
> to be the historic mission of the four Powers – the Soviet Union, Italy,
> Japan and Germany – to adopt a long range policy and to direct
> the future development of their peoples into the right channels by
> delimitation of their interests for the ages.[79]

Molotov was duly invited to Berlin for discussions with the Nazi leaders,
discussions which Ribbentrop clearly felt held out good prospects for
success.[80] At the close of his letter to Stalin he mooted the possibility of a
further visit to Moscow 'to discuss – possibly with representatives of Japan
and Italy – the bases of a policy which would be of practical advantage to
all of us'.[81] Significantly, Stalin eagerly accepted the invitation for conversations in Berlin but was notably more reserved about the prospect of
becoming involved in negotiations with the Italians and the Japanese.[82] As
was to become apparent during Molotov's visit, the Soviets were much more
interested in clarifying their relations with Germany down to the last detail
rather than engaging in vague discussions about world coalitions or continental alliances. For the time being at least, the presence of German troops
in Finland and Romania was a more pressing matter for the Russian leaders
than the revision of the Straits Convention or aggrandisement at the expense
of the British empire.

The Soviet–German conversations of 12–13 November 1940 rank
amongst the most significant negotiations of the entire war. Had they followed the course that Ribbentrop intended, Great Britain and, indirectly,
the USA would have been faced with an overwhelming aggregate of power
in the form of an alliance between Germany, Italy, Japan and the USSR,
to which would be added as associated powers Spain, Vichy France and
Germany's satellites and client states in central and south-eastern Europe.

Moreover, the position of certain neutrals, notably Turkey, would have been seriously compromised. Although it is impossible to speculate upon how long the Germans could have held together such an artificial coalition, or upon the effect it might have had upon American policy, there can surely be no doubt that Great Britain's already precarious strategic position at the turn of 1940–1 would have been further, and perhaps fatally, undermined, at least as far as the Mediterranean and the Near and Middle Eastern theatres were concerned.

However, even as Molotov's train rolled into Berlin's *Anhalter Bahnhof*, the prospects for Ribbentrop's scheme for Soviet accession to the Tripartite Pact were rapidly diminishing. Hitler's enthusiasm, if it can so be termed, for the project of a *Kontinentalblock* and for the peripheral strategy – having reached a high point in October 1940 when he met Laval and Pétain at Montoire and Franco at Hendaye – was now definitely on the wane. Gradually he was returning to the idea which lay at the root of all his calculations in the field of foreign affairs – the attack on the USSR – and was seeking to explain it to his military leaders with a variety of different and often contradictory reasons.[83] Even if Ribbentrop had been able to secure agreement with Russia during Molotov's visit, it is clear from Hitler's attitude that it would have been purely transitory in nature and would certainly not – as Ribbentrop had hoped – have formed the basis for a lasting, mutually profitable partnership. Military studies about the feasibility of an attack on the USSR had been underway since the late summer of 1940, and at a gathering of military leaders on 4 November it was made clear that the preparations for the operation were to continue despite the impending visit of the Soviet Foreign Minister.[84] Ironically, Directive No. 18 on the conduct of the war was issued on the very day of Molotov's arrival in the German capital. As far as Russia was concerned it read: 'Political discussions have been initiated with the aim of clarifying Russia's attitude for the coming period. Regardless of what outcome these discussions will have, all preparations for the East which already have been orally ordered, are to be continued.'[85]   That the contents of this directive were kept from the German Foreign Minister can be taken as certain. Indeed, although Ribbentrop was aware of Hitler's growing suspicion of Soviet policy, the *Auswärtiges Amt* was not kept informed of the details of military planning and was hardly ever represented at the crucial conferences between Hitler and his military leaders. In these circumstances it seems unlikely that Ribbentrop himself was aware of Hitler's irrevocable decision to smash Russia before he attended the conference at the Berghof on 8–9 January 1941, when the Führer left his audience in absolutely no doubt about his future intentions.[86] During his discussions with Molotov, therefore, Ribbentrop developed in detail the arguments which he had outlined in his recent letter to Stalin, in an attempt to patch up the faltering Soviet–German relationship. Germany, Japan, Italy and Russia, he believed, could find their *Lebensräume* without coming into conflict with one another if each power chose to expand in a southerly direction. With Great Britain already defeated, there were rich pickings to be had for Japan in South-East Asia; for Italy in the Mediterranean; for Germany in Equatorial Africa; and for the USSR in the Persian Gulf and India. Therefore the only sensible course was for the four powers to reach agreement along these lines in order to clarify their interests 'for the future on a very long-range scale'. As a further sweetener Ribbentrop dressed up his proposal by hinting that under such an arrangement the Soviet Union could expect a more favourable position in the Arabian Sea and at the Straits.[87] Molotov, however, was markedly reserved. He seemed far more interested in tying the Germans down to specifics on the Balkan and Scandinavian questions. As far as Russia's possible accession to the Tripartite Pact was concerned, Molotov told Hitler on 12 November 1940 that such an arrangement 'appeared to him entirely acceptable in principle ... But the aim and significance of the Pact must first be more closely defined, particularly because of the delimitation of the Greater East Asian Sphere.'[88]

The following day was one of intense bargaining between Hitler and the Soviet Foreign Minister. Their discussion ranged over numerous topics from the German guarantee to Romania to the question of southern Bukovina, and from German troop movements in the Baltic to a possible Russian guarantee of Bulgaria, an issue which particularly perturbed Hitler, who fudged it by repeatedly asking whether the Bulgarians had requested such a guarantee.[89] The Führer's concern over Finland and Bulgaria was understandable in view of his decision to make the final break with Russia in the spring of 1941. Finland had been assigned specific tasks in the military planning of *Barbarossa*, while Bulgaria, as well as being envisaged as a source of supplies for the forthcoming German advance into Russia, had recently assumed even greater importance in view of Mussolini's Greek débâcle, which threatened to provide the British with bases from which to launch bombing raids on the Ploesti oilfields. Moreover, Hitler understood full well that if Bulgaria were pressed to accept a Soviet guarantee then not only would it prove exceedingly difficult to help the Italians in Greece should that become necessary, but also that the first hint of a Russo-German conflict would lead to the occupation of that country by the Red Army. Having staked his claim to Romania, thereby increasing German influence in the Balkans, Hitler was adamantly opposed to allowing Russia to take a similar step with regard to Bulgaria, which the Soviets insisted lay within their security sphere. The whole discussion was heated, circuitous and, in terms of concrete agreements, entirely unproductive. Ribbentrop attempted to introduce a conciliatory note into the exchanges by declaring, rather pathetically, that perhaps the Soviet and German Governments simply misunderstood each other, and that in fact 'if one considered matters realistically there were no differences between Germany and Russia'.[90] No amount of eyewash, however, could disguise the fact that there were indeed numerous and serious points of friction between Berlin and Moscow which, thus far, Molotov's visit had done precious little to ease. At each point in the conversation between Hitler and the Soviet Foreign Minister when it became obvious that no progress could be made on the specific questions of Russo-German relations, the negotiators lapsed into generalisations about the booty to be had from the British empire – a subject which neither Hitler, in view of his preoccupation with the Eastern problem and his sentimental attachment to the idea of an eventual 'partition of the world' with England, nor Molotov, owing to the very real Soviet concerns about German policy in northern and south-eastern Europe, appeared to speak about with any great conviction.

Nevertheless, it was a subject to which Ribbentrop himself returned with a vengeance in the final round of the negotiations on 13 November 1940. The Nazi Foreign Minister repeatedly pressed his Soviet counterpart to consider the possibility of co-operation between Germany, Japan, Italy and Russia, and the latter's accession to the Tripartite Pact, even going so far as to reveal to Molotov certain clauses of a draft treaty intended to fix the spheres of interest of the Axis, Japan and the USSR, and to repeat his offer to mediate between Moscow and Tokyo. Molotov listened politely but refused to become engaged in a detailed discussion. As firmly as Ribbentrop stuck to his point about the proposed *Kontinentalblock*, so Molotov continually raised those difficult subjects upon which the Soviet Government sought satisfaction. What, he asked, did the Axis intend with regard to Turkey, Romania, Bulgaria, Yugoslavia, Greece, Poland, Sweden and Finland? Even the normally stubborn Ribbentrop became exhausted with Molotov's detailed interrogations, finally complaining that he had been *überfragt* (queried too closely) on these issues and confining his response to the glib and, in Moscow's view, wholly unconvincing assurance that everything that Germany undertook was directed against Great Britain. As Gustav Hilger noted, Ribbentrop

> could only repeat again and again that the decisive question was whether the Soviet Union was prepared and in a position to cooperate with us in the great liquidation of the British empire. On all other questions we would easily reach an understanding if we could succeed in extending our relations and in defining the spheres of influence.[91]

Molotov might well have harboured reservations about Ribbentrop's grandiose plans for the dismantling of the British empire. This final conversation had taken place in an underground bunker, owing to an inconvenient appearance of the RAF over the German capital. While Ribbentrop was delivering the usual monologue about how Germany had already won the war, Molotov interrupted and impishly enquired that if that really was the case then he would be interested to learn whose bombs were currently raining down on Berlin.[92] Two weeks later Molotov informed the Germans that Russia was prepared to associate itself with the Tripartite Pact, provided that it obtained satisfaction over Finland – which meant the withdrawal of German troops and the cancellation of the Transit Agreement – over Bulgaria – which meant the conclusion of a mutual assistance pact and thus an acceptance by Germany that that country lay firmly in the Soviet sphere of influence – plus further concessions in the Persian Gulf and northern Sakhalin.[93] None of these conditions, especially those pertaining to Finland and Bulgaria, were acceptable to Hitler, and, despite repeated requests from the Soviet Government, no response to this communication was ever received before the launching of *Barbarossa*.[94]

Although the November negotiations had achieved nothing in terms of political agreement, the Germans derived the impression that, for their part, the Soviets were not seeking a conflict with the Reich.[95] On the other hand, Hitler was determined to strike against the USSR in the spring of 1941 and even Ribbentrop, the champion of German–Soviet co-operation, appears to have been shaken by the intransigence and tenacity displayed by Molotov during the Berlin conversations. In January 1941 Ciano found him 'extremely sceptical' as regards Russian good faith and fearing that the Soviets, who had recently appeared enthusiastic about improving their relations with Rome, were attempting to gain influence in Balkan affairs by seeking to ingratiate themselves with Mussolini.[96] Nevertheless, convinced that Germany's future could best be assured through collaboration with Italy, Japan and the USSR against Great Britain, Ribbentrop stuck tenaciously to his policy of Soviet–German friendship in the hope that something could still be salvaged. During a conversation with the Chancellor in December 1940 he discussed in detail the points put by Molotov the previous month and strongly urged concessions to the USSR and a joint settlement of Balkan questions. 'My insistent representations', he later wrote, 'had at least one result, he [Hitler] did not absolutely reject the demands. Indeed, before we parted after our long conversation ... Hitler said something that gave me hope of an eventual compromise with Russia: he said: "Ribbentrop, we have achieved many things together, perhaps we shall also pull this one off together." '[97] Of course, there was no sincerity in this alleged statement. In all likelihood Hitler was merely deceiving his Foreign Minister, in the hope that by holding out some prospect of an improvement in relations with the USSR Ribbentrop would have something to chew over and it would put a stop to his incessant requests for audiences. In any case, by 18 December, when Hitler signed Directive No. 21 for *Barbarossa*, the die was cast.

Ribbentrop watched helplessly as Soviet–German relations continued to deteriorate in the first months of 1941. Not only did Stalin and Molotov receive no satisfaction of their demands about Finland and Bulgaria, but they were incensed by the dispatch of German troops to Bulgaria as part of the build-up for operation *Marita* and by Bulgaria's accession to the Tripartite Pact in March. The following month the Russians replied by seeking to improve their position in the Balkans by signing a friendship treaty with the Simović Government of Yugoslavia which had seized power following a *putsch* ousting the pro-German régime of Prince Paul and reversing his policy of alignment with the Axis in the Tripartite Pact. In view of these developments, Ribbentrop's representations were less likely than ever to make any impression upon the Führer. Hitler, he later recalled, became 'more and more negative' as far as Russia was concerned. Indeed, Ribbentrop felt that 'in my attitude to Russia I stood alone'.[98] Even Ribbentrop's references to the Russian policy of Bismarck, with whose achievements Hitler had more than once favourably compared those of his own Foreign Minister, could not diminish the Führer's determination to act. 'I left no stone unturned to achieve a German – Russian alliance', Ribbentrop reflected in 1946.

> Perhaps I would have succeeded in the end had there not been that resistance on ideological grounds which always made the conduct of a foreign policy impossible. It was these ideological considerations, coupled with Russia's political actions, her military preparations, and lastly her demands, which painted in Hitler's mind a picture of a monstrous danger threatening Germany. In view of this, my arguments counted less and less'.[99]

At this juncture Ribbentrop received assistance in his efforts to avert a German–Soviet conflict from the officials in his own Ministry, whose advice he had persistently shunned during previous crises.[100] Ernst von Weizsäcker had viewed with growing concern the deterioration in Russo-German relations since the autumn of 1940.[101] This able and dispassionate diplomat could see no reason for a breach with the Soviets, particularly as it would leave Great Britain undefeated in Germany's rear. Russia, he felt, posed no threat to the Reich, and he had been struck by the obvious desire of Molotov and his delegation for further Soviet–German co-operation which had been on show almost to the point of ostentation during the Berlin negotiations.

On 17 November 1940 he wrote: 'Why should she [Russia] not stew in her stagnant Bolshevism alongside us? As long as she is governed by the type of people we saw here, we have less to fear from that country than we did when it was ruled by the Tsars.'[102] Two months later later he commented further:

> Would this war [against Russia] bring us any closer to our goal as regards England, even if it went entirely according to plan? Either we smash England, in which case we don't need to become embroiled in the East, or we fail to force England to capitulate, in which case a war in the East will be of no use to us.[103]

On 14 April 1941 Weizsäcker informed Ribbentrop that he was opposed to war with Russia,[104] and that he was supported in this view by the German ambassador in Moscow, Count Friedrich Werner von der Schulenburg.[105] Two weeks later, under instruction from Ribbentrop, Weizsäcker drafted a memorandum setting out in all clarity the arguments against a breach with the USSR. Reflecting the views which Ribbentrop had put to him two years earlier, the State Secretary wrote that everything must be directed to ensure the collapse of Great Britain. 'A German attack on Russia', he concluded, 'would only give the English a new moral lift. It would be interpreted there as German uncertainty as to the success of our fight against England. We would thereby not only be admitting that the war was going to last a long time yet, but we might actually prolong it in this way, instead of shortening it'.[106]

On the very day that Weizsäcker was preparing his memorandum, Schulenburg, who had been summoned to Berlin by Ribbentrop in order that he might explain personally to Hitler the situation as seen from his post, was received in the Reich Chancellery. Even by Hitler's standards, it was an astonishing interview. Mustering all his powers of analysis and his experience of the Soviet mentality and political system, Schulenburg attempted to deflect the Führer from his collision course.[107] Hitler, never at his best when exposed to the sober evaluations of career diplomats, asked some questions in a tone which was patently hostile to the Soviet Union, heard Schulenburg out and then terminated the conversation with the remark 'Thank you, this was extremely interesting.'[108]

It was perhaps Hitler's discourteous and disinterested reception of Schulenburg which finally convinced Ribbentrop that the Führer was determined to strike and that his own Russian policy was therefore doomed to collapse.[109] The whole point of summoning the Ambassador to Berlin and of having Weizsäcker draw up a memorandum arguing against the attack had surely been to present as strong a case as possible for at least the postponement, if not the abandonment, of *Barbarossa*, which remained

Ribbentrop's goal throughout the spring of 1941. It is in this context that his efforts to interest Hitler in the possibility of further collaboration against Great Britain with Vichy France and Japan are best understood. Indeed, as Weizsäcker noted as late as 29 April, Ribbentrop himself was 'fundamentally opposed to war with Russia'.[110] Two days later, therefore, Weizsäcker was understandably horrified to learn that Ribbentrop had expressed his full support for the impending attack in a memorandum to Hitler.

It is of course highly unlikely that Ribbentrop's innermost convictions had undergone an overnight transformation. Ever fearful for his own position, and aware of the relative weakness of the Foreign Office in the endless struggles for authority which, above all else, characterised the internal dynamics of the Third Reich, it is quite likely that Ribbentrop simply did not have the courage to stand up for those convictions when the crunch came. After all, had not years of co-operation with the Führer proved the latter's genius time and time again? And to oppose him now, in the greatest decision of his life, might well have disastrous consequences for the Foreign Office and its minister. And equally, if Hitler said that Russia would collapse in six weeks, then so it would prove. Perhaps then Germany would be in a position finally to crush that 'ramshackle empire',[112] the heart of which lay across the North Sea.

Yet if Berezhkov's claims are true, even when it came to the declaration of war Ribbentrop could not conceal his displeasure at the turn of events and was at pains to ensure that the Soviet leaders should know that he himself had opposed the decision. Perhaps at that fateful moment Ribbentrop realised the full magnitude of what was being undertaken and recognised that Germany was embarking upon a war which it could not possibly win. Perhaps, as Berezhkov suggests, Ribbentrop was even thinking that this wholly undiplomatic demonstration might be useful in his defence if he was ever brought to trial for his deeds.[113] Of one thing we can be certain. Ribbentrop was opposed to the German attack on the Soviet Union in June 1941. As had happened so many times before, however, he had bowed to Hitler's implacable will and, once the conflict came, resolved to do all in his power to ensure the destruction of the USSR.[114]

Ribbentrop's predecessor and role model, the Iron Chancellor, Otto von Bismarck, had not crumbled so easily when in 1890 Kaiser Wilhelm II had wantonly sacrificed Russian friendship by refusing to renew the secret German – Russian Reinsurance Treaty. Six years later Bismarck had revealed the contents of that treaty to the entire world, much to the fury and embarrassment of the monarchy.[115] Six years after Hitler sacrificed his alliance with Stalin in a similar act of wantonness, Ribbentrop had been executed for war crimes, the 'thousand year Reich' lay in ruins and Soviet troops occupied German territory from Frankfurt an der Oder to points as far westwards as Halle, Erfurt and Magdeburg.

Notes

1. 'War Ribbentrop gegen den Angriff auf Russland?' *Frankfurter Allgemeine Zeitung*, 21 August 1965. In his recently published memoirs, Berezhkov has repeated this claim. See V.M. Bereschkow, *Ich war Stalins Dolmetscher: Hinter den Kulissen der politischen Weltbühne* (Munich, 1991) p. 290. It should be noted that none of the other witnesses present on this occasion have reported this alleged outburst by Ribbentrop.
2. J. von Ribbentrop, *The Ribbentrop Memoirs* (London, 1954) p. 158.
3. See W. Michalka, *Ribbentrop und die deutsche Weltpolitik 1933–1940: Aussenpolitische Konzeptionen und Entscheidungsprozesse im Dritten Reich* (Munich, 1980) pp. 278 ff.
4. See Ribbentrop to Hitler and Neurath, 28 Dec. 1937. Published in A. von Ribbentrop, *Die Kriegsschuld des Widerstandes: Aus britischen Geheimdokumenten 1938–39* (Leoni am Starnberger See, 1974) pp. 61–74; Memorandum by Ribbentrop for the Führer, 2 Jan. 1938, Documents on German Foreign Policy (hereafter DGFP), D, I, no. 93.
5. G. Ciano, *Ciano's Diary 1937–1938*, Trans. Andreas Mayor, Introduction by Malcolm Muggeridge (London, 1952) p. 24.
6. On the evolution of Hitler's attitude towards Great Britain during the mid-1930s, see G. T. Waddington, 'Hitler, Ribbentrop, die NSDAP und der Niedergang des Britischen Empire 1935–1938', *Vierteljahreshefte für Zeitgeschichte*, 40, no. 2, 1992, pp. 273 ff.
7. Minutes of the Conference in the Reich Chancellery, 5 Nov. 1937, DGFP, D, I, no. 19.
8. See Michalka, *Ribbentrop*, pp. 50 ff.
9. Ibid. pp. 138 ff. See also K. Hildebrand, *Vom Reich zum Weltreich: Hitler,* NSDAP und koloniale Frage 1919–1945 (Munich, 1969) pp. 357 ff., pp. 491 ff.
10. E. Kordt, *Nicht aus den Akten. Die Wilhelmstrasse in Frieden und Krieg: Erlebnisse, Begegnungen und Eindrücke* (Stuttgart, 1950) p. 151.
11. See Michalka, *Ribbentrop* p. 298; K. Hildebrand, *The Foreign Policy of the Third Reich* (London, 1973) pp. 48–9.
12. This information is contained in a paper headed 'Henry Noble ° The Baronet', 19 Apr. 1937, Churchill Archives Centre, Churchill College, Cambridge, Christie Papers, CHRS 1/21A.
13. See Memorandum by Schmidt, 13 Nov. 1940, DGFP, D, XI, no. 325. During the conversation Ribbentrop also referred to a possible Sino-Japanese reconciliation.
14. Henderson to Sargent, 22 Aug. 1939, Public Records Office, London (hereafter PRO), FO 800/279.
15. G. M. Gilbert, *Nuremberg Diary* (London, 1948) p. 41.
16. F. Wiedemann, *Der Mann, der Feldherr werden wollte* (Velbert-Kettwig, 1964) p. 144.
17. Memorandum by Dörnberg, 12 Dec. 1939, DGFP, D, VIII, no. 448; Memorandum by Schmidt, 13 Nov. 1940, DGFP, D, XI, no. 325.
18. L. E. Hill (ed.), *Die Weizsäcker Papiere 1933–1950* (Frankfurt am Main, 1974) pp. 125–6; E. von Weizsäcker, *Memoirs* (London, 1951) p. 126.
19. Kordt, *Nicht aus den Akten* pp. 225–6. See also: FO Minute (Sir R. Vansittart), 23 May 1938, PRO, FO 371/21721, C4851/1941/18; FO Minute (Mr Ashton-Gwatkin), 28 June 1938, PRO, FO 371/21663, C6577/62/18.

20. On the course of the negotiations see T. Sommer, *Deutschland und Japan zwischen den Mächten 1935–1940. Vom Antikominternpakt zum Dreimächtepakt: Eine Studie zur diplomatischen Vorgeschichte des Zweiten Weltkriegs* (Tübingen, 1962) pp. 116 ff.

21. Hill, *Die Weizsäcker Papiere* p. 126.

22. Memorandum by Vansittart, July 1938, PRO, FO 371/21708, C7007/1180/18. The memorandum contains information received in the Foreign Office on 30 June. Although it lacks a precise date, internal evidence indicates that it was prepared before 15 July. Similar arguments were advanced in May 1939. On the strength of a conversation with an official of the German embassy in Moscow 'Chips' Bohlen telegraphed to the State Department on 20 May: 'On his return from Tehran the German Ambassador in Moscow was told by Ribbentrop, *obviously reflecting Hitler's views*, that in the opinion of the German Government, Communism had ceased to exist in the Soviet Union; that the Communist International was no longer a factor of importance in Soviet foreign relations, and that consequently it was felt that no real ideological barrier remained between Germany and Russia.' (My italics.) See J. von Herwarth, *Against Two Evils: Memoirs of a Diplomat-Soldier during the Third Reich* (London, 1981) p. 155.

23. Ribbentrop, *Memoirs*, p. 109.

24. See, for example, Phipps to Hoare, 10 Dec. 1935, PRO, FO 371/18860, C8198/234/18.

25. See Ciano to Ribbentrop, 31 May 1939, DGFP, D, VI, no. 459.

26. See Memorandum by Plessen, 4 Sept. 1939. Enclosed in: Mackensen to Weizsäcker, 5 Sept. 1939, DGFP, D, VIII, no. 11. At the same time that he was threatening the Japanese with such a course of action, Ribbentrop was also seeking to drop hints in Moscow of his readiness to mediate a settlement between Moscow and Tokyo. See the draft telegram of late May 1939 to the German embassy in Moscow, DGFP, D, VI, no. 441.

27. Coulondre to Bonnet, 22 May 1939, *French Yellow Book: Diplomatic Documents 1938–39* (London, n.d.) no. 127, p. 148.

28. See, for example, FO Minute (Mr Collier), 24 Jan. 1936, PRO, FO 371/20346, N477/187/38; Minute by Wigram, 9 Oct. 1936, PRO, FO 371/19913, C7072/4/18.

29. FO Memorandum, 'The Strength of the Franco-Soviet Pact and the Chances of a Rapprochement between Germany and the USSR', 5 Mar. 1938, PRO, FO 371/21626, C2209/95/62. The memorandum was drawn up by the Central and Northern Departments of the Foreign Office in response to an American request for British views on the subject.

30. See FO Minute (Mr Peake), 23 Jan. 1939, PRO, FO 371/23686, N492/243/38.

31. Henderson to Halifax, 24 Apr. 1939, PRO, FO 371/22989, C5975/16/18.

32. Minute by Kirkpatrick, 6 May 1939, PRO, FO 371/22972, C6794/15/18.

33. Law to Sargent, 8 June 1939, PRO, FO 800/285.

34. FO Memorandum (Sir R. Vansittart), 16 May 1939, PRO, FO 371/23066, C7169/3356/18.

35. Stanhope to Halifax, 19 May 1939, PRO, Prime Minister's Office (PREM) I/409.

36. Memorandum by Hencke, 24 Aug. 1939, DGFP, D, VII, no. 213.

37. Ibid.

38. P. O. Schmidt, *Statist auf diplomatischer Bühne 1923–1945: Erlebnisse des Chef-dolmetschers im Auswärtigen Amt mit den Staatsmännern Europas* (Bonn, 1949) p. 444.

39. Rosso to Ciano, 25 Aug. 1939, cited in: M. Toscano, *Designs in Diplomacy: Pages from European Diplomatic History in the Twentieth Century* (Baltimore, 1970) p. 119.

40. F. von Sonnleithner, *Als Diplomat im 'Führerhauptquartier': Aus dem Nachlass* (Munich and Vienna, 1989) p. 98.

41. Ribbentrop, *Memoirs*, p. 130.

42. See I. Fleischhauer, 'Der deutsch-sowjetische Grenz- und Freundschaftsvertrag vom 28 September 1939: Die deutschen Aufzeichnungen über die Verhandlungen zwischen Stalin, Molotow und Ribbentrop in Moskau', *Vierteljahreshefte für Zeitgeschichte*, 39, no. 3, 1991, pp. 468–9.
43. See Sommer, *Deutschland und Japan*, pp. 296 ff.
44. Ott to the Auswärtiges Amt, 16 Oct. 1939, DGFP, D, VIII, no. 264.
45. Ribbentrop to Ott, 9 Sept. 1939, ibid. no. 40.
46. See Memorandum by Knoll, 25 Sept. 1939; Memorandum by Dörnberg, 12 Dec. 1939, ibid. nos. 132 and 448; Aufzeichnung über das Gespräch des Herrn Reichsaussenministers mit Herrn Y. Aikawa (Präsident der Mandschurischen Schwerindustriegesellschaft), 4 März 1940, Bundesarchiv, Koblenz, NS/10.
47. Memorandum by Knoll, 1 Feb. 1940, DGFP, D, VIII, no. 590.
48. G. Ciano, *Ciano's Diplomatic Papers*, ed. Malcolm Muggeridge, transl. Stuart Hood (London, 1948) p. 316.
49. Memorandum by Schmidt, 2 Oct. 1939, DGFP, D, VIII, no. 176.
50. G. Ciano, *Ciano's Diary 1939–1943*, edited with an Introduction by Malcolm Muggeridge (London, 1947) p. 159.
51. Ibid. p. 158.
52. Mussolini to Hitler, 3 Jan. 1940, DGFP, D, VIII, no. 504.
53. See, for example, Mackensen to Ribbentrop, 2 Dec. 1939, ibid. no. 410.
54. Memorandum by Ribbentrop, 10 Jan. 1940, ibid. no. 518.
55. Ciano, *Diary 1939–1943*, p. 162.
56. Sommer, *Deutschland und Japan*, p. 308. In this connection see also the draft telegram from Weizsäcker to Mackensen, ? Jan. 1940, and Weizsäcker to Ott, 24 Jan. 1940, DGFP, D, VIII, nos 549 and 567.
57. Ciano, *Diary 1939–1943*, p. 190.
58. Memorandum by Schmidt, 10 Mar. 1940, DGFP, D, VIII, no. 665.
59. Ibid.
60. Hitler to Mussolini, 8 Mar. 1940, ibid. no. 663. Ribbentrop later claimed that during the winter of 1939–40 he made strenuous efforts to bring Hitler around to his way of thinking as regards the changes which Stalin was allegedly effecting within the USSR, and believed that his arguments were not without effect. See Ribbentrop, *Memoirs*, p. 133. However, despite the fact that Hitler appears to have been prepared to use Ribbentrop's arguments as a means of appeasing Mussolini and others, there are no indications that he ever seriously considered adopting Ribbentrop's pro-Soviet anti-British course. For an indication of his continuing hostility towards Russia see: Memorandum of a Conference of the Führer with the Principal Military Commanders, 23 Nov. 1939, DGFP, D, VIII, no. 384.
61. Ciano, *Papers*, p. 356.
62. See Memorandum by Schmidt, 17 Mar. (*sic*) 1940, DGFP, D, IX, no. 1.
63. Toscano, *Designs in Diplomacy*, pp. 146 ff.
64. Mackensen to Ribbentrop, 17 Aug. 1940, DGFP, D, X, no. 357.
65. Ciano, *Papers*, p. 392.
66. See Memorandum by Ribbentrop, 24 June 1940, DGFP, D, X, no. 10.
67. A. Rossi, *The Russo-German Alliance: August 1939 – June 1941* (London, 1950) p. 133.
68. See A. Hillgruber, *Hitler, König Carol und Marschall Antonescu: Die deutsch-rumänischen Beziehungen 1938–1944* (Wiesbaden, 1965) pp. 89 ff.
69. On these issues see G. L. Weinberg, *Germany and the Soviet Union, 1939–1941* (Leiden, 1954) pp. 125 ff.
70. Ribbentrop to Tippelskirsch, 26 Sept. 1940, DGFP, D, XI, no. 109.
71. In this connection see Tippelskirsch to Ribbentrop, 27 Sept. 1940, ibid. no 113.
72. R. Cecil, *Hitler's Decision to Invade Russia 1941* (London, 1975) p. 71.
73. See Editor's Note, DGFP, D, X, p. 373.
74. Hildebrand, *Foreign Policy*, p. 102.

75. See A. Hillgruber, *Hitlers Strategie: Politik und Kriegführung 1940–41* (Frankfurt am Main, 1965) pp. 178 ff.
76. Ribbentrop to Stalin, 13 Oct. 1940, DGFP, D, XI, no. 176.
77. Ribbentrop, *Memoirs*, p. 150.
78. Ibid.
79. Ribbentrop to Stalin, 13 Oct. 1940, DGFP, D, XI, no. 176.
80. See, for example, his remarks to Ciano on 4 Nov. 1940, Ciano, *Papers*, p. 406.
81. Ribbentrop to Stalin, 13 Oct. 1940, DGFP, D, XI, no. 176.
82. Schulenburg to Ribbentrop, 22 Oct. 1940, ibid. no. 211.
83. See Cecil, *Hitler's Decision*, pp. 69 ff.
84. Weinberg, *Germany*, p. 137.
85. Führer Directive No. 18, 12 Nov. 1940, DGFP, D, XI, no. 323.
86. See Editor's Note, ibid. pp. 1056 ff. Ribbentrop himself claims that he was never informed about military questions and did not realise Hitler's intentions towards Russia until after the Yugoslavian campaign. See Ribbentrop, *Memoirs*, p. 152.
87. Memorandum by Schmidt, 13 Nov. 1940, DGFP, D, XI, no. 325.
88. Memorandum by Schmidt, 16 Nov. 1940, ibid. no. 326.
89. Memorandum by Schmidt, 15 Nov. 1940, ibid. no. 328.
90. Ibid.
91. Memorandum by Hilger, 18 Nov. 1940, ibid. no. 329.
92. K. Young (ed.), *The Diaries of Sir Robert Bruce Lockhart 1939–1965* (London, 1980) p. 557.
93. Schulenburg to Ribbentrop, 26 Nov. 1940, DGFP, D, XI, no. 404.
94. G. Hilger and A. J. Meyer, *The Incompatible Allies: A Memoir-History of German–Soviet relations 1918–1941* (New York, 1971) p. 324.
95. Weinberg, *Germany*, p. 144.
96. Ciano, *Papers*, p. 419.
97. Ribbentrop, *Memoirs*, pp. 151–2.
98. Ibid. p. 151.
99. Ibid.
100. There had been mounting concern within the Auswärtiges Amt about the deterioration of Soviet–German relations and the possibility of further crises developing into an open conflict since mid-1940. The most active groups opposed to a breach with the USSR were the diplomats in the German embassy in Moscow and the circle headed by Ernst von Weizsäcker, which included Erich Kordt and Hasso von Etzdorf. See M. Thielenhaus, *Zwischen Anpassung und Widerstand. Deutsche Diplomaten 1938–1941: Die politischen Aktivitäten der Beamtengruppe um Ernst von Weizsäcker im Auswärtigen Amt* (Paderborn, 1984) pp. 213 ff.; R. Gibbons, 'Opposition gegen *Barbarossa* im Herbst 1940: Eine Denkschrift aus der deutschen Botschaft in Moskau', *Vierteljahreshefte für Zeitgeschichte*, 23, no. 3, 1975, pp. 332 ff.
101. Hill, *Die Weizsäcker Papiere*, pp. 216 and 219.
102. Ibid. p. 226.
103. Ibid. p. 232.
104. Ibid. p. 248.
105. Ibid. p. 249.
106. Memorandum by Weizsäcker, 28 Apr. 1941, DGFP, D, XII, no. 419.
107. Memorandum by Schulenburg, 28 Apr. 1941, ibid. no. 423.
108. Herwarth, *Against Two Evils*, p. 191.
109. Ribbentrop received a copy of Schulenburg's record of his conversation with Hitler during the afternoon of 29 April.
110. Hill, *Die Weizsäcker Papiere*, p. 251.
111. Ibid. p. 252.

112. A statement attributed to Ribbentrop shortly after Munich. See Memorandum by Halifax, 21 January 1939, PRO, Papers of the Foreign Policy Committee (FP) (36) 75, Cab 27/627.
113. Bereschkow, *Stalins Dolmetscher*, p. 291.
114. Ribbentrop, *Memoirs*, p. 158.
115. E. Crankshaw, *Bismarck* (London, 1985) p. 411.

Chapter 2

The Yugoslav *Coup D'État*, 27 March 1941

DUŠAN BIBER

The purpose of this chapter is to analyse two problems which were discussed or even misinterpreted as early as 1941: Was the Barbarossa plan known to the Yugoslav authorities and was it disclosed to Prince Paul by Hitler at Berchtesgaden on 4 March 1941? Was the German attack on the Soviet Union delayed or postponed through the impact of the Yugoslav *coup d'état* of 27 March 1941?

THE DISCLOSURE OF HITLER'S PLANS

In his official history of British foreign policy Sir Llewellyn Woodward wrote:

> On the night of March 31 – April 1 a report was received from Belgrade that Hitler had told Prince Paul of Yugoslavia that he intended to attack Russia on June 30 ... On the night of 2–3 April Lord Halifax telegraphed that Mr. Welles had given him a report of the statement by Hitler to Prince Paul of his intention to attack Russia.
>
> On 6 April Mr. Eden telegraphed from Athens that the King of Greece had said that Prince Paul was quite clear that Hitler had spoken strongly against Russia and had explained that he would have to take military action in order to secure the raw materials which he needed. Hitler had said that he would choose his own time for the attack.[1]

Sir Stafford Cripps, the British ambassador in Moscow, suggested to Dr Milan Gavrilović, the Yugoslav minister in Moscow, that he should pass this information to the Soviet authorities and that he, Cripps, 'had told Stalin and Molotov of Hitler's statement to Prince Paul'. That was accomplished on the night of 6–7 April 1941, and Mr Eden repeated this information on 16 April to Mr Maiskii, the Soviet ambassador in London.[2]

'Well-informed' German sources had spread gossip in Belgrade immediately after March that Prince Paul had visited Hitler. The Associated Press duly reported this item. However, nothing was said regarding the Soviet Union.[3]

The American minister in Belgrade, Arthur Bliss Lane, reported on 30 March 1941 at 1 p.m.:

> With regard to Prince Paul's meeting with Hitler at Berchtesgaden on March 4 or 5 (not 11) I am informed by a reliable source that Hitler said to Prince Paul during a 2-hour interview Yugoslavia must sign the Tripartite Pact in her own interest as in June or July he was going to attack Russia. British Minister says foregoing fits in with information he has.[4]

However, this report should be seen in the light of Bliss's previous report of 29 March, after his discussions with the Yugoslav foreign minister, Dr Momčilo Ninčić, and his report on the minister's views. 'He said that Yugoslavia could not count on Soviet support unless the Soviet Union were in danger of being attacked by Germany. In that case the Soviet Union would probably offer Yugoslavia a military alliance.'[5]

The conclusion seems obvious. The 'reliable source' must have been someone in Yugoslav military intelligence instructed by the Yugoslav Foreign Minister and possibly the prime minister himself, Army General Dušan Simović. The most likely explanation is that the intention was to impress the Soviet Union indirectly, using British and American channels, and thereby · facilitate the forthcoming negotiations for a pact of friendship and mutual assistance between Yugoslavia and the Soviet Union. The point was that mutual assistance was not accepted by the Russians, who agreed only to a pact of friendship and non-aggression, signed on 6 April 1941 but dated 5 April.

On his way back from Moscow, the Yugoslav minister Dr Gavrilović stopped over in Ankara. From the American embassy in Turkey, Mr Kelley, the first secretary, reported the content of his conversation with the Yugoslav minister on 16 June 1941:

> The Führer stated that Germany was undertaking operations in the Balkans in connection with its campaign against Russia, and that as soon as the Balkan campaign was finished, he would proceed against the Soviet Union. Gavrilović stated that this was the most effective argument to use with Prince Paul on account of the latter's hatred of

the Soviet Union. When Mr. Gavrilović subsequently had occasion to
tell Molotov of this conversation, the latter stated, 'We are ready'.[6]

In a conversation between Prince Paul and King George of Greece nothing
of this was mentioned. The British minister in Athens, Sir Michael C. Palairet,
reported on 31 March 1941:

> Prince Paul had given some account of his interview with Hitler which
> appears to have taken place at Berchtesgaden early this month. Hitler
> had spoken like a warlord and used threatening language about those
> countries whose attitude displeased him ... The King formed the
> impression that Prince Paul had been considerably scared at this inter-
> view.

Mr Nicholas minuted on 1 April: 'I think the worst count in the indictment
against Prince Paul is that he did not tell us the truth about this visit.'[7] Nor
did Sir Terence Shone, Anthony Eden's special envoy, give any hint of this
in his memorandum on Prince Paul dated 28 March 1941:

> With the departure of 'our friend' the hand which has guided Yugoslav
> foreign policy for the last six years has been removed and we have lost
> what has been until lately the most valuable source of information and
> the best medium for exerting our influence on Yugoslav policy which
> we have possessed since the days of King Alexander.[8]

Sir Winston Churchill did not repeat in his memoirs the story of Hitler's
'revelation' to Prince Paul.[9] Prince Paul explicitly denied the story in his
letter of 15 March 1968, answering the query posed by Dr Ilija Jukić.[10] As
Barton Whaley sagely concluded:

> Whatever the source, the Americans and British were deceived. Quite
> aside from the inherent unlikelihood of Hitler making such an early
> disclosure of BARBAROSSA to Prince Paul, no record of it has been
> found in the German files ... Hitler's alleged revelation of BAR-
> BAROSSA was only a rumor, one that probably originated in the
> Simović – Gavrilović circle.'[11]

After the war Colonel Vladimir Vauhnik, who in 1941 was serving as a
Yugoslav military attaché in Berlin, told the historian Jacob B. Hoptner that
during the second week in March he had warned the aide-de-camp of Prince
Paul and the Yugoslav General Staff of the impending German attack on the
Soviet Union. No answer was received from Belgrade and Colonel Vauhnik
therefore informed Dr Ivo Andrić (the Yugoslav minister in Berlin), the
British (through the Swedish Military Attaché) and General Tupikov (the

Soviet military attaché), who was already aware of this information. After the Yugoslav *coup d'état* Colonel Vauhnik passed this information to Colonel Bernard Paxton, the United States military attaché in Berlin and also to his assistant Captain John Lovell. Colonel Vauhnik actually disclosed some of his sources, giving their full names: Count Sigismund Bernstorff, the Count's cousin Albert, and Willy Pabst, formerly a major in the *Wehrmacht* High Command (OKW).[12] However, in Colonel Vauhnik's memoirs published posthumously, these persons were identified only by initials.[13] The historian J. B. Hoptner mentioned Admiral Canaris, the powerful head of the German *Abwehr* and his deputy General Hans Oster as the most valuable sources for Colonel Vauhnik, who supplied this information himself but gave no further details.[14]

The official history of British intelligence in the Second World War states: 'By 1 April, it appears, the Yugoslav Military Attaché in Berlin had got wind of the German plan and his government had passed this information to Moscow via London.'[15] This date should perhaps be corrected to mid-March, if Colonel Vauhnik is to be believed. As far as Yugoslav historians know, not a single report by Colonel Vauhnik on *Barbarossa* has survived. Nor did the German Sonderkommando von Kuensberg enjoy any success in searching Yugoslav documents captured in Belgrade and in other cities. The German Sicherheitsdienst interrogated Colonel Vauhnik thoroughly; he was first released in Belgrade, then rearrested and taken to Gestapo headquarters in Berlin. In his letter of 15 August to Ribbentrop, Reinhard Heydrich described the main source of Colonel Vauhnik's achievement as 'social espionage'.[16]

After the war, General Petar Kostić was interrogated. In his statement made to the Yugoslav War Crimes Commission he quoted Hitler's words to Prince Paul: 'You can't go to war with Russia if war starts between us [Germany] and Russia, because your people are against it as they are against the war with England. We don't ask you to take part in the war on our side.'[17]

THE YUGOSLAV COUP D'ÉTAT

Colonel William Donovan, director of the American OSS (Office of Strategic Services) visited Belgrade in February 1941, and among other high-ranking government officials he talked to General Dušan Simović, the commander of the Yugoslav air force. General Simović was the only individual who speculated on possible German actions in the future. Colonel Louis J. Fortier, the United States military attaché, minuted:

Germany would attack Russia for the purpose of seizing the Ukraine initially, and eventually overpower south-east Europe. After all, this had always been Germany's primary aim ... Once these forces had become over-extended, then Russia would attack Germany ... In General Simović's opinion, plan three is the more likely one to be adopted by Germany, with an initial, main effort against Russia.

Simović believed that the British Isles, North Africa and Russia formed the German target list.[18]

After the defeat of Yugoslavia in May 1941 and the German occupation, the Yugoslav Royal Government escaped to Greece, Palestine and finally to London. Prime Minister General Simović delivered a lengthy 50-minute speech on the BBC for Serbian National Day, 28 June:

> This German action might have had very serious military consequences. However, the attack against Turkey, the Near East and Russia was postponed by the events following upon March 27th, when Yugoslavia became her chief enemy ... Yugoslavia frustrated the plans of the German General Staff, forced it to lose time, and thereby saved Allied Turkey and the Near East and made impossible the envelopment of Russia from the south and the attack on it from the rear over the Caucasus to the east of the Caspian sea, and forced Hitler to limit himself to a frontal attack.[19]

Mr Dixon of the Southern Department of the Foreign Office read this speech in advance and minuted on 27 June: 'General Simović would have it that Yugoslav resistance saved Turkey from this attack, prevented the encirclement of Russia and forced Hitler to attack Russia from the front. All this may be a bit fanciful but it is good propaganda.'[20]

The press subsequently made frequent reference to this argument, to a degree that the repetition became almost a myth in its own right – Yugoslavia saved Moscow, and saved the Soviet Union.[21] Little wonder that General Milan Nedić and the Serbian quisling press reacted almost immediately, describing General Simović in ironic terms as the 'saviour of Bolshevism'.[22]

At the Nuremberg International Military Tribunal the minutes of Hitler's conference in the Reichskanzlei on 27 March 1941 were considered to be the final proof. Hitler was enraged and decided to punish and destroy Yugoslavia: 'In this connection the beginning of Operation Barbarossa will have to be postponed for anything up to four weeks'.[23] Professor Hugh Seton-Watson observed: 'Yugoslavia's action compelled Hitler to bring up additional troops for his Balkan campaign. The campaign took longer and required more men than had been anticipated. The consequent modification of plan and change of troop movements lost Hitler one valuable month of campaigning weather in Russia.'[24]

Elizabeth Wiskemann, referring to the meeting in the Reichskanzlei, came to a similar conclusion: 'The attack upon Russia was originally to have taken place in the middle of May, but the crushing of Yugoslavia delayed it for about five weeks.'[25]

Hugh Dalton, Minister of Economic Warfare – whose responsibilities included superintendence of SOE (Special Operations Executive) – expressed his own belief that 'the effect of this coup, disappointing as it was in military terms in Yugoslavia itself, delayed the German attack by a precious fortnight'.[26]

In his plea for Draža Mihailović in 1946, David Martin came to the following conclusion: 'The Germans were able to overcome the Yugoslav Army in twelve days. But the revolution of 27 March cost them the war.'[27]

Cordell Hull is more restrained in his memoirs when he speculates along the lines of 'what if'.[28] Max Beloff takes issue with Goering's claim that 'the German attack on Russia might not have taken place but for the alleged complicity of the Russians in the Belgrade *coup*'. He went on to conclude: 'The Balkan campaign following the *coup d'état* in Yugoslavia did, in fact, have the effect of postponing the date of the attack on Russia, originally intended for 15 May.'[29]

Hamilton Fish Armstrong described the German delay as decisive: 'Thus the *coup d'état* in Belgrade, carried out by men who were as thoroughly anti-Communist as they were anti-Nazi, had the ironical result of saving the Communist capital.'[30]

The well-known American writer Louis Adamić, quoting James Klugman's *Yugoslavia Faces the Future*, believed that mass demonstrations actually delayed Hitler's attack on the Soviet Union for five full weeks.[31] William Shirer quoted Field Marshal Friedrich von Paulus to the effect that Hitler's decision to destroy Yugoslavia postponed the beginning of *Barbarossa* by 'about five weeks'.[32] P. D. Ostović, referring to Liddell Hart, nevertheless doubted this: 'General Halder, the Chief of the German General Staff at that time, and other German officers maintained that the attack against Russia could not have started before the middle of June, 1941 as the ground was not sufficiently dry before that date.'[33] Professor Butler, writing in *Grand Strategy*, was both cautious and inclined to be critical when he set down these conclusions:

> Nevertheless, there is no mention in the German records of a post-ponement of 'Barbarossa' until the *coup d'état* of 27 March in Belgrade, which led Hitler to undertake 'Operation 25' against Yugoslavia. On

that day the Russian adventure was put off for about four weeks, and on April 7 Brauchitsch issued an order stating that the development of the situation in Yugoslavia, with the necessary deployment of greater forces in the south-east, required changes in the course of preparations for 'Barbarossa'. The postponement would be from four to six weeks: all preliminary plans would be completed in such a way as to make it possible to start the offensive about June 22. This date was finally confirmed on April 30.

These details are of great significance: for the argument seems valid, that, if as result of the delaying influence of Operation 25 the High Command were already on 7 April contemplating launching 'Barbarossa' on 22 June and confirmed this date on 30 April, then events occurring in the intervening period could scarcely have caused an additional 'postponement'.[34]

Walter Ansel was apparently thinking along the same lines:

Time was of the essence for more reasons than one: the digression into Yugoslavia could retard Barbarossa. Without any quibble Hitler faced up to a four-week delay. This alone established Marita's importance as a part of Barbarossa: elimination of Yugoslavia had become essential. A delay of nearly six weeks did result from all causes – Yugoslavia, weather and others. In fact, Barbarossa could not have gained these weeks by starting earlier because during this period bad weather in the east would have mired any start.[35]

Martin van Creveld undertook a professional analysis of the complicated military aspects of *Barbarossa* and concluded that the Germans concentrated their troops in the east even earlier than was originally laid down. German troops were withdrawn from Greece through Yugoslav territory, which according to the treaty signed in Vienna was not part of any previous plan.[36]

Finally, we can call Herr Hitler himself as a star witness. Major Engel noted his conversations with Hitler on 24 March 1941 on the eve of the Vienna ceremony and three days before the Belgrade *coup d'état*:

F. [uehrer] ist sehr ungluecklich und besorgt ueber die Lage auf dem Balkan. Das bevorstehende Eingreiffen werfe ihm sein ganzes Konzept ueber den Haufen, die grossen Ziele muessten alle verschoben werden, und in der zweite Haelfte Mai die Sowjetunion anzugreiffen, waere unmoeglich. An sich waeren ein paar Wochen frueher oder spaeter nich so schlimm, aber man duerfte auf keinen Fall in den russischen Winter kommen. Jetzt sei fruehster Termin Ende Juni, und man weiss nie, wann der Sommer aufhoert. Diesen ganzen Bloedsinn verdankte

man leider den Italieneren ... In diesem Zusammenhang fielen harte Woerte ueber den Duce.[37]

[The Führer is very unhappy and worried about the situation in the Balkans. The planned intervention throws his entire concept into confusion, the major objectives must be completely displaced, and to attack the Soviet Union in the second half of May may prove to be impossible. As regards that matter a few weeks earlier or later is not so bad, but under no circumstances do we want to hit the Russian winter. Now the earliest deadline should be the end of June, but we never know when summer comes to an end. For all this complete nonsense we have unfortunately the Italians to thank. In this respect some strong language was used about the Duce.] (trans. J. Erickson)

Notes

1. Sir Llewellyn Woodward, *British Foreign Policy in the Second World War* (HMSO, London, 1970) vol. I, pp. 604, 605 and 609.
2. See also Earl of Avon, *The Memoirs of Anthony Eden: The Reckoning* (Collins, London, 1965) pp. 220, 229, 230 and 265.
3. Public Record Office (PRO), FO 371/29779, R 2158, R 2372/113/67.
4. *Foreign Relations of the United States* (FRUS), vol. II, 1941, p. 973. Cf. Constantin Fotitch, *The War We Lost* (The Viking Press, New York, 1948) p. 58; Alfredo Breccia, *Jugoslavia 1939–1941* Giuffrè, Rome, 1978) pp. 503, 505, note 51; Dušan Biber, 'Knez Pavle u britanskoj konfinaciji' ('Prince Paul in British Confinement'), in *Casopis za suvremenu povijest*, II–III, 1976, p. 26.
5. FRUS, II, 1941, p. 972.
6. FRUS, I, 1941, p. 315.
7. PRO, FO 371/30255, R 3308/2752/92.
8. PRO, FO 371/30270, R 4320/3617/92.
9. Sir Winston Churchill, *The Second World War*, vol. III (*The Grand Alliance*) (Cassell, London, 1950) p. 141.
10. Ilija Jukić, *The Fall of Yugoslavia* (Harcourt Brace Jovanovich, New York and London, 1974) p. 82.
11. Barton Whaley, *Codeword Barbarossa* (The MIT Press, Cambridge, Massachusetts and London, 1973) pp. 58–60 and 28. A Leak from Berchtesgaden? Alfredo Breccia, *Jugoslavia 1939–1941*, p. 503 is cautious regarding Hitler's statements ('sembra ... avrebbe confidato'). Nevertheless, later he seems to accept this story at face value.
12. Jacob B. Hoptner, *Jugoslavija u krizi 1934–1941* (*Jugoslavia in Crisis 1934–1941*) (Otokar Kersovani, Rijeka, 1972) pp. 231–2.
13. Vladimir Vauhnik, *Nevidna fronta* (Ljubljana, 1972) pp. 141–52.
14. Jacob B. Hoptner, *Jugoslavija*, p. 272, note 53.
15. F. H. Hinsley et al., *British Intelligence in the Second World War*, (HMSO, London, 1979) vol. I, p. 453, note 102, referring to M. R. D. Foot, *Resistance* (HMSO, London, 1976) p. 188. Edward Beneš, *Paměti* (Prague, 1948) p. 229 claims that he conveyed to the Yugoslav minister in London Mr Subbotich Colonel Moravec's information about German preparations for the attack on the Soviet Union and plans for the partition of Yugoslavia. No trace was found in the files of Yugoslav legation in London. General Simović stated on 14 June 1951 (Archives of Yugoslav Armed

Forces 21/2-2) that in mid-March he had twice warned Prince Paul that Hitler was going to attack the Soviet Union and perish there.

16. V. Vauhnik, *Nevidna fronta*, p. 170, App.
17. Archives of Yugoslav Armed Forces, Belgrade, 2/1-231.
18. The National Archives and Records Administration, Washington DC, RG 59, Decimal File 74.00118, European War 1939/52. Enclosure) 7 to Despatch) 1109 of 1 February 1941, 'Visit of William J. Donovan to Belgrade'.
19. PRO, FO 371/30210, R 6732/73/92. The same document is also in the Archives of Yugoslavia (Arhiv Jugoslavije) AJ 103-24-160.
20. Ibid.
21. *The Times*, 11 August 1941; *The Times*, 27 March 1942: 'The coup certainly delayed the attack on Russia for six weeks; and this delay had an enormous, probably a decisive effect, bearing on the fortunes of that mementous campaign.' Similar arguments were repeated on the BBC on 28 February 1942 and 3 March 1942, and in Livingston Hall on 31 March 1943 (Archives of Yugoslav Armed Forces, 8-6/1-1).
22. *Obnova* (Belgrade) 2 December 1941.
23. IMT, Nuremberg, XXVIII, p. 23 (1746-PS), Besprechung über die Lage in Jugoslawien.
24. Hugh Seton-Watson, *Eastern Europe between the Wars 1918–1941* (CUP, Cambridge, 1946) p. 408.
25. Elizabeth Wiskemann, *The Rome – Berlin Axis* (New York and London, 1949) pp. 257 and 260.
26. Hugh Dalton, *The Fateful Years: Memoirs 1931–1945* (London, 1957) p. 375.
27. David Martin, *Ally Betrayed* (New York, 1946) p. 18. However, in his latest book *The Web of Disinformation* (Harcourt Brace Jovanovich, San Diego, New York and London, 1990) p. 22, he reduces the delay to 'two or three weeks', and still believes that 'it may very well have saved Moscow'. He changed his conclusion into 'may have cost the war'. Julian Amery, *Approach March* (London, 1973) p. 229 believes: 'It may even have saved Moscow.' Peter II, King of Yugoslavia, *A King's Heritage* (London, 1953) p. 62 repeats the story: 'Because of this war Hitler was forced to delay his plan to attack Russia. This delay was an invaluable contribution to the Allied cause.'
28. Cordell Hull, *The Memoirs of Cordell Hull*, (New York, 1949) vol. II, p. 933.
29. Max Beloff, *The Foreign Policy of Soviet Russia*, (OUP, London, 1949) vol. II, p. 366.
30. Fish Hamilton Armstrong, *Tito and Goliath* (New York, 1951) p. 10.
31. Louis Adamić, *The Eagle and the Roots* (Garden City, 1952) pp. 428–9.
32. William Shirer, *The Rise and Fall of the Third Reich* (Secker & Warburg, London, 1960) p. 830.
33. P. D. Ostović, *The Truth about Yugoslavia* (New York, 1952) p. 165.
34. Ramsay Montagu Butler, *Grand Strategy*, vol. II (*September 1939 – June 1941*) (HMSO, London, 1957) pp. 540–1.
35. Walter Ansel, *Hitler and the Middle Sea* (Duke University Press, Durham, NC, 1972) p. 124.
36. Martin van Creveld, *The Balkan Clue: Hitler's Strategy 1940–1941* (London, 1973) pp. 170–6.
37. Hildegard von Kotze (ed.), *Heeresadjutant bei Hitler 1939–1943: Aufzeichnugen des Majors Engel* (Deutsche Verlags-Anstalt, Stuttgart, 1974) p. 98.

Ribbentrop and Stalin, 23 August 1939.

Below: A delighted Ribbentrop accepts the plaudits at Koenigsberg following the signature of the Nazi-Soviet Pact, 24 August 1939.

The Yugoslav
coup, Belgrade,
27 March
1941.

Opposite: 'Decree of the Supreme Soviet: declaring a state of war', 22 June 1941.

У К А З

ПРЕЗИДИУМА ВЕРХОВНОГО СОВЕТА СССР
О военном положении

Prince Paul, with Hitler (below), on a military parade, Berlin, 1941.

Chapter 3

British Intelligence and Barbarossa

H. F. HINSLEY

On 31 May 1941, just when they were completing their arrangements for the occupation of Syria, the commanders-in-chief in the Middle East were informed by the Chiefs of Staff that Germany was concentrating large army and air forces against Russia, was demanding concessions from the Soviet Government and would march if its demands were refused. As may be judged from the date and the contents of this telegram, the Whitehall authorities had been slow to reach agreement on the conclusion that Germany would make an attack on Russia, an undertaking which it had been preparing throughout the previous winter. Even when they finally settled these differences – a bare three weeks before the attack – the Whitehall authorities were still failing to understand that Germany had not just been preparing war in the event of the breakdown of negotiations and after the dispatch of an ultimatum, but an unconditional invasion, a surprise assault.[1]

One reason for their slowness was that speculation about the possibility of a German attack on Russia had run ahead of Germany's preparations – ahead, indeed, of Hitler's first instructions to prepare the attack. By giving rise to rumours before there could possibly be any foundation for them in intelligence, the disbelief with which they later greeted genuine pointers to Germany's intention was strengthened.

As early as 14 June 1940 – the day on which Paris fell – the Foreign Office, prompted by the wish to get on to closer terms with Russia, was advising Sir Stafford Cripps, the newly appointed ambassador to Moscow, that the Russians were alarmed by Germany's victories in France. Cripps then told Molotov that 'according to our information' Germany would be forced to turn east if France collapsed.[2] On 26 June, the Prime Minister sent – via Cripps – a warning to Stalin to the same effect.[3] There is no ground for doubting whether these warnings were sincere. On 27 June the Prime Minister expressed his opinion to Smuts: 'If Hitler fails to beat us here he will probably recoil eastwards. Indeed, he may do this without attempting invasion ...'[4] But the views expressed by Cripps and the Prime Minister had not been advanced by the intelligence branches. On the contrary, a divergence between their views and those of the Foreign Office emerged during the preparation of a Joint Intelligence Committee (JIC) paper on Germany's intentions that was issued on 2 July. While the Foreign Office cast some doubt on Germany's determination to invade the United Kingdom and, though not expecting it at once, allowed for a German move into the Ukraine, Military Intelligence (MI) insisted that Germany would give absolute priority to *Sealion*.[5]

After the beginning of July, when it became manifest that Germany was preparing for *Sealion*, the conviction of the Service staffs that the defeat of Great Britain was Germany's overriding objective was universally accepted. On 5 August 1940 the JIC concluded unanimously, with no trace of dissension, that Germany and Russia both had the best of reasons for avoiding an open clash.[6] By the middle of October, however, when the threat of invasion was receding, Cripps and the Prime Minister had returned to their earlier speculations, and the earlier dissension between the Foreign Office and MI had reappeared. Cripps now told the Foreign Office that the Russians were so consumed with fear of Germany and Japan that it was unnecessary for him to warn them of the dangers of an Axis attack; and at the end of the month, his response to the news that Molotov was going to Berlin was to repeat that in the long run, probably during 1941, the fundamental hostility between Germany and Russia would reassert itself.[7] On 31 October, the Prime Minister – this time in verbal briefing of senior military commanders – took the view that Germany would inevitably turn on Russia during 1941 for the sake of its oil.[8] By then this view had recovered ground in the Foreign Office. On 29 September MI had asserted that 'the time will never come ... when it will be safe to say that invasion of the UK is off', and on 7 October, in a letter to the Director of Military Intelligence (DMI), the Foreign Office Chairman of the JIC had protested that his assertion was 'irrational' and that MI's attitude was 'crippling our strategy'.[9]

Until the end of October 1940, the reluctance of MI to believe that Germany could cease to regard Britain as its main enemy was justified not only by the knowledge that it was giving priority to the *Sealion* front, but also by the state of intelligence about its intentions towards Russia. In June Cripps had supported his warning to Molotov by referring to 'our information', but no such information had been received in Whitehall. Nor was any obtained during the next three months, a fact which is not surprising in the light of the state of Germany's preparations.

On 21 July, soon after he had issued his *Sealion* directive and learned that the British Government had rejected his peace offer, Hitler had ordered preliminary studies for an attack on Russia. On 29 and 30 July he had decided that preparations should begin for a five-month *Blitzkrieg* against Russia from May 1941, in case major operations against the United Kingdom had to be deferred. On 5 August, the High Command of the German Armies (OKH) had received a first study for the operation. As yet, however, the German planning was confined to Hitler and a handful of his senior officers, so that Sigint was silent on the subject, and the other sources – the Secret Intelligence Service (SIS) and British diplomatic reports – merely duplicated the speculation in which people in Whitehall were themselves engaging.

In July 1940, the SIS reported that the Soviet Military Attaché in Berlin had warned his government that Germany was preparing to attack Russia. In the same month, however, another SIS agent concluded that war with Russia 'was out of the question at present'. The reports from diplomatic sources were no less contradictory, some claiming that Russia and Germany were both preparing for a clash, and others claiming that Hitler had renounced his earlier eastern aspirations. Among the latter, one dwelt in some detail on the German anxiety to refute Cripps: the German embassy in Moscow was saying that the warning he had put about was based on the movement of German divisions to Poland, and was explaining that these divisions were not first-line troops and had been sent east because they could not be maintained in France. This might have been the basis for suspecting that Germany was protesting too much, but it would have been a flimsy basis and any tendency to make much of it must have been checked by the Russian Government's response to the warnings from Cripps and Churchill: on 1 August it denounced the attempts of Great Britain to drive a wedge between Russia and Germany.

By the end of October the number of German divisions facing Russia had been increased from 15 to 33 (including 5 armoured, 2 motorised and 1 cavalry), and the logistic preparations in the east – the establishment of training centres and airfields, the transfer of supply depots and the development of communications – had begun in earnest. During September, following a concentration of Russian troops against Finland, Germany had negotiated the passage of German troops through Finland and increased its forces in north Norway. Germany was concerned with the protection of the Romanian oil and the Finnish nickel in the event of Russian moves against them, but its attempt to explain its eastward deployments as being defensive and its insistence that the logistical preparations were being made for economic, not military, reasons did not wholly satisfy the Russians. By mid-September another problem was creating friction between the two countries. In consequence of Hitler's orders at the end of July, that the German army be raised to 180 divisions, German deliveries to Russia were falling so far behind what had been promised in the trade agreement of February 1940 that the Russians temporarily cancelled all long-term projects for exports to Germany. By 1 November they were complaining that Germany could apparently deliver war material to Finland but not to Russia. Alongside these developments, which were increasingly difficult to conceal from the Russians, Germany had taken highly confidential steps to further the preparations for a Russian campaign. On 28 September, Hitler had confirmed his verbal orders for the expansion of the Army and the creation of new divisions for the east, and had laid down that these were to be ready by 1 May. Also in September, the *Abwehr* had been instructed to improve its neglected coverage of Russia – though Hitler had vetoed OKH's wish to begin photographic reconnaissance of Russia for fear that this would disclose his intentions. By mid-October Army Group East had been set up in Poland and OKH had moved its HQ from France to Zossen.[10]

On these developments Whitehall received several reports from the SIS and diplomatic sources. Some contained rumours of a breakdown in Russo-German trade relations. In particular, an SIS source reported that Mikoyan was opposing the export of materials which the USSR needed for its own defence. Other reports claimed that Russia was putting pressure on Finland (for such things as demilitarisation of the Aaland Islands) and that Germany was sending troops to Finland, garrisoning the nickel mines there and signing an agreement with Finland for the transit of German troops to north Norway. But the reports put different interpretations on these developments. Some spoke of an increase in Russia's military precautions against a German attack and indicated that some circles, particularly the Swedish Government, were convinced that a German attack on Russia would not be long delayed. Others said that Germany was only reacting to a Russian threat and was taking every possible care not to antagonise Russia. Up to the last day of October, when the War Office weekly intelligence summary reported that the Russians were undertaking large-scale manoeuvres in order to improve standards in their army,[11] the intelligence branches had commented on none of these reports. But given the nature of the reports they can scarcely be blamed for their reticence.

Up to the same date, Whitehall had received two other items of intelligence to which it, arguably, paid too little attention. One came from A-54. On 22 August he reported that he had learned from an OKH officer that the intelligence branch responsible for the Russian area – OKH's Foreign Army East – had been expanding since June; that the *Abwehr*'s counter-intelligence activities against Russia were also to be increased as a matter of urgency; and that the *Abwehr* in Romania had been reinforced by specialists on the southern Ukraine, the Crimea and the Caucasus. None of the intelligence branches drew the attention of the JIC, the chiefs of staff or the Cabinet to this item. By the end of September, however, A-54 was predicting that Germany's occupation of Romania was imminent, and would be followed by German advances through Turkey and Spain.[12]

The second item of intelligence that might have been thought significant concerned the eastward deployment of German divisions. On 27 August, MI accepted that a very considerable addition to the troops in Poland was taking place, and quoted reports of a total of sixty divisions there. The figure was a considerable over-estimate; the number of German divisions in Poland reached twenty-five in September and did not increase till 1941. But MI concluded that not even sixty divisions constituted an undue concentration of German forces in the east: the Germans had to keep their spare divisions somewhere, and from Poland they could use them to intervene anywhere in Europe.[13] In thus rejecting any association between information about the German order of battle and the rumours about a German attack on Russia, MI was basing itself on the belief that Germany was giving priority to *Sealion*.

After the German entry into Romania in October 1940, the German threat to the Middle East replaced *Sealion* as the chief ground for the conviction that the defeat of Britain was Germany's chief priority, and thus for the view that rumours about German preparations for an attack on Russia should be ignored.

At first, it is true, MI had some difficulty in deciding what to make of the growing evidence that the German army was expanding and embarking on a large mechanisation programme. On 31 October it recognised that

> Germany is preparing for a campaign in areas suitable for operations by mechanised forces on a large scale.... These areas might equally well be Russia or the Middle East. Furthermore, ... in the Ukraine Germany can find her raw materials. In addition to which there have been signs recently of increasing nervousness on the part of the Russians as to Hitler's future intentions.

To MI, however, it seemed probable that Hitler, yielding reluctantly to the advice of his military advisers, had decided to postpone *Sealion* and prepare for an advance through the Balkans to Turkey. Its conclusion was that Hitler 'sees dangers in this policy which may bring him into conflict with Russia and dislikes it because it will not yield quick results, but he is wise enough to see that he may have to adopt it'.[14]

Once it had accepted that Hitler had temporarily turned away from *Sealion* and was contemplating operations against Great Britain in the Balkans and the Mediterranean, MI supplemented its belief that Germany would not wish to tackle Russia until it had disposed of the United Kingdom with the argument that it nevertheless had to prepare against the possibility of a Russian attack on itself while it was engaged in the south and the south-east. On 27 October, MI was using the argument to explain the move of German troops to Finland – of which it then had 'confirmed evidence' – and the German – Finnish transit agreement of September – of which it had now obtained the details.[15] On 3 November, Air Intelligence (AI) adopted the same line: the move to Finland had completed Germany's European bulwark against Russia.[16] On 6 and 12 November, MI extended the explanation to cover the German deployment in eastern Europe. The purpose of this, as of the move to Finland, was to hold Russia off while Germany advanced through Bulgaria and Thrace to the Middle East and helped Italy to subdue Greece.[17] On 16 December it declared that 'Germany thinks that 58 divisions in Poland and 10 in East Prussia, as well as fortifications in Poland and a potential base in Finland, will keep Russia quiet.'[18] On 24 December it repeated the same view: Germany did not want a two-front war and would not fight Russia until it had disposed of Great Britain.[19] On 1 January 1941, by which time a recently established network of Polish agents had disclosed that a considerable amount of west – east road and rail construction was taking place in Slovakia, MI's explanation was that Germany was preparing to move troops from Poland and the Protectorate to Romania for the attack on Greece.[20]

On 9 January 1941, the first inter-departmental study of German intentions that had been attempted since early November followed the line laid down by MI: German forces in eastern Europe had been moved there to guard against a Russian attack while Germany advanced into the Balkans; until it had defeated Great Britain, Germany would not wish to fight Russia 'except in dire necessity'.[21] On the same day, Hitler reaffirmed his intention to invade Russia at the middle or the end of May 1941, despite expressions of anxiety about the undertaking from OKH and Admiral Raeder. Their doubts had increased as they had watched Hitler's plans take shape in a series of decisions and directives during the previous two months. In a directive, on 12 November – at the outset of Molotov's visit to Berlin of 12–13 November – he had confirmed the verbal orders for the preparation of the invasion which he had issued on 31 July. After the Molotov visit he had decided that there should be no attempt to reach a negotiated settlement with Russia: diplomatic exchanges should be continued only for the purpose of deception and as a means of preserving the advantage of a surprise attack. The release of the *Barbarossa* directive had followed on 18 December. Based on plans submitted to Hitler by OKH on 5 December, this laid down that Soviet Russia was to be defeated in one rapid campaign 'even before the conclusion of the war with England'. The Army was to assign all available units to this task, subject only to the protection of the occupied countries. The German Air Force (GAF) was to release units for the support of the Army in an eastern campaign in such strength as would ensure that land operations were brought to a rapid conclusion and that eastern Germany suffered as little as possible from enemy air attack. This concentration in the east was to be limited only by the need to protect supply bases and operational areas as a whole against air attack and to ensure that the offensive against Britain, and in particular against its supply routes, was not brought to a standstill. Orders for deployment against Russia would be issued eight weeks before the operation was due to start. Preparations requiring a longer period, if they had not started already, would be put in hand at once and be completed before 15 May 1941. It was 'of decisive importance that the intention to attack should not become known'. Knowledge of these further decisions was confined to the highest levels in Germany, and no whisper of them reached Whitehall. Two obstacles nevertheless stood in the way of a total acceptance of inter-departmental appreciation of 9 January.

The first was the fact that rumours about German preparations for an attack on Russia had been increasing. During November and December 1940, the SIS was reporting that its contacts among the Balt aristocrats were openly saying that they would soon regain their estates 'in the wake of the German army'. From November the world's Press – notably the *Neue Züricher Zeitung* and the *Chicago Daily News* – began to carry stories of a coming Russo-German war.[22] By the end of November the eastward deployment of the German army was the subject of constant and nervous speculation among the diplomatic corps in Moscow.[23] In November, the SIS man in Helsinki reported that he had heard from *Abwehr* officers that Germany would attack Russia in the spring.

In an appreciation issued on 17 January 1941, MI noted that there had been 'a number of suggestions lately that Germany may be intending' an attack on Russia and proceeded to examine them in the light of what was known about the deployment of the German army. The three German divisions in north Norway were probably there to guard against the danger of British raids. There were 1,500 troops in Finland – this was a lines-of-communication contingent. The six divisions in Slovakia evoked no comment. Of the presence of German divisions on the Romanian frontier with Russia there was no evidence. Improvements were being made to the communications between Germany and Russian Poland – these were 'probably intended for implementing more rapidly recent economic agreements rather than for any military purpose in the immediate future'. Similar work in Romania indicated preparation for operations in the south-east rather than against Russia. As for Poland, the number of German divisions there had now climbed to seventy in MI's estimates but most of them had been there since the previous summer and many of them were internal security divisions, not part of the field army. Apart from the fact that the Germans were undertaking a good deal of work on fortifications on the Russo-German frontier – which made it unlikely that Germany contemplated any offensive action in the area–German dispositions and preparations in the neighbourhood of Russia's frontiers 'cannot at the moment be described as anything but normal'.[24]

The second obstacle was the lingering suspicion elsewhere in Whitehall that military order of battle intelligence was not everything – that there was some substance to the persistent rumours. This suspicion had flared up again in November 1940, at the time of Molotov's negotiations in Berlin in which Molotov had insisted on Russia's interest in Finland and the Balkans and resisted Hitler's suggestion that Russia should expand in the direction of Persia and India. Though the negotiations had been commented on in countless reports from British embassies, the British Government had learned little about their true purpose or their outcome, and the speculation of MI and the Foreign Office on these subjects had diverged. For MI, Molotov's visit to Berlin had been made necessary by the need for closer contact between the Russian and the German Governments at a time when German troop concentrations on the Russian frontiers – made by Germany in order to secure her rear – were alarming the Russians, and when the Germans were anxious to know Russia's attitude to their extension of the war into the Balkans and against Turkey.[25] In the opinion of the Foreign Office, the important points had been that Russian policy in the Balkans was running counter to German designs and that Russia had not responded to Germany's attempt to get it to support a German move into the Middle or Near East.[26]

By 22 January, when it had learned that Russia and Germany had renewed their economic agreement and signed a Pact of Friendship, the Foreign Office was commenting with approval that in the appreciation of 17 January MI had on military grounds reached the same conclusion as it had itself reached on political grounds: that there was no reason to expect an early German attack.[27] This view was not shared by the Prime Minister or Cripps. On 6 January, the former had again referred to the possibility that Hitler would turn east. 'A great campaign in the east of Europe', he wrote, 'the defeat of Russia, the conquest of the Ukraine and an advance ... to the Caspian would none of them, separately or together, bring him victorious peace.'[28] On 20 January, no doubt on his initiative, the Defence Committee of the Cabinet debated, inconclusively, whether, beyond Bulgaria, Germany's object was to operate against the British or to drive into the Ukraine and the Caucasus.[29] On 24 February he commented that Russia was now in an unenviable position and that its attitude was one of making concessions to Germany in order to gain time.[30] Cripps, meeting the Foreign Secretary and the Chief of the Imperial General Staff (CIGS) in Ankara at the end of the month, found that the CIGS believed that Germany was still giving priority to *Sealion*. In contrast, he himself was still convinced that Germany would attack Russia first, and that it would do so 'not later than the end of June'.[31] Early in March the rumour was circulating around the embassies in Moscow that on his return from Ankara Cripps had told Vyshinski, the deputy foreign minister, that in his personal opinion – based on reliable sources–Germany would turn on Russia after defeating Greece, Yugoslavia and Turkey.

What, since it did not exist in Whitehall, was the source of his 'reliable' information? A possible answer is provided by what is known of American intelligence about the *Barbarossa* preparations. According to some American published accounts, the United States Commercial Attaché in Berlin had been kept informed of the initial planning between August and December 1940 by a senior member of the Nazi Party, and some time between early January and mid-February 1941 he was given full details of Hitler's *Barbarossa* directive of 18 December and of the Führer's conference on the subject of 9 January 1941. According to the same accounts, Washington received this information on 21 February and gave it to the Russian Ambassador in Washington on 1 March – the further delay being in part due to consultations with the United States Ambassador in Moscow and to his advice that the Russians would distrust a warning and regard it as a provocation.[32] Cripps was perhaps informed of this development by his American colleague. There is no evidence, however, that Whitehall received any information at this time from the United States Government. Moreover, what was subsequently received was not as precise as is suggested by the above accounts. The Foreign Office files show that on 21 March and 17 June 1941, secret documents, obtained from the State Department and dating from the previous January and April, were sent to London by the British embassy in Washington. The June documents were not received until 25 June, after the German attack had begun. Only the April documents survive in the files now. They consist of very generalised accounts of German intentions and strategic objectives in the Mediterranean as well as against Russia, and the plans for the attack on Russia are only in broad outline.[33] The documents dated January and received from Washington in March were presumably no more revealing; at least in the Service intelligence branches they received no more attention than did the many other rumours that were coming in about *Barbarossa*. In the second half of March, MI was reaffirming the assessment it had formed in January.

It is true that a further advance in Germany's preparations did not go entirely unnoticed by the intelligence sources. For obvious reasons the German army staggered the eastward movement of its formations and HQs, those headed by well-known generals remaining in the west for as long as possible. The GAF, whose forward airfields and other installations had been under construction since October, deferred till April and May the deployment of the signals and administrative troops needed for the reception of its operational formations. The latter themselves were used against the United Kingdom or kept in Germany for refitting until a yet later date; like the Army's main mechanised formations, they were not transferred to the east until the last three weeks before the opening of the offensive. At some levels, however, the German eastern build-up had to be intensified after the *Barbarossa* directive of 18 December 1940, and particularly after 3 February 1941, when OKH incorporated that directive into an operational order. On 3 February the Army group commanders were appointed and indoctrinated. The number of divisions facing Russia grew from 34 in mid-January to 46 by 5 April after allowing not only for dispatch of 28 divisions from Poland to the south-east for the Balkan campaign, but also for the transfer of some divisions from the east to western Europe. In March the GAF intensified its vast programme for the construction of airfields and accommodation in the east.[34]

From the beginning of February, reports on some of these activities began to reach Whitehall. One SIS report, dated 31 January, said that preparations for the invasion of Russia were almost open; troops were arriving in Poland from France; Russian speakers were being recruited into the Army and Russian *émigrés* into German intelligence units, regardless of suitability; preparations for operations by the GAF were particularly striking and included the construction of a continuous chain of aerodromes along the railway line from Poznan to Lódź. On 5 February MI commented on another report that large numbers of German troops, mainly armoured, were reaching East Prussia and that there was rail congestion between Berlin and Warsaw. Its comments were in the old vein: there was no other evidence to suggest that Germany was preparing for action against Russia, and these moves were probably being made in order to keep Russia quiet while Germany occupied Bulgaria.[35] On 6 February, its comments on items which dealt with the German garrison in north Norway also conformed to MI's earlier views: the garrison was not large enough to suggest that Germany was contemplating a descent on Iceland but it was not excessive as a safeguard against the danger of a Russian or a British attack.[36] On the same day, however, the DMI attached another appreciation to a letter he wrote to the Chairman of the JIC and the other Directors of Intelligence. This said that the German army, calculated by MI to be about the size of 250 divisions, was 'stronger than is necessary for actual operations, excluding a war against Russia which is unlikely for the present'.[37] At first sight the wording suggests that no change of ground had taken place; but the phrase 'for the present' had at last replaced the phrase 'until Germany has disposed of Great Britain'.

On 7 February MI issued another ambiguous appreciation. This stated that 250 divisions would be enough to hold off Russia if Germany attacked Turkey, but it added that 'Hitler is an opportunist'.[38] The implication behind this phrase might have been that Hitler was unlikely to undertake a venture which, like an attack on Russia, required long preparation. But it is possible that MI felt that he might switch to a surprise attack on Russia if it suited him.

A further sign of uncertainty – perhaps also of division of opinion – in MI occurred on 14 February, when it notified the General Staff that a 'most reliable source' had recently reported an increase in German intelligence activity in the Near East, particularly against Turkey, Syria, Egypt, Iraq, Persia and Russia, at the expense of the intelligence staffs in west Germany. In the previous August it had received similar information from A-54 and had not drawn it to the attention of the higher authorities (see p. 000 above). It now took this step in part because the latest information had come from an even better source, the hand cypher of the *Abwehr* which the Government Code and Cypher School (GC and CS) had broken during December 1940. No doubt for the same reason, its comments on the information – though primarily about Germany's intentions in the Balkans and the Middle East – included remarks about Russia which departed from its earlier views. One of them was that, although it would be 'dangerous' to let the information cast doubt on 'the serious intention of Germany to invade Great Britain in the coming months', 'it does certainly suggest that invasion is not imminent'. Another read as follows: 'The present changes do not seem to have the effect of weakening the intelligence centres charged with action against Russia' and 'they may be significant of German intentions in the later months of 1941'.[39] Given that the information was such as to foster Whitehall's grave anxiety about Germany's intentions in the Balkans, Syria and Iraq – that the DMI, indeed, in handwritten comments on it, dwelt only on its relevance to the danger in the Middle East – these remarks constituted no mean concession from MI's previous standpoint.

On 5 March it paid more than its usual attention to SIS and diplomatic reports suggesting conflict between Germany and Russia, including one to the effect that the Hungarian General Staff was convinced that Germany planned to attack Russia in June and July, and another which claimed that the Germans had asked the Romanian Government to supply plans of all bridges crossing the Pruth and the Dniester – the frontier rivers with the USSR. MI thought that the first of these reports 'must be taken with reserve' but that the second was 'significant'. It also noted that the mobilisation of the Romanian army was possibly relevant, and added the comment that Romanian and Hungarian forces could serve as a deterrent to Russian action in the Balkans 'for the time being, irrespective of a more active role in the near future'.[40]

But if MI was now on the alert, it was now, also, that Germany's deception measures had some impact on it. On 10 January, in a directive announcing that *Sealion* and *Felix* were to remain temporarily postponed, and again on 6 February after approving OKH's operational order for *Barbarossa*, Hitler had ordered an intensified effort to disguise the *Barbarossa* preparations as preparations for invasion of the United Kingdom in 1941. The intensified effort involved actual movements and operations, beginning in March with the westward deployment of twenty-one divisions, mostly of second-class quality, from eastern Europe to Belgium and northern France, and incorporating especially heavy GAF raids on the United Kingdom in May. On 5 March MI noted SIS reports of the beginning of this east – west movement and, according to post-war testimony, was deeply divided as to what to make of it.[41] Some of the specialists on the German order of battle were sure that the troops belonged to training formations which had been moved east before the attack on France; moreover, they suspected that their return to the west might be a pointer to Germany's intention to turn on Russia. The DMI, by their account, dismissed this view as wishful thinking. By 11 March a compromise view had been adopted. On that date MI noted that the westward movement of troops was continuing, and concluded – from the concurrence of westward and eastward movements – that the German army was being redistributed, rather than concentrated in any one area.[42]

This conclusion paved the way for MI's return to its earlier position. On 18 March, noting the continuing rumours of Germany's intention to attack Russia, it conceded that 'the whispering campaign appears to have intensified', and that 'there are indications that Germany is less friendly, even on the surface'. But it felt that some of the rumours arose from the fact that the Germans had been moving troops to Poland during the past three months, and that these troops 'may be to replace those which have moved to Romania and to dispose of some of Hitler's new divisions'. Its final conclusion was that 'so long as Germany has her hands full elsewhere, however, an attack on Russia is most unlikely'.[43]

On 19 March this was reaffirmed in a further inter-departmental report. The key to Germany's intentions after the end of the Balkan campaign was, this paper said, its determination to try to defeat Great Britain during 1941, and it would not attack Russia before it had defeated Great Britain. If Great Britain had not sued for peace by June, Germany would give priority to a march through Syria to Suez and would do all it could to increase the strain on British resources by encouraging Japanese intervention, by stirring up insurrections in Latin America and by mounting such diversionary operations as an attack on Freetown. The report admitted that it might also be contemplating other campaigns, in areas 'suitable for operations by mechanised forces where petrol was available'.[44] But in the week following the report, the Service intelligence branches continued to discount the rumours which conflicted with it. On 23 March AI was unconvinced by an SIS report that Germany intended to turn on Russia after occupying Greece, Yugoslavia and European Turkey in April: in its view the GAF was consolidating for a renewed onslaught on the United Kingdom[45] and Germany would need three months to prepare for an attack on Russia.[46] Two days later, in an appreciation devoted mainly to the situation in Libya and the invasion threat to the United Kingdom, MI agreed with AI that *Sealion* was now unlikely unless renewed air attack and intensified blockade failed to reduce Great Britain, but it felt that Germany was in earnest about a Balkan campaign. It mentioned the fact that reports continued to show that Germany was busy in Finland and to suggest that it intended to attack Russia in the summer. But the activity in Finland was 'possibly with a view to containing Soviet troops; possibly to distract Soviet attention from the Balkans'. As for the rumours about an attack on Russia, they 'were not convincing'.[47]

In defence of the intelligence branches, it must be conceded that, rumours apart, they had as yet received few items of information that could have been set with any confidence against their strategic assumptions. Nor did Churchill dissent from their conclusions. As he wrote later:

> Up till the end of March I was not convinced that Hitler was resolved on mortal war with Russia, nor how near it was. Our intelligence reports revealed in much detail the extensive German troops movements towards and into the Balkan states ... But none of these necessarily involved the invasion of Russia and all were readily explainable by German interests and policy in [that area] ... Our information about the immense movement taking place ... towards the main Russian front ... was far more difficult to acquire. That Germany should at that stage and before leaving the Balkan scene, open another major war with Russia seemed to me too good to be true ... There was no sign of lessening German strength opposite us across the Channel. The German air raids on Britain continued with intensity. The manner in which the German troop concentrations in Romania and Bulgaria had been glossed over and apparently accepted by the Soviet government, the evidence we had of large and invaluable supplies being sent to Germany

from Russia, the obvious community of interest between the two countries in overwhelming and dividing the British Empire in the East, all made it seem more likely that Hitler and Stalin would make a bargain at our expense rather than war upon each other.[48]

For him, however, the intelligence picture underwent a substantial change at the end of March. On 26 March the Enigma disclosed that German army formations previously ordered to move from the Balkans to the Cracow area included three armoured divisions and two important HQs. On 27 March, immediately after the *coup* in Belgrade, the Enigma revealed that this transfer was being halted. For the Prime Minister and for some of the intelligence bodies this intelligence provided the first confirmation that Germany's main preparations were directed against Russia. On 28 March, the head of AI's German section issued the following minute:

> It is significant that the day after Yugoslavia signed the Tripartite Pact orders were issued for the transfer of a large proportion of the German 'Balkan' forces to the Russian front. This, together with other reports and events such as the Lend-Lease Bill and the development of airfields in the east, leads me to believe that Germany's intention is to move into the Ukraine in the near future. A Balkan conflagration would necessarily postpone this. We have always believed that for economic reasons Germany must if possible avoid a war in the Balkans. On the other hand for the same reasons she may be forced to occupy part of Russia. A considerable time must, however, elapse before she could gain any appreciable economic advantages. There is therefore a possibility that Germany will accept diplomatic defeat in the Balkans and ... concentrate on preparations for an aggressive policy against Russia.[49]

On 30 March, GC and CS also concluded that the Enigma evidence pointed to the possibility of some large-scale operation against Russia, 'either for intimidation or for actual attack'.[50] By then the Prime Minister had reached the same conclusion. But on 28 March, at the news of the Yugoslav *coup*, he had thought that 'if a united front were formed in the Balkan peninsula Germany might think it better business to take it out of Russia observing that we have had many reports of heavy concentrations in Finland and intrigues in Sweden and Finland'.[51] Thereafter, according to his subsequent account, the receipt of the Enigma intelligence

> illuminated the whole Eastern scene in a lightning flash. The sudden movement to Cracow of so much armour needed in the Balkan sphere could only mean Hitler's intention to invade Russia in May. This seemed to me henceforward certainly his major purpose. The fact that

the Belgrade revolution had required their return to Romania involved perhaps a delay from May to June.[52]

This account is confirmed by the fact that on 30 March he put the following conclusion in a telegram to the Foreign Secretary in Athens:

> My reading of the intelligence is that the bad man concentrated very large armoured forces etc to overawe Yugoslavia and Greece, and hoped to get former or both without fighting. The moment he was sure Yugoslavia was in the Axis he moved 3 of the 5 Panzers towards the Bear, believing that what was left would be enough to finish the Greek affair*. However, the Belgrade revolution upset this picture and caused the northward movement to be arrested in transit. This can only mean, in my opinion, the intention to attack Yugoslavia at earliest, or alternatively [to] act against the Turk. It looks as if heavy forces will be used in Balkan peninsula and that Bear will be kept waiting a bit. Furthermore, these orders and counter-orders in their relation to the Belgrade coup seem to reveal magnitude of design both towards southeast and east. This is the clearest indication we have received so far. Let me know in guarded terms whether you and Dill agree with my impressions.[53]

On 3 April he sent a message to Stalin:

> I have sure information from a trusted agent that when the Germans thought they had got Yugoslavia in the net, that is to say after March 20, they began to move three out of the five Panzer divisions from Romania to southern Poland. The moment they heard of the Serbian revolution this movement was countermanded. Your Excellency will readily appreciate the significance of these facts.[54]

To the Prime Minister's indignation, this message did not reach the Russian Government till 19 April.[55] One reason for the delay was Cripps's belief that the Russian Government would regard it as provocative.[56] Cripps did not doubt that a German attack was imminent, and already at the end of March he had again urged Whitehall to open discussions with the Russian Government. During the delay he stressed to Vyshinski the seriousness of the German threat to Russia and the advisability of Russian support for the Balkan States.[57] On 19 April he gave Vyshinski both the Prime Minister's message and his own. The latter stated that in view of 'the many indications we have received from usually reliable sources ... a seizure by force of the sources of supply in the east is not a hypothesis at all, but part of the planned German development of the war for the spring of this year'.[58] By then, the embassies in Moscow were alive with rumours of an early German invasion and Cripps may have heard that the Swedish embassy had informed his American colleague on 24 March that it had good grounds for believing them to be accurate.[59]

Unlike Cripps and the Prime Minister, the Foreign Office remained unconvinced. On 1 April, having received from the embassy in Belgrade the rumour that Hitler had told Prince Paul that he would attack Russia on 30 June, it decided not to forward it to the Russians. Its reasoning was that, as the Soviet Government felt safe until Great Britain had been defeated, warnings would only encourage it to remain subservient to Germany unless they contained incontrovertible evidence that Germany intended to attack regardless of Russian concessions.[60] No doubt on similar grounds, the Foreign Secretary counselled the Prime Minister against sending his warning of 3 April.[61] Although this relied on evidence that was, to say the least, more plausible than the rumour about Prince Paul, the Foreign Office did not accept his interpretation of it. It was not a regular recipient of Enigma decrypts and was in no position to judge their significance; but it had the authority of MI for believing that the decrypts of 26 and 27 March were not a decisive pointer to Germany's plans. A Foreign Office minute early in April approved the 'very same point of view' expressed by MI at a meeting on 31 March, that Hitler would not attack Russia if he could avoid it.[62]

The Foreign Office soon changed its mind. On 11 April the Foreign Secretary instructed Cripps to urge the Russians to do their utmost to encourage the Balkan States to resist Germany, and his message said that 'the German attack [on Russia] of which there are so many signs' would not be prevented by 'the fact that he [Hitler] is in conflict with us'.[63] On 16 April he told the Soviet Ambassador in London of the Prince Paul rumour and discussed with him the possibility of an Anglo-Russian *rapprochement*.[64] MI, on the other hand, continued to be sceptical. On 1 April it conceded that the Enigma decrypts were 'of interest', but it also insisted that 'there is as yet no reason to believe the numerous reports that Germany intends to attack Russia in the near future'. On the contrary, 'the German object is undoubtedly to exert military pressure on Russia to prevent Russian interference in German Balkan plans'.[65] This conclusion MI repeated to the Chiefs of Staff on 3 April, when it added that the rumours of an impending attack might be being put about by Germany in order to influence Russia's diplomatic decisions.[66] On 2 April, in its widely circulated weekly intelligence summary, it had indeed pointed out that the German army now had 250 divisions; that this was the maximum that Germany could sustain without damage to its war production and supply; that it could not sustain so large a number in a long campaign; and that 'this policy seems to indicate that the

German General Staff either contemplate in 1941 a short rapid campaign for which 250 divisions are considered sufficient, or hope to achieve their ends by an overwhelming display of force and ... thereafter expect a period of quiescence'. In this paper, too, however, MI indicated its preference for the second of these interpretations by again referring to Germany's interest in holding off possible threats.[67] On 9 April, again in the War Office weekly intelligence summary, it considered that reports of a German attack on Russia might well be German propaganda 'as part of a war of nerves against Russia during the Balkan campaign'.[68]

In the next inter-departmental intelligence assessment – a paper on 'German Strategy 1941' issued by the JIC on 10 April – MI's views prevailed. On this occasion, as so often before, the intelligence bodies concluded that Germany's main objective remained the defeat of Great Britain during 1941, by blockade and air attack if possible, by invasion if necessary. It was beyond question that it also planned a drive through the Balkans as far as the Straits, but so long as it saw any chance of defeating the United Kingdom during 1941 it would not continue her advance as far as Syria, Egypt or Iraq – the more so as this would antagonise Turkey and Russia. As for Russia, a 'direct' German attack was unlikely at present. Germany would continue military preparations in the east with the double purpose of keeping Russia amenable and of enabling itself to take immediate action when necessary. In the long run, of course, a Russo-German clash was inevitable unless Germany was defeated in the war with Great Britain. Germany undoubtedly had its eyes on the Ukraine and the Caucasus; Russia was fully aware of this. But Russia would do all it could to avoid the clash and so would Germany. The many rumours to the contrary were probably designed to frighten Russia. Concentration and movements of German troops in the east – of which there was considerable intelligence – could have been undertaken for the same purpose, and such preparations would enable Germany to move against Russia if it later decided that its chances of eliminating Great Britain during 1941 were receding.[69]

After the completion of this report MI showed signs of wavering. On 15 April it stressed that there was still no indication that Germany was increasing its total forces on the Russian frontier. But it also noted reports that the Russians were moving troops to the frontier; added that these 'suggest that they, at least, are taking the German threat seriously'; and concluded that the rumours of a German attack 'were consistent both with a war of nerves and with an intention actually to invade'.[70] In the War Office weekly intelligence summary of 16 April MI repeated this admission: it was impossible to tell whether the 'persistent rumours coming from so many quarters ... are merely being spread by Germany as part of a war of nerves or have some more solid basis in fact'.[71] It repeated it in the chiefs of staff résumé on 17 April.[72] Nor did it dissent when, after discussions with the Service intelligence departments and the Ministry of Economic Warfare (MEW), the Foreign Office reached the same judgement in an appreciation of the latest intelligence for dispatch to Cripps on 20 April.

At the end of March the Polish underground organisation in eastern Europe had reported that Germany would attack on 15 April,[73] and SIS's representative in Geneva had heard from a well-placed source with contacts in German official circles that Hitler would attack Russia in May. In the middle of April some diplomatic sources were predicting that the attack would be early in June and suggesting that Russia had some knowledge of the German plans. By then these sources – the Poles, the SIS and the diplomatic reports – had also sent in considerable detailed intelligence to support the general warnings. Germany had ordered a further call-up of men for military service and was developing airfields in Poland, mapping the Russo-German frontiers by air photography, training Russian refugees in Romania for administrative work; organising Ukrainian and White Russian *émigrés*, printing Russian currency notes and continuing preparations for fifth-column activity in the Ukraine and the Caucasus. In the past month it had also increased its divisions in East Prussia and Poland. In commenting on this evidence to Cripps on 20 April, the Foreign Office admitted that Whitehall did not know what to make of it. The reports might be part of a German war of nerves. A German invasion would result in much chaos throughout Russia and the Germans would have to reorganise everything in the territories which they might occupy. Meanwhile they would lose their supplies from Russia. The loss of material transferred across the Trans-Siberian railway would be even more important. Although the resources of Germany were immense, they would not allow it to continue its campaign in the Balkans, maintain the existing scale of air attacks against the United Kingdom, take the offensive against Egypt and at the same time invade and reorganise a large part of the USSR. All these arguments pointed against a German attack. On the other hand, a rapid success in the Balkans would enable Germany to throw most of its fifteen armoured divisions against Russia. There was as yet no information about the movement of German aircraft towards the Russian frontiers; if the necessary preparations had been made in Poland, aircraft could be moved there at the shortest notice. The appreciation concluded by saying that the German General Staff appeared to be opposed to a war on two fronts and in favour of disposing of Great Britain before attacking Russia, but the decision rested with Hitler.[74]

The apparent unanimity of this appreciation concealed, however, a serious divergence of opinion between MI and the Foreign Office, which was becoming more convinced that Russia was soon to be attacked. This became clear when the Chiefs of Staff called for a verbal discussion with the JIC on 22 April. In a brief for the CIGS, in advance of the discussion, MI dwelt mainly on *Sealion* and discounted the rumours of a German attack on Russia because there were 'no immediate signs of the essential troop moves in the direction of the USSR'.[75] Another MI appreciation of 22 April stated that 'it appears certain that preparations for an eventual war with Russia are continuing, but there is absolutely no confirmation that Germany will attack this summer'.[76] These assertions were strictly correct: partly because Germany was deferring the eastward movement of its armour, and partly because for communications connected with the eastern deployment – as opposed to those connected with the Balkan campaign – it could use landlines and forbid references to operational matters in messages going out by WT, so there were 'no immediate signs', 'no confirmation'. At the discussion itself, the Foreign Office Chairman of the JIC argued only that a threat to Russia might well develop as soon as the Greek campaign was over. But the DMI insisted that this development could be excluded. There was no advantage to Germany in attacking Russia before the invasion of the United Kingdom; if it did so it would be after the harvest.

A typewritten note is attached to the archive copy of DMI's brief for the CIGS, in which an unidentifiable writer commented: 'If Germany can beat us, Russia is in the bag. Russia does not represent an obstacle to Germany in her battle with Great Britain. A pincer movement (on Suez) is the most likely course'.[77]

At the meeting of 22 April, of which only a brief record survives, the two schools at least agreed that, if and when a German intention to attack Russia was confirmed, the movements of Germany's armoured divisions would provide the important evidence. In the event, however, Enigma decrypts relating to the GAF provided the next pointers to Germany's intentions.

On 24 April, the Enigma disclosed that a Signals Regiment was ordered from the Channel front to Poland, to come under Fliegerkorps V which had hitherto been in France. On 30 April AI summarised decrypts pointing to a considerable programme for the construction of airfields and fixed GAF installations in Poland – including a signals-and-aircraft-reporting system – and noted that, while this was 'probably for training purposes', the GAF could now transfer a substantial operational force to Poland at short notice.[78] On 3 May the Enigma revealed that aircraft of Fliegerkorps VIII, previously active in Greece, were to be hurriedly refitted in Gatow and that one of its units was to join a rail movement to Cracow a week later. It added, on 5 May, that the air component of the 12th Army was to join a movement for Oderberg, a major concentration point near Cracow, on 22 May; on 7 May, that the GAF was over-flying Finland;[79] on 13 May, that Fliegerkorps II, which had been under Luftflotte 3 for attacks in the United Kingdom, was subordinated to Luftflotte 2, already associated with the eastern build-up. On 17 May it disclosed that Luftflotte 4 signals troops in the Athens area were ordered to withdraw from operations and entrain for Moldavia between 20 and 25 May, and that elements of Fliegerkorps IV (hitherto in France) were ordered to the Bessarabian frontier and given an operational area from the south Carpathians to the Black Sea. On 18 May, elements of Fliegerkorps VIII were ordered to join a rail movement to Oderberg on 28 May. This move was delayed by the operation against Crete, which nearly delayed the already postponed *Barbarossa* campaign, but the final urgent withdrawal of this formation to the eastern front was reported in the Enigma on 1 June. By 19 May Flakkorps I and II, previously associated with the *Sealion* preparations, had been ordered to be brought up to more than war strength, and the élite Flakregiment 'Hermann Goering' had been told to proceed to a point east of Cracow and place itself under Flakkorps II. By the same date it was known from the Enigma that GAF and army units carrying bridging equipment were to join a movement starting for Moldavia on 5 June.

Meanwhile, the first mention of code-name *Barbarossa* had occurred in the Enigma on 8 May in connection with Luftflotte 4, and the first reference to Plan or Contingency B (*Fall-B*) was received on 14 May, when the GAF Enigma associated it with the 12th Army. By that date, Whitehall had obtained a considerable amount of information – even about German army movements – from the GAF Enigma and the Railway Enigma. On 26 April it learned that the movement of ground forces from the Balkans to the Cracow area, halted at the end of March, had been resumed. By 5 May it knew that up to five motorised divisions were involved. As always, the GAF Enigma information on army movements was fragmentary and its interpretation was anything but a straightforward matter. By 19 May, only about a dozen of the divisions known to be on the move had been identified, and their destinations remained unknown. Even so, it was clear by then that many of the divisions that had taken part in the Greek campaign had either left the Balkans or would soon be doing so; that unidentified formations were also on the move; and that the moves were taking place with some urgency. There was also little doubt that most of the moves were towards the Russian frontier. The accompanying GAF signals and other units were known to be going to widely dispersed points in eastern Poland and Moldavia, and Posen had been established as the HQ of Army Group B. The 12th Army – later to be taken out of operation – had been connected with the Cracow area and it was known that three of its corps were taking part in the movements. Moreover, as early as 5 May, it had been learned from the

Enigma that on 22 May a POW cage from the 2nd Army at Zagreb was to join a movement on its way to a division at Tarnow, east of Cracow.

It was not only the evidence of the Enigma traffic that indicated that exceptional activity was afoot. From the beginning of May the SIS's Polish connections reported on a series of eight railway movements, all named after Polish rivers, of which only one was mentioned by name in the Enigma. In addition, after the middle of April the SIS supplied from its Polish, Czech and Yugoslav connections a steady stream of individual reports about German troop movements to the east and about the formation by the Germans of civilian administrations for the territories to be captured.

By the middle of May it could thus no longer be questioned either that exceptional German military preparations were in train or that they were aimed at Russia. But at that juncture the picture being built up by the military evidence was blurred by the diplomatic evidence – or rather by the assumptions of the diplomatic world.

From the middle of April, embassies throughout the world were not only claiming that Germany was preparing to turn on Russia, they were also canvassing the possibility of a new Russo-German agreement. The rumour, which was without foundation, was given colour by the resumption of trade negotiations between the two countries, and it soon swelled into the belief that Germany was making stringent demands such as control of the Ukraine, and would attack if they were rejected. At first few of the commentators believed that Stalin could yield to the demands, but none doubted that Germany was making them; and even the suggestion that Russia was giving way was circulating by the middle of May. A report to this effect was broadcast at that time by Rome Radio, though it was publicly denied in Berlin and privately to the British Government by the Soviet Ambassador.[80]

The Sigint evidence available up to the middle of May was not absolutely incompatible with these rumours. By that date, however, GC and CS had concluded that it indicated that Germany planned an invasion and was not merely seeking to intimidate the Russians. It was particularly impressed by the revelation that a POW cage was being moved to Tarnow; by the urgency with which Fliegerkorps VIII was being prepared for dispatch to Poland; and by the news that Flakkorps I and II were also being transferred. The latter had played a decisive forward role during the invasion of France.[81] By 23 May AI had reached the same conclusion on receiving the news from the Enigma that Fliegerkorps II and other components of Luftflotten 2 and 3 were now moving from France to the east. Although it admitted that German preparations might be intended only to intimidate Russia, it now believed that they pointed to a decision to 'satisfy German military requirements by occupying western USSR' – Hitler having concluded that an early victory over Great Britain had become impossible – and estimated that the GAF would probably commit 1,070 aircraft (excluding army co-operation).[82] In MI, however, the Enigma evidence again failed to carry the day.

On 25 April, before the Enigma clues had begun to accumulate, MI had produced for the first time a full-length appreciation devoted solely to Russo-German relations. In this paper it had conceded that there was 'an actual threat' to Russia, but had still discounted a German intention to attack. Apart from feeling that Germany's preparations sprang from the wish to contain Russia while Germany was fighting in the Balkans – an argument which it now used for the last time – MI remained convinced that Germany's chief aim was the defeat of the United Kingdom. It was putting itself in a position to attack Russia, but its reasons were that it needed to ensure Russia's continuing economic collaboration, that it wished to keep Great Britain and Turkey guessing and, possibly, that it was feeling it would have to invade Russia ultimately, if it failed in the Battle of the Atlantic.[83] On 15 May MI was somewhat more hesitant. It now had to consider not only the Enigma evidence but also diplomatic reports that German – Romanian staff talks were in progress and that Russian maps had been issued to Romanian officers, and SIS reports that pro-German governments were being organised among émigrés from the Ukraine and the Baltic States. It accepted that 'preparations for operations against Russia will soon be complete'; it listed not only the strategic arguments that should deter Germany from turning on Russia, but also, for the first time, those that might persuade it to do so – the need to free most of its ground and air forces before invading Britain; and it expressed the wish to forestall Russian intervention in Finland, Scandinavia and the Balkans. It also conceded that the presence of two Flakkorps in Poland and the movement of armoured divisions pointed to an offensive. But it still concluded that Germany had not yet decided whether to threaten Russia into complying with its demands or to attack it.[84] Fundamentally, MI could not bring itself to believe that an attack would make sense.

On 21 May, its weekly intelligence summary was pointing out that it was difficult to find a logical reason why Hitler should attack unless he had 'made up his mind ... to dispose of the Red Bogey once and for all'. Because it did not believe that Hitler had done such a thing, it allowed its attention to be deflected from Sigint and the military evidence by the diplomatic reports that were suggesting that Germany's object was only to intimidate the Russians and was succeeding.[85] On 22 May, in the chiefs of staff résumé, it conceded that even the diplomatic reports suggested that the situation remained tense: 'Two reports state that Hitler has not finally decided whether to obtain his wishes by persuasion or force of arms, and another indicates that the latter alternative will be chosen if the former does not give results by the end of May.' 'Nevertheless,' the résumé added, 'some reports of rapprochement suggest that German threats have been successful and that arrangements for German control of the dispatch of supplies from Russia have been accepted by the latter country. German propaganda which was recently spreading rumours of war is now stressing co-operation.'[86]

It was in this situation that the JIC brought together all the intelligence in the first study it had specifically devoted to 'Germany's intentions against the USSR'.[87] Issued on 23 May, the study recognised that the Germans could not fight Russia at the same time as invading England, but that *Sealion* was unlikely in the immediate future. More than that, it acknowledged that 'the domination of Russia was a fundamental German objective', and that it was in Germany's interest 'for matters to be brought to a head as soon as possible'. These were the arguments which underlay the JIC's first conclusion: 'Germany cannot fight a long war without obtaining greater economic help from Russia than she is now receiving. She can only obtain this by an effective agreement or war.'

Which of these courses would Germany take? The JIC recapitulated all that had been said in recent weeks of the disadvantages that Germany would incur by attacking Russia, adding only the new consideration that a war forced on Russia would strengthen the Soviet Government's hold on the Russian people. Against these disadvantages, it set down the arguments that might induce Germany to attack, and these now included – alongside Germany's growing economic requirements for strategic purposes – the consideration that an invasion would enhance Germany's military prestige, which might be useful in off-setting the danger that the USA might enter the war, and enable Germany to resume 'the role of anti-Bolshevist champion – thus facilitating the consolidation of the "New Order" in Europe'. After weighing up these pros and cons, the JIC reached its second conclusion: 'the advantages ... to Germany of concluding an agreement with the USSR are overwhelming'. After all, Germany might do as much for its military prestige by imposing an agreement on Russia as by making an attack on it.

In its third conclusion the report considered one of the reasons why it was impossible to be certain that Germany would take its 'natural course', which 'would be to exert extreme pressure, backed by the threat of force, to obtain by negotiation from the USSR the concessions she requires'. The Soviet Government's 'natural course' was to try to avoid a clash by yielding to German demands; but it would refuse to sign any agreement that endangered its effective control of Russia, and it was making extensive preparations to meet the German threat should the worst happen. All depended on how much Germany demanded: 'If in the course of negotiations she sees no prospect of reaching agreement she will implement her threat of force.'

Before reaching these conclusions, the JIC summarised the Enigma evidence about Germany's military preparations and was in no doubt that they were taking place on a gigantic scale. But it omitted just those items – the POW cage and the hurried withdrawal of key GAF formations from the Balkans – which had persuaded GC and CS that Germany was not negotiating about its demands. On the other hand, the assumption that it was negotiating with Russia appeared as a statement of fact: 'With her usual thoroughness Germany is making all preparations for an attack so as to make the threat convincing.' Moreover, the body of the report had a section added to it under the heading 'Latest Intelligence' and this announced that there were indications that Hitler and Stalin had reached an agreement on military as well as economic and political collaboration.

These indications had been received from, among other sources, the British Ambassador in Washington. On the day the JIC report was issued, Lord Halifax reported that, according to information obtained from Berlin on 21 May, German troops were assembled in force on the Russian frontier, but that the Russian Government had recently assented to German demands for a large increase in supplies and that the economic agreement might have military implications, with Russia allowing the passage of German troops and material to areas east of Suez and committing itself to take action against India.[88] It is reasonable to suppose that it was this rumour which prompted the JIC to add a sentence to its final conclusion at the last minute. After saying that Germany would implement its threat if it saw no prospect of reaching agreement, the JIC ended its report with the observation that 'from present intelligence agreement is the more likely event'.

For the next fortnight this belief continued to close Whitehall's eyes to the possibility that Germany was preparing an unconditional attack.

It is fair to add that the entire diplomatic world continued to share the belief. On 22 May, a decrypt from the Japanese Ambassador in Moscow reported that Germany was unlikely to attack as long as Russia continued to acquiesce. Other Axis diplomatic decrypts pointed unequivocally in the same direction; in one, decrypted on 25 May, the Japanese Ambassador in Berlin mentioned the German interest in threatening India by advancing through Turkey and the Middle East. Other embassies agreed: Russia would yield and the Germans would then march to Suez via Syria; and Germany was still determined to attempt an invasion of the United Kingdom. At the same time the rumour that the Germans were proposing direct participation

in the Soviet economy – a rumour which had been circulating in the diplomatic community in Moscow for some time – continued to reach London
up to the middle of June. There were even suggestions that Germany and
Russia had reached agreement on the joint development of the Ukraine and
direct German control of the sources of supply from some areas of Russia.
On 2 June, the Foreign Office's explanation for the apparent lack of negotiations in Moscow was that they might be taking place in Berlin so that
Stalin could keep from his colleagues what was going on.[89]

To set against this stream of reports, on 23 May Whitehall received from
A-54 the warning that Russo-German negotiations were 'just a delaying
mechanism'; he also gave further details about the alternative regimes that
the Germans were organizing for Russian areas. From 27 May, GC and CS
was supplying a steady flow of evidence on military preparations. On 27
May the GAF Enigma revealed that Fliegerkorps II was asking for maps of
Latvia, Lithuania, most of Poland and north-east Romania. On 29 May it
showed that the commanders of Luftflotten 1 to 5, AOC Centre, Fliegerkorps
I, II, IV, V and VIII, Flakkorps I and II and Fliegerführer Baltic were, together
with the GAF Liaison Officer with OKM, all invited to attend a conference
with their Intelligence Officers on 4 June. By then there was ample evidence
from the GAF and the Railway Enigma of an assembly for attack behind the
Bessarabian frontier, and the assumption that Moldavia was to be a jumping-
off point had been confirmed in two ways. A newly identified army authority,
the Commander-in-Chief of the High Command of the German army troops
in Romania, planned to fly along the line of the frontier river. Siebel ferries
and an assault-boat company which had previously been in the English
Channel were being included in a rail movement destined for Moldavia. Of
the many rail movements known to be running to Poland, the contents and
destinations were identified in only a few cases, but these few left no doubt
that GAF and army units were being deployed along practically the whole
length of the frontier. In north Norway the Enigma had by now revealed the
arrival of further reinforcements and had provided some indications that the
Germans were preparing to attack. During the first week of June the GAF
Enigma established that the transfer of Luftflotte 2 from northern France to
the east was substantially completed, that the delayed departure of Fliegerkorps VIII from Greece was at last taking place and that the units of
Fliegerkorps VIII were not to transfer to their advanced landing grounds for
Fall-B before 16 June. In a signal decrypted on 8 June, Luftflotte 2 told
Fliegerkorps VIII not to mention operational matters on WT or landline till
further notice. On 10 June, in a further decrypt, Goering summoned the
commanders of all the GAF formations that had been mentioned in the
Enigma signals to a conference at Karinhall, his personal HQ, for 15 June.[90]

For GC and CS this further evidence converted the probability that Germany might be planning a surprise invasion into a virtual certainty. On 31 May it issued a special paper surveying the Enigma intelligence to that date:

> It becomes harder than ever to doubt that the object of these large movements of the German army and air force is Russia. From rail movements towards Moldavia in the south to ship movements towards the Varanger Fjord in the far north there is everywhere the same steady eastward trend. Either the purpose is blackmail or it is war. No doubt Hitler would prefer a bloodless surrender. But the quiet move, for instance, of a prisoner-of-war cage to Tarnow looks more like business than bluff. It would no doubt be rash for Germany to become involved in a long struggle on two fronts. But the answer may well be that the Germans do not expect the struggle with Russia to be long. An overwhelming eastward concentration, a lightning victory, an unassailable supremacy in Europe and Asia – such may be the plan behind this procession of troop trains from the Balkans to the eastern frontier.[91]

On 7 June, by which time it had worked out the GAF order of battle on the Russian front, identifying the rough operational areas of most of its units, and had calculated that well over 2,000 aircraft were involved, GC and CS issued another special report. It concluded that there was little doubt that Germany was planning 'a very large-scale operation against Russia with the main front of attack in Poland and East Prussia'. On the evidence that Fliegerkorps VIII was not to transfer to advanced landing grounds for *Fall-B* before 16 June, it calculated that Germany would be ready by 15 June.[92]

These were not the only Sigint developments. During the first week of June, GC and CS reported that five new naval WT frequencies had been introduced in the eastern Baltic and also noted that 'the introduction of army and GAF type call-signs into naval traffic pointed to imminent co-operation'. From about the same time, it noticed that the GAF in the west was employing a form of radio deception (dubbed 'Sham') in an attempt to conceal the eastward movement of its formations. From the quality and regularity of the transmissions, and with the aid of Direction Finding (DF), it was able to detect that ground stations were broadcasting signals which simulated those normally passed between aircraft and their ground controllers.[93]

In Whitehall the intelligence organisations put a different interpretation on the Enigma clues. For them every new indication of the scale and urgency of Germany's military preparations was further proof that Germany was determined to get its way in the negotiations, and they equally feared that Russia might yield. But they could no longer exclude the probability that

Germany's determination would lead to war. On 30 May the JIC was as convinced as before that agreement was being sought, but less inclined than in the report of 23 May to believe that an agreement would come. It concluded that 'although many reasons exist why Germany should decide, after her success in Crete, to exploit her success by action toward Egypt, all the evidence points to Germany's next move being an attempt to enforce her demands on the Soviet by means of a threat of force which can immediately be turned into action'. In an annex the report noted that the GAF preparations were so thorough that they could 'only portend such drastic demands on the Soviet government that Hitler is doubtful of their acceptance and is, therefore, prepared to implement his threat of force by actual operations'.[94] It was at this point, on 31 May, that the Chiefs of Staff warned the commanders-in-chief in the Middle East that Germany was demanding drastic concessions from Russia and would march if they were refused (see above, p. 43).

On 31 May and again on 2 June, the Permanent Under-Secretary in the Foreign Office noted in his diary that, while he agreed with the Chiefs of Staff that Germany was fully prepared for an attack on Russia, he still believed that Russia would give way.[95] But by 9 June opinion in the Foreign Office had hardened into conviction that, as the Foreign Secretary then told the Cabinet, 'all the evidence points to attack',[96] and a Foreign Office minute described Hitler's apparent decision to attack Russia as 'the most astonishing development on the grand scale since the war began'.[97] The Foreign Office was presumably influenced by a decrypt, obtained on 3 June, in which the Italian Ambassador in Moscow had reported that his German colleague had assured him that Germany was not negotiating with Russia, and by the fact that on 7 June the Swedish Government had warned it that Germany would bring force to bear about 15 June.[98]

On 10 June, following the Cabinet meeting of the previous day, the Foreign Secretary gave the Russian Ambassador full details of the intelligence available about Germany's military dispositions and elicited from him the reassurance that no political negotiations were proceeding between Russia and Germany and that there would be no Russo-German alliance.[99] But at its next meeting, on 12 June, the Cabinet remained hesitant. After being informed by the Foreign Secretary that Cripps, on a visit to London, did not know whether Russo-German political negotiations were taking place but expected Germany to issue an ultimatum when its military build-up was completed, it felt unable to decide whether Germany would prefer to destroy Russia's military forces or to demand complete control of the Ukraine and the Caucasus in the hope that Russia would yield. If Russia gave way to this demand, it noted, Germany would have outflanked Turkey to the north.[100] But no sooner had it broken up on this uncertain note than GC and CS decrypted a message sent out by the Japanese Ambassador in Berlin on 4 June. It was part of a long account of the interview he had just had with Hitler. Hitler, the Ambassador reported, felt that the Soviet attitude, though outwardly friendly, was habitually obstructive, and he had decided that communist Russia must be eliminated. If sacrifices were not made now they would be twenty times greater in five or ten years' time. Romania and Finland would join Germany against Russia, and the campaign would soon be over. 'If Japan lagged behind when Germany declared a state of war against Russia, it was quite open to her to do so.' The Ambassador added that, though neither Hitler nor Ribbentrop mentioned a date, the atmosphere of urgency suggested that it was close at hand.[101]

This information finally convinced the JIC that Germany intended to turn on Russia. In a short paper, issued on 12 June, it announced that 'fresh evidence is now to hand that Hitler has made up his mind to have done with Soviet obstruction and intends to attack her. Hostilities therefore appear highly probably, though it is premature to fix a date for their outbreak.'[102] On 13 June – presumably on the strength of the same information – the Foreign Secretary, after consultation with the Prime Minister, told the Russian Ambassador that the evidence for a German offensive was increasing and offered to send a military mission to Moscow;[103] the Chiefs of Staff instructed the Joint Planners and the JIC to make arrangements for the dispatch of a mission when Germany attacked.[104]

Between 14 June and 22 June (the day on which Germany launched the offensive), the Enigma, without disclosing the actual date, left no room for doubt about the imminence of the attack.

On 14 June GC and CS decrypted messages which issued code-names for operations against Russia from Norway and Finland and carried most secret orders in connection with the arrival of a 'Chief War Correspondent' at Kirkenes. On 15 June, an aircraft-reporting unit at Kirkenes was instructed to prepare to cross into Finland but in no circumstances to occupy its posts there until authority was given. By 18 June decrypts had revealed that there were GAF battle staffs and special-operations staffs at Kirkenes and that the latter was receiving information about Russian orders for the camouflage and dispersal of aircraft. On 20 June, three decrypts dealt with the crossing of the frontier. One lifted the ban on flying over the prohibited frontier zone, but limited flying there to the movement of aircraft to airfields near the frontier. Another warned the special operations staff at Kirkenes that, since mine-laying was to be carried out before the crossing, surprise would not be possible. In a third, Kirkenes was instructed that any aircraft flying over the frontier before the general crossing must do so at a great height. Apart from these messages to north Norway, there had been other indications in the Enigma. On 14 June the staff of Luftflotte 4 received instructions to be at their new battle HQ, ready to operate, from 17 June. On 19 June, Luftflotte 1 was told that it could carry out mine-laying before 'general crossing of the frontier'. On 21 June, GC and CS decrypted a message in which Luftflotte 4 gave Fliegerkorps IV a target for the first attacks.[105]

To the end, however, Whitehall found it difficult to discard the belief that Germany would present Russia with demands and an ultimatum. On 16 June MI, noting that there had been rumours about Russo-German relations reaching a crisis about 20 June, did confess that much obscurity surrounded the nature of the German demands, but it still suggested that 'Germany anticipates the necessity of using force, possible because she feels certain that Russia cannot bow to the very drastic demands she wishes to make.'[106] The Foreign Office was never wholly convinced that 'Germany intended to attack Russia and not merely to use diplomatic and military pressure to intimidate the Soviet Government' – that Hitler had decided to invade Russia 'without giving her the chance to surrender to the most stringent demands'.[107] As for Cripps, who had predicted so early and for so long that Germany would attack, his suspicion that Russia would give way to pressure increased as the crisis mounted. When he attended the Cabinet on 16 June, still expecting a German ultimatum, he spoke at some length and with much uncertainty about whether Russia would or would not meet German demands.[108]

Like the long-standing assumption that Russia and Germany were negotiating, the feeling that Russia might even now give way to Germany's demands owed something to the policy which Russia had adopted towards the threat from Germany since the beginning of 1941. It had been increasing its defensive preparations and issuing political warning, backed by military movements, against Germany's expansion to the south-east; but it had also been doing its utmost to propitiate Germany – renewing the trade agreement in January, resuming its supplies to Germany and increasing them month by month, acquiescing in extensive German violations of its airspace, withdrawing recognition of the Belgian, Norwegian and Yugoslav Governments in May, and maintaining towards other western governments not merely an uncommunicative attitude, but even a pose of unconcern which culminated on 14 June in its public denial of the rumours that Germany was about to attack it. In relation to the German threat, this policy was no doubt well considered. It is sufficiently explained by the need of the Russian Government to gain time and by its wish to make it plain in Russia and to the world, in the event of a German invasion, that Russia had not provoked it.[109] In Whitehall, however – as for other governments that watched from outside – it necessarily created uncertainty as to whether Russia would resist if

Germany increased the pressure and all the more so because of another consideration.

Cripps's hesitation owed much to his conviction that, as he told the Cabinet on 16 June, Russia would be unable to hold out for more than 3–4 weeks if Germany did attack. In this belief he was at one with all the Whitehall departments, where the lack of intelligence about Russia and information from Russia was well-nigh complete. On 9 June the JIC allowed Germany 4–6 weeks to occupy the Ukraine and reach Moscow; in a revised version of this paper, issued on 14 June, it changes its estimate to between three and four weeks at the shortest but possibly as long as six weeks.[110] In MEW's opinion 'the Germans would not incur heavy casualties or any high degree of military exhaustion in defeating the Red Army'.[111] The Foreign Office held much the same view. Only the Prime Minister did not wholly share the prevailing pessimism about Russian powers of resistance.

From the middle of June, as the Enigma pointed more clearly every day to the imminence of *Barbarossa*, and as doubt about Russia's readiness to withstand German political pressure was replaced by certainty that it could not survive a German attack for long, Whitehall's latent anxiety about *Sealion* returned to the surface. On 14 June the JIC calculated that, on the assumption that Germany reached Moscow in 3–4 weeks, there would be an interval of 4–6 weeks before it could attempt an invasion of the United Kingdom; if it took as long as six weeks to defeat Russia this interval would be between six and eight weeks.[112] On 17 June MI noted that the SIS's sources, including the valued Polish network, were reporting that further German troop movements into France were about to take place on a large scale.[113] It was in these circumstances that on 25 June – three days after the opening of *Barbarossa* – urged on by the Prime Minister, the Chiefs of Staff ordered the anti-invasion forces in the United Kingdom to be kept on the alert and be brought to their highest state of efficiency by 1 September.[114] It was not until 23 July that the JIC concluded that an invasion attempt was unlikely before 1942. It based this view on the obvious ground that, with the improvement of British defences, invasion was becoming an increasingly hazardous operation and that, given the need for redeployment from Russia, it had become a complex undertaking. It supported it with the argument that Sigint and photographic reconnaissance contained no sign of German redeployment.[115] The JIC repeated this view on 1 August,[116] and on the following day the Prime Minister and the Chiefs of Staff decided to withdraw the directive in which they had required the highest state of readiness from the beginning of September.[117]

Notes

AI	Air Intelligence Branch, Air Ministry
APS	Axis Planning Section
CIGS	Chief of the Imperial General Staff
COS	Chiefs of Staff
D of I(O)	Director of Military Intelligence
FO	Foreign Office
FOES	Future Operations (Enemy) Section
GC and CS	Government Code and Cypher School
JIC	Joint Intelligence Committee
MI	Military Intelligence Branch, War Office
VCIGS	Vice-Chief of the Imperial General Staff
WO	War Office

1. COS(41) 196th Meeting, 30 May; 197th Meeting, 31 May; W. L. S. Churchill, *The Second World War* (Cassell, London, 1950) vol. III, p. 318.
2. L. Woodward, *British Foreign Policy in the Second World War* (HMSO, London, 1970) vol. I, pp. 463–5.
3. Churchill, *Second World War*, vol. II, p. 120.
4. Ibid. pp. 227–8.
5. JIC(40) 143, 144 (Revise), 144 (Final) and COS(40) 518 (JIC) of 27 June to 2 July, CAB 80/14.
6. JIC(40) 225 of 4 Aug.
7. Woodward, *British Foreign Policy*, vol. I, pp. 489, 491, 495 and 498.
8. DO(40) 39th Meeting SSF, of 31 Oct., CAB 69/8.
9. Letter from Cavendish-Bentinck to DMI, 7 Oct. 1940 (MI 14 Appreciations File), WO 190/892.
10. B. Whaley, *Codeword Barbarossa* (MIT Press, Cambridge, Mass. and London, 1973) pp. 30–1, 33 and 136.
11. WO Weekly Intsum no. 63 of 31 Oct. 1940, WO 208/2258.
12. C. Amort and I. M. Jedlica, *The Canaris File* (Allan Wingate, London and New York, 1970) pp. 96–7; F. Moravec, *Master of Spies* (Bodley Head, London, 1975) p. 202.
13. MI 14 Appreciation, 27 Aug. 1940, WO 190/891.
14. MI 14 Appreciation, 31 Oct. 1940, WO 190/891.
15. MI 14 Appreciation, 27 Oct. 1940, WO 190/891.
16. AI3 Summary of Minutes, vol. II, Minute of 3 Nov. 1940, AIR 40/2321.
17. MI 14 Appreciation, 6 and 12 Nov. 1940, WO 190/891.
18. Notes for VCIGS, 16 Dec. 1940 (MI Appreciations File).
19. MI 14 letter to FOES, 24 Dec. 1940 (MI 14 Appreciations File).
20. WO Weekly Intsum no. 72 to 1 Jan. 1941, WO 208/2258.
21. COS(41) 23 (FOES(41) 1, Revise) of 9 Jan., CAB 80/25.
22. Whaley, *Codeword Barbarossa*, pp. 180 and 182.
23. Ibid. p. 27.
24. MI 14 Appreciation, 17 Jan. 1941.
25. MI 14 Appreciation, 24 Nov. 1940.
26. Woodward, *British Foreign Policy*, vol. I, p. 497.
27. FO 371/29470; N286/78/38.
28. Churchill, *Second World War*, vol. III, p. 10.

29. DO(41) 6th Meeting, 20 Jan., CAB 69/2.
30. WM(41) 20 CA, p. 4, 24 Feb. 1941, CAB 65/21.
31. Whaley, *Codeword Barbarossa*, pp. 35–6.
32. Ibid. pp. 37–40 and 227–8; US Department of State, *Foreign Relations of the United States* (US Govt. Printing Office, Washington, DC, 1958) vol. I, 1941, pp. 712 and 714; Cordell Hull, *Memoirs* (Hodder & Stoughton, London 1948) pp. 968–9; W. L. Shirer, *The Rise and Fall of the Third Reich* (Fawcett, Greenwich, Conn., 1959) ch. 23.
33. PRO: EO 371/26521; C6928/C7205/78/38.
34. G. E. Blau, *The German Campaign in Russia* (US Department of Army, Washington, 1955) p. 26.
35. WO Weekly Intsum no. 77, to 5 Feb. 1941.
36. COS(41) 78, Résumé to 6 Feb. 1941, CAB 80/25.
37. MI 14 Appreciations File; Letter from DMI to Cavendish-Bentinck and the other Ds of I, 6 Feb. 1941, WO 190/893.
38. MI 14 Appreciation, 7 Feb. 1941.
39. MI 14 Appreciation, 14 Feb. 1941.
40. WO Weekly Intsum, to 5 Mar. 1941.
41. MI 14 Appreciation, 5 Mar. 1941.
42. MI 14 Appreciation, 12 Mar. 1941.
43. Summary of MI 14's Indications, 18 Mar. 1941, WO 190/893.
44. FOES(41) 5 of 19 Mar. 1941, CAB 81/64.
45. Summary of AI3 Minutes, vol. II, minute of 13 Mar. 1941, AIR 40/2232.
46. Ibid., minute of 23 Mar. 1941.
47. Summary of MI 14's Indications File, 25 Mar. 1941.
48. Churchill, *Second World War*, vol. III, p. 317.
49. AI3 Summary of Minutes, vol. II, minute of 28 Mar. 1941, AIR 40/2232.
50. GC and CS. CX/JQ/57 of 30 Mar. 1941.
51. Churchill, *Second World War*, vol. III, p. 151.
52. Ibid. p. 319.
53. Churchill, *Second World War*, vol. III, pp. 319–20.
54. Woodward, *British Foreign Policy*, vol. I, p. 604.
55. Churchill, *Second World War*, vol. III, p. 323.
56. Woodward, *British Foreign Policy*, vol. I, p. 605.
57. Ibid., vol. I, pp. 606–7.
58. Ibid., vol. I, pp. 608–9.
59. US Department of State, *FRUS* pp. 133 and 723.
60. Woodward, *British Foreign Policy*, vol. I, p. 604.
61. Ibid. vol. I, p. 606.
62. FO 371/29479; N 1367/78/38.
63. Woodward, *British Foreign Policy*, vol. 1, p. 605; Churchill, *Second World War*, vol. III, pp. 320–1.
64. Woodward, *British Foreign Policy*, vol. I, pp. 609–10.
65. Summary of MI 14's Indications File, 1 Apr. 1941.
66. COS(41) 221, Résumé no. 83 to 3 Apr. 1941, paras 18, 20 and 23.
67. WO Weekly Intsum to 2 Apr. 1941.
68. Ibid. to 9 Apr. 1941.
69. JIC(41) 144 of 10 Apr. 1941, covering APS(41) 3 of 5 Apr. 1941.
70. Summary of MI 14's Indications File, 15 Apr. 1941.
71. WO Weekly Intsum no. 87, to 16 Apr. 1941.
72. COS(41) 248, Résumé no. 85 to 17 Apr., para. 23.
73. Whaley, *Codeword Barbarossa*, p. 48.
74. Woodward, *British Foreign Policy*, vol. I, p. 612.

75. MI 14 Appreciations File, DMI Memo to CIGS, 22 Apr. 1941.
76. Summary of MI 14's Indications File, 22 Apr. 1941.
77. COS(41) 143rd Meeting, 22 Apr., CAB 79/11.
78. Air Ministry Weekly Intelligence Survey, to 30 Apr. 1941, AIR 22/74.
79. Air Ministry Weekly Intelligence Survey, to 7 May 1941. For the following evidence from the Enigma, see F. H. Hinsley et al., *British Intelligence in the Second World War* (HMSO, London, 1979) vol. I, pp. 460–1.
80. Whaley, *Codeword Barbarossa*, p. 180.
81. F. H. Hinsley et al., *British Intelligence*, p. 465.
82. DD13 Minute to D of I(O), 23 May 1941 (in MI 14 Appreciations File), WO 190/893.
83. MI 14 Appreciation, 25 Apr. 1941.
84. COS(41) 311, Résumé to 15 May, paras 30, 34 and 35; MI 14 Brief for APS, 15 May 1941 (in Appreciations File).
85. WO Weekly Intsum to 21 May, WO 228/2259.
86. COS(41) 325, Résumé to 22 May 1941, paras 27–8.
87. JIC(41) 218 of 23 May.
88. Woodward, *British Foreign Policy*, vol. I, p. 615.
89. FO 371/29481: N 2498/78/38.
90. F. H. Hinsley et al., *British Intelligence*, pp. 472–4.
91. Ibid. p. 474.
92. Ibid. p. 474.
93. Ibid. pp. 474–5.
94. JIC(41) 229 of 30 May 1941.
95. D. Dilks (ed.), *The Diaries of Sir Alexander Cadogan* (Cassell, London, 1971) pp. 382 and 385, diary entries for 31 May and 2 June 1941.
96. WM(41) 58 CA, 9 June, CAB 65/22.
97. FO 371/26521: C6668/19/18.
98. FO 371/29482: N 2673/N2680/78/38; Woodward, *British Foreign Policy*, vol. I, p. 620; Whaley, *Codeword Barbarossa*, p. 106.
99. Woodward, *British Foreign Policy*, vol. I, p. 620.
100. WM(41) 59 CA, 12 June.
101. F. H. Hinsley et al., *British Intelligence*, p. 478.
102. JIC(41) 252(0) of 12 June.
103. Woodward, *British Foreign Policy*, vol. I, p. 621.
104. COS(41) 210th Meeting, 13 June, CAB 79/12.
105. F. H. Hinsley et al., *British Intelligence*, pp. 479–80.
106. Summary of MI 14's Indications File, 16 June 1941.
107. Woodward, *British Foreign Policy*, vol. I, p. 620; J. R. M. Butler, *Grand Strategy* (HMSO, London, 1957) vol. II, p. 544.
108. WM(41) 60 CA, 16 June 1941.
109. Woodward, *British Foreign Policy*, vol. I, p. 595; Whaley, *Codeword Barbarossa*, pp. 32–3.
110. JIC(41) 234 of 9 June.
111. Woodward, *British Foreign Policy*, vol. I, p. 615 (n).
112. JIC(41) 234 of 9 June.
113. MI 14 Appreciation, 17 June 1941.
114. COS(41) 224th Meeting, 25 June.
115. JIC(41) 295(O), 23 July.
116. JIC(41) 307(O), 1 Aug.
117. COS(41) 274th Meeting, 2 Aug.

Chapter 4

The German Attack, the Soviet Response, Sunday, 22 June 1941

DMITRI VOLKOGONOV

A month and a half before the giant clash of the Great Patriotic War, the German and Russian heads of government could be heard in their respective capitals, at that time still linked by the German–Soviet Boundary and Friendship Treaty of 28 September 1939. Hitler appeared at the Reichstag on 4 May 1941; Stalin in the Kremlin the day after. Both spoke of war. But neither mentioned what forthcoming war would mean for Europe.

Hitler, a man whose conscience was a sham and to whom human life meant nothing, evidently gave a very long speech.[1] 'Deputies! Members of the German Reichstag! At a time when action means everything and words nothing I have no intention of appearing before you, representatives of the German people, more often than is necessary ...' He subsequently gave the deputies a detailed account of how Poland was smashed, followed by Norway, Belgium, Holland, France, Yugoslavia and Greece. In his expansive speech 'the first Aryan' endlessly reviled Winston Churchill, resorting to the crudest imprecations and insults directed at the British Prime Minister.

In the closing part of the speech Hitler declared that in the course of the subjugation of Europe,

> the German armed forces have truly surpassed even themselves. Infantry, armoured and mountain divisions, as well as SS formations, competed without a rest, in bravery, endurance and stubbornness to achieve their goals. The work of the General Staff has been outstanding. The air force has added to its historic glory, new heroic deeds ... Nothing is impossible for the German soldier!

His closing phrases are regarded as significant and frank:

The German people will firmly maintain superiority of the armaments and under no circumstances will they allow any decrease in their supremacy ... This is the greatest process of arming in the history of the world. Vital measures, in that respect, will have to be undertaken, with future approval and determined support of the National-Socialists ... The German empire and its allies constitute a power, which no coalition in the world can surpass. German armed forces will unremittingly intervene in the course of the events whenever and wherever it will be required.

In the conclusion, Hitler assured the deputies that he 'looks at the future with tranquillity and utmost confidence'.[2]

Those listening to the speech were not yet aware that his words about 'the utmost confidence in the future' related directly to Directive No. 21, known under the code-name *Barbarossa*. Choosing the name of the redbearded German king seemed a good omen to Hitler. True, on return from a routine expedition, Barbarossa, in a rather mundane fashion, drowned crossing a ford, but his military campaigns were so successful ...

Directive No. 21 formulated the operational plan with the utmost clarity:

The German armed forces must be prepared *to crush Soviet Russia in a quick campaign* (Operation *Barbarossa*) even before the conclusion of the war against England.

I. *General Purpose*: The mass of the Russian *army* in western Russia is to be destroyed in daring operations, by driving forward deep armoured wedges, and the retreat of units capable of combat into the vastness of Russian territories to be prevented.

In quick pursuit a line is then to be reached from which the Russian air force will no longer be able to attack German Reich territory. The ultimate objective of the operation is to establish a defence line against Asiatic Russia from a line running approximately from the Volga River to Archangel.[3]

One of the principal architects of the war plan devised in the German High Command was Major-General Friedrich von Paulus, whose name became better known to the Soviet people after February 1943 and the German surrender at Stalingrad.

The full scope of the German plans was revealed to the Soviet leadership after the war, when Colonel-General Jodl of the German High Command handed Major-General Trusov, representative of the Control Commission in Germany, a file of top-secret documents entitled 'Concerning the Conduct of the War in the East'.[4]

On 5 May Stalin appeared in the Kremlin, at the graduation of the students of the Military Academy, still unaware of the *Führer*'s speech and *Barbarossa*. The Soviet dictator's address was extraordinary in its content. According to General N. G. Lyashchenko, who was present at the reception, Stalin had sheets of paper in front of him. However, the original text is not available, but a shorthand record of the speech was ordered. After the war, when preparations to publish volumes 14 and 15 of the *Vozhd*'s (leader's) works began, the notes taken by the research assistant of the People's Commissariat for Defence – K. Semyonov – were accepted as the basis for the text. Few people know that, in addition to the speech, Stalin also gave three toasts, the last one being of greatest interest. Strictly speaking, it was more an addition to the toast given by one major-general, who proposed: 'To the peaceful Stalinist foreign policy!' But Stalin interrupted the speaker:

> Permit me to correct you: that kind of policy has guaranteed the peace for our country. Peaceful (foreign) policy – that is a good thing. For the time being, up till now, we followed a defensive line, and we did not re-arm our Army, we did not provide it with the modern means to fight ... But if we are to defend our country, we are obliged to adopt an offensive posture ... We must reform our education, our propaganda, political instruction, we should adopt an offensive posture. The Red Army is a modern army, and a modern army is an offensive army.

In his speech, having congratulated the students of the Academy on the completion of their studies, Stalin declared, 'on your return into the Army, you will not recognise it'. Waving his good hand now and then, the orator stated that the Army had learnt the lessons from the Soviet – Finnish war and from the events in the west. Unexpectedly, while describing the qualitative growth of the Army, he mentioned the existence of 'Top-Secret' documents and a 'Special File', the latter being especially significant. 'Currently we have 300 divisions in our Army', said the leader of the Party and the Government. The *Vozhd* painted an optimistic picture of the condition of the Red Army, and on this occasion he depicted the process of rearmament with the new military technology as if it were an actual fact.

'Why is Germany presently winning in the west?' Stalin asked himself. Looking around with his yellow eyes, he lingered on an explanation of the secrets of its successes.

> First of all the Germans have learnt the lessons of their defeat in the First World War, when they allowed themselves to fight on two fronts. The military thought of the German army has advanced. The Army has been equipped with the new technology. The Germans have 'politically

prepared' themselves for the war, having acquired a 'sufficient number'
of allies.

Did Stalin think this was not the case for the USSR? Had he changed his mind
after signing the treaty of 'friendship' with Germany, his most recent ally?

But Stalin declared that the German army was not invincible, because
'The German army possesses nothing special in the way of tanks, artillery
or air force. A significant part of the German army is losing the ardour that
it had at the beginning of the war ...' Stalin continued highlighting the
weaknesses of the German war machine: 'Boasting, complacency and conceit
are beginning to surface in the German army. Their military thinking is not
advancing any longer, their war technology is lagging behind ours. The
German army has lost the taste for any further improvement of their military
technology ...'

In his order – signed that very day – the People's Commissar for Defence,
S. K. Timoshenko, expressly praised Stalin as a 'great leader and teacher'.[5]
The reader is free to judge this degree of analytical 'perspicacity'.

Those were Stalin's views, the views of a man who determined the policy,
the military organisation, the strategy of the defence of the country, single-
handed. On the order of Stalin, the Chief of the Main Political Propaganda
Administration of the Red Army, Army Commissar (second rank) Zaporozhets, began preparing the new directive, 'The Tasks of the Political Propaganda in the Red Army in the Immediate Future'. It was finished round
about 20 June, but Stalin had no opportunity to see it, nor did the People's
Commissar for Defence manage to sign it. The war found it on Stalin's desk.
The gist of the document contained the main elements of Stalin's May speech.
'The great leader' supposed that, after the German attack, the war waged
by the Soviet Union would only be an offensive one. The draft of the directive
suggests that 'political propaganda should be made a priority at present in
the Red Army. All forms of propaganda, political agitation and education
should be directed towards a single cause – the political, moral and military
preparation of personnel in order to wage a just, offensive and war-short-
ening war.'[6] In addition, the directive correctly concluded that 'Germany is
waging war in order to establish its supremacy in Europe' and it aspired to
create 'a large colonial empire'.

Stalin believed, as he had stated in his toast on 5 May, that in the event
of a German attack – which he considered unlikely, as it would have meant
war on two fronts – the Red Army would be in a position quickly to shift
from 'defensive to offensive action'. But did he really not know about the
'top-secret' directive of the People's Commissar for Defence, No. 34678 of
17 May 1941, in which the Marshal of the Soviet Union, S. K. Timoshenko,

had evaluated the results of combat readiness? It stated that the requirement and the provisions for 'the winter period of 1941 had not been met in a significant number of formations and units'. The Main Military Soviet, for example, assessed the readiness of the Red Army air force as 'unsatisfactory'. The documents with these appraisals, which were well known to Stalin, were signed by S. K. Timoshenko, A. A. Zhdanov and G. K. Zhukov.[7] Incidentally, after this evaluation the Chief of the Main Administration of the air force, Pavel Vasil'evich Rychagov, was relieved of his command, arrested and shot that same year.[8]

The special inspection of the Kiev, the Western and Baltic Special Military Districts, and the Odessa Military District, which was carried out from 23 May to 5 June 1941, ascertained the readiness of the forces as unsatisfactory. The coded telegram, addressed to the military soviets of the districts and the armies, and signed by Timoshenko and Zhukov, presents an alarming evaluation of the condition of the units.[9] A little earlier, A. Zaporozhets had reported the same findings in a special account to Stalin and other members of the Politburo, 'concerning the condition of the fortified districts on our western frontiers', namely that 'the majority of the troops deployed in the fortified districts on our western frontiers are not battle ready'.[10] Yet only a month and a half before the beginning of the war, Stalin was insisting that in the event of a German attack, the USSR would quickly go over to the offensive.

Even to this day there are people in the USSR who claim that 'thanks to the Party's action and attention', the country had basically been ready to repel the aggression, but for the treachery by Hitler, which brought on the catastrophe at the beginning of the war. What readiness indeed! The report by Timoshenko and Zhukov – addressed to Stalin, Zhdanov and Voznesensky, and signed after Stalin's boastful speech of 5 May – states that in all the most important categories 'of arms and weapons and equipment, meeting the plan of delivery from the industry is totally unsatisfactory.'[11]

The country was preparing itself for war, yet it was not ready for it. The Soviet people, the greatest heros and martyrs of the approaching war, sacrificing their all, exerted every effort in order to increase the defensive potential. The spiritual resolve of the people to protect their fatherland was high. But the errors of the top leadership in foreign policy, the supremacy of the bureaucracy and dogmatism, Stalin's decapitation of the Army, and the unquestioning subordination to every wish of the autocrat who was considered infallible predetermined – to the highest degree – the most unsuccessful beginning of the war for the USSR.

At that time Stalin was receiving a constant stream of dispatches, via various channels, about the concentration of the German troops at the frontier. The reports sent to Stalin were based on numerous sources of information, gathered by the secret service and the intelligence units. The report of the intelligence section Headquarters of the Western Special Military District, signed on 4 June 1941 by Colonel Blokhin and Major Samoilovich, reads: 'On the basis of reliable sources from the secret service, the military preparation of Germany for the war against the USSR lately, and especially since 25 May, has been intensified.' The report also gives details about the continuous arrival on the frontier of new units, one after the other, especially tank and mechanised units. It further delineates:

> All the civil medical establishments both in large and small localities – to be occupied by the hospitals ... The secret mobilisation of the officials who would be performing their duties in the western regions of the USSR has ceased. These officials have been fully briefed, and are only waiting for the beginning of the war. There are courses run for parachutists who will be dropped in the rear of Soviet Belorussia, whose aim would be sabotage. The possibility of an attack on the USSR by Germany in June has not been ruled out ...[12]

Also enclosed with the report is the interrogation document of Frentsel Jozef Jozefovich, who crossed over to the Soviet side on 4 June', from which it is plain that the German army intended to attack the USSR imminently.[13]

The abundance of many similar reports reassured Stalin, since he considered the Germans could not be so unconcerned about their preparations, and that the deserters were just provocateurs. But all the statements by Timoshenko and Zhukov, he rebuffed tersely: 'Do not succumb to provocation ... Are the Germans capable of fighting on two fronts?' It seemed as if he did not wish to understand that, strictly speaking, there was no 'front' in the west after the defeat of France.

As Marshal Zhukov told Konstantin Simonov, it was some time in the spring of 1941, when the stream of reports about the concentration of German troops in Poland considerably increased, that Stalin wrote a personal letter to Hitler asking for an explanation of the situation. In a 'confidential' reply the *Führer* reported to the Soviet leader that the information was accurate; it was true that large military formations were concentrated in Poland, but being confident that it would go no further than Stalin himself, Hitler was duty bound to make it clear to him that the formations in Poland were not directed at the Soviet Union. He said that the territories of west and central Germany were being subjected to heavy British bombing; hence the reason for removing a considerable part of his troops and placing them in Poland. Stalin believed that the *Führer* intended to adhere strictly to the

Pact, which had been guaranteed by the very honour of the head of government. It appears, said Zhukov, that Stalin believed in Hitler's argument. What the Soviet leader did not know at that time was that at the beginning of 1941 Germany had carried out a huge disinformation effort, Operation *Sealion*, with the aim of convincing the Soviet Union about large-scale preparations for a landing operation on the British Isles. The realisation of this plan was clear from an 'accidentally lost' map of the German invasion of England, and the statement by the German military attaché, General Koestring, who importunately repeated to the Soviet officials attending formal meetings that the German forces in Poland 'must be thoroughly rested, before they go and finish off England'.[14]

But under the pressure of the military, Stalin had decided to put several defensive measures into effect. In May 1940, Major-General Vasilevski, on the order of Timoshenko, completed in his own handwriting one copy ('High priority. Top secret. Personal only') of the 'Plan for the Defence of the State Frontier', and delivered it to Stalin and Molotov. The plan stated that 'it might be possible that the conflict would be limited to our western frontiers only, but the possibility of the attack by Japan on our Far-Eastern frontier is not excluded'.[15] As a result of a discussion in the narrow circle of Stalin's office, the conclusion was reached that the first echelon in the west should contain 57 divisions, the second 52, and the reserve 62 divisions. Here, under the pressure of Stalin, a huge strategic mistake was permitted: the main forces were concentrated on the south-western axis (around 100 divisions). Stringing out divisions of the strategic echelon in the interior, frequently far from the frontier, permitted the aggressor to deal with separate elements of the defence in piecemeal fashion. The main blow was expected in the south-west, but Hitler attacked the centre, on the western axis. This should have been expected: in all the previous campaigns, the German forces went into action aiming towards the capitals of the conquered states, along the shortest possible axis.

After the plan for the defence was approved, General Zhukov was appointed chief of the General Staff in January 1941. It so happened that in just half a year, this was already the third appointment of a chief of the General Staff. In August 1940, K. A. Meretskov replaced B. M. Shaposhnikov, and now the former was replaced by Zhukov. This leapfrogging was hardly conducive to well-thought-out strategic understanding of the menacing situation.

The military managed to persuade Stalin to undertake a big step: at the end of May and beginning of June 1941, 793,000 reservists were called up for training, which made it possible to replenish some formations in the front line 2–3 weeks before the start of the conflict. In general terms, at the beginning of 1941, the strength of Red Army units – measured against a requirement for a full complement (100 per cent) – was as follows: medium tanks – 74 per cent, artillery weapons – 76 per cent, aircraft – full complement, but in the main these machines consisted of old models.

The war was rapidly approaching. According to various sources Hitler moved the date of the start of the offensive several times. In May, the 14th, 15th and 20th were consistently favoured, but in the month of June first it was the 15th, and finally it was the 22nd. Hitler estimated that the war would last five months at most.[16]

Stalin, sensing the lack of readiness for war, strove in every possible way to demonstrate his loyalty to Hitler. In June, when German aircraft began to violate the Soviet frontier in great numbers, the Soviet leader issued a directive: the flights 'are not carried out deliberately. During the infringements German planes do not carry weapons.'[17] In cases when the aircraft had a 'forced landing', the crew was permitted to take off again, unimpeded. However, reports about German preparations for an attack were rolling in like an avalanche. Stalin suggested to Molotov that he should try a probe. A statement issued by Tass on 14 June was published; it contained a delicate reproof to Germany with regard to its adherence to the conditions of the Pact, but nevertheless in the conclusion it stated: 'Germany is as steadfastly sticking to conditions of the Soviet–German Non-Aggression Pact, as is the Soviet Union.' Stalin and Molotov were essentially offering Berlin new talks, which, should they last a month or two, would remove any possibility of war during 1941.

On the day when *Pravda* published the Tass statement, Hitler held a meeting of the High Command of his Army, at which he listened to the commanders of Army Groups' report on readiness for 'Drang nach Osten'. The *Führer* confirmed the new date for the invasion: 22 June 1941. But the time of the attack was shifted from 3.30 to 3.00 hours.[18] Goebbels, Minister of State for Propaganda, wrote in his diary: 'In Moscow they are preoccupied with guess work, it looks as if Stalin is slowly beginning to understand what is what.' But basically 'he has not changed his view [about Germany], just like a rabbit views a snake'.[19]

On the same day, life continued as usual in the forces of the 7th, 14th and 23rd Armies of the Leningrad Military District, the 8th, 11th and 27th Armies of the Baltic Special Military District, the 3rd, 10th, 13th and 4th Armies of the Western Special Military District, the 5th, 6th, 26th and 12th Armies of the Kiev Special Military District, and in several corps of the Odessa Military District. Combat machines were being driven, shells were bursting on the firing ranges, new aerodromes and fortified areas were being constructed; staff officers, in accordance with the instruction given by the

General Staff, were finalising the plans for the defence of the state frontiers
and the localities of anti-aircraft defence. In accordance with the directive
issued by the People's Commissariat for Defence on 13 May 1941, four
armies (the 16th, 19th, 31st and 22nd) were to continue the move forward
from the interior. The completion of the forward deployment was planned
for the middle of July. Generally stressful, military life continued, controlled
and managed rigidly – as is usually the case in this type of military system –
from the centre. The pulse of the military organism was beating faster. The
announcement of 14 June brought, it seemed, a calming influence into the
tense atmosphere of the Soviet existence. And life continued as ever. At
ammunition factory No. 80, for example, the interruption of the delivery
plan was investigated; the Moscow Commission was engaged in the Podol'sk
factory, trying to find out why hull armour had cracks in it; specialists asked
the People's Commissar of the Shipbuilding Industry, Nosenko, why the
military had been supplied with only three ferry boats instead of nine.[20] But
that day, they were also occupied with the ending of the *chistka* (purge) in
the ranks of 'suspicious' persons amongst the local population: 'To the
commander of the Baltic Special Military District. To the commander of the
2nd Army. On 14 June at 18.00 hours, 115 men were arrested. Only a few
are left. Everything is going successfully. The work is nearing the end. Major-
General Kurkin.'[21]

As the fateful day was approaching, how did they greet it on the German
side?

The last-minute preparations for the attack by the German forces were
nearing completion. The communication links between Hitler's headquarters – now relocated in Rastenburg – and the staffs of the Army Group
were checked out. Hitler's personal message (Ed.: *An den Soldaten der
Ostfront*) was sent to the troops, calling upon them 'to eliminate the Bolshevik threat to Germany in the east'. The trains, which were switched over
to the accelerated schedule of traffic, continued to deliver the troops and
freight to the frontier. During the second half of 21 June, Luftwaffe aeroplanes arrived one by one on the border aerodromes. Sabotage units sent
prearranged signals about the onset of the attack on 22 June to the many
secret agents previously emplaced within the frontier districts. Many of them
became subversive elements while wearing Red Army uniforms.

At the end of the day, Ribbentrop sent a long telegram 'Urgent! State
secret!' to the German Ambassador, with the instruction to report its contents to the Soviet leadership the following morning. The declaration stated
that the treaties of 23 and 28 September 1939 'brought great advantages in
the field of foreign policy to the Soviet Union'. But, as became clear, it went

on, 'the ratification of the agreements turned out to be a tactical man'uvre for obtaining an arrangement favourable only to the Soviet Union'. In a four-page document by the German Ministry of Foreign Affairs it was emphasised that 'the Soviet actions against the Baltic States, against Finland and Romania, where Soviet claims reached as far as Bukovina, demonstrated' the aim to 'bolshevise and annexe those countries'. The document asserted that: 'The occupation and bolshevisation by the Soviet Union of the countries conceded to it as its sphere of influence seems to be a direct infringement of the Moscow Agreements ...' It further accused the USSR of the 'intention to attack Germany from the rear', and the Ministry of Foreign Affairs reported, 'that is why the *Führer* ordered German armed forces to confront that threat with all the means at their disposal'.[22] Almost at the same time, during the second half of 21 June, Hitler wrote to Mussolini:

> I am writing you this letter at a time when the many months of long, hard thinking and the constant nervous waiting has ended, as I have now made the most difficult decision of my life. I think that it would be wrong to suffer the situation any longer, having received the report about the picture and the conditions in Russia, and also after acquainting myself with many other dispatches ... As regards the war in the East, Duce, it will definitely be hard. But not for a minute do I doubt our success.... the final decision will be made today at 7 o'clock in the evening ...[23]

Hitler did not know yet that starting the war would be easier for him than ending it.

But what was happening that evening in Moscow?

Poskrebyshev, assistant to the Chairman of the Soviet People's Commissariats, was constantly delivering reports from the western border to Stalin's table, each one more worrying than the previous one. The report signed by the Chief of Staff of the Baltic Special Military District, Lieutenant-General Klenov, stated: 'The Germans have finished the construction of the bridges across the Niemen.... The civilians have been advised to evacuate to a depth of 20 kilometres from the frontier ...'[24] The Chief of Staff from the Western Special Military District, Major-General Klimovskikh, reported: 'barbed wire along the frontier on the route Augustov – Seiny, while in place during the day, was pulled down towards the evening. In the woods, there is a sound of engines.'[25] Colonel-General M. P. Kirponos, commander of the Kiev Special Military District, reported to the effect that war would begin in a matter of hours.

Stalin wavered. He had always been a prisoner of politics, and took decisions only after a great deal of inner struggle. At that moment he did not want the war; he knew he was not ready. However, there are moments when it is necessary to act with great resolution and fast, so that history cannot leave time for failure. Having occupied the position of earthly God, his perception of the surrounding events became so distorted that Stalin did not want to believe anything could happen that would contradict his forecast and his wishes.

In the evening of 21 June, Stalin ordered Molotov to invite the German ambassador, Schulenburg, in order to explain the situation on the frontier. He insisted this should be done in Berlin: the Soviet Ambassador was to meet Ribbentrop. Schulenburg, who had been instructed to destroy the embassy secret papers, listened to Molotov with an inscrutable expression. He expressed astonishment that 'the Soviet Government is not in a position to understand the reasons for German dissatisfaction ...' The Soviet Minister, Molotov, having been one of the main architects of the Soviet–German policy, was expecting reassurance. Instead, Schulenburg coldly replied: 'I cannot give you an answer to that question, and I shall transmit it to Berlin.' Ribbentrop refused to receive the Soviet Ambassador, and dispatched him to the State-Secretary, von Weizsäcker. When the Soviet ambassador, Dekanozov, asked about the incidents of German planes flying over Soviet territory, the State-Secretary rudely interrupted him, stating: 'Since my view differs, it is necessary to wait for the reply from my government ... There will be a delay of one day.'[26] Indeed, in a few hours the German Government would be giving 'the reply' in the form of an unprecedented invasion of Soviet territory.

In Moscow – after lengthy discussions in Stalin's study, with Timoshenko and Zhukov present – it was decided to send the forces an order issued by the Main Military Soviet, known as 'Number One'. After it was coded, it was sent to the Headquarters of the Military Districts during the first half of the night of Sunday, 22 June. This order read: 'In the course of 22–23 June 1941, sudden attacks by the Germans on the fronts of Leningrad, Baltic Special, Western Special, Kiev Special and Odessa Special Military Districts will be possible. The task of our forces is not to yield to any provocations likely to prompt major complications.'[27] But that timid directive did not reach many units. The forces of the border districts – numbering 170 divisions, containing more than 3 million men – were stationed at too great a depth, and were caught unawares by the tactical suddenness of the German forces. The latter, numbering around 4 million men, and having concentrated their troops on a few basic axes, obtained a 3:1 superiority. On the first day of war alone, the Western Special Military District lost over 1,200 aircraft – most were destroyed on the ground. In the initial hours the Germans had established superiority in the air.

Soviet forces at the frontier, caught out by the unexpected, were desperately overwhelmed, and their efforts were uncoordinated and spontaneous. In the first few hours, communication links and command and control were paralysed.

It is interesting to look at the initial days of the war through the eyes of the participants. After the death of Stalin, several military leaders charged with reaching a common understanding of the initial period of the war submitted their recollections to the General Staff. The former commander of the 8th Army, Lieutenant-General P. P. Sobennikov, reports that a specific 'defensive plan did not get to the troops'. No written orders either before or after 20 June were received from the Headquarters of the District. 'On 21 and 22 June, the Command Post received conflicting orders over the telephone and the telegraph, about mines and the organisation of the sector. Moreover, one set of orders instructed that the measures be taken immediately, the others revoked them, then they were again confirmed, then repealed ...'

During the night of 22 June 'I personally received an order from the Chief of Staff of the Front, Lieutenant-General P. S. Klenov, in a highly unequivocal form – "at daybreak of 22 June, move the troops away from the frontier and take them out of the trenches" – which I categorically refused to do....' One could feel a high degree of nervousness, lack of co-ordination, vagueness, fear of 'provoking' the war. Indeed, at daybreak on 22 June 'almost the whole air force of the Baltic Military District was burnt out on the aerodromes'. The General, who very shortly had to assume the command of the whole north-western front, sorrowfully concluded: 'The staff of the army was not battle ready ...'[28]

The commander of the 8th Mechanized Corps, Lieutenant-General D. I. Ryabyshev remembered that on 22 June 'out of 939 tanks at the disposal of the corps, only 169 were of the new type (KV and T-34); the other stock obsolete machines T-26, BT-5, BT-7.' After reconnaissance in the frontier regions, with the aim of determining the route for the tanks, General Ryabyshev recalled,

> 'I observed massive infringements of the frontier by the German air force and reported this to the Chief of Staff of the 26th Army, General I. S. Varennikov, to indicate the German forces' preparation for the attack. General Varennikov categorically brushed aside my opinion and assured me that should there be something serious, then we should receive timely confirmation.... Nobody had any ideas about war.'[29]

Further, Ryabyshev remembers that in the earliest days he received orders one after the other from Front and Army Headquarters, amounting to endless requests to move the corps over considerable distances. Having received one order to move the troops of the corps into the reserve of the Front and having begun its execution, he suddenly received another about an attack on the enemy in the direction of Brody and Dubno. By then, the columns were already on the march. 'The KP [Command Post] of the corps was visited by the member of the Military Soviet of the south-western front, Corps Commissar N. I. Vashugin, who requested the immediate execution of the front commander's last order about the departure of the corps to the Dubno region, and threatened me with execution.... Exerting an enormous effort, the forces of the corps were regrouped and turned round, and engaged in heavy battle, even though it was later established that the previously planned advance had been cancelled earlier.' The units of the corps found themselves encircled. When in the end the remnants of the formations managed to extricate themselves from the enemy grip, their composition contained only 10 per cent of the original strength of the tanks. 'The aimless transfer of the corps in the initial days,' Ryabyshev recalled with bitterness, 'the lack of stable communications, the frequent changing of tasks – without the realistic consideration of the resources and the time factor – and the absence of the air cover and co-ordination with the neighbouring units, in spite of the exceptional courage of the troops'[30] predetermined large failures and defeats.

On the central sector of the Soviet–German Front, events took a most serious turn. At 7.15 in the morning, having received the report of the attack by Hitler's Germany, the forces received one more directive, signed by Timoshenko, Zhukov and Malenkov, to this effect: 'The troops, with all their might and means, are to overwhelm the enemy forces and destroy them in the regions where they have infringed the Soviet frontier. The ground forces are not to advance and cross the frontier without special authorisation.'[31] In the Kremlin they did not even contemplate that in six days the German forces would be in Minsk.

Having received muddled, fragmentary reports from the front, another new and totally unrealistic directive was prepared on the initiative of Stalin. It was addressed to the Military Soviets of the north-western, western, south-western and southern fronts, and ordered them to encircle – 'by powerful concentric blows' – and destroy the Suvalki concentration of the enemy; and encircle and destroy the invading troops in the region Vladimir-Volynsk and Brody: 'towards the end of 24 June take possession of the Lublin region'. One of the paragraphs dictated personally by Stalin announced: 'On the front from the Baltic Sea to the Hungarian frontier I authorise the crossing of the state frontier and operations, without taking the frontier into account.'[32]

In one phrase, the word 'frontier' was repeated three times. Stalin was agitated, but not yet in shock, which was going to paralyse him psychologically for two or three days by the end of the week. Incidentally, this is confirmed in the 'Comrade Stalin's visitors' book' (*Kniga zapisi lits, prinimaemykh tovarishchem Stalinym*) in the Kremlin. After 28 June till 1 July no one visited Stalin; he did not receive anybody.[33] It was on 28 June he learnt that, east of Minsk, two German tank groups had linked up and encircled the main forces of the western front. Having found themselves encircled, the Russian forces fought with selfless devotion to the end of the first ten days' period in July.

At the beginning of July the dictator was to be found close by his dacha, shaken by the picture of the beginning of the war, painted by the members of the General Staff. The enemy tank formations were breaking through towards Leningrad, Moscow and Kiev. On some days the German troops advanced 30–40 kilometres in 24 hours. Thus, Stalin's orders 'to cross the border' only underline his total ignorance of the real situation.

The most tragic situation occurred on the western front, as documents signed by the commander of the western front, Army General D. G. Pavlov, and his Staff testify. Fate had allotted him only one week as a commander of the front. Then, exactly a month after the beginning of the war, General D. G. Pavlov, the Chief of Staff V. E. Klimovskikh, Chief of Signals A. A. Grigor'ev, commander of the 4th Army A. A. Korobkov were all to be convicted and shot the same day. The artillery commander N. A. Klich was shot later. The initiator of the 'exposure' of the front's leadership, who found 'criminal activity' had taken place, was L. M. Mekhlis. As a response to that initiative, Mekhlis and all who supported him received a telegram of approval from Stalin. The destiny of the 44-year-old Pavlov and his comrades had been sealed. Some documents signed by Pavlov and his circle have been left for posterity.

In the evening of 22 June, Pavlov and Klimovskikh reported to Moscow that the troops of the 3rd and 10th Armies had fallen back only negligibly, and that the 4th Army 'is fighting, it is estimated, on the line Mel'nik – Brest – Vlodava'.[34] Essentially unaware of the situation, as a result of having lost control of the troops, the commander of the front was reporting his 'estimates'.

In the morning of the 23rd, a cipher was sent to the troops of the front, signed by Pavlov, Fomin and Klimovskikh, stating:

> Experience of the first day of war demonstrated lack of co-ordination and carelessness of many commanders, including senior commanders. They do not think of providing fuel and artillery rounds, or replenishing infantry ammunition, until the ammunition is running out, and there is a mass of vehicles engaged in evacuation of families into the country,

and all this is done by the Red Army soldiers, men from combat units. They are not evacuating the wounded from the battle fields, they are not organising a break for the officers and soldiers....[35]

Another cipher from Pavlov to the commander of the 10th Army asked:

> Why did Mechanised Corps not advance, whose fault was it? Go into action immediately, do not panic, but take command. The enemy has to be beaten in an organised way. We must not allow ourselves to run away without any direction. You must know each division, where it is, when, what it is doing and with what results ...[36]

Within 2–3 days Pavlov realised that the troops of the 3rd and the 10th Armies were 'in the bag'. Under these circumstances the commander made a big, and as we can see, correct decision: on the Minsk axis there remained a corridor 50–60 kilometres wide. There was still a small chance to save the troops.

> To commanders of the 13th, 10th, 3rd and 4th Armies. Today during the night of 25 and 26 June, not later than 21.00 hours, begin the withdrawal, prepare the units. Tanks to the front, and cavalry and reinforced PTO [antitank defence] to the rear.
>
> Conclude the forthcoming march swiftly in a day and a night, under the cover and with the support of the rearguard. Effect breakthrough on a wide front. The first march-manoeuvre should cover 60 km. in 48 hours and more ...
>
> Pavlov, Ponomarenko, Klimovskikh[37]

But it was not possible to effect a rapid 'withdrawal march'. All the fuel depots had either been bombed or had fallen into enemy hands.

Having fought bravely in Spain, Pavlov left a few similar instructions for posterity, but thanks to the circumstances as presented by Stalin, Pavlov was depicted as the chief culprit of the catastrophe of the first few days. Another dispatch – by the Secretary of the Brest Oblast Committee of the Communist Party of Belorussia, M. N. Tupitsin – was sent to Stalin, and received within three days of the beginning of the conflict:

> The Oblast Committee of the Communist Party of Belorussia considers that the command of the 4th Army [commander A. A. Korobkov] was revealed as unprepared to organise and conduct military operations ... From the start of the military actions, units of the 4th Army began to panic. Finding themselves under sudden attack, officers lost their heads. One could see thousands of officers (beginning with majors and colonels, ending with subalterns) and soldiers turning to flight. The

danger is that the panic and desertion have not yet ceased, and military command has not taken any decisive steps so far.[38]

As we know, Stalin did take 'decisive measures'. For the errors, which primarily should lie on his conscience, the Soviet dictator very quickly began to 'bring order' into the Army. Several generals were arrested: F. K. Kuz'min, V. A. Melikov, A. G. Potaturchev, F. N. Romanov, I. V. Selivanov, V. V. Semashko, N. I. Trubetskoi, P. G. Tsyrul'nikov, I. I. Alekseev, B. I. Arushanyan, V. S. Golushkevich, F. S. Ivanov and other senior commanders. But not all had the same fortune. On the eve of the war, as a consequence of the previous bloody purges, many had quickly climbed to the high ranks without having mastered the necessary expertise; others became sacrificial lambs, and had heaped upon them all the failures, of which there were many in that period of 1941.

But it would be dishonest to write the history of these first few days only in dark colours. The spirit of heroic conduct and selflessness did not leave the Soviet soldier and commanders in the most tragic hour of battle. On 29 June, Colonel-General Halder wrote in his dairy: 'Everywhere, the Russians fight to the last man. They capitulate only occasionally. It is striking that at the point of capture of the artillery batteries, only a few are captured. Some Russians fight until they are killed, others run away, they take off their uniforms, and try to get out of the encirclement, posing as peasants.' Already on the first day of the war, so ill-fated for Soviet aviation, the air force pilots L. G. Butelin, S. M. Gudimov, A. S. Danilov, I. I. Ivanov, D. V. Kokorev, A. I. Moklyak, P. S. Ryabtsev, and other pilots rammed the enemy aircraft.

I. I. Kopets behaved differently, having commanded a squadron in Spain and having fought bravely in the Spanish skies. Very quickly, the command of the aviation of the whole Western Special Military District fell on his shoulders. He could not bear the blow when, in the course of the first day, the western front lost 738 aircraft, 528 of them still on the runways.

A telegram was sent to Moscow, to the Main Office of Political Propaganda, reading: 'At 17.00 hours on 22 June, in his own office, the commander of VVS [Soviet Air Force] Western Special Military District, Major-General Ivan Ivanovich Kopets, committed suicide, his faint-heartedness was a result of private failure and comparatively heavy losses in aviation ...'[39] The telegram was signed by Lestevym, the chief of the Political Propaganda Administration. It is quite clear that 'faint-heartedness' and 'private failures' were standard forms of explanation.

A frighteningly huge gap on the western front yawned on the map lying in Stalin's office. First he sent the Marshal of the Soviet Union, B. M. Shaposhnikov, to the western front; then, one after the other, two more marshals, G. I. Kulik and K. E. Voroshilov; and after the encirclement, two remaining marshals – S. K. Timoshenko and S. M. Budenny. But even such an impressive 'commando raid' of marshals could change very little by their one appearance, and the strategic initiative belonged to the Germans.

As the fiery avalanche of war was speeding eastward, the country and its leaders began to act. On 23 June, Stavka of the High Command was formed, headed by Timoshenko, and consisting of seven members. The following day, the Evacuation Soviet, headed by L. M. Kaganovich, and the Bureau for Military-political Propaganda, headed by a loyal Stalinist, Mekhlis, were formed. By the second or third day of the war, the machinery for preparing the edicts/decrees of the Central Committee and the Soviet of People's Commissars began to function and it worked without stopping. Orders were issued: 'Regarding the evacuation from Moscow of state reserves, precious metals, precious stones, the Diamond Fund of the USSR, the valuables from the Armoury in the Palace of Kremlin', 'Regarding the procedure of removal and disposition of population contingents and material wealth', 'Regarding the transfer from Moscow of People's Commissariats and Main Administrations ...' People's Commissariats had to move in part or as a whole, to Astrakhan, Vladimir, Stalingrad, Ivanovo, Kirov, Omsk, Ufa, Syzran', Saratov, Tomsk, Ul'yanovsk, Sverdlovsk, Molotov, Gor'kii, Chelyabinsk and other cities. Stalin was mustering everyone, in order to hold a Central Committee Plenum. But it was never held and he had no need for it throughout the whole war. Only once, in 1944, was Stalin's Areopagus convened. Stalin's system needed the Party only as an executive organ. Stalin appeared to have no need at all of the utopian communist idea, and he turned to the ghosts of Nevski, Donskoi, Minin, Pozharski, Suvorov and Kutuzov, with the aim of relying on the strength of the nation's patriotism. But he was soon in need of church and nationalistic consciousness, though he did not turn to the Comintern for anything.

The country was being dragged into the most difficult, exhausting war, in which merciless millstones of war would grind over many men's fates. Towards the middle of July, i.e. only three weeks into the war, troop losses amounted to one million dead and wounded, and the same number taken prisoner. At the beginning of the war, two-thirds of men on the western front were killed, wounded or taken prisoner. The Valkyrie – warrior maidens from German mythology, whose occupation is to distribute victories and deaths – were merciless towards the Soviet soldier. In those weeks, in the occupation zone, more than 20 million Soviet citizens faced drinking that most bitter draught of German slavery. On the battlefields, 3,500 tanks were left burned or knocked out; more than 6,000 aircraft destroyed; and much else in the way of military equipment and weapons lost. The Soviet navy sustained heavy losses, especially in the Baltic.

I doubt that, after such a paralysing blow, any other country could have continued to fight. And so, the initial period of the war was finally lost. But the greatness of the Soviet people was proved, since they did not break, weaken or bow down. And when Hitler – assuming that the USSR was going to be finished within the next week – started appointing *Gauleiters* of Ukraine, Belorussia and the Baltic Region, counting on annexing those Soviet countries to the Reich, a great invincible patriotic movement for the salvation of the motherland was beginning to gain momentum and expand immensely across Russia.

The tragedy of the beginning of the war lies not only in Hitler's treachery, but also in the evil of the Stalinist system, in which only one man could take all decisions, one political power had the monopoly of governing, and the Leader's blunders and crimes were treated unquestioningly as 'great deeds'. Had Stalin listened to Zhukov, Timoshenko, and even Pavlov, when they were asking for permission – even one week before the fateful beginning – to place troops at battle readiness and take defensive positions in good time, the war could have begun very differently. Stalin's mistakes, personifications of the totalitarian system, were mourned by millions of Soviet people's lives. They did not live to love and grow old, but crossed the invisible line, separating existence from non-existence, whence there is no return. Looking at it in a historical context, it was a defeat of the Stalinist system, but not of the people. The Soviet people found unbelievable spiritual strength within themselves, and this permitted them to pass through the darkest part of the valley of death, and yet not lose the will to fight and win. But victory was frighteningly distant. The very ability of the people to endure those incredible ordeals gave hope that sooner or later the aggressor would be conquered.

When I look at the middle-aged man with his 'salad dressing' row of medals from the Great Patriotic War, I frequently catch myself trying to imagine him when young, to capture in the wrinkled face, ash-grey hair and weary eyes something that existed in him *then*. This is easier done when leafing through reports and orders from the front, in the military archives, reading the yellowed pages of letters from the front or listening to reminiscences of veterans, who were on the border on 22 June 1941. It is all the same, even if one looks through binoculars from the opposite end. It is all so far away now. Half a century has passed since that fateful day ... Yet it will remain with us eternally, but only as something out of the past.

Notes

1. *Völkischer Beobachter*, no. 125, 5 May 1941.
2. Tsentralnyi arkhiv Ministerstva Oborony (TSAMO) (Ministry of Defence Central Archive), coll. 32, inv. 11306, file 5, pp. 501–22.

3. TSAMO, coll. 500, inv. 12462, file 7, pp. 1–2.
4. TSAMO, coll. 500, inv. 12462, file 7, p. 2.
5. Tsentralnyi Gosudarstvennyi arkhiv Sovetskoi Armii (TSGASA) (Central State Archive of the Soviet Army), coll. 4, inv. 12, file 97, pp. 545–6.
6. TSAMO, coll. 32, inv. 11309, file 101, p. 24.
7. TSAMO, coll. 32, inv. 11309, file 3, pp. 85–95.
8. TSAMO, coll. 8, inv. 794, file 31, p. 61.
9. TSAMO, coll. 208, inv. 2513, file 70, pp. 424–6.
10. TSAMO, coll. 15, inv. 725588, file 36, p. 241.
11. TSAMO, coll. 67, inv. 12001, file 141, p. 48.
12. TSAMO, coll. 127, inv. 12915, file 16, pp. 307–14.
13. TSAMO, coll. 127, inv. 12915, file 16, pp. 317–19.
14. TSGASA, coll. 33988, inv. 4, file 36, p. 56.
15. TSAMO, coll. 16, inv. 2951, file 232, p. 2.
16. F. Galder (F. Halder), *Voennyi dnevnik* (Moscow, 1968) vol. 2, pp. 80–1. (This is the Soviet translation of Colonel-General Halder's *Kriegstagebuch*.)
17. TSGASA, coll. 33987, inv. 3, file 1368, p. 246.
18. F. Galder, *Voennyi dnevnik*, vol. 2, pp. 576–7.
19. *Der Spiegel*, as quoted in *Za rubezhom*, no. 26, 1989.
20. TSAMO, coll. 67, inv. 12001, file 141, pp. 48–63.
21. TSAMO, coll. 140, inv. 680086, file 7, p. 165.
22. 'SSSR–Germaniya 1939–1941gg. Dokumenti i Materialy', *SShA*, 1983, pp. 167–70.
23. Ibid. pp. 170–3.
24. TSAMO, coll. 221, inv. 2467, file 39, p. 70.
25. TSAMO, coll. 208, inv. 2454, file 26, p. 34.
26. 'SSSR–Germaniya 1939–1941', p. 174.
27. TSAMO, coll. 229, inv. 164, file 1, p. 71.
28. TSAMO, coll. 15, inv. 881474, file 12, pp. 246–53.
29. TSAMO, coll. 15, inv. 881474, file 12, p. 179.
30. TSAMO, coll. 15, inv. 881474, file 12, p. 187.
31. TSAMO, coll. 5, inv. 11556, file 1, p. 4.
32. TSAMO, coll. 48-A, inv. 1554, file 90, pp. 260–2.
33. See: *Izvestiya TsK KPSS*, no. 6, 1990, p. 216.
34. TSAMO, coll. 208, inv. 10169, file 4, p. 23.
35. TSAMO, coll. 208, inv. 2513, file 71, p. 203.
36. TSAMO, coll. 208, inv. 2513, file 71, p. 203.
37. TSAMO, coll. 15, inv. 725588, file 36, p. 239.
38. *Izvestiya TsK KPSS*, no. 6, 1990, pp. 204–5.
39. TSAMO, coll. 208, inv. 2513, file 71, p. 131.

Part 2
Strained Alliances, Flawed Strategies

Introduction

'An Alliance of Sorts' (Chapter 5) aptly describes not only the hurriedly improvised diplomatic bridge built between Great Britain and the Soviet Union after June 1941, but also the great variance of both interest and perspective between the two powers. A widely accepted view has been that the 'Grand Alliance' came seriously adrift towards the end of the war, the divisions, sparked off by the acrimonious debates in 1942–3 over the timing of the Second Front, and the disputes marring the summit conferences in 1944 and 1945. On the eve of the German attack, the Foreign Office, belatedly recognising the seriousness of the military threat to the Soviet Union, was forced to face the likelihood of Britain fighting alongside the Soviet Union and the 'unpleasant situation' of great sympathy being generated for the Russians. 'Strong pressure' to treat Russia as an ally would be encountered: 'This should be resisted.'

Nor, with *Barbarossa* in full swing, did the British show any great degree of confidence in the ability of the Soviet Union to survive for any length of time. Only slowly and painfully did the British overcome their caution, an attitude much condemned by Sir Stafford Cripps, who was at pains to underline the importance, 'the enormous and absolutely vital importance' of the Russian front, 'our one insurance against the future'.

The Soviet Union did not collapse, however near the brink it came. But 'the seeds of contention' had been planted, nourished by a mutual suspiciousness and a barely concealed animosity which had deep, historical roots. The picture of an unalloyed Churchillian magnanimity countering a grasping and uncompromising Stalin is not one which is commonly accepted. With the opening of the Russian archives it is likely that a much more comprehensive picture of the politics of the 'Grand Alliance' will continue to emerge, enlarging on the multi-volume documentary collections published in Moscow in the 1970s and 1980s dealing with Anglo-Soviet, Soviet – American and Soviet – French wartime relations, together with the documentary publications covering the Soviet Union and the wartime summit conferences. Already a start has been made with the limited release of materials involving the activities of General Burrows with the British Military Mission in Moscow and his relation with the Soviet high command.

Of Stalin and his infamy there seems to be no end to the revelations. Professor Mertsalov, a veteran of the battles of Moscow, Stalingrad and Kursk, looks at the roots of the colossal tragedy which Stalin heaped on the Soviet people – a tragedy with which even now many find it impossible to come to grips or merely substitute a pallid 'bureaucratised' history, dangerously near a form of apologia for Stalin and Stalinism. Much is made at the moment of the need to fill in the 'blank spots' in Soviet history, yet a neo-Stalinist 'bureaucratic' approach does little to remedy the situation.

Nowhere is that need more urgent than with respect to the military history of the 'Great Patriotic War of the Soviet Union, 1941–5', a need earlier recognised by none other than the former Defence Minister himself, Marshal Dmitrii Yazov, but it was a matter of 'too little, too late'. There are grave questions to be answered. While blame is heaped on Stalin himself, what of the responsibility of those senior commanders – the much-lauded Zhukov and others, like Timoshenko and Shaposhnikov – who for all practical purposes connived at this Stalinist mayhem and involved themselves (and millions of men) in a strategic nightmare? Even those who purport to uncover the truth have been selective with it or have shrunk from its implications and fail to confront key questions. Why, for example, did Stalin strike down those who were his natural allies in any struggle against aggression; what was the price for the abandonment of established Leninist principles, or rather their complete distortion which ruled out compromise of any kind?

The cult of the war, the 'Great Patriotic War', played an important role in reinforcing the legitimacy of the Soviet regime. At the same time, it not only showed up the hollowness of 'Stalinist strategy' – itself a ramshackle assembly of crudely misunderstood ideological notions – but war shattered it completely. It was a bankrupt strategy contrived by political troglodytes, not only Stalin himself but also his unlettered acolytes, and practised with baleful consequences by military dinosaurs. The limited disclosures do not as yet comprehend the magnitude of this tragedy. That rationale for sustaining Soviet rule has now vanished, a mere cult no longer suffices as either explanation or justification, but the need to find the proper national position of the war with its tragedies and especially its triumphs is pressing.

One of the mightiest dramas of the war on the eastern front was the battle of Stalingrad, a symbol of Soviet resilience and a sign of coming German defeat. But the exhaustion of the *Blitzkrieg* and the deep crisis of German strategy had occurred much earlier, the result of the defeat of the German armies before Moscow in the winter of 1941–2. Almost inevitably, the battle of Moscow and its far-reaching repercussions have long been overshadowed by the titanic struggle at Stalingrad, but Lieutenant-General Reinhardt points to October 1941 as the time when sober reckoning had to consider that a successful outcome of the war for Germany was a diminishing (if not actually diminished) prospect, and for those who might have doubted this the German defeat at Moscow made it unmistakably plain. That defeat impinged not only the German army in the field but had grave consequences for the German armaments industry, already strained to the limit. The raw materials which Hitler had hoped to have at his disposal through his conquests in Russia did not and could not now materialise. And so, the whole strategic picture changed. It was no longer a case of 'forcing through victory', rather of prolonging resistance to a superior enemy coalition.

Against the odds, that coalition did hold together, its fissures, animosities and fundamental contradictions notwithstanding. After the defeat at Moscow, Germany could not fail to observe its strategic arteries becoming ever more hardened, with its flexibility and adaptability on the decline, and ultimate collapse – however postponed – inescapable. Stalingrad only confirmed more gruesomely what Moscow had presaged.

Chapter 5

An Alliance of Sorts

Allied Strategy in the Wake of Barbarossa

GABRIEL GORODETSKY

In retrospect, the rift between the Allies and Russia which emerged at the end of the war has often been seen as responsible for the nature of Europe's ultimate political settlement. It is, however, almost impossible to comprehend these events properly without referring to the Allies' differences which arose when Hitler attacked Russia on 22 June 1941, and when the Soviet Union became Britain's only fighting ally. This chapter sets out to examine a set of interrelated issues: were the British and Russians able to reconcile their respective interests by discarding mutual suspicions and misunderstandings? Were the new allies able to take advantage of the changing fortunes of war to lay sound foundations for a collaboration to stem Nazism?

Our understanding of the emergence of the Grand Alliance derives mostly from Churchill's own authoritative but highly distorted and tendentious memoirs. Both western and Soviet historians have tended uncritically to accept Churchill's assertion that, whereas the Chiefs of Staff were cautious and lacked any definite policy, he himself shed his known hostility towards the Soviet Union and launched into a steadfast partnership. The ample British archival material, read in conjunction with the documents released by the Soviet Foreign Ministry, relay a different picture.

Contrary to what is believed, British intelligence did not fully realise the likelihood of a German–Soviet war until the end of May 1941. Like Stalin, they believed that the Germans deployed their forces in the east as a prelude to negotiations with the Soviet Union. The Joint Intelligence Committee (JIC) considered the probability of war for the first time on 23 May. Weighing the *pros* and *cons*, it still maintained that 'collaboration [with Germany] was the most likely course'. On 31 May, the acquisition of fresh reports from intercepts of the *Wehrmacht* communications (known as the Ultra) cast some doubts on this interpretation. Although it was still anticipated that Germany would exploit its recent successes and consolidate its position in the Middle East, it was now considered that Germany was determined 'to enforce her demands on the Soviet by means of a threat of force which [could] immediately be turned into action'.[1]

The probability of war was examined solely through the destabilising effect which a war might have on British interests in the Middle East and India.[2] British determination to maintain supremacy in the area was demonstrated by the occupation of Syria in early June and Churchill's urging of Wavell to launch *Battleaxe*, his counter-offensive against Rommel, in the middle of the month.[3] Moreover, the Commander-in-Chief of the Middle East was instructed to prepare for the occupation of Iraq, which would enable the Royal Air Force to make 'the biggest blaze ever' in the Baku oilfields.[4] Likewise, Eden's famous conversations with Maiskii, at the beginning of June, were therefore not aimed at laying down foundations for a collaboration but rather at safeguarding Britain's status quo in the Near East.[5]

Once the war had become almost a certainty, the prejudices and poor information available to the Chiefs of Staff led them to the evaluation that the *Wehrmacht*, employing the usual *Blitzkrieg* tactics, would conduct a leisurely campaign, lasting between three and six weeks. The campaign was expected to lead to the capture of Moscow and the annihilation of the bulk of the Soviet army. This assessment was cardinal to the co-ordination of future strategy with the Soviet Union. The interest of the Chiefs of Staff now centered on the implication that a German invasion would delay the attempted invasion of Britain for at least eight weeks, and thus provide opportunities for the British army to sustain the defence of the Near and Middle East and intensify the warfare in North Africa.[6]

Thus, even before Germany had invaded the Soviet Union, the gloomy prognosis of Soviet prospects, the anticipation of a breathing space and pursuance of the peripheral strategy did not mitigate a full-blooded alliance, but rather 'a rapprochement of some sort ... automatically forced upon us'. The Chiefs of Staff were advised that, rather than hinting at an alliance, they should express 'sympathy with the new victims of German aggression'.[7] Less than a week before the outbreak of hostilities even Eden, though favourably disposed towards an association with the Russians, made the important distinction that rather than becoming 'allies of the Soviet Union' Britain would 'have a common enemy and a common interest – i.e. to do Germany all the harm we can'.[8]

Within this context, arguments were brought forward against any 'effective assistance' owing to geographical constraints; or naval assistance owing to the closure of the Baltic and Black Sea to the British fleet. In a note to Churchill, Eden conceded that with the British forces 'fully engaged' in the Middle East, little could be done beyond the intensification of air raids over France.[9] Even when measures were finally contemplated, the JIC – almost to the day of the launching of the German offensive – pursued its examination of the possibility of a German–Soviet agreement, which by definition was bound to have a clearly anti-British nature and place the Soviet Union on the other side of the barricade.[10] On the whole, collaboration was therefore to be confined to the exchange of information and the dispatch of army representatives to Moscow.[11]

The most important operative conclusion of the War Cabinet, reached a few days before the outbreak of hostilities, has been entirely neglected by British historians. The common belief in an early fall of the Moscow Government was accompanied by an estimate that the most proficient part of the Red Army – stationed in Siberia – would form a nucleus of resistance, which would extend Britain's breathing space. Therefore, the British decision on 13 June to send a military mission to Moscow – often used by historians as an example of British commitment to the alliance – was aimed, as the Chiefs of Staff explained, to 'keep the "pot boiling" '. The limits of the association were explicitly contained in instructions to the commanders-in-chief of the various theaters: 'Co-operation will not extend to military alliance nor are there any plans for dispatch of military forces or supply of war material.'[12]

The expectations from the military mission paralleled the nature of the economic assistance contemplated on the eve of the war. In an inter-departmental meeting held on 17 June, it was agreed that the only British contribution could be a 'forthcoming and welcoming attitude'. The relief to be expected from a war in the east was again tempered by the assumption of an imminent Soviet collapse. The Cabinet was thus encouraged to exploit the unexpected respite to 'stage operations on the West to act as diversion', but advised against providing the Russians with supplies in view of the scarcity of resources and difficulties in communication.[13]

Finally, Churchill's own detailed survey of the war situation in the Defence Committee, on the very eve of the war, clearly reflected his rigid strategic thinking. Notwithstanding the anticipated major shift in the course of the war, Churchill continued to pursue the residual Middle Eastern strategy single-mindedly.[14] Once limits to co-operation had been drawn, Churchill informed the Cabinet of his intentions to present Germany 'as an insatiable tyrant that had attacked Russia in order to obtain material for carrying on the war'.[15]

To the Russians the probability of an alliance with Britain seemed equally

remote. Stalin did not expect the Germans to fight on two fronts. He anticipated that Hitler would seek concessions from Russia,[16] or reach an agreement with Britain before launching his offensive. Soviet suspicions of British
connivance in the German attack were expressed by prominent members of
the Soviet embassy in London on several occasions, even after Churchill's
speech. 'All believed', recalled Litvinov in Washington a few months later,
'that the British fleet was steaming up the North Sea for a joint attack, with
Hitler, on Leningrad and Kronstadt.'[17] Mesmerised by the recent German
successes in the Balkans, Stalin was even more reluctant to make the slightest
move, which might be interpreted by the Germans as provocation.

This explains the ominous silence and confusion which engulfed Maiskii
in the early days of the war, when Stalin vanished from the scene for at least
a week. Maiskii learnt of the invasion from the BBC morning news and even
had to postpone a meeting with Eden until he had become acquainted with
Soviet policy through Molotov's radio address.[18] When finally meeting Eden
later in the day, he seemed to be obsessed with a separate peace only, seeking
assurance in this respect. Maiskii's frequent conversations with Eden in the
earlier days of the war focused on marginal topics, such as the expansion of
cultural relations and the improvement of the Soviet image in the British
media.[19] The initially restrained Soviet approach enabled both Eden and
Churchill to get away with vague undertakings and promises to bolster the
war effort.[20]

Churchill's famous broadcast on the night of 22 June is perhaps the most
outstanding example. Churchill's speech and own account of these early
hours of the new war have deflected historians of all persuasions from a
more accurate presentation of the origins of the alliance. Churchill's poignant
oratory is often presented as an illustration of his ability to shed lifetime
prejudices and animosity against Communism when the future of Britain
and western civilisation so dictated. Churchill's now famous comment to his
secretary, 'If Hitler invaded Hell I would make at least a favourable reference
to the Devil in the House of Commons',[21] is wearily quoted to depict him as
the architect of the Grand Alliance. This deep-rooted 'genesis' myth is hardly
corroborated by archival evidence. As Eden astutely commented a few days
later, Churchill, far from spontaneously committing Britain, told the world
'after his own unrivalled fashion' of decisions which had been reached
earlier.[22] However, the speech reveals Churchill's political genius, which was
masterly engaged in reconciling conflicting tendencies and satisfying the
expectations of opposed political poles. As shown, the motives for pledging
aid to Russia, its nature, and particularly its limitations, had all been worked
out before. Indeed, an examination of Churchill's opening phrases in this
light reveals his anxiety about a Soviet collapse being 'only a stepping-stone'

towards Asia – more specifically India and China – and an attempt to seize the oil resources, indispensable for the running of the German war machine. Historians have been further deflected from the crucial debate which focused on the means to be employed in the war by Churchill's pledge to fight Nazism to the bitter end. Here, Churchill's rhetoric concealed the absence of any major shift in strategy by referring to the more pressing Soviet anxiety (of which he had learnt from Maiskii earlier on that day): 'We will never parley, we will never negotiate, with Hitler or any of his gang. We shall fight him by land, we shall fight him by sea, we shall fight him by air ...' Throughout the speech, adhering to the Foreign Office's advice, Churchill refrained from using the term 'ally'. Aid to Russia was promised in qualified terms, which were not immediately apparent to listeners because of the inspired oratory: 'Any man who fights against Nazism will have our aid ... It follows, therefore, that we shall give whatever help we can to Russia and the Russian people.' Technical or economic assistance was plainly reduced to 'whatever is in our power'. The clue to British strategy, however, is to be found, not in these frequently quoted statements but rather in the final evaluation that the invasion of Russia was 'no more than a prelude to an attempted invasion of the British Isles'. It followed therefore, as Churchill concluded, that Russian danger was British danger.[23]

Rather than Churchill's speech, his directive to the Chiefs of Staff, the next day, reveals the limits set to co-operation and the concrete actions undertaken by the British Government in the wake of *Barbarossa*. On the face of it the directive appears as a very early appeal – perhaps even the first – for launching a 'second front' in France. In reality Churchill, sharing the Army's apprehension about a German invasion of Britain, literally followed their earlier recommendations on the need to exploit the temporary German preoccupation in the east. 'Now the enemy is busy in Russia', he wrote, 'is the time to "Make hell *while* the sun shines".' His operative instructions were based on the short-term advantages which the British army might derive from the conflict. They therefore aimed at disrupting the German preparations for the invasion of the French coast.[24]

The more cautious Chiefs of Staff favoured a small raid, which at best would have 'a considerable nuisance value'. But they virtually concurred with Churchill that any available army forces or equipment would be most profitably employed in the Middle East, and insisted that troops and equipment earmarked for other operations in planning should not be diverted to operations in Europe. Although such operations were consistently presented as the main impediment to any diversionary action on the Continent, they were still in an embryonic stage. Cadogan attests that as late as 21 July, members of neither the Cabinet nor the Chief of Staff could tell how far the

Canary Islands were from the mainland: 'Ye Heavens! After Namsos and Crete! Alexander said 500 miles (I had said 120). Pound measured it roughly on a Mercator's projection of the world hanging up on the wall. Said he made it about 150! This is really shattering.'[25]

A preliminary study concluded that it was questionable whether a raid would in fact draw major German forces from the eastern front. Attention was focused on the short-term advantages which the British army might derive from the conflict. The gloomy prospect of a Soviet collapse meant that 'in view of the short time which may be available' the preparation and execution of a minor raid 'should be treated as of the utmost urgency'. The objectives chosen were clearly designed to upset the German preparations for an invasion: 'Dunkirk – Dumps, stores and barges[;] Cap Griz Nez – Railway guns[;] Pt. Aux Oies – Stores depots[;] Forêt d'Hardelot–Invasion barges, military Headquarters'[26]

The Director of Combined Operations, whose troops were earmarked to execute the raid, revealed the obstacles which made the attainment of even these limited objectives unfeasible. The restrictions imposed on the Chiefs of Staff meant that only sufficient assault craft to land at best a brigade could be made available, certainly not the 20,000 men envisaged by Churchill. They therefore favoured the initial idea of co-operation with the Special Operations Executive in launching subversive activities in Russia and in the demolition of Soviet oilfields.[27]

In the mean time Lieutenant-General Mason Macfarlane, a highly eccentric intelligence officer, was appointed as head of the British military mission to Moscow. The mission left for Russia, entirely sceptical about the prospects of Soviet survival. The directives to the mission lay bare its aims. A firm collaboration was viewed only as an unlikely remote possibility, while the instructions concentrated on the more likely event of a 'serious defeat'. The mission was stripped of any authority to embark on negotiations concerning concrete assistance and strategy. Its primary task was to overcome Soviet distrust and encourage the prolongation of Soviet resistance. Macfarlane was advised to split up his mission and organise guerrilla warfare, once Russia collapsed. If resistance proved hopeless, Macfarlane's orders were 'to try to reach India, over the Pamirs. "But this", General Dill, the chief of staff, admitted wryly, "would be a very long walk".' The Naval Section was likewise expected to impress on the Russians the need to destroy all port facilities, to make them 'unusable' and convince the Soviet navy to either ship the Arctic Fleet to British waters or scuttle it.[28] No wonder the mission felt so sceptical about the prospects of Soviet survival. Hugh Dalton, the Minister for Economic Warfare, noticed that on leaving Britain Macfarlane had been 'very pessimistic and didn't want to go. He doesn't like the Russians anyhow ... He went out thinking that the Russians could not last three weeks.'[29]

The military mission was flown in Catalinas to Archangel in a 19-hour uninterrupted flight by the only direct route open for communication between the two countries. They were received by Admiral Kuznetsov, commanding the naval forces in the White Sea. Macfarlane's initial address reflected the pattern of the mission's activity, aimed at verbally boosting Soviet morale and invigorating their resistance. Great Britain and Russia, stressed Macfarlane, 'were now fighting side by side against a common enemy'. The presence of a mission was 'a proof of the desire of the three British Services to bring every possible assistance to the fighting forces of the Soviet Union'.[30]

Shortly after arriving in Moscow, Cripps introduced the members of the military mission to Molotov. Like Macfarlane, he stressed the moral value of the mission's presence in Moscow, reflecting the 'determination of the British people to co-operate to the utmost with the citizens of the Soviet Union in what had now become their common struggle'. He further excused the rather small size of the mission by the poor air communications. The faint commitment was, however, overlooked by the Russians. In these early days of the war they seemed to be entirely bedevilled by fanciful expectations of British connivance in the war or a slackening of the British war effort. Astute observers in Moscow noticed that 'mistrust and suspicion of Britain continues'. The military mission seemed to be 'tolerated rather than fully utilized'.[31] Indeed, when Molotov met Cripps after his return from London, he was interested only in assurances concerning Rudolf Hess's flight to Britain – purportedly on a peace mission – a month earlier.[32]

Besides their deeply embedded suspicions about possible German–British peace talks, the Russians faced a difficult dilemma. Fully aware of Britain's expectations of a catastrophe, they rightly suspected that the British incessant quest for intelligence was aimed at evaluating the duration of the 'breathing space'. They were fully aware that the Chiefs of Staff might not risk the dispatch of material and manpower in view of the severity of the situation at the front. They were thus compelled to walk the tightrope of both alerting Britain to the severity of the situation and simultaneously inspiring confidence in their own ability to survive.

But the Russians soon registered success in striking the right balance, as is evident from Cripps's diary: 'As each day passes and we are able to remain in Moscow it is encouraging and raises my hopes. [The Russians] seem calm and confident as to the immediate result though they are fully conscious of the tremendous pressure that is being exerted upon them.'

Macfarlane's and Cripps's swift reappraisal of the Soviet scene did not derive from first-hand knowledge of the situation on the battlefield, but rather from the sense of determination and confidence displayed by the Kremlin. The differing evaluations of Soviet prospects in Moscow and London thus became the focal point of the strategic and political debate.[33]   In his memoirs, Churchill put historians on a wrong track by suggesting that the difficulties encountered in launching the alliance resulted from Stalin's insistence on the execution of a second front, which was a strategic folly. In reality it took quite a while before the second front emerged as the bone of contention in Allied strategy. The idea of a second front in France was first raised in London even before Stalin had emerged from his retreat; and promoted by Maiskii, Lord Beaverbrook – who now appeared as the champion of assistance to the Soviet Union – agreed that if proper pressure was exerted on the British Cabinet it could do more by way of diverting the British navy to the region of Murmansk, while the Army could 'execute major raids on the French coast'.[34] Indeed, Beaverbrook hastened to challenge the Chiefs of Staff's assumptions that:

> it would be folly to denude our still slender resources to aid an ally whose armies, though not in actual disarray, were none the less everywhere in retreat. The more supplies we sent ... the more would fall into enemy hands. And we should find our own tanks and aircraft turned against us in the West. The most that Russia could afford us was a breathing space in which to build up our own armaments to the furthest extent.[35]

In order to prompt Stalin to cement an alliance, Maiskii presented his own ideas of a second front as Beaverbrook's 'personal suggestion'. As a result of Maiskii's initiative, Soviet strategy was now exploring two parallel avenues. An attempt was made to evaluate Beaverbrook's proposal of a major raid in France. This suggestion, however, did not tally with available information on the British disposition. Further, Stalin also had a low opinion of British infantry and therefore did not pursue the idea.

The other avenue seemed much more concrete and urgent and fitted in with Soviet priorities which were based on a long-range strategy. Stalin's high assessment of the British navy led him to seek the protection of the naval route to the west, which was indispensable for free communications and supply. It is worthwhile noting, therefore, that in the first month following the invasion, the Russians did not direct their efforts towards the attainment of a 'second front', but towards what was dubbed as the 'Murmansk operation'. The operation called for an extension of British naval presence in the North Sea, the disruption of German traffic in the Norwegian fjords, and a flank protection of Soviet troops engaged in action with the German forces in the approaches to Murmansk. Admiral Miles, the head of the British naval mission, was quick to raise various objections to such an operation. But the objection really stemmed from the Admiralty's pessimistic outlook. Their exclusive concern was to extricate the Soviet Northern Fleet from what they believed would be a certain destruction by the Germans.[36]

Early on it dawned on the Russians that the military mission was not authorised to initiate a genuine military collaboration. Despite the general improvement in atmosphere, military affairs, as Cripps commented in his diary, remained 'very sticky'.[37] Cripps was becoming increasingly frustrated by the Cabinet's position: 'They want all the advantages of cooperation without giving anything ... The Russians are being very cooperative and helpful and friendly in all matters. The job at the moment is to make our people equally cooperative in London.'[38]

Cripps and Macfarlane suggested therefore that a breakthrough could only be effected in London.[39] The two had become convinced that the success of further negotiations depended on a revision of British grand strategy. Before the Soviet military mission set off for London, Cripps addressed Churchill personally:

> What is required now above all is some action by us to demonstrate our desire to help even at some risk to ourselves if necessary ... In my view some immediate action by us with the specific object of helping them, beyond the intensification of air bombardment, is essential. It may be that we can do no more than make a demonstration at Murmansk or on the coast of France, but such a demonstration made quickly would I am convinced bring in a huge dividend in the morale and determination of these people. They realise what their fighting means to us and not unnaturally they look to us to do something practical to reciprocate the help they are giving.

Harping on the fears prevalent in London, Cripps concluded with a warning that Britain was 'in danger of encouraging collapse if we do not fully and frankly give the Russians everything possible to help and strengthen their resistance'.[40]

Macfarlane followed suit, challenging the strategic premises of the Chiefs of Staff, which rested on the assumption of an early Russian collapse. He too stressed the 'critical value' of diversionary operations from the 'political point of view'. In London, Eden called upon Churchill to weigh carefully the advantages to be derived from the subsidiary operations as compared with a strike against the German-occupied coastline in France. He expressed doubts whether Churchill's verbal commitments would convince Stalin 'unless they were accompanied by definite promises of military assistance'.[41]

The Chiefs of Staff were little moved. General Dill regarded the association with the Russians mostly as a liability. He warned that Britain was 'being manoeuvred into a false position and may be forced to undertake unsound military action for political reasons'. 'It is the Russians', he cabled to Macfarlane

> who are asking for assistance: we are not. If they are going to fight they will fight – but for their own lives and not to help us to defeat Germany. Accordingly I feel that the line we should take is as follows: – 'We are doing quite nicely against Germany, particularly in view of ever increasing American aid and the practical certainty that USA will sooner or later come into the War. All our forces are now being devoted to the accomplishment of a definite strategy for winning the war without having allowed for Russian aid.'[42]

The Chiefs of Staff, therefore, held fast to their original objectives of prolonging the Soviet resistance, collating intelligence, and above all denying the Caucasian oilfields to the Germans. 'If the Hun push reaches the Caucasus,' Dalton argued, 'the destruction of the oilfields will be of vital importance to us.'[43]

The strategic debate, however, was revitalised in London by the unrelenting Soviet demands for operations in the north, and by the increasing criticism of Cripps, Macfarlane, Beaverbrook and Eden. The debate was further fuelled by the growing American willingness to provide the Russians with material relief, which threatened to throw British strategy into disarray. It had become obvious in London that some real sacrifice would have to be made. The immediate controversy focused on whether the Navy or the War Office were to bear the brunt. For the first time since the outbreak of hostilities in Russia, the Defence Committee was convened in early July to consider the Soviet demands. In a strongly worded memorandum, the War Office warned that 'priorities had to be maintained'. Any contribution was bound to be allocated 'at the expense of security at home, and we cannot afford further delay in completing our minimum anti-invasion programme'.[44] Admiral of the Fleet Pound, as if oblivious to the Soviet idea of a lavish and extensive supply programme, referred only to the Soviet request for protection of their flank in the defence of Murmansk, which he strongly opposed. Instead, he opted for a marginal operation by an aircraft carrier aimed primarily at assaulting German ships berthed in the fjords near Petsamo.

The discussion manifested how tightly related and interdependent were naval assistance, raids on the French coast, and the continued reinforcement of the Middle East. Churchill, alerted once again by the Chiefs of Staff to the fact that any major raid would necessitate a reallocation of forces and the abandonment of operations in planning, withdrew his earlier recommendation and endorsed Pound's idea of limited naval assistance. Despite Eden's mild protest, Churchill ruled out even a minor raid, which he regarded as 'most inadequate and out of proportion in the general war situation'.[45]

Churchill further demarcated the limits to collaboration in a highly rhetorical message to Stalin. His admiration of the Soviet 'strong and spirited resistance' and the 'tenacity of the soldiers and people' was followed by a distinctly qualified promise to do 'everything to help you that time, geography and our growing resources allow'. While avoiding reference to diversionary activities in France, Churchill alluded to a possibility of limited concerted plans in the Arctic. The bait appeared at the end. A promise that 'the longer the war lasts the more help we can give' aimed at encouraging the Russians to pursue their struggle, thereby extending the respite for England.[46]

As Eden feared, Stalin was not decoyed by Churchill's vague promises. On recovering the reins in the Kremlin after his apparent nervous breakdown, Stalin complained that Churchill's verbal assurances did not really bind Britain. His moderate response was governed, however, by an obsessive fear of a British–German reconciliation. He aimed therefore at committing Britain to a treaty of a 'purely general nature' which would 'create a basis for our joint efforts'. The treaty was duly signed in the Kremlin on 12 July. It pledged in very vague and general terms mutual assistance 'without any precision as to quantity or quality' while each country undertook not to conclude a separate peace.[47]

As Harold Nicolson witnessed, the views of the War Office seemed to be still 'coloured by political prejudice and by the fact that Stalin [had] murdered most of his senior officers'.[48] In view of their meagre expectations, the War Office did not pursue any preliminary discussions on combined strategy. Consequently, the guidelines set by the Chiefs of Staff for the forthcoming negotiations with the Soviet military mission were based on the assumption that the main British object was to keep Russia fighting for as long as possible. The feigned cordiality was intended 'to encourage' the Russians and conceal the fact that Britain was 'not allied with Russia' and did 'not entirely trust that country'.[49] To counteract the tendency of the War Office 'to deprecate the arrival of the military mission', the Foreign Office made extraordinary efforts to allow a smooth sailing of the negotiations. The Chiefs of Staff were advised to display at least an 'outwardly cordial treatment of the Russians ... In order to give an atmosphere of friendliness we should be as lavish as possible in entertaining this mission, and the luncheon given in their honour should be as large as possible.' Considering the fact 'that Russians are extremely partial to alcoholic drink', the Chiefs of Staff were encouraged to throw frequent cocktail parties in honour of the mission.[50]

The Soviet military mission, headed by General Golikov, the deputy chief of staff, arrived in London on 8 July. The next day it held a series of meetings with Eden, David Margesson (the Secretary for War) and the Chiefs of Staff. Golikov unfolded Stalin's directives, which again leave one in little doubt as to his priorities. The foremost need was to 'launch a common front in the north of Europe together with the British'. Stalin had explicitly instructed Golikov that such an operation was 'indispensable for securing sea communications both between the USSR and Great Britain, and between the USSR and the United States'. The 'French operation' and an offensive in the Balkans were assigned a 'marginal role in terms of both time and investments involved'.[51] Accordingly, the occupation of Spitsbergen and the Bear Island, a vital strategic asset for securing British maritime presence in the north and safe passage to Murmansk, became the focal point of the negotiations.[52]

The meetings with the armed services hardly concealed their deep-rooted mistrust. Margesson refused to shake hands with the mission and left them standing throughout the short meeting. He clearly conveyed the feeling that he 'hardly believed in the Red Army's victory nor in the viability of the Soviet political system'.[53] Though more cordial, the meeting with the Chiefs of Staff, chaired by Pound, did little to break the ice. Pound resorted to Churchill's methods of expressing 'admiration ... for the way in which the Russian forces were fighting', but to the Russians he actually gave the impression that he was 'horrified' to be in their company, was in a rush, and had 'more significant issues to look after than negotiations on "hare-brained" schemes with Bolsheviks'.[54]

The next morning Pound easily induced the Chiefs of Staff to reject the Soviet proposal for operations in the north which, he said, 'amounted to a considerable commitment'. It was felt that the Russians seemed to be oblivious to 'the magnitude of the administrative problems' involved. The ingenious ploy decided on was to present them with a questionnaire which would not only provide the Chiefs of Staff with information but would help 'to educate the Russians in the problems involved'.[55]

This decision, however, had to be modified as a result of the growing American involvement in the Anglo-Soviet dialogue. A division of labour had promptly been devised in Moscow, by which the economic onus would fall on the Americans while the transport of supply, and military co-ordination in general, would be sought in London.[56] On 29 June a colossal list of requirements was submitted to both the British and the Americans. The massive aid contemplated implied that the Russians expected to run an organised convoy system – similar to the Anglo-American convoys operating in the Atlantic – in the North Sea.[57] By the beginning of July General George Marshall, the American army chief of staff, had succeeded in casting doubts in Roosevelt's mind about the soundness of British strategy in the Middle East. Consequently Roosevelt proposed the reallocation of American resources through the setting-up of a Tripartite Committee with the British.[58] Harry Hopkins, Roosevelt's powerful intimate adviser, who was soon to leave for London, told the Soviet Ambassador in Washington that the British should be 'sensible enough' to realise that the Soviet Union was entitled to a share of American resources. He further provided the Russians with an adequate picture of the political rivalries in Washington, and encouraged them to enlist the help of key figures in industry and the military to overcome opposition to collaboration.[59]

Churchill became acquainted with the shift in Roosevelt's attitude when negotiations with the military mission were already under way. He was informed by Halifax that Roosevelt believed the German attack on Russia to imply that the situation 'would now boil up very quickly, and that there would very soon be shooting'.[60] He was further informed that the American General Staff was of the opinion that, although the defeat of Russia could not be excluded, the immediate situation was pretty good, and that the Russians were holding remarkably well.[61] Churchill was also alerted to increasing insinuations by Maiskii and Cripps of a possible separate peace, which he feared might come as a terrible disappointment to the public. But above all he was aware of the advantages to be reaped if the Russians could stay on in the battlefield and continue with the war, at any rate until the winter closed in.[62]

So, his decision to opt for massive supply to the Soviet Union and limited action in the north was the least of two evils. Thus the Navy came to carry the brunt of co-operation with the Russians. Shortly after the Chiefs of Staff had turned down the Soviet proposals, Churchill overruled Admiral Pound and instructed him to send a small naval squadron to the Arctic. Its task, significantly described in vague terms, was 'to form contact and operate with the Russian naval forces'.[63]

In view of the futility of the negotiations in London and the breakthrough achieved in Washington, the Russians now clearly assigned primary import-ance to supply and looked up to Washington. Golikov was summoned back to Moscow for consultations in which it was decided to press on with the execution of two operations: a combined naval and air operation, supported by Soviet infantry, against the German forces in northern Norway, and the occupation of Spitsbergen and the Bear Island.[64] Both were, as Golikov said after emerging from a conference with Stalin, 'indispensable for the establishment of reliable communication between the USSR and England and the USSR and the USA'. But the key for supplies lay in Washington to where he was hastily dispatched.[65]

Erroneous reading of these events has led historians to emphasise Stalin's demands on Churchill – on 21 July – to open a second front in France. The demand was qualified by an admission of 'the difficulties involved in the establishment of such a front'. In fact, the message was leading to an assertion that, in view of the difficulties, 'it was easier to establish a front in the north. Here, on the part of Great Britain, would be necessary only naval and air operations, without the landing of troops or artillery.'[66]

The main Soviet objective of such an operation – securing communication routes as a basis for long-term massive and prolonged collaboration – was completely lost on the British. The Chiefs of Staff continued to maintain that Britain could not allocate naval and air forces 'without large scale diversion from other and more pressing commitments'.[67] Aware, however, of Churchill's constraints they conceded that co-operation was justified 'not so much from the point of view of what is most advantageous to us militarily, but having in mind the political and psychological effect of us "joining hands" with the Russians'. Most reluctantly they opted for a short-term lamentable operation in Spitsbergen, leading eventually to the evacuation of Soviet and Norwegian miners from the island and to the dispatch of two air squadrons to Murmansk.[68]

Churchill assumed that such measures would alleviate the immediate pressure for opening a second front and suspend a decision on a more concrete and continuous naval commitment in the north. For that reason he also enthusiastically welcomed the joint occupation of Iran, which fitted all too well into British strategy in the Middle East. To tie British hands even further, Churchill also exerted extraordinary pressure on Auchinleck to launch his offensive in North Africa.[69]

It now remained for Churchill to enlist his rhetorical skills in breaking the various decisions to Stalin. After turning down the idea of a major raid in France, he once more begged Stalin to 'realise limitations imposed upon [England] by resources and geographical position'. To attempt a landing, he concluded, 'would be to encounter a bloody repulse, and petty raids would only lead to fiascoes'. In view of the limitations imposed by the Chiefs of Staff on operations in the north, Churchill, rather than committing himself, depicted a 'step by step' programme depending on 'changing variants'. The permanent presence of the British fleet in the north – the quintessence of Soviet strategic needs – was vaguely alluded to as a remote possibility.[70] Churchill's stream of telegrams to Stalin at the end of July, and his presentation of Hopkins as his own representative in Moscow, clearly indicate his determination to ward off the Soviet demand for a combined strategy with moral support and offer of supply. Eden disapproved of Churchill's course, consistently pursued since the outbreak of war. The rhetoric, he thought, seemed to be losing its effect, as the

> style is becoming so sentimental and florid ... it will have the worst effect on Stalin who will think-guff no substitute for guns. It is worrying how little we apparently can do by way of military operations to help Russia ... The slowness and lack of imagination of our Chiefs of Staff are enough to frighten one.[71]

The limits of rhetoric were evident when on 23 July Golikov stopped over in London *en route* to Washington. He gained the clear impression that the war in the east had not altered the premises of British strategy. He further gleaned that the arguments about a second front and operation in the north were tied up with British plans to resume the battle in the Middle East.[72]

The shift towards the United States was manifested in Stalin's instructions to Golikov to proceed to Washington 'to deal more expeditiously with the question of military supplies'. Admiral Kharlamov was shortly to assume Golikov's place as the head of the mission. His naval background and the command post he had held in northern waters clearly indicated the primary significance the Russians attached to the organisation and shipping of supplies to Russia.[73]

Likewise, in a frank conversation with Eden and Pound on 23 July, Golikov – resigned to the fact that a second front in France was not feasible – reiterated the demand for creating a supply route in the North Sea. The operations in the north, he bluntly admitted, were a prerequisite for the 'establishment of the route Greenland–Iceland–Spitzbergen for the transit of supplies to Russia'. Pound left Golikov in no doubt about the transient nature of the naval operation, stressing that all ships 'must return when they had carried out their mission, as they would be required for other operations'.[74]

Crushed between the hammer and the anvil, Churchill called upon the Chiefs of Staff to make every effort on their part 'to assist and encourage' the Russians.[75] In the War Cabinet he overruled Pound's opposition to the dispatch of three air squadrons to Murmansk, assuming that the dispatch of British ships to Murmansk would 'make the whole difference to our effective co-operation with the Russians in this area'.[76] However, such a gesture fell short of Soviet expectations.

While military operations had in fact been ruled out, the incessant Soviet demands for 'supply of war material' could no longer be ignored. Maiskii clearly impressed on Eden that if the 'difficulties of taking any action in

France were, as the Prime Minister said, insuperable, surely [England] could
do more to assist Russia with supplies'.[77] Hopkins's visit to London had
finally driven home the realisation that the Americans were favourably
disposed to a redistribution of resources, and it was therefore felt that 'there
would be advantage in joint discussion between the United States authorities
and ourselves as to the extent and methods of the material help to be sent
to Russia'.[78]

Soviet successes in securing American material supply were apparent
when, at the beginning of August, the Americans set up an independent
machinery with the Russians to discuss quotas of production and shipping.
These early moves prepared the ground for Harriman and Beaverbrook's
visit to Moscow in late September, and the establishment of the convoy
system.[79]

British strategy towards the war in Russia had been formulated on the
assumption of an early Soviet defeat. The continued Soviet resistance and
establishment of an alliance of sorts did not bring about a major shift.
Consequently even the limited aims of the Russians, the securing of a long-
term commitment through the execution of the 'Murmansk operation', by
far exceeded the Chiefs of Staff's anticipations, which were confined to a
successful Soviet withdrawal or scuttle of their fleet in the north.

The protracted war in the east at best removed the immediate threat to
Britain and afforded it a much-needed respite for preparing the offensive in
the Middle East. The long-range strategy was therefore left intact and
assumed that British air, naval and economic resources, sustained by American armaments, would suffice seriously to weaken Germany and throw it
'on the defence' in 1942. British strategy therefore called for the tightening
of the economic blockade while maintaining British assets in the Middle and
Far East. The Russians were expected to 'save themselves just as we saved
ourselves in the Battle of Britain and in the Atlantic'.[80]

As prospects of Soviet survival brightened, pressure increased for fostering
the alliance – both for political and military reasons. Naturally the pressure
emanated from the Russians themselves, but it was advocated just as vocifer-
ously from within the British Cabinet. Cripps was the first openly to reproach
the Government for 'underestimating the enormous and absolutely vital
importance of this front to [Britain] as our one insurance against the future'.
He hit the nail on the head by complaining that 'the total war directive [was]
lacking in realisation of the fact that this front is as much a front of ours as
the home front or that in the Middle East'. And he concluded:

> So far, the whole atmosphere has been one of caution, as if we expected
> the Russians to collapse at any moment and as if we were always

waiting to see where the next German success was going to be, so that we could then make arrangements to try counter the next but one. This is a defeatist attitude which is always postponing our help till it is too late to make it of the critical value that it might be.[81]

Hindsight often leads historians to view the fierce debate on the second front in 1942–3, and the summit conferences at the end of the war, as the major causes of the rift within the Alliance. Generations of historians have adhered to the myth, cultivated by Churchill, of the genesis of the alliance. This version, drawing on Churchill's voluminous history of the war, depicted Churchill's foresight in anticipating the invasion and the determined efforts undertaken by him to accommodate British strategy with the changing circumstances. Churchill's benevolence was further contrasted with Stalin's ingratitude, to explain the gradual drifting apart of the partners.[82]

It seems, however, that the seeds of contention were planted at the very birth of the Grand Alliance. The Russian front was regarded by the British solely as a welcome but ephemeral respite. The notion of coalition warfare, let alone the remote political vision of the Soviet position in the post-war period, was foreign to British strategic thinking. In their debate with Churchill and the Chiefs of Staff, Cripps, Eden and Beaverbrook were the obvious losers. And yet their premonitions of the post-war domestic and international order were the clearest and earliest harbingers of events yet to come.

Various factors contributed to the false start of the alliance. Naturally the Russians could not assume anything but final victory and therefore conceived a long-term association. The British, anticipating an early defeat, were bound to consider the short-term tactical advantages which the new war seemed to provide. But beyond this differing appreciation of the prospects of the war lay substantial strategic and political dissensions which fed on a legacy of mutual suspicion and animosity. Indeed, both the Soviet Union and Great Britain entered the enforced association while considering one another as both potential allies and potential enemies. And they continued to harbour suspicion throughout the war.

The formulation of British strategy towards the Soviet Union was determined in the first place by the wish to safeguard underlying strategic concepts. This was facilitated by the slim Soviet chances of survival. Notwithstanding departmental differences, the Chiefs of Staff shared the belief in the need to tighten the economic siege of Germany while executing peripheral operations. The prospect of a final frontal assault on Germany, which assumed a co-operation with a continental ally, was suppressed after the fall of France. Despite occasional tactical disputes with the Chiefs of Staff, Churchill appeared as the champion and spokesman of the peripheral strategy, which was inflamed to quite a degree by the imperial dream he still cherished. It provided Churchill with an opportunity to establish and secure a British presence in Egypt, Syria, Iraq and Iran, thus guarding the route to India and assuring British control of vital raw materials. However, this pattern, once established, meant that the means employed became an end in itself.[83] In the British plans for the final defeat of Germany there was little room for a Soviet contribution. The plans rested on a gamble, reflecting Churchill's belief that the Americans would eventually join the war and decide the battle in Europe as they had done in 1917–18.

The Soviet strategy aimed in the first place to repel the Germans and to recover control of the buffer zone gained in 1939. Though such claims were voiced by Stalin, they were low-key, in view of the conditions prevailing at the outset of the war. Stalin, moreover, discerned soon enough the primary role of the Americans and could not afford to defy Roosevelt's determination to postpone territorial settlements until the end of the war. The first month of the war convinced the Russians that Britain's defeatist outlook and determination to pursue subsidiary operations in the Middle East rendered a second front in France unlikely. As we have seen, contrary to Churchill's account, Stalin did not, therefore, press for an immediate diversion. The primary Soviet objective was the execution of operations in the north, which were a prerequisite for establishing communication with the west and allowing a smooth flow of supply. The technique employed by the Russians with some success at the beginning of the war, and pursued in 1942, was trading off the demands for territorial arrangements and the 'second front' against supplies.

Both Britain and Russia could boast successes in the immediate aftermath of the German invasion. These, however, eroded the very foundations of the emerging alliance. As if oblivious to the changing fortunes of war, Churchill succeeded in preserving British strategy. He further established a strategic mould which he forced the Americans to pursue until well into 1943. The Russians succeeded in diverting American resources to the eastern front while securing a continued British commitment to the war effort. And yet they were reluctantly obliged to concede that the onus of the actual fighting would fall on them.

Notes

1. Quoted in F. H. Hinsley, *British Intelligence in the Second World War*, (London, 1979) vol. 1, p. 477.
2. WO (War Office) 208/1761, JIC (Joint Intelligence Committee) (41)234 (1st draft), 31 May 1941, and comment by MI 14.
3. M. Gilbert, *Finest Hour: Winston S. Churchill, 1939–1941* (London, 1983) ch. 57,

and M. Howard, *The Mediterranean Strategy in the Second World War* (London, 1968) ch. 2.

4. FO (Foreign Office) 954/24, minutes by Warner, Strang and Cadogan, 31 May; CAB (Cabinet Papers) 79/86 COS (Chiefs of Staff) (41)197, including War Office to C.-in-C. Middle East and India, 31 May 1941.

5. FO 371/29466 N2570/3/38, Eden to Cripps, 2 June; CAB 65/18 (Cabinet Conclusions) 56(41), 2 June 1941. See also A. Eden, *The Reckoning* (London, 1965) p. 266.

6. WO 208/1761, JIC(41)234 (1st draft), and comment by MI 14; final draft in FO 371 29483 N/2906/78/38 and comment by Cavendish-Bentinck, 15 June in N3047/78/38; see also JIC(41)218, 23 May in FO 371 29483 N/2893/78/38, 31 May. For the undecided nature of MI appreciation see WO 190/893, 2 June 1941.

7. FO 371 29484 N/3040/78/38, minutes, 17 June 1941.

8. CAB 122/100, Eden to Halifax, 18 June 1941.

9. PREM (Churchill's private papers) 3/395/16, Eden to Churchill, 9 June 1941.

10. FO 371 29484 N3046/78/38, JIC(41)251 (Final), 'Some Effects of German–Soviet Collaboration', 13 June 1941.

11. FO 371 29466 N2889/3/38, FO memorandum and minutes, 8 June 1941.

12. CAB 65/22 60(41), 16 June; CAB 79/12 COS(41)210, and CAB 84/32 JP (Joint Planners of the Chiefs of Staff) (41)451(S), 13 and 14 June; CAB 79/12 COS(41)218 and JP(41)465, 19 June; WO 193/666, WO to C.-in-C. ME, 29 June 1941.

13. Beaverbrook papers, B/338, Colville to Beaverbrook, 5 Aug., 1960; Harvey papers, diary, Box 56397, 17 June 1941; on the limited nature of the economic collaboration see FO 371 29560 N3084/3014/38, Warner (FO) to Postan (Head of the Russian section in the Ministry of Economic Warfare), 18 June; FO 371 29560 N3092/3014/38 MEW (Ministry of Economic Warfare) to Halifax and minutes by Postan, 19 June 1941.

14. CAB 69/2 (Defence Committee) DO(41)42, 17 June 1941.

15. CAB 65/18 61(41)7, 19 June 1941.

16. This was explicitly stated in all interviews with Soviet officials in the aftermath of the German invasion.

17. The Library of Congress (Washington, DC), Ambassador Davies Papers, Box 11. See also Halifax's Papers, York County Library (York,), A.7.8.9, diary, 11 Dec. 1941.

18. I. Maiskii, *Memoirs of a Soviet Ambassador: the War 1939–43* (London, 1967) pp. 156–60.

19. FO 371 29466 N3207/29/38, Eden to Baggallay, 26 June 1941.

20. FO 371 29560 N3056/3014/38, Eden to Cripps, 22 June. The assurances sought in that respect are even more conspicuous in Maiskii's cable to Moscow, MID (Soviet Ministry of Foreign Affairs), *Sovetsko-Angliiskie otnosheniia vo vremiia Velikoi Otechestvennoi Voiny, 1941–1945* (Moscow, 1983) vol. I, pp. 45–7, and fn. 1, p. 553. Harvey, Eden's private secretary, who was present at the interview, witnessed that Maiskii's 'only anxiety' was that England 'might now go in for peace!' Harvey papers, diary, Box 56397, 22 June 1941; Eden in *The Reckoning*, p. 270 conveys the same sense. On the same day, the British Chargé d'Affaires found Vyshinskii cautious and 'exceedingly nervous', FO 371/29466 N3018/3/38, Baggallay to Eden.

21. W. S. Churchill, *The Second World War: the Grand Alliance* (London, 1950) vol., p. 331. Churchill kept walking on the thin thread. On 15 July 1941 he told parliament: 'Let no one say that we are now in league with Communists and are fighting the battle of communism ... If Hitler, in his insane megalomania, has driven Russia to fighting in self-defence, we bless her arms and wish her all success, without for a moment identifying ourselves with her communistic creed.', quoted in FO 418/87 C7951/3686/62.

22. *Parliamentary Debates – House of Commons*, vol. 372, col. 971.

23. FO 371 29484 N3212/78/38.

24. CAB 80/58 COS(41)116(O), 23 June 1941; the document is saturated with emphasis on the temporary nature of the conflict: 'As long as we can keep Air domination over the channel ...', or 'as long as it proves profitable'.
25. D. N. Dilks (ed.), *The Diaries of Sir Alexander Cadogan 1938–45* (London, 1971) p. 393.
26. CAB 84/32 JP(41)481(S), 24 June. The persistent lamentable appreciation of the situation by the Cabinet is well reflected in CAB 65/18, 64(41)1, 65(41)1, 69(41)1, 30 June, 4 and 14 July 1941.
27. CAB 79/12 COS(41)222, 24 June; CAB 84/32 JP(41)485, 'Action Against Northern France', 25 June 1941.
28. JP(41)482, 'Directive to the Head of the Liaison Mission to Moscow', 24 June; ADM (Admiralty) 1/11158, 'Instructions to Naval Section of Military Mission', 23 June 1941. A candid description of Macfarlane's mission is in E. Butler, *Mason-Mac: the Life of Lieutenant-General Sir Noel Mason-Macfarlane* (London, 1972) ch. 12.
29. Dalton papers, diary, 1 July 1941.
30. WO 178/25 55882, War Diary of Military Mission in Moscow, 26 June 1941.
31. *Foreign Relations of the United States*, 1941, vol. I, pp. 176–7, Steinhardt to Hull, 21 and 28 June 1941.
32. FO 371 29466 N3250/3/38, Cripps to FO, 27 June; WO 178/55 55882, War diary, 27 June, and *Sovetsko-Angliiskie otnosheniia*, vol. I, pp. 47–50, Molotov to Maiskii, 27 June 1941. On Soviet suspicion see G. Gorodetsky, 'The Hess mission and Anglo-Soviet relations on the eve of "Barbarossa" ', *English Historical Review*, CI, no. 399, April 1986.
33. Cripps Papers, diary, 29 June, 1 and 3 July 1941.
34. *Sovetsko-Angliiskie otnosheniia*, vol. I, pp. 52–3, Maiskii to Molotov, 28 June 1941, and Maiskii, *Memoirs of a Soviet Ambassador*, pp. 160–2.
35. Beaverbrook papers, D/541, 'Second Front', 28 June 1941. See also A. J. P. Taylor, *Beaverbrook* (London, 1972) pp. 160–2.
36. ADM 199/1106 and WO 178/25 55882, 2 July 1941. On the Admiralty's decision to refrain from action in the north see ADM 1/12671 and ADM 1/11158, Appreciation of Action in North by C. R. W. Lamplough, Director of Military Intelligence, draft reply and reply to Military Attaché in Moscow 1800/23, and Admiral Tom Philips to C.-in-C. Home Fleet, 1 July 1941.
37. Cripps Papers, diary, 30 June 1941.
38. Cripps papers, diary, 29 and 30 June, 1 and 3 July 1941.
39. ADM 1/11158, Macfarlane to COS, 30 June 1941.
40. PREM 3/395/16, Cripps (hand written personal letter) to Churchill, 6 July 1941.
41. WO 193/644, Macfarlane to Dill, 10 July; FO 371 29561 and 29486 N3669/78/38 and N3463/3014/38, Cripps and Macfarlane, 5 and 6 July 1941.
42. WO 193/666, memorandum by MO1 (Military Operations), 10 July 1941.
43. CAB 66/17 WP (War Cabinet Papers)(41)145, Memorandum by the Minister of Economic Warfare, 30 June 1941.
44. WO 193/666, WO Note for Cabinet.
45. CAB 69/2 DO(41)45, 3 July 1941.
46. FO 371/29486 3539/78/38, Churchill to Stalin, 7 July 1941.
47. FO 371 29485 N3527/78/38, and 29467 N3528 and 3529/3/38, Cripps to Eden, 8 July 1941; see also *Sovetsko-Angliiskie otnosheniia*, vol. I, pp. 69–73, and Cripps's diary, 9.7.41.
48. CAB 79/12 COS(41)235, 6 July 1941.
49. CAB 84/32 JP(41)523, Moscow telegram no. 729 from 5 July; COS(41)235 in ADM 1/11158, 6 July 1941.
50. COS(41)235 in FO 371 29561 N3559/3014/38; see also FO minutes, and note by Churchill, 9 July 1941.

51. N. M. Kharlamov, *Trudnaia Missiia* (Moscow, 1983) pp. 32–3. On Admiral Miles's evidence on the significance attached by the Russians to the operations in the north see ADM 199/1106, War Diary, Naval Mission, 10 July 1941. Stalin's briefings to Golikov are described in Golikov's 'Sovetskaia voennaia missiia v Anglii i SShA v 1941 g.', *Novaia i noveishaia istoriia*, 3, 1969, pp. 102–3.
52. CAB 80/58, 9 July 1941.
53. Kharlamov, *Trudnaia Missiia*, p. 37.
54. CAB 80/58, 9 July 1941, and Kharlamov, *Trudnaia Missiia*, p. 34.
55. CAB 79/12, COS(41)239, 10 July; for the discouraging nature of the questionnaire see CAB 80/58, Hollis (COS) to the Soviet Mission, 10 July 1941.
56. *Sovetsko-Amerikanskie otnosheniia*, vol. I, pp. 45–6, Exchanges between Umanskii and Molotov, 26 and 29 June 1941.
57. FO 371 29466 N3239/3/38, Macfarlane to COS, 29 June; ADM 1/11158, Cripps to FO, 30 June and Macfarlane to COS, 6 July 1941.
58. *Sovetsko-Amerikanskie otnosheniia*, vol. I, pp. 49–56, telegrams exchanged between Umanskii and Molotov, 30 June, 3 and 8 July 1941. On the origins of the American strategic feud with the British see M. Stoler, *The Politics of the Second Front* (Conn., 1977) ch. 1.
59. *Sovetsko-Amerikanskie otnosheniia*, vol. I, pp. 58–71, 10 July 1941.
60. CAB 122/100, Halifax to Eden, 7 July 1941.
61. FO 371 29564 N3613/3084/38, Halifax to FO 3256, 10 July 1941.
62. Quoted in W. Kimball (ed.), *Churchill and Roosevelt: the Complete Correspondence* (Princeton, NJ, 1984) pp. 212, 215–17 and 220–1, exchange of telegrams between Roosevelt and Churchill, 12 July 1941.
63. ADM 199/1934, note by Churchill and Admiralty minutes, 10 July 1941. Eden's genuine appreciation of the unsatisfactory nature of the negotiations was recorded by Harvey: 'what is important is not so much these paper undertakings but the action here which we can take to help the Russians. Here the PM is less helpful. The Navy are non-cooperative about operations in the North, *War Diaries*, p. 17.
64. Golikov, 'Sovetskaia voennaia missia', p. 106.
65. *Sovetsko-Angliiskie otnosheniia*, vol. I, pp. 83–4, memo on Molotov's meeting with Cripps, 15 July 1941, is by far a fuller version than Cripps's telegram to Eden in FO 371 29467 N3738/3170/38.
66. FO 371/29615 N3955/78/38, exchange of telegrams between Churchill and Stalin, 19 July 1941.
67. CAB 84/33 JP(41)557, 17 July 1941, and WO 106/1998, COS to Macfarlane, 19 July 1941.
68. CAB 79/13 COS(41)253; CAB 80/58 COS(41)145(O), 20 July, and CAB 79/13 COS(41)260, 24 July 1941. On the new nature of the operation as designed by the Ministry of Economic Warfare, see ADM 1/11158, Soviet Merchant Shipping, MEW to ADM 5 July, minutes by Postan 11 July 1941.
69. A full discussion of the operation is in J. Beaumont, 'Great Britain and the rights of neutral countries: the case of Iran, 1941', *Journal of Contemporary History*, 16, 1981, 214–28.
70. *Sovetsko-Angliiskie otnosheniia*, vol. I, pp. 88–9, and FO 371 29615 N3955/78/38, Churchill to Stalin, 21 July 1941.
71. Harvey, *War Diaries*, p. 24; PREM 3/170/1, Churchill to Stalin, 28 and 31 July 1941.
72. FO 371 29487 N3933/78/38, and 26756 C8028/3226/55, Eden to Cripps, 18 July; Golikov, 'Sovetskaia voennaia missiia', p. 107, and *Sovetsko-Angliiskie otnosheniia*, vol. I, pp. 86–9, 19 July 1941.
73. FO 371 29561 N3855, N3856 & 3927/3014/38, telegram exchanges between Cripps and Eden and minutes, 18 and 19 July 1941.
74. FO 371 29488 N4025/78/38, Eden to Cripps, 23 July 1941. Macfarlane's information

that 'the only departments that are functioning properly are Naval and Economic. Military, Air ... are none of them at all good' clearly reveal Soviet priorities, FO 371 29562 N4070/3014/38, 25 July. Miles's attitude is clearly reflected in ADM 199/1106, Naval Mission, war diary, 3 Aug. 1941

75. CAB 79/13 COS(41)259, 23 July 1941.

76. CAB 65/23 73(41)3, 24 July 1941. On execution of the limited plan see CAB 79/13 COS(41)263, 26 July 1941.

77. A number of books have been written on the issue of supply. The most updated and revealing is J. Beaumont, *Comrades in Arms: British Aid to Russia, 1941–1945* (London, 1980).

78. FO 371 29487 N3956/78/38, Eden to Cripps, 21 July; CAB 65/19 72(41)1&2, 22 July 1941. On soviet views see Kharlamov, *Trudnaiia Missiia*, pp. 63–4.

79. FO 371/29562 N4271/3014/38, Halifax to Eden, 4 and 5 Aug. 1941.

80. WO 193/644, COS to Macfarlane, 14 July 1941.

81. FO 371/29489 N4647/78/38, Cripps personal to Eden, 14 Aug. 1941.

82. This myth was further bred by Churchill's biographer, Martin Gilbert, *Winston S. Churchill: Road to Victory, 1941–1945* (Boston, 1986). For a critical examination of the biography see T. Garton Ash, 'In the Churchill Museum' and 'From World War to Cold War', *New York Review of Books*, 8 May and 11 June 1987, and Warren F. Kimball, *The New York Times*, 12 Dec. 1986.

83. See argument in S. Lawlor, 'Britain and the Russian entry into the 'war', in R. T. B. Langhorne (ed.), *Diplomacy and Intelligence during the Second World War: Essays in Honour of F. H. Hinsley* (Cambridge, 1985), p. 183.

Red Army parade, Moscow, 7 November 1941. The Germans were closing in.

The Battle of Moscow, December 1941.

Marshal G. Zhukov's command post, Battle of Moscow, December 1941.

Below: Destroyed German vehicles, Moscow, 1941.

Above: Officers from the US Army Air
Force and Soviet Air Force make
contact.

The surrender of Field Marshal von
Paulus, Stalingrad, February 1943.

Top: General Gerhard Matzky with Japanese associates, unveiling the bust of the first German military advisor to Japan.

Middle: Celebrating the start of the Pacific War, Officers Club of the Imperial Japanese Navy, 15 December 1941.

Opposite: 'Kodama, Yoshio, No. 414, Sugamo Prison, 28 March 46.'

Chapter 6

Barbarossa and the Soviet Leadership

A Recollection

STEPAN A. MIKOYAN

Let me begin at once by apologising for my English and at the same time take this opportunity to introduce myself and my family. It might be appropriate to say something of my father Anastas Ivanovich Mikoyan, born in 1895 in Armenia, who worked with every Soviet leader from Lenin to Brezhnev, who was for several decades deputy chairman of the Council of People's Commissars (in effect deputy prime minister) and subsequently First Deputy Chairman of the Council of Ministers. He became the formal head of the Soviet state during 1964–5 when he was appointed chairman of the Presidum of the Supreme Soviet. At the age of thirty he was appointed People's Commissar for External and Internal Trade and then Commissar for Supplies. He was also a member of the Politburo, the highest policy-making body, and during the war a member of the GKO, (the State Defence Committee), that central command agency for the whole of the USSR, which played a vital role in the rapid and greatest possible mobilisation of physical and human resources to achieve final victory. Of this, however, more anon.

Our family was one of all boys, five of us, with myself as the eldest. Three of us, with the exception of the two youngest, fought in the war, all as fighter pilots. The second son of the family was killed in action, an air battle near Stalingrad when he was only eighteen years old. The third son went to the front in the second half of the war. My war service began at the end of the battle for Moscow, where during one of our sorties my own aircraft, a Yak-1 fighter, was shot up and caught fire. I made a crash-landing on a snow-covered field, in the process suffering severe burns and a fracture of one of my bones. After recovery from these injuries I took part in the battle for Stalingrad together with my brother and then later fought on the north-western front and in the Moscow Air-Defence command.

After the war I studied at the Air Force Engineering Academy and after graduation entered the Air Force Flight Test Institute. There I served as a test-pilot and as commanding officer (flight tests manager) for twenty-seven years. For more than a decade now I have been Deputy General Manager with an aviation firm responsible for flight testing and for cockpit ergonomics, incidentally, the same firm which designed the Soviet Space Shuttle designated *Buran* ('Snow-storm').

It will be readily seen that I am not a historian, so my comments are based on my own experience, from what I learned from my father and from other sources. I was a teenager before the war and can well recall the atmosphere of the times. In spite of the repressions, all too sorrowfully acknowledged, the spirit of enthusiasm which had originated with the October Revolution was to a certain degree still alive. It was generally accepted that we were building socialism and that our country was surrounded by unfriendly, even hostile countries. Most youngsters actually looked forward to serving in the armed forces and, if necessary, defending the motherland. In the expectation that war might be forced on it, a great deal of attention was paid in the Soviet Union to strengthening military power in the days before 1941. When Hitler embarked on his expansionist policies and the likelihood of war increased, efforts to prepare for war received a particular boost.

Under this programme new models of aircraft, tanks and artillery pieces were designed and built. Large formations of parachute troops were organised. Production of munitions, combat vehicles and military equipment greatly increased. A number of those shortcomings in the organisation of the Red Army, its equipment and structures, so recently exposed in the 1939–40 Soviet – Finnish war, were in the process of being corrected. In one of his last articles my father wrote that not long before the beginning of the war Stalin charged him, as a deputy people's commissar and at the same time responsible for foreign trade, with making purchases abroad of those strategic materials which we lacked entirely or were short of, such as rubber, tin, lead, aluminium, nickel, diamonds, and different types of alloys among other items. All had to be stored in the greatest secrecy. In the same article he also stated that, taking advantage of the Soviet–German Non-Aggression Treaty of 1939, the Soviet Government placed an order – one of many – for machine-tools needed in the Soviet defence industry. This particular order amounted to 200 million Deutschmarks, but several months before the war of 1941 the Germans cancelled part of the order we had placed.

The tragedy of the country gripped by Stalin's internal policy of repression also had its effect on military capability, especially the purge of the command staff which began with the infamous case of Marshal Tukhachevskii and other top commanders in the spring of 1937. Many thousands of officers, from battalion commanders and upwards, were arrested, most of them vanishing for ever. To replace them, a large number of relatively young, inexperienced officers were promoted to senior posts, thereby weakening the leadership of the Army. It is also worth bearing in mind that the purges had an effect on all the officers who had survived; conscious as they were of the danger, most of them lacked sufficient assurance and initiative, qualities vital for commanding officers of a fighting army. At the same time the purge of qualified technical personnel seriously affected those sections of industry associated with the military and R&D institutes. A number of promising projects were held up or even dropped, simply because the leading personnel had been arrested. I have in mind the fate of the rocket project which was being developed by the group including Sergei Korolev.[1]

After the conclusion of the 1939 'Molotov – Ribbentrop pact', Soviet circles displayed a certain self-assurance. The threat of war seemed to have receded. However, Soviet leaders – including Stalin himself – at the beginning of 1941 were made aware of the many signs together with pieces of information, which revealed Nazi Germany's intention to attack the Soviet Union. Among all these numerous items I will recall only a few. Two of my acquaintances who were then serving at the Soviet embassy in Berlin told me (much later, in the 1950s) that they had personally written a report on the transfer of German troops to the Soviet border some two months before the actual German attack. Three days before war broke out a telegram was sent from the Soviet embassy to Moscow in which the specific day and hour of the German attack was reported, based on information gained from intelligence. Prime Minister Winston Churchill had much earlier also sent a warning of German intentions to Moscow.

My father told me of a strange occurrence in the port of Riga two days before the war. Here it is in his own words:

> Two days before the war (at that time as a deputy chairman of the Council of People's Commissars, I was also in charge of the merchant navy), between approximately 7 and 8 o'clock in the evening, Chief of the port of Riga, Yu. S. Laivin'sh telephoned me: 'Comrade Mikoyan, we have here around twenty-five German vessels: some are loading, others are unloading. We have learnt that they are all getting ready to leave the port tomorrow, 21 June, in spite of the fact that neither the loading nor the unloading will be completed. I am asking for orders: should I hold the vessels or allow them to go.'
>
> I said that I would have to ask him to wait, as it was necessary to consult about this question. Immediately I went to see I. V. Stalin. There were several members of the Politburo with him. I told him

about the telephone call from the Chief of the port of Riga, and I suggested that we hold the German vessels, as the situation resembled the preparation for the beginning of war. This had never happened before, that all the vessels, not yet loaded and the ones not unloaded should leave on the same day.

Stalin said that should we detain the vessels, Hitler could regard it as a provocation justifying war. We were not to hinder the departure of the vessels. I delivered the corresponding instruction to the Chief of the port of Riga.[2]

Finally there was a deserter from the German army who actually swam the Dniester late in the evening on the very eve of the German attack and provided information on the exact timing of the forthcoming assault. When they received this very latest information, the Defence Commissar Marshal Timoshenko and General Zhukov, chief of the General Staff, went straight away at midnight to Stalin to ask him once again to sign an order to bring Red Army troops up to a state of readiness. Stalin hesitated but because of the position taken by the military, supported by members of the Politburo, he did sign an order but watered it down by demanding that there should be no yielding to 'provocations'. In any event it was too late. The commanders in the field received this order just as the German attack opened.

Throughout the whole period preceding the outbreak of war Stalin had been very much afraid that some event or instance could 'provoke' the Germans and thus precipitate war. He was not inclined to believe that Hitler would break the Non-Aggression Pact if left unprovoked. Stalin considered that the Soviet Union was much weaker than Germany which had conquered most of Europe, and he dreaded the prospect of war at a time such as this. He convinced himself that Hitler would keep his word and moreover that he, Hitler, would not risk making war on Russia before he had defeated Great Britain. Though Stalin received alarming information about German preparations, he also convinced himself in this matter that here was either a cunning plot on the part of the Germans, or else an attempt by the British to bring about a war between Germany and Russia. He never for a moment trusted Prime Minister Churchill. Stalin was by nature extremely mistrustful and cunning, ever ready to believe in meanness or treachery in others.

The losses of Soviet armed forces at the very beginning of the war were substantially increased because the German attack developed so unexpectedly for Red Army troops. In terms of aircraft, more than 800 were destroyed on the ground on the first day of the war without ever taking to the air, and about 400 were shot down in aerial battles. Communications between armies and divisions and with Moscow in most instances broke down. At the front, scattered units either hid in woods or were surrounded by German troops. On this first day the Soviet navy did not suffer any losses and here I must mention that this was because Admiral Kuznetsov, commander of the Soviet Navy, acting on his own responsibility, issued orders for full operational alert during the night of the German attack.

After a week of war the Soviet leadership had almost no information whatsoever about the situation on the western front. Stalin and several members of the Politburo visited Supreme Headquarters to find out just what was happening. They were shocked to learn that the General Staff had almost no information. With Stalin and Beria (head of the People's Commissariat for Internal Affairs (NKVD)) making so many demands, the situation became so tense that General Zhukov, chief of the General Staff, according to my father, ran from the room in tears. The Politburo members left for the Kremlin but Stalin left for his own dacha in the suburbs of Moscow and stayed there in a state of collapse.

The following evening the members of the Politburo, having worked out certain measures for the creation of governmental bodies to operate in wartime, called on Stalin. Stalin was sitting in an armchair when the visitors entered and, as my father said, he was evidently frightened – apparently having decided that his guests had come to depose and arrest him. Let my father tell the rest of the story in his own words:

> In the evening, on 29 June, several members of the Politburo were gathered with Stalin in the Kremlin. They were all interested in the situation on the western front, especially in Belorussia, where during the previous evening German-Fascist forces had occupied Minsk. Communications with the Belorussian Military District had been interrupted. No fresh reports about the situation in Belorussia at that time were coming through. What was certain was that there was no contact with the forces on the western front. Stalin rang up Marshal Timoshenko at the People's Commissariat for Defence. However, he could not give any concrete information about the situation on the western front.
>
> Anxious about the developments, Stalin suggested to us all that we go to the Defence Commissariat and investigate the situation there. In the office with Timoshenko was G. K. Zhukov, N. F. Vatutin and several other generals and officers of the General Staff. The conversation was very grave. Only at that time did Stalin properly understand the whole seriousness of the assessments of the force, time-factor and consequences behind the attack by Hitler's Germany. It was decided to send responsible representatives from the Stavka to establish contact with the Belorussian Military District immediately.

The following day around 4 o'clock, N. A. Voznesenskii was in my office. Suddenly there was a call from V. M. Molotov's office asking us to go and see him. With Molotov were already several members of the Politburo. They were considering a suggestion about the need to create, on the model of the Leninist Soviet of Workers and Peasants Defence, an extraordinary wartime organ – the State Committee for Defence (GKO), which would have total control of the country. We, together with Voznesenskii, agreed with that recommendation. We all concurred that Stalin should head the GKO. We decided to visit him. He was in the so-called 'nearer' dacha, in the forest of Poklonnaia Gora, where he had been now for several days.

We found Stalin in the small dining-room, sitting in an armchair. He looked at us quizzically and asked us: 'Why have you come?' One could sense that he was worried, but that he was taking care to appear calm. Molotov, as our spokesman, said that it was necessary to concentrate the power into one organ that would be called upon to decide all the questions of operations and to organise the mobilisation of all the country's forces for the resistance against the occupiers. That kind of organ had to be headed by Stalin.

Stalin looked somewhat astonished, but after a short pause said: 'Very well ...'

Thereafter we considered how many members there should be in the GKO and who should be in it. There were two suggestions: the GKO should consist of either five or seven members. Stalin favoured the second option which would have included myself and Voznesenskii. But not all agreed.

In order to speed up the decision, I proposed: 'Let there be five members in the GKO. As regards myself, in addition to the functions which I currently hold, give me the responsibility in the military-economic area where I have better expertise than the others. I am therefore asking that you appoint me as a plenipotentiary of the GKO with the same authority as any member of the GKO in the field of supplies of the front: rations, clothing and fuel." This is what they decided finally. On his own suggestion, Voznesenskii was given responsibility for the production of arms and ammunition. Molotov was to manage the production of tanks, and aviation industry was to be Malenkov's responsibility.'[3]

Eventually Stalin acquired confidence in his role as Supreme Commander (Verkhovnyi Glavnokommanduyushchii). His authority during the war was extraordinary. The vast majority of the population did not associate him personally with the disasters and believed in him absolutely. It might be argued that the totalitarian political system of the country, reprehensible though it was, did furnish certain advantages in wartime, though there were many negative by-products and unfortunate consequences. A high price usually had to be paid in order to reach particular targets. On more than one occasion Stalin took strategic or even tactical decisions without weighing the opinions of senior military officers, leading frequently to unnecessary losses.

A case in point was the defence of Kiev in 1941. Powerful German forces were poised to cross the river Dnieper both north and south of the city with the aim of encircling the armies of the south-western front, commanded by Colonel-General Kirponos. The chief of the General Staff, General Zhukov, twice visited Stalin, insisting on the abandonment of Kiev in order to save Soviet armies.[4] But Stalin, completely ignoring the real situation, hoped to hold the German advance on the line of the river Dnieper and forbade any withdrawal. As a result, the armies of the south-western front were routed, largely scattered, encircled piecemeal and then made prisoner. This disaster greatly facilitated the easterly advance of the German army while the threat to Moscow also grew appreciably.

In 1942, at a time when Kharkov, the second biggest city in the Ukraine, was held by the Germans, the Red Army launched an offensive to recapture it. Nevertheless, it soon became apparent to the front command that a flank attack by German Panzer divisions was inevitable and that advancing Red Army troops were very likely to be encircled. General Bagramyan at front headquarters failed to persuade Marshal Timoshenko, front commander, to call Stalin for permission to call off the Soviet advance. Bagramyan then contacted Khrushchev, at that time the political member of the Military Soviet attached to the Front, to ask him to telephone Stalin. But Stalin, according to my father who was present on this occasion, refused to talk to Khrushchev, saying that Khrushchev understood nothing of these matters.[5] The result was a vast encirclement of the Red Army, giving the German army what was virtually an open road to drive into the Caucasus and strike on to the Volga. In my view, had these blunders not been committed, the city of Stalingrad would never have been besieged.

As for those repressions in the armed forces, there were fewer than previously, but even the most senior commanders and generals were very often replaced or dismissed following frontline failures which might vary in degrees of seriousness.

Perhaps I might turn now to another wartime topic. Because of enemy occupation of vast regions of our territory, mainly the industrial regions, thousands of plants and factories had to be evacuated to the east. In spite of the fact that many of these enterprises began production at the new sites – in many cases out in the open – the industrial output dropped dramatically.[6]

During 1941 and 1942 we had a shortage of almost all of the items needed to wage war. Our western allies, mainly the United States and Great Britain, were willing to help and began supplying the Soviet Union under the terms of Lend-Lease. The first British convoy carrying aircraft arrived in the northern port of Archangel as early as August, 1941. The deliveries of aircraft during the first two years of war were, in my opinion, of the utmost importance to us. At first we got Hurricanes from Great Britain which were somewhat out of date, but then the Spitfire arrived – an excellent fighter aircraft. From the United States the best machines we obtained were the Airacobra and Kingcobra fighters and the Douglas A-20 Boston and North American B-25 Mitchell bombers.[7] The significance of the tanks delivered to the Soviet Union was much less because the Red Army rapidly acquired increasing numbers of the Soviet T-34 tank, recognised as the best medium tank of the Second World War.

The Soviet Union also received many strategic items under the Lend-Lease arrangement, materials such as aluminium, copper, lead, rubber and so forth. Deliveries of food products were also very helpful. As a fighter pilot I also had first-hand experience of items delivered through western aid. When I served with the Moscow Air-Defence command, our fighter aircraft were equipped with American radios and artificial horizons. We were vectored on sorties by British ground radars. We were even wearing western flying-suits. Finally I should point out that perhaps the most important item of western deliveries for the Soviet ground forces were the lorries, the Studebakers and the Fords, which transformed our horse-drawn artillery into towed artillery.

I hope that I will not appear immodest if I mention that all of the activities connected with Lend-Lease deliveries were carried out under the supervision of my father Anastas Mikoyan in his capacity as a member of the State Defence Committee, responsible for supplying the armed forces with all manner of items including ammunition. I might add that as deputy chairman of the Council of People's Commissars, deputy prime minister as I have described him, he was also responsible for the supervision of supplies to the whole of the Soviet population.

My father played an important role in the first conference on Lend-Lease supplies, the circumstances of which he has described himself:

> On 27 September 1941 I sent a memorandum to the Central Committee of the Communist Party with a list of supplies from the USA and Great Britain itemised under 69 points, covering the period from October 1941 to the end of June 1942. In this were included aeroplanes, tanks, anti-aircraft guns, anti-tank weapons, aluminium, tin, lead, steel, machine-tools, equipment, wheat, sugar etc.

On 28 September 1941, the British delegation led by Lord Beaverbrook arrived in Moscow, together with an American one headed by Harriman. V. M. Molotov was in charge of the Soviet delegation at this conference. It included: Marshal K. E. Voroshilov, V. A. Malyshev (deputy chairman of the Council of People's Commissars of the USSR), Admiral N. G. Kuznetsov (People's Commissar for the Navy), A. I. Shakhurin (People's Commissar for the Aircraft Industry), General N. D. Yakovlev, (Chief of the Main Artillery Administration), M. M. Litvinov (Deputy of the Supreme Soviet of the USSR), General F. I Golikov (Deputy Chief of the General Staff of the Red Army) and myself as the deputy chairman of the Council of People's Commissars and People's Commissar for Foreign Trade. During the opening of the conference on 29 September the order of business was established and six commissions were formed. I was included in the Commission for raw materials and equipment. We had only two days at our disposal – 29 and 30 September. It was envisaged to hold the closing session of the conference on 1 October.

The Commission for raw materials and equipment held a session on 29 September and two sessions on the following day. Its work was complicated. Within the USA as well as in Britain, there were statesmen who publicly opposed granting us any aid. In connection with this I shall quote the USA representative in our Commission, Butt (with whom I had lengthy discussions). In his broadcast on the American radio on 2 November 1941 after his return from Moscow, Butt said: "Five weeks ago the President asked me to visit Moscow as part of an Anglo-American mission to hold a meeting with the Russians and discuss the possibility of giving aid to the Soviet Union. I must admit, that at the time I was not convinced in the expediency of handing over to Russia a substantial quantity of material and equipment ... Like many Americans I supposed that the Russians were good agricultural, but poor technical, workers. It was said that should we send valuable machine-tools and equipment to the people who do not know how best to use them, then it would be tantamount to throwing them to the wind. I was also informed that in the opinion of many military experts, Russian resistance would be counted in days. I also knew that many Americans refrain from giving aid to Russia, because they do not like the Soviet form of government ...

Before my visit I thought that the Russians were clumsy in the mechanics, and slipshod. However I have established that they are resourceful, capable, technically educated people. They do not waste money on materials and equipment, they use these to the full."

On 1 October, the conference of the three states representatives concluded its work. According to the agreed statement by our Commission, on 1 October 1941, the USA and Britain undertook to send to the Soviet Union every month, beginning immediately after the signing of the agreement: 400 aeroplanes, 500 tanks, also aluminium, tin, lead, some equipment etc. All this, of course, satisfied only our minimal needs.

During November – December 1941, the USSR received in the form of Lend-Lease supplies from America 545,000 dollars worth, only 1 per cent of the supplies which the USA had promised to send to the Soviet Union for that year. Let us note that all the other countries received, on average – every month during 1941 – various military equipment to the value of 61.7 million dollars.'[8]

In conclusion I would like to say that the Soviet people survived an exceptionally difficult war and suffered unbelievable hardships, which were made the more severe because of the failings of the system and Stalin's own mistakes. Our losses need not have been so great. But in spite of this the Red Army managed to expel the enemy from the country, advance through eastern Europe and together with the Allies crush the Third Reich. Thus was Europe liberated and the world freed from fascism and racism.

Notes

1. In 1933, Sergei Pavlovich Korolev became deputy director of the new rocket-propulsion research institute, but was arrested in June 1938. His release came only in July 1944, and in 1945 he was sent to Germany to examine German V-2 rockets. He then became chief designer of long-range missiles and headed Soviet work on space flight.
2. See A. I. Mikoyan, V pervye mesyatsy Velikoi Otechestvennoi voiny' in *Novaya i noveishaya istoriya*, no. 6, 1985. A. I. Mikoyan's memoirs prepared for publication here by S. A. Mikoyan.
3. More from A. I. Mikoyan himself, published in the above.
4. On the Kiev operations in 1941, see Marshal G. Zhukov, *Vospominaniya i razmyshleniya* 10th edn (Novosti, Moscow, 1990) pp. 121–46.
5. For the published documents see the series 'Vot gde pravda, Nikita Sergeyevich' in *Voenno-istoricheskii zhurnal*, no. 12, 1989, pp. 12–20; no. 1, 1990, pp. 9–18; and no. 2, 1990, pp. 35–46. See also Marshal I. Kh. Bagramyan, *Tak shli my k pobede* (Voenizdat, Moscow, 1988) pt. 2, ch. 2, pp. 305–57.
6. On the Evacuation Soviet and the role of A. Mikoyan, see his 'V Sovete po evakuatsii' in *Voenno-istoricheskii zhurnal*, no. 3, 1989, pp. 31–8 from his personal papers.
7. See 'Aviatsionnyi lend-liz' in *Voenno-istoricheskii zhurnal*, no. 2, 1991, pp. 27–9 on

aircraft deliveries to the Soviet Union. Figures taken from the Main Staff of the Soviet Air Force (see table p. 28), 9,681 US fighter aircraft and 2,771 bombers.

8. A. Mikoyan's own account as published in *Novaya i noveishaya istoriya*, no. 6, 1985 (see Note 2 above).

Chapter 7

The Collapse of Stalin's Diplomacy and Strategy

ANDREÏ MERTSALOV

As we approach the fiftieth anniversary of the end of the Second World War, what might be identified as Soviet historiography has reached the widely held but mistaken view that 'we know all about it'. Yet at the same time here is a historiography whose real success in actual research must be described as modest. The statement that up till now in the USSR at large there is no 'full and clear picture' must be accepted as correct. The issue, however, is not the 'grandeur' of the events or the scale of the problems; the reasons for this unsatisfactory state of affairs lie elsewhere. Even now, after loud declarations by the new Russian leadership about the declassification of documents, researchers are still being denied access to them. Previous official historiography made no use of the memoirs already completed by scores of writers devoted to their subject. Many participants in the war – especially officers and soldiers, who above all had to compensate with their own blood for the defects and errors of the high command – have already passed away, without leaving written or, even more importantly, printed testimonies. The majority of Soviet specialists writing on the war appear poorly equipped. They are not masters of the methodology of dialectical materialism. Even their knowledge of Marx, Engels and Lenin is derived basically from the interpretation of others. Several generations of Soviet historians were unfamiliar with the standard works of Jomini, Clausewitz and other representatives of military-historical thought. Names such as A. A. Svechin[1] and other significant Soviet specialists of the 1920s and 1930s are forgotten, as well as the attainments of contemporary foreign and Soviet scholars of differing persuasions, who up to the present time remain out of favour.

Beginning with Stalin, ill-educated rulers and their obedient 'experts in historical science' distorted history by way of apologias. Anything 'the Boss' did was praised as a great achievement. However, historiographical studies made their mark between 1985 and 1991, when problems which needed further research were identified. But nevertheless a great deal of time was squandered, in particular as a consequence of the muddle-headed attempts of administrators to organise a successor to the 12-volume history of the war by producing a 10-volume dinosaur. This proved to be a failure.[2]

In 1992 academic and popular writing was severely curtailed. By order of the newly created 'ideological department', publishers returned authors' work when it did not meet with the approval of this department – even if it had already been prepared for print. The approaching fiftieth anniversary of the victory has received no publicity. Simply telling the truth confers no propaganda advantage. How can one possibly agree with this absurd thesis of the 'red – browns' (red = Communists, Brown shirts = Fascists)? How is it that the two main powers of the opposing coalitions during the period of 1939–45 suddenly joined forces in 1992? How can one overlook the genuine merit of millions of Party members – members of the Communist Party, which is currently regarded as 'illegal' – in defence of Moscow and the capture of Berlin?

B. N. Yeltsin's speech of 8 May 1992 demonstrates the current view. 'At that time it was inappropriate to have doubts even about inhumane and the most cruel orders, and no useless reproaches were heard regarding the mistakes which were unavoidable during those complex, critical conditions.' What can we read into that phrase? Is it (a) approval for Stalin's actions, which almost brought about the ruin not only of the state but also of the Soviet people, (b) a tendency to please the conservative leanings of the veterans, or (c) a brushing-aside as 'empty/useless' the prevailing reproaches about the 'mistakes' committed in those 'critical conditions'?

The very essence of science consists exactly of doubts. Without them one cannot make either positive or negative deductions, yet to do so is invaluable. During the war, in actual fact, all doubts were brutally and disgracefully eradicated. But that does not mean there were no such doubts or that these were 'inappropriate'. It is important to emphasise that the point of view expressed here, or a similar point of view regarding Soviet military historiography, is shared by other historians such as B. Bonwetsch, V. I. Dashichev, R. V. Davis, V. M. Kulish, N. G. Pavlenko, A. M. Samsonov, V. A. Sekistov, J. Erickson, and other leading Soviet and foreign specialists.[3]

Interpretation of the 1941 events naturally followed the same course as the rest of the military historiography. The aspirations of Stalin and his accomplices to hide the genuine cause of the catastrophe of the Soviet forces, namely delusions of Politburo members and the Soviet marshals, was most influential and worked on the assumption that patriotism can be taught only by 'positive examples'. Since June 1941, right up to the present, a complacent

ignorance persists about the former enemy: we Russians talk about the
Red Army actions, but we do not study the Soviet–German war. Official
historiography lacks any theoretical basis. It has not yet answered many
questions about the surprise of 1941. During the years of *perestroika*, a
second wave of falsification of wartime events took place, new in form, but
old in its application of bias. Judging by the conversation I had with the
Marshal of the Soviet Union D. T. Yazov at the beginning of 1991, I
concluded that certain leaders of the Party and the Army understood the
necessity for reconstructing the study of the war. But that understanding
came, obviously, too late. It is no accident that anti-Soviet and separatist
groups have gained powerful influence in current Russian literature.

The events of 1941 on the eastern front are both complex and contradictory. It is enough to say that they represented the ruination of both Stalin's
plans and Hitler's regime. Stalin was saved through the enormous efforts of
the people, who rose up to defend their country. Hitler went through agony
for several years more. It is a mistake to reduce this conflict to an encounter
of two kindred authoritarian regimes, as the most reactionary elements in
the west did, but in vain. Nowadays the hopeless, latter-day followers of
this view in the Russian Federation repeat it, in order to gain doubtful
political capital. It is true that both regimes were alien to the people, but
people in the USSR were not indifferent to the kind of war waged by Hitler.
One can never justify Fascists by referring to Hitler's anti-communism. The
latter does not by any means define the essence of fascism. It was inevitable
that this war should grow and develop into the collision of two big states –
the USSR and Germany – because the main aim of fascism during that period
of its aggression was the creation of a 'German India' in eastern Europe, as
a base for the continuation of war in order to gain supremacy in the whole
world.[4]

The already compromised doctrine of totalitarianism in the west has
nothing in common with the genuine criticism of Stalinism. However, in the
Russian Federation attempts to bring totalitarianism back to life are being
made. It is very tempting to label everything fascist, which was the case until
August 1991, and then put the blame for the crimes of Stalinism and Hitlerism on millions of Soviet and German citizens. A. N. Yakovlev goes even
further, asserting that 'we are all guilty'. However, not all the Germans were
fascist. A significant proportion of them fought against it, and an even bigger
part of them was indifferent. Just like Hitlerism, Stalinism was by its nature
immoral and aggressive. It was backed by part of the population through
lies and oppression. However, after 22 June 1941 its immediate foreign-
policy intentions basically coincided with the just aims of the Soviet people.
This conclusion cannot be nullified even using Professor Hans-Adolf Jacobsen's thesis already expressed during the 1950s: in 1941 Stalin had not

decided on aggression, but it is uncertain how he would have conducted himself at Hitler's first point of failure in his war against Britain. Examining the alternatives, the academics none the less cannot equate events that actually happened with the ones that might have happened. No newly published documents regarding Stalin's plans can cover up Hitler's crimes, particularly not those in eastern Europe. In this light, speculation about 'preventive war' by Germany or even 'two preventive wars' – one German, presumably one Soviet – makes no sense.

Looking at the aggression of 22 June 1941 from the point of view of military-political security, it is very hard to find anything similar in the new histories. The Soviet Government – object of the aggression, – was totally isolated, and its military forces were paralysed by the nasty and foolish will of a tyrant all of its own. Of course, soon after 22 June a series of other governments declared that they were prepared to join the Soviet Union, but their armies were not committed to direct action against Germany until much later. And so the anti-Fascist coalition was born, though not without a certain delay. True, it was hardly thanks to Stalin's diplomacy; the deciding factors were fascist imperialist characteristics and actions, extreme aggressive aims and the means accompanying these. As Churchill said, he was ready to form an alliance with the devil himself, if this meant that Hitler would end up in hell. At the time when the coalition was formed, the main forces of the fascist bloc were concentrated against the Red Army. The overall burden of the alliance was very unevenly distributed. The bloodiest and messiest part of all the actions fell on the Red Army. To a great extent, this explains the ratio of human and *matériel* losses of the members of the coalition.

Much praised by Stalin's propaganda, the most significant offspring of his diplomacy – the Non-aggression Pact with Germany and its specific meaning for the Soviet state – have to be studied with care. But even now it is possible to ascertain that this agreement allowed Germany to select the most favourable time, place and method to attack the USSR. And then there was the analogous treaty with Japan, signed in April 1941 – another asset of Stalin's diplomacy. But this treaty was not enough to restrain Japan from direct entry into the Soviet–German war. The Smolensk defeat inflicted on the German army in the late summer of 1941 was a vital factor, according to A. Hillgruber from the Federal Republic of Germany. Only after that defeat did Japan accept the 'southern variant' of aggression, following the failure of *Barbarossa* and persuaded by the permanent presence of very large Soviet armies in the Far East. Of course, during the 1941–5 period, Japan used all its growing might to crush the United States, Great Britain, China and its other enemies. In the main it was Soviet armed forces that kept the Soviet Union's neighbours to the south, such as Turkey, out of the war rather than Soviet diplomacy itself. But these forces were therefore diverted from the blood-letting Soviet–German front.

When interpreting the failure of Stalin's diplomacy, one cannot ignore the roles of Ribbentrop's, Himmler's and Keitel's departments. The Nazis easily turned mistakes and frequently blundering diplomacy to their advantage. German supremacy in northern, south-eastern and eastern Europe obviously went against the interests of the smaller countries in those regions. Their governments were also responsible for the situation which developed. One of the most important factors of the crisis that occurred before the war in Europe – the Munich policy – deserves wholly separate treatment. I only wish to comment that it is impossible to justify such appeasement solely by referring to the viciousness of Stalinism. After Stalin's massive repressions, primarily of the Red Army leadership, followed by the decimation of the defence industry, Prime Minister Neville Chamberlain and his supporters had good grounds for doubting that the Soviet Union would make a reliable ally. But in the final analysis, supporters of the Munich policy miscalculated the Soviet Union's defence capability. The populations of the western countries paid dearly for the blindness of their governments. Prior to crushing the fascist bloc they also had to suffer defeats and bury their dead, which is especially unforgivable. Unlike Stalin, several leading statesmen in the west understood, even prior to the war, that the long-term fundamental interests of their countries were the same as those of the USSR, and that their forces should be united against the oppression of the so-called 'puppet governments'.

However, the main causes for the failure of Soviet foreign policy in 1941 lay elsewhere. The reasons were: massive dilettantism, dogmatism, adventurism, sectarianism, the provincialism of Stalin and his followers, and disregard of the national interests in order to satisfy their lust for power. They were ignorant of the world around them; they did not understand capitalism with its complex processes; they totally repudiated its potential, as yet untapped for progress. In capitalism they saw only reactionary attributes. They were unable to understand the new quality which was inherent in reactionary movements. I am thinking particularly of fascism. Having given themselves airs and graces in the Party and in the Comintern, the Soviet leadership could not understand that the collision of the Party with fascism represented not just a collision with a new capitalist movement eager to criticise the Party. In fact, fascism was an enemy of civilisation, of all mankind; Stalin was possibly able to come to an understanding of this only during the course of the 1941–5 war.

Stalin and his acolytes were unable to grasp the axiom expressed in the Manifesto of the Communist Party regarding the ability of capitalism for self-improvement, or to comply with Lenin's continual appeals to study capitalism. In actual fact, Lenin's reconsideration in 1915 and 1916 of the thoughts of Marx and Engels regarding the simultaneous victory of the revolution in all the developed countries as the necessary condition for the successful establishment of socialism was also forgotten. This is how the idea of world revolution was formed, an idea which Lenin and his followers had already abandoned in 1919 as their slogan. However, Stalin's continuous evocation of this idea greatly damaged Soviet foreign policy, especially where relationships with other governments were concerned. The call for a purely proletarian revolution throughout the world damaged the process of uniting the anti-Fascist movements – democratic, liberal, Christian and pacifist movements. In reality, during the 1930s Stalin conducted a traditional imperialist policy – agreement with Germany about border demarcation on the Vistula, a war of aggression against Finland, to mention but two instances. According to I. M. Maiskii – the Soviet ambassador in London – as the 1930s drew to a close, Winston Churchill, bitterly opposed to the idea of world revolution, considered that this was no longer a prime Soviet objective. Nevertheless, Stalin and his immediate circle took no account of the modification to the whole concept of world revolution undertaken by Lenin himself. The theoretical limitations of Stalin and his advisers frequently had speedy adverse consequences on diplomacy. Because of his incomprehension of the political and other differences within the capitalist world, he formed an erroneous notion about the supposed 'contradictions' in the Anglo-American relationship being the most significant within foreign countries. Such incomprehension gave rise to the Soviet–German Non-Aggression Pact, which in turn seriously delayed the establishment of the anti-Fascist coalition. In addition to Lenin's theory, Stalin also spurned his tactics, and in the first instance his stipulations teaching about compromises. On the whole it is thanks to Stalin that Communists were faced with the prospect of confining themselves solely to their own bloc. Stalin had little need to attack the 'middle ground'. 'The main enemies' embraced precisely every natural ally of the Communist Party in the fight against fascism – beginning with left-wing Socialists and ending with Churchill's supporters. Stalin's stance of spreading conflict amongst the enemy was widely publicised. This was the position of 'the by-stander rejoices', but it turned back, like a terrible boomerang, against the country whose head of state he was. In fact, those who did the 'rejoicing' in these circumstances were the very persons who stood back or stood aside at a time of great crisis, ending up by saying 'let the Germans and the Russians kill each other, the more the merrier.'

The limitations of Stalin and Molotov as diplomats are clearly reflected in the unfolding of Soviet–German relations from 1939 to 1941. The many steps they undertook to appease Germany far exceeded the obligations contained in the Nazi–Soviet agreement of 1939. One example is the severing of relations with those countries occupied by the *Wehrmacht*. It would appear that after 23 August 1939, Stalin and Molotov regarded Great Britain as their main enemy and stupidly burnt their bridges.

One of the many shameful pages that comprise Stalinist history is the 'Katyn incident'. From a legal and moral viewpoint there is no difference between the murders carried out on the orders of Hitler or Stalin, whether one has in mind the Germans from the Ruhr, or the Jews in the Baltics, the Ukrainians from Poltava or the Russians from Nizhnii Novgorod. But the murder at Katyn in 1940 of thousands of Polish army officers, prisoners of war in the Soviet Union, was of a different order; at Katyn it was a professional military force which was annihilated, men who would have made natural allies of the Soviet Union in that war which Hitler subsequently unleashed within a year. I note that the 'Katyn incident', used as a propaganda instrument for anti-Communist or anti-Soviet purposes, was first exploited by Goebbels, and its use has shamefully continued to this day.

Rejecting the endeavours of the apologists who suggest that even though Stalin and his followers did not manage to prevent the Second World War, at least they certainly created the most favourable conditions for the future victory of the anti-Fascists, we should not go to the other extreme. A fresh examination of Soviet relations with Spain, Austria Czechoslovakia and Yugoslavia is increasingly necessary. It is becoming apparent that not everything in Stalin's diplomacy was negative. For example, it is necessary to reassess Stalin's policy with respect to foreign liberation movements, but most immediately it is necessary to emphasise the significant role of the Resistance in defeating Fascism.

The incompetence of Stalin and his advisers in foreign policy brought about many military-strategic blunders. In the final analysis, because they failed to understand that governments are as likely to become allies as they may turn into enemies, they created a false assessment of the aggressor, his might and intentions. During the first six months of war in 1941, when it was absolutely essential to concentrate fully available forces and means for the resistance against the aggressor, this semi-literate leadership was overcome by shock. Stalin's confusion predetermined the outcome of the fighting during the summer and autumn. However, it hardly needs saying that the overall picture was much more complex. There was open criticism of Stalin's diplomacy by F. F. Raskol'nikov;[5] there was despicable opportunism displayed by the generals who carried out Stalin's criminal orders without dissent. Stalin's own behaviour had veered wildly in his attempts to appease the aggressor; economic bribes and conciliatory military gestures followed each other in quick succession. But in the last resort the determining factor was the inertness of the Soviet leadership at a time when circumstances demanded the most energetic action. Both the scholarly and other literature have accorded a special place to this extraordinary phenomenon.

Stalin and Stalinists invested a great deal of effort into obfuscating just how catastrophe befell the Workers – Peasants Red Army in the initial period of the war, just where the responsibility for it lay and what its consequences were. Even so, they succeeded in creating only a very weak set of arguments: deliberate emphasis on 'the treachery of the Fascists'; ambiguous assertions regarding the surprise factor without any explanation of its nature or who was responsible in responding or not responding; false premiss about the military-technical superiority of the *Wehrmacht* over the Red Army at the point of attack and about German use of total military-economic potential of the occupied countries by 22 June 1941. There were other arguments influenced by external conditions, such as total mobilisation of the *Wehrmacht* and its mastery of contemporary combat experience; effects of the rapid defeat of France and the absence of the Second Front; 'complacency', 'placidity' of the population and the Army, 'undisciplined soldiers of the Red Army and their commanders', 'frightened intellectuals', the incompetence and personnel changes of generals and pathetic attempts to create a framework about 'peace-loving and aggressive' nations, not to mention counter-attack as panacea. Of special significance is the assessment that, had the Red Army been brought up to battle readiness, the Germans would have had a 'pretext' for an attack on the Soviet Union, when in fact the whole world knew by then that aggressors themselves create a necessary 'pretext' and the attacks take place for deep-seated reasons not 'pretexts'. The tactics of 'not giving a pretext' resulted in a great deal of sorrow. The Tass announcement of 14 June 1941, an official Soviet statement hinting at the possibility of talks with Germany, and other similar actions only served to disorientate the population of the USSR and to spur on the aggressor.

Several Soviet and foreign historians have demonstrated that the combined forces of the *Wehrmacht* and its allies were not greater than the manpower and the weapons of the Soviet frontier districts. The supremacy of the *Wehrmacht* arose only after the catastrophe of the Red Army. In the books edited by bureaucrats of literature like G. A. Kumanev and others, Stalin's established thesis is upheld through forgery. They take into account the total number of German tanks – old and new – but count only the new ones when talking about Soviet tanks.[6] Yet in the initial period both countries successfully used both the old and the new equipment. German specialists consider that on 22 June Germany was drawing only on its own resources. In essence the potential of the occupied countries was not being employed.

It is significant that prior to total mobilisation the *Wehrmacht* was winning, but after mobilisation it began to suffer defeats. The rigid application of the experience gained in the western campaigns proved to be inappropriate when used against the Soviet Union. The Red Army had mastered not only the lessons drawn from its own combat experience but also those derived from the experience of other countries. However, Soviet practitioners of these ideas, forward-looking commanders, were eliminated by Stalin and his cronies.

Stalin cursed the rapid defeat of France and the fall of Paris in 1940, and assailed the absence of the Second Front later in the war. But why should the defence of the USSR have depended on the steadfastness or the mercy of foreign countries? Stalin, in his Victory Day speech on 25 May 1945, mentioned in passing 'mistakes' made by the government, and he thanked the Russian people for their 'endurance'. But that was utter hypocrisy. 'The Boss' knew how that acquiescence was achieved. P. A. Zhilin[7] and others attempted to 'improve' the arguments, and suggested that in the first instance the reasons for the defeats should be divided into objective and subjective factors. But even after the closest examination, they appear entirely subjective. All could be explained as a result of faulty leadership. The premiss that 'history gave the Soviet Union little time' cannot be sustained either. The development of the Soviet economy during the war demonstrated its full potential and how badly the government was utilising it. According to some, repression and the Red Army's lack of readiness for war in June 1941 returned the country to the economic conditions prevailing not only in the middle of the 1930s but those of the early part of that decade.

Stalin lied: not only Stalin but millions knew about the high-speed attack, especially in the frontier regions. Secondly, having information does not exclude surprise. The essence of surprise is in the inability of troops to engage in battle immediately. Currently some historians admit to a greater or lesser degree surprise – in a 'tactical and operational' or a 'morale-psychological' meaning of the word. It is not possible to agree with that entirely. Surprise was total; it defeated the Army, the rear, and swept over the worker, the Red Army soldier, 'the Boss', his Defence Commissars and his generals. Surprise left a mark not only on individual battles but on the whole war, the whole life of the nation.

The origins of surprise are a subject of many contrived explanations. Not only the 'perfidious enemy', but also the irresponsible Soviet Government stands accused. Because of them, mobilisation did not take place, troops were not brought to battle readiness and the war started with the slaughter of unarmed sleeping men, unprotected even by simple buildings. To encounter the war in barracks and tents, on aerodromes familiar to the enemy, is the best way to lose one's army or to have it captured. The reasons for all this go deeper. The leadership of the USSR was in a state of shock, but not only immediately before the attack. One cannot talk about any kind of 'sober assessment of the internal and foreign-policy position of the USSR'.[8] Stalin demonstrated this earlier by cutting the supplies to Germany, calling up reservists, then again grovelling to the Fascists. Berlin laughed at the Tass announcement suggesting talks. Throughout the whole of this time, the leadership of the Red Army disregarded accurate information about the enemy and its plans. Constrained by Stalin, the leaders either did not act or they undertook clearly inadequate measures. Conclusion about the shock has been substantiated by many documents and memoirs. Shock was communicated in Stalin's conduct and that of his circle – the whole of the People's Commissariat for Defence, the General Staff, the Stavka – in the muddle-headed orders of 'the Boss' and his readiness to surrender Leningrad and even Moscow.

Errors were committed by the heads of all three great powers of the wartime coalition. President Roosevelt made a grievous error, and the result was defeat at Pearl Harbor. But that is insignificant in comparison with the catastrophe of the Red Army. The main culprit for the attack turning into a surprise attack was Stalin. This absolute ruler categorically forbade his military men to carry out elementary duties when the circumstances indicated that the war was imminent. Stalin's appeal for vigilance, in the face of the approaching threat of the new campaign against the Soviet Union, has a hollow ring. Other leaders of the Red Army, Timoshenko, Zhukov, and commanders of the Military Districts, were also responsible, though the latter only to a lesser degree. Under the conditions of the cult of personality, in the opinion of Dmitrii Volkogonov, 'it is hard to blame the People's Commissars for Defence, the Main Military Soviet ...'. In actual fact, the conditions of tyranny explain the blind compliance of Politburo members and People's Commissars for Defence, marshals and generals, but in no way do they justify it. When tens of millions of one's countrymen's lives are at stake, Zhukov's words about 'faith in Stalin's infallibility' are reminiscent of childish talk. Even more so since he already knew of Stalin's great military embarrassment, for example in Finland and the failure of the Red Army during the 'Winter War' of 1939–40.

Responsibility for the surprise assumes an even larger significance when considering that in this case one is talking about very simple things. In the opinion of the nineteenth-century Russian strategist General A. Jomini, it became very difficult to carry out a surprise attack after the invention of firearms. It is feasible only in the case of an army forgetting the basic requirements of their own standing orders, in which case the army is reduced simply to holding outposts. This historian stressed that measures to be taken against a surprise attack are provided in the standing orders of all armies. All that is necessary is to put them into effect. Jomini states that, in 1812 at Tarutin, Murat was attacked suddenly and was beaten by Kutuzov, and as a consequence he tried to justify himself. In the opinion of Jomini, Murat was taken unawares only through his own unforgivable blunder.[9]

Effects of the enemy's surprise attack cannot be limited to the framework of 1941 alone. The main consequences were that, in the course of several months, the enemy destroyed or captured 90 per cent of the troops in the western military districts, which was the core of the regular army. He destroyed or captured huge amounts of arms and ammunition, including almost all the tanks and aeroplanes. The Soviet Union lost a huge proportion of its population and vast territory, including those areas which were the most economically developed. Evacuation of industry to the east played a part, but at what cost, and how much was saved, nobody knows to this day. According to some data, there was a 60 per cent loss of steel. Assuming that before the war over 145 thousand vehicles were produced, then in 1942 there were only 35 thousand. Production in some industries fell to zero.[10] The aggressors realised the old principle of 'war feeds war'. The direct consequence of the surprise attack was starvation in Russia. In the opinion of V. Moskoff the majority of Soviet citizens lived at that time 'on the edge between life and death'.[11]

Operation *Typhoon* was also a surprise attack for Stalin and his advisers. That baleful factor, surprise, pursued the Soviet Union for the entire duration of war. It is necessary to reject Stalin's premiss (his Order of the Day, on Red Army Day, 23 February 1942), that 'the time of surprise and unexpectedness has passed, equally German-Fascist reserves have been totally expended', and that the fate of the war will be decided henceforth by the 'permanently operating factors'.[12] This awful legacy of surprise attack permeated all post-war decades. In the long term, the dreadful effects of the loss of population and material resources cast a huge shadow over the country. It is impossible to research these separately here. But even now one can say that there is not a single sphere of social life in Russia where one cannot see the consequences of that catastrophe. Consider particularly the '1941 syndrome', under whose influence (and not only in the former Soviet Union) the most extravagant military programmes were, even up to the present, developed – the response to the 'surprise factor'.

Surprise was, to a certain extent, neutralised by the exceptional spiritual strength of the people and the Army. The geopolitical factor played a significant role in 1941–2, in particular the vast territory and a developed economy. In the following years, the influence of the various national anti-Fascist movements on the western allies grew larger. The Russian patriotic upsurge, which has been widely talked about, is only part of the picture. The newly opened archives from the secret collections also present a mixed picture. In the summer and autumn of 1941, one could hear comments like: 'Hitler will do no harm to the Russians, he will only kill the Jews'; 'It is all the same to me, whether it is Hitler or the Soviet Government', 'the sooner they hang all the Communists, the sooner will come the end of the Soviet Government'. There was a false conclusion in circulation regarding Fascism and its aims in eastern Europe: 'The war exists between the German Government and our government, but the people of both countries fight because they are forced to.' In October 1941 especially, manifestations of anti-Sovietism and anti-Semitism increased, and the confusion of the leadership and of the population became even greater. 'In Moscow', they were saying to each other, 'we should do just what the French did, open the door and let the Germans in.' Documents mention rumours about 'the treason' of Timoshenko, Pavlov and even Stalin himself. It is not possible to consider all this just emanating from German propaganda only. Events themselves led people to an anti-government position. I have never forgotten the angry words spoken to me by a young teacher from Novokhoperska, where the 1110th Regiment of the 329th Rifle Division was formed: 'Where are your promises to fight on foreign soil now that the Germans are on the very brink of capturing Voronezh?'

Recently, a Red Army General Staff's document of 15 May 1941 has become available. It concerns two interesting issues and I therefore intend to deal with it in greater detail. Certain historians, both in the Soviet Union and elsewhere, attempted to present its contents as sensational. The document itself is a report sent to Stalin by Defence Commissar Timoshenko and General Zhukov, chief of the General Staff, drafted by Vasilevskii and Vatutin, the latter both deputy chiefs of the General Staff. The report drew the conclusion that Germany was completing its preparation for war and aimed to 'pre-empt us [the Red Army] in deployment and effect a surprise attack'. Contrary to Marshal Shaposhnikov's earlier assessment submitted in 1938 and 1939, the authors stated that the main German forces were concentrated south of the Pripet marshes. They deemed it imperative to 'forestall the enemy in deployment and to attack the German army'. 'The strategic aim of the Red Army's action' was 'defeat of the main forces of the German army.' The main Soviet attack would be carried out by the south-western front forces in the direction of Cracow – Katowice. One of the aims was to cut Germany off from its southern allies.

From the political point of view, this document hardly contains anything essentially new. Within the Soviet Union, in the 1930s and the beginning of the 1940s, there was constant loud talk about the Red Army's offensive intentions to 'defeat the enemy on his own territory'. Stalin again stressed this in his speech delivered to the graduates of the Red Army military academies on 5 May 1941. In reality he also attempted to 'defeat the enemy' in subjugated Poland and in Finland. One should not, as some authors now do, simplify events, and claim that it was Stalin who incited aggression by calling for the proletarian revolution. In propaganda, in army regulations and other documents, the prevailing formula was: 'should an enemy attack,... we shall respond by a blow three times stronger against the warmongers' and more of the same. V. B. Rezun,[13] a former officer of the GRU (Soviet Military Intelligence), and his ardent sympathisers in the Soviet Union, allude to this lecture. Discounting Hitlerite aggression, they strive to represent the eastern campaign in the form of defensive measures. But, when defining the political character of a war, scholarship does not address the methods of actions, but the aims of the warring countries. Jomini had already tackled that problem at the beginning of the nineteenth century. He demonstrated that an attack does not always equal aggressive war. One should not confuse the offensive (a form of military operations) with aggression (which is the political aim of the war at large). It is not a matter of who 'pre-empted' whom, who 'attacked' whom, or whose forces are on whose territory. In 1944–5, the USA 'attacked' Germany, and the Soviet Union 'attacked' Japan. However, history does not brand them as aggressors, and not simply because they won.

In a purely military sense, the document of 15 May does not have great significance. It is completely normal that Staffs work out different variants of operations, in the event of war. They are certainly not always conditioned by the political aims of the government. In the case of the Soviet General Staff, the matter is not just the fact that they planned for attack. What is dreadful is that these or other optimum operational variants were tackled too late and amongst too narrow a circle; thus to realise and execute these plans on 22 June was impossible as they were not ready. It is lamentable that the Soviet forces in the main proved incapable of active operations.

The report had scarcely any substantial influence on the approach adopted towards the origins of the war, or the defeats of 1941. It is not possible to repudiate the thesis about errors committed by Stalin and his advisers, concentrating the main forces on the southern flank at the time when the enemy was planning to attack in the centre. In the opinion of B. N. Petrov,[14] this concentration was not a result of errors, but rather of the intention to crush the enemy on his own territory. According to military records, in the 'Lwów salient' which jutted westwards there were 4,200 tanks, including the bulk of the most modern tanks available in the western military districts. But were the main forces of the *Wehrmacht* not, in fact, in the centre while the Red Army was concentrated in the south? Did the Red Army high command not err in judging the direction of the enemy's main attack? Was it not so that on the Minsk axis the Red Army was quickly crushed, whereas on the Kiev front resistance was more stubborn? Publication of the new document only reinforces the opinion that the Soviet leadership was in a state of shock and that there were different tendencies, some realistic alas too few, others reckless and inclined to appeasement, with the latter prevailing in the final resort.

Surprise gave rise to a Stalinist method of war management, even though one should look for the underlying causes in the massive political murders of the 1930s, and finally in his despotism. In my view that management was characterised by incompetence, anti-democratism – especially bureaucratism – and immorality, which frequently turned into cruelty. These traits are organically tied with each other, which can best be seen in the following facts. In the Central Archive of the Ministry of Defence in the series 'Data on Examining Experience of Operations', there is a report written by Colonel K. F. Vasil'chenko, prepared in the western sector of the operations directorate of the General Staff, mentioning the attempt of the forces under the command of Zhukov to destroy Army Group Centre. In the main the author analyses the actions of the 33rd and 43rd Armies on the Vyazma sector. In the official works of Zhukov that question is either avoided, or is interpreted from only one point of view. The greatest distortion of official history occurs in the case of the destruction of four divisions of the 33rd Army, fulfilling the reckless orders issued by Stalin – Zhukov. Vasil'chenko's reports as well as many other documents and recollections show that, even in 1942, Soviet leadership knew neither the enemy nor its capabilities. The forces and the means apportioned to any designated operation were extremely inadequate. Stalin's leadership tried to compensate for the gigantic loss suffered in the summer and autumn of 1941 in the first instance by taking harsher disciplinary control of the army.[15]

The true nature of Stalin's leadership is abundantly revealed in Order No. 227 issued on 28 July 1942. It exposes the bureaucratism of the regime. The essence of the order lies in the restrictions of the rights of commanders of all ranks, the most extreme centralisation of the military leadership, in which bureaucratism is inherent. But it was also immoral, as it contained the attempt by Stalin to find a scapegoat. His was an extreme cruelty. In Order No. 227 one can see a reflection of the non-professionalism of both Stalin and his advisers. Contemporary war is inconceivable without all commanders exercising initiative. But it was precisely this which the author of the order was aiming to destroy.[16]

It is also necessary to emphasise the direct link between surprise attack and the excessive price of victory. To the latter can be apportioned losses directly caused by the unpreparedness of the western military districts in the summer of 1941, and by those primitive methods of leadership during the subsequent years which were greatly affected by surprise. The greatest controversy is generated by looking at the correlation of military losses of the Red Army and the eastern front of the *Wehrmacht*. The authors of the six-volume history of the Great Patriotic War give the figure of 14 million dead Red Army soldiers. They seem to be close to the real figure as this number coincides with the calculations of several foreign scholars. *Wehrmacht* dead, according to German data, numbered in excess of 4 million, and in that number is included 2.8 million on the eastern front. This means a correlation of 5:1. Global numbers of fatalities among the civilian population of the Soviet Union and Germany stand at 27 million and 6 million respectively, a correlation of 4.5:1.

It is impossible to accept the deductions of those who compiled the statistical collection on Soviet losses, *Grif sekretnosti snyat*, published in Moscow in 1993 as the final scholarly word on this matter.[17] It is obvious that they are not dealing with complete data, that they minimise Soviet combat losses and maximise those of the enemy. They disregard previous work by scholars who studied this problem, ignore the connection between the level of losses and the Army's military art, and also the responsibility for the excessive losses of the Red Army. But even so, this collection has been useful. It has dispelled the myth about the superiority of Stalin's military leadership school and about the turning-point in the development of military leadership after the victory at Stalingrad. According to the data of the compilers, losses of both countries were approximately equal, whereas the losses of the Red Army in 1943–5 by comparison with 1941–2 were not decreased.

To conclude, in the history of the Soviet–German war the year of 1941 was not only 'heroic and tragic', as some authors deemed it. It was also the time of downfall of Stalinist diplomacy and strategy, which to a great extent governed the distribution of roles within the anti-Fascist coalition which emerged in 1942. It was a strategy driven by an ignorant direction of the Soviet war effort, resulting in huge Soviet human and *matériel* losses. The pride of the Soviet people, who inflicted the most grievous damage on the common enemy, and the recognition of the people, liberated from fascism by the Red Army, cannot take away the bitterness of the sacrifices and losses suffered by them.

At the same time, the year 1941 brought about the downfall of *Barbarossa* and checked the pace of the *Blitzkrieg*. Germany, with its limited economic potential and weak allies in support of its pretensions to world domination, could count only on a series of short-lived wars against an isolated enemy. Failure to achieve a quick victory and the establishment of a kind of balance, which the *Wehrmacht* never managed to overwhelm in spite of all its efforts, doomed any plans to conquer the world. The course of the war had slid out of Germany's control. At the end of 1941, one could no longer argue that Germany *might* be defeated, only about *when* it would be defeated.

Notes

1. Aleksandr Svechin, *Strategiya* (Voennyi Vestnik, Moscow, 1927). Translated as *Strategy* (East View Publications, Minneapolis, 1993).
2. The 12-volume work in question is *Istoriya vtoroi mirovoi voiny 1941–1945*, published in Moscow by Voenizdat between 1973 and 1982, edited first by Marshal A. A. Grechko and later by Marshal D. F. Ustinov. The '10-volume dinosaur' refers to the new history of the war planned in ten volumes, *Velikaya Otechestvennaya voina sovetskogo naroda* (Voenizdat, Moscow). The first volume was duly prepared and presented for discussion by General D. Volkogonov, and resulted in extremely acrimonious exchanges. The stenographic report of the session of the Editorial Commission on the 10-volume history was published in *Nezavisimaya gazeta*, 16 June 1991, with a foreword by V. Tretyakov, entitled 'Generals and History'.
3. See *Der Zweite Weltkrieg* (Munich, 1990); *Die Umwertung der sowjetischen Geschichte* (Göttingen, 1991); R. W. Davies, *Perestroika und Geschichte* (Munich, 1991); *Aus Politik und Zeitgeschichte* no. 24, 1991; J. Erickson, 'New Thinking about the Eastern Front in World War II', *The Journal of Military History*, 56, no. 2, April 1992, pp. 284–6.
4. *Hitlers Krieg?* (Cologne, 1989) pp. 114–15.
5. See Z. V. Grebel'skii, *Fedor Raskol'nikov* (Moscow, 1988) pp. 174–83.
6. See, for example, *Sovetskii tyl v pervyi period Velikoi Otechestvennoi voiny* (Nauka, Moscow, 1988) pp. 49–50.
7. See A. A. Grechko and D. F. Ustinov (eds), *Istoriya vtoroi mirovoi voiny 1939–1945*, 12 vols (Voenizdat, Moscow, 1975), vol. IV, p. 482.
8. See O. V. Vishlev in *Novaya i noveishaya istoriya*, no. 1, 1992, p. 91.
9. A. Jomini, *Kratkoe nachertanie voennogo iskusstva* (St Petersburg, 1840), pts 1–2; also his *Ocherki voennogo iskusstva* (Oborongiz, Moscow, 1939), vols 1–2, p. 33.
10. See statistical survey *Goskomstat SSSR* (Moscow, 1990).
11. V. Moskoff, *Bread of Affliction: Food Provision in the USSR during the Second World War* (Cambridge University Press, Cambridge, 1990), ch. XIII, pp. 234–5.
12. 'permanently operating factors': (1) stability of the rear, (2) morale of the Army, (3) quantity and quality of divisions, (4) armament, and (5) organising ability of commanders.
13. Viktor Suvorov (pseud. of V. B. Rezun), *Icebreaker: Who Started the Second World War?* (Hamish Hamilton, London, 1990).
14. See B. N. Petrov, 'O strategicheskom razvertyvanii Krasnoi Armii nakanune voiny', *Voenno-istoricheskii zhurnal*, no. 12, 1991, pp. 10–20.
15. See, for example, TSAMO (Ministry of Defence Central Archive), arch. 27, coll. 333, file 3.
16. See Ministry of Defence Central Archive, arch. 228, coll. 3947, file 5, pp. 200–15. See also 'Prikaz Narodnogo Komissara Oborony Soyuza SSR No. 227 28 iyuliya 1942 g. g. Moskva', signed by J. V. Stalin, in *Voenno-istoricheskii zhurnal*, no. 8, 1988, pp. 73–4.
17. See Colonel-General G. F. Krivosheyev (ed.), *Grif sekretnosti snyat* (Voenizdat, Moscow, 1993).

Chapter 8

The Imperial Japanese Navy and the North – South Dilemma

JOHN CHAPMAN

'A war with Russia would be ruinous for Japan whatever outcome the war might have.'
    Japanese Navy officers, in conversation with the German Naval Attaché in Japan, December 1936
'Russia must be destroyed, once and for all.'
    Adolf Hitler, in conversation with Japanese Ambassador Ōshima, 14 July 1941

THE CHANGING HISTORIOGRAPHICAL CONTEXT

In November 1991, a special conference was convened at Lake Yamanaka on the slopes of Mount Fuji to mark the fiftieth anniversary of the outbreak of the Pacific War and to use the occasion to undertake a reappraisal of the validity of the findings of an earlier joint US–Japanese conference of historians concerned with the subject at Lake Kawaguchi in July 1969.[1] A major departure from the previous conference lay in the extension of invitations to historians from Europe, China, Korea, the Soviet Union and the South-East Asian countries to participate in these deliberations. That very fact reflected the crumbling structure of antagonism that had sustained the Cold War. That the Cold War had really ended had just been graphically signalled by Boris Yeltsin to the conveniently located television cameras in August, and the writing on the wall for the disintegrating historiographical infrastructure underpinning the US–Japanese alliance against the USSR was already evident in the pressures for reform of the Japanese political system – symbolised in the tentative efforts of Prime Minister Kaifu and the new Emperor to reject the denial of collective responsibility for Japan's past record as a brutal and cruel neighbour.

    Faced with the prospects of President Bush's 'new world order', the ruling party feared that the fiftieth anniversary of the outbreak of the Pacific War might lead to an abandonment of the old consensus, and the election of Mr Miyazawa – the leader of the faction most closely identified with the US alliance – represented a last effort to shore up the old domestic order, as well as to preserve what could be preserved of the legacy of the Cold War order. Although US and Japanese historians largely reaffirmed the historically orthodox explanations of the outbreak of the Greater East Asian War (*Dai Tōa Sensō*) that had been employed to accommodate Japan within the ambit of the US system of post-war alliances, and although the fiftieth anniversary of the Pacific War (*Taiheiyō Sensō*) – with its focus on Japanese aggression against the western powers – passed off without any significant manifestations of anti-Japanese animus, the studied cynicism of the ruling élite was undermined by the sight of elderly Korean 'comfort women' reliving before the cameras the torment of their shameful ordeal, backed by revelations of the existence of archival evidence for state responsibility for their subjection to sexual conscription.

Perhaps more importantly, however, this coincided with yet more manifestations of a seemingly ineradicable corruption of the political system and its 'iron triangle' of power that had remained virtually untouched by the reforms of the US Occupation. Just as the USA had encouraged and tolerated the Mafia in Italy and rescued it from Mussolini's grip, so in Japan the USA had given up on early efforts to purge the influence of organised crime (*bōryokudan*) and had settled for a tacit acceptance of strident assertions in favour of preserving society from communist and socialist subversion as a good enough justification for permitting financial brokerage of the system to become dominated by sinister and corrupt influences. The Lockheed scandal of 1972 provided the clearest evidence of US complicity in promoting graft and violence by groups who had already plied their nefarious trade among the very militarists condemned as war criminals. The current statements of determination to break the old system mirror the reformist rhetoric of the immediate post-war era, except that the exercise of choice is less subject to dependence on external forces than in 1945 and is perhaps more conducive to greater historiographical heterodoxy.

OLD RHETORIC, NEW MASTERS, SAME SELF-INTEREST

Japan's situation in 1945 seemed extremely bleak. The rhetoric of the leadership about a life or death struggle, which had been employed to justify aggression against their neighbours, had the character of a self-fulfilling prophecy not just for the armed forces, but for the whole of the society, faced with a stark choice between mass suicide and survival. The preference for survival was tied ineluctably with hope for reconstruction and a more prosperous future. First, the desire to appease and soothe the victors was strongly fuelled by the recognition that the victors held the key to the most advanced technologies and the greatest sources of wealth. Secondly, the Japanese had suffered from the perceived bad faith of Stalin in denouncing the Soviet–Japanese Neutrality Pact prematurely, in the slaughter of thousands of Japanese troops even after the surrender of Japan in August 1945[2] and in the brutal treatment of captured Japanese nationals detained for a decade afterwards in labour camps.[3] Stalin and others could readily point in turn to Japanese behaviour in 1904, to the brutalities of the Japanese intervention in Siberia[4] and to the aggressive role of the Japanese army along the borders of the Soviet Union and its ally, Outer Mongolia, in the latter part of the 1930s.[5] Well before the end of the Second World War, it is clear that anti-Soviet sentiments remained strong within the ranks of the military in the USA (and Britain), and officers who had had experience of contacts with the Imperial Japanese Army prior to 1941 (including General MacArthur) found it quite readily possible to revert to pre-war assumptions about the cardinal importance of isolating and neutralising the Soviet Union. Anglo-American officers regretted that the Japanese army had not been permitted to have its strategic head in setting national goals, just as many individuals had been far from unsympathetic to the anti-communist and anti-Soviet arguments put forward by Hitler in the 1930s. Japanese General Staff officers could claim that they had been reluctantly drawn into the anti-American strategy of the Japanese navy, and the exponents of pre-emptive strikes against the USSR could espouse the hope of assisting the USA to succeed where they themselves had failed. The army factions which had adopted the anti-Soviet strategy as the top priority were by no means unwilling to collude with the US Occupation in making scapegoats of General Tōjō Hideki, his associates in the War Ministry and his collaborators among the party, business and bureaucratic élites.[6] The US Occupation authorities, for their part, consciously decided to limit the numbers of prosecutions in order to facilitate early reconciliation, and blocked demands from other Allied countries for many other charges to be incorporated in the prosecution at the Tokyo Tribunal.

The dominant role in the US Occupation of Japan was played by the US army. The US navy was largely marginalised. MacArthur appointed his own historians, who gathered material in collaboration with the 1st Demobilisation Bureau, run by former General Staff officers. Former Japanese navy officers in the 2nd Demobilisation Bureau and US navy officers sent to Japan to gather material for the US official naval history found themselves in peripheral positions.[7] Officers from the Counter-Intelligence Corps (CIC) of the US army provided most of the manpower for the interrogation of former

Japanese government and military personnel, including navy personnel. While the most prominent of the Japanese fleet commanders failed to survive the war and hence made prosecutions of navy figures a lesser priority, (CIC) officers nevertheless showed a less than vigorous interest in dealing toughly with surviving admirals who had been involved in pre-war planning and policy compared to surviving generals.[8] The fact that the Dutch judge, Röling, entered a dissenting judgement at the Tokyo Tribunal, in which he argued the case for the execution of three Japanese admirals, highlights the selective nature of Allied decision-making and reflects the determining role of MacArthur and the US military.[9] While the central theme of an Axis conspiracy to commit aggression provided a means whereby the Soviet Union could participate in the conduct of the Allied prosecution, it soon became clear that Soviet prosecution demands and methods were treated with scepticism and circumscribed accordingly through the management of the Tribunal.[10] More summary justice, however, was meted out to Japanese war crimes' suspects overseas by both US and other Allied military tribunals by contrast with the main show trial in Tokyo.[11]

US post-war strategy in Asia was based on the assumption that control of Japan was of key importance for a future in which US forces would avoid any major involvement on the Asian mainland and that the USSR was to be isolated and neutralised if it made any attempts to dominate the Asia – Pacific region. While control of Japan through occupation could be achieved so long as economy and society remained shattered by war, that position could scarcely be sustained forever. A compromise had to be made that would form the basis of future collaboration most suited to the wider international context within which the two countries were most likely to be operating. Since the security scenario held to be most likely by the US War Department envisaged the USSR as the key opponent to US interests, it was logical that those groups in Japanese society that had been most respectably anti-Soviet and anti-communist would receive the most favourable hearing and treatment. Respectability was enhanced if individuals and groups had demonstrated that they had not been involved in any significant anti-American activity prior to 1941. The surviving Japanese General Staff personnel involved in the anti-Soviet strategy were mostly individuals who had been involved in collaborative relations with Nazi Germany against the USSR, though there remained a not insignificant number of officers who had retained links with the earlier generation of anti-Soviet strategists who had worked with the French, Poles, British and Americans.

The latter were the most favoured and some of them formed an unofficial group of military advisers to the Occupation and the Yoshida administration that was described in the 1950s as the *KATO KIKAN*. This was an acronym

based on the first letters of the names of four former senior intelligence
officers who had served as military attachés abroad and in General Staff
intelligence posts in Tokyo prior to 1945. The letter K stood for Lieutenant-
General Kamata Senzō, who had served in the Japanese embassy in Washington in the early 1930s; A stood for Lieutenant-General Arisue Seizō, a
former attaché in Rome who was head of the Intelligence Division of the
General Staff at the end of the war;[12] T stood for Lieutenant-General Tatsumi
Eichi, who had worked as military attaché in London in the late 1930s when
he had served under Yoshida as ambassador; O stood for Major-General
Onodera Makoto, military attaché in Riga and Stockholm.[13] While posted
in London, Yoshida himself had sought to work closely with the Conservative Party Central Office, the City, the Treasury and the War Office on
an Anglo-Japanese–German alignment against the USSR, but this had fallen
on deaf ears in the Foreign Office. Anthony Eden and his officials, privy
to much of Yoshida's diplomatic communications through control of the
Government Code and Cypher School (GC and CS) and to information
obtained from the Soviet defector Krivitsky – about Yoshida's attempts to
work with members of the radical anti-Soviet group within the Japanese
foreign service (*kakushin-ha*), headed by Shiratori Toshio – rejected Yoshida's advances with withering condescension.[14] But from a position of post-
war strength, Yoshida renewed his overtures to leading pro-Axis figures
within the *Gaimushō*, such as Ushiba Nobuhiko and Furuuchi Hiroo, who
found employment with the Central Liaison Unit and later were appointed
ambassadors to Washington and Djakarta respectively.[15]

Many of those who expected to be blamed and punished for the disastrous
war with the USA committed suicide at the time of the surrender or were, in
some cases, set up as scapegoats and betrayed by other individuals arrested
by war crimes investigators. There was a deep resentment within the Army
and the ruling élite for the repressive political control exercised by General
Tōjō Hideki – who served as War, Home and Prime Minister and briefly as
Chief of General Staff – and those who supported him. Old scores were
settled within the walls of Sugamo Prison, and many against whom hard
evidence was difficult to find – as a result of the deliberate destruction of
swathes of government archives or because they exercised their right to
silence – went unpunished. Those army officers and civilians closely identified
with the policy of subjugating China and promoting the advance into the
Pacific were selected as targets, while those who had been most closely
identified with pre-emptive war against the USSR or had some experience
that seemed of value to the US authorities for the future were often shielded
from prosecution, even when evidence of war crimes or atrocities against
Allied personnel existed.[16] The Japanese navy more generally escaped lightly

from the prosecution process and from the public obloquy heaped on the Army.

The accounts of pre-war and wartime strategy and operations were reconstructed by the army and navy historical teams working directly for the G-2 Section of Occupation Headquarters. These formed the basis of the archival material and of the subsequent production of the official history published by the Defence Agency in Tokyo between the late 1960s and early 1980s.[17] This largely embellished and corroborated the earlier post-war historical explanations which were reflected in both the Kawaguchi and Yamanaka conference proceedings. With the ending of the Cold War and especially the fall of the Liberal Democrat regime, the way has been opened for a far more independent revision of pre-war Japanese history and of Soviet–Japanese relations than joint US–Japanese orthodoxy could permit. Given the political uncertainty that now reigns, however, it is impossible to predict if the new stance of the Japanese Government will remain more than superficial or if it heralds the first steps in a more thorough revisionism. But if the system is to be broken, it cannot be done without significant historiographical change.

SOVIET–JAPANESE RELATIONS AND THE OLD ORTHODOXY

The logic of the assumption that the key role in Japanese expansionism lay with the Japanese army tended to dictate that the conduct of policy and strategy towards the USSR was primarily a matter for the Army General Staff; and, by extension, that the nature of Soviet–Japanese relations and the role of the USSR in Japanese foreign policy was determined by the behaviour of the Japanese General Staff. While there is much evidence to suggest that the General Staff did seize the political initiative in national decision-making on foreign policy in the years after 1931, the direct impact of the changes fell squarely on China rather than on the USSR. Even at that early stage of Japanese expansionist tendencies, the January 1932 landing of Japanese marines at Shanghai indicated a clear attempt by the Japanese navy to shift the focus of national strategy from north to central China, with the result that Britain and the USA were just as alarmed by the changes as the USSR. In domestic politics, it is also clear that navy as well as army officers were directly involved in the efforts at 'government by assassination' at this period, when the dynamics of the political system indicated a tendency for a shift away from civilian control to military control of government decision-making. From 1934 to 1936, civilian politicians had sought to co-opt navy senior personnel as a means of protecting themselves against the more radical ambitions of the Army and its political allies. But in the events surrounding the 'mutiny' of the Tokyo garrison in February 1936 (*ni-ni-roku jihen*), from which the Navy was excluded and in which retired admirals were targets and victims, a very serious jolt was given to the system which came close to being shattered by an internecine Army – Navy conflict.[18] Thereafter, a delicate balance had always to be maintained between the interests of both parties and a consensus carefully nurtured, both in terms of domestic and external policy.

Although individual writers have drawn attention to the role of the Navy in Japan–Soviet relations,[19] the negative attitude it adopted towards the risk of being drawn into conflict with the USSR has not been very clearly elucidated as a fundamental and systematic principle guiding navy policy and strategy all through the pre-1945 era. While navy leaders were happy to accept that the General Staff had every right and duty to pursue a *defensive* strategy *vis-à-vis* the Soviet Union, they fought tooth and nail to deny the demands of those within the Army who favoured an *offensive*, pre-emptive policy. This opposition was clearly demonstrated as far back as the period of intervention in Siberia from 1918 to 1923, but had already emerged after the ending of the Russo-Japanese War and the period of Russo-Japanese economic co-operation between 1907 and 1917 which had been highly profitable for Japanese business and industry. The savagery of the atrocities and counter-atrocities that had characterised the later stages of Japanese army involve-ment in the Russian Civil War provided some of the earlier examples of the breakdown of discipline in the Army and of the fanaticism that was engen-dered by experience of ideological and guerrilla warfare. Many of these lessons had to be relearned as a result of army campaigns in China, especially after the organisation of guerrilla warfare by the Chinese Communist Party following the end of the Long March in 1935–6 and the formation of the united front in the wake of the Xian Incident.

THE NORTH–SOUTH DICHOTOMY IN JAPANESE STRATEGY

The dichotomy between an army-led northern strategy and a navy-led sou-thern strategy was a recurrent feature of Japanese policy that attracted the attention of Soviet policymakers at least as early as 1932. In the 1920s, Soviet policymakers had been preoccupied by the indefatigability of the Japanese army's anti-Soviet and anti-communist credentials and were con-stantly concerned to observe all the signs of Japanese efforts to get close to the White and nationalist minority *émigré* groups abroad and to potential allies among the countries along the Soviet borderlands fearful of any threat of Soviet expansionism. France and its east European allies constituted the basis of just such a two-front threat involving Japan, particularly at those times when the constellation was expanded to involve Britain and the USA.

Even when Stalin's policy of non-aggression pacts successfully detached France, its allies and the USA from Japan and an anti-Soviet encirclement strategy, Soviet propaganda continued to try to warn of the threats of capitalist encirclement and reinforce the Japanese General Staff's perceptions of Soviet fears of the threatening strategy that could create the greatest danger to the existence of the regime. The Japanese army had publicly acknowledged as early as the spring of 1931, that Poland was far too weak to be considered a credible bulwark even against Soviet expansion into eastern Europe (as it had achieved against all the odds in 1919–20), let alone a force that could restrain any Soviet offensive forays in Asia (even on the very limited scale of intervention against the warlord of Manchuria in 1929).[20] The resort to collaboration with the French in 1918 had resulted in part from the unexpected collapse of Germany and the German army's decision to collaborate with the Bolsheviks rather than to seek their downfall, but a large section of the Japanese officer corps (which had seriously toyed with the idea of ditching the Allies in favour of Germany) continued to view the German rather than the French army as a role model despite the inimical secret collaboration between Germany and the USSR (and the latter's protégé, Chiang Kai-shek).

Hopes for change in German foreign policy were partly sustained by the willingness of the small German navy to engage in collaborative projects with its Japanese counterpart and increased after 1928 with growing signs of unease and dissatisfaction attending German–Soviet relations. The more Stalin's First Five-Year Plan unfolded and his willingness to dangle economic incentives before Germany's enemies in exchange for *détente* adversely affec-ted Germany's economic and military security, the more possible it became for Japanese army officers to get a foot in the door with officer exchanges and secondments under an agreement of 1930.[21] The onset of the Great Depression emphasised German as well as Japanese insecurity, as the reduction of US trade with Japan and the withdrawal of US capital investment in Germany helped deepen economic, social and political unrest in both countries. Even before the Japanese incursion in Manchuria, the Japanese General Staff unsuccessfully signalled to the *Gaimushō* its desire to support German demands for greater equality of treatment at the forthcoming Geneva Disarmament Conference and indicated its hopes for an accord with Germany as a future ally against the USSR.[22]

The relentless rise in the electoral fortunes of the Nazi Party and Hitler's repeated public and private assurances of approval of the Japanese solution to the Manchurian Incident, together with the effects of the Japanese take-over on German trade in the area, provided incentives for a much earlier implementation of German–Japanese collaboration than anyone had antici-pated.[23] Reports of contacts between the Japanese and the Nazis and aware-ness of Nazi links with some of the same radical-right *émigré* groups in Europe and China were the subject of Soviet comment from the spring of 1932.[24] Interest in Japanese army intelligence contacts with the Nazi Party and other right-wing groups also attracted the attention of German military counter-intelligence (*Abwehr III*) at precisely the same time.[25] The *Abwehr* also requested the support of German consular missions in collecting military reports that might throw light on the prospects for Soviet–Japanese conflict. Its signals-monitoring division (*Abwehr II*) focused on diplomatic and mili-tary communication networks in the Far East and it dispatched military and naval intelligence agents to the Far East from October 1931 onward, to reinforce its existing contacts in the area to provide on-the-spot reports of the developing crisis.[26] The German General Staff was already extensively represented in Moscow and continued to receive numerous inside reports from the Soviet side until 1934. Feelers about the dispatch of German military and naval attachés to other capitals were put in train via diplomatic circles. Japanese approval in principle for the secondment of German army and navy officers to Japan was indicated as early as the spring of 1931, but it was not until December 1932 that a firm proposal to implement this was indicated from the German side, following agreement with the Foreign Ministry that appointments of attachés to the major capitals – including Tokyo – would be systematically instituted during 1933.[27]

Recipients of the circular proposing the dispatch of a German army officer on secondment to an active Japanese unit included the head of the Armed Forces Section in the War Ministry (*Wehrmachtsabteilung*), Lieutenant-Colonel Eugen Ott, who had served as a close aide to the Defence Minister and Chancellor, General von Schleicher, particularly in the political nego-tiations with the Nazi Party leading up to Hindenburg's invitation to Hitler to replace von Schleicher in January 1933. Ott's close association with the discredited von Schleicher put him in a delicate political position once Hitler took over, and the army commander-in-chief, General von Hammerstein, decided to reassign him. Ott told the Office of Strategic Services (OSS) after the war that he was warned that he should go as far away from Berlin as possible and first thought of an appointment to a regiment in southern Bavaria, but it was suggested to him by his wife that he follow up the idea of the secondment to the Far East to look into the problem of Manchuria and he duly received von Hammerstein's approval.[28]

After the war, two contact people of the *Abwehr* in Tokyo spoke to CIC officers and drew attention to the fact that Mrs Ott had been married before to a German architect who was a prominent local member of the German

Communist Party in Frankfurt.[29] Interestingly, too, a daughter of General von Hammerstein who went to Japan in the mid-1930s was accused of being a member of the Communist Party and was the subject of a report to the Gestapo.[30] East German sources have also claimed that during the period of her first marriage Mrs Ott met Dr Richard Sorge – the head of the Red Army covert intelligence unit in Shanghai from 1929 to 1932 and in Tokyo from 1933 to 1941 – at a Communist Party function in the Ruhr area and danced with him.[31] On 12 January 1933, the German Foreign Ministry instructed Ambassador Voretzsch to inform the *Gaimushō* that it was planned to dispatch a naval attaché to Tokyo, but regretted financial reasons prevented the dispatch of a military attaché. On 17 March, the Defence Ministry contacted the Foreign Ministry, and Ott approached the Japanese military attaché in Berlin, Colonel Banzai Heihachirō, direct, asking him to pass on his request in principle for a six-month secondment. On 12 April, the Defence Ministry reported that Ott had specified to Banzai that he wanted to be in Japan from June to December 1933, but had also asked for secondment to an artillery regiment and for permission to 'join a Japanese army unit in Manchuria to learn about conditions there'. Ott left on board the steamer *Leverkusen*, arriving at Shanghai on 29 May where he was scheduled to spend a few days before moving on to Tokyo.[32]

It is not known if Ott was accompanied by his wife on this trip, but it has been claimed – mistakenly – that it was during Ott's secondment to an artillery regiment at Nagoya that he first met the Soviet agent Dr Sorge. The latter in fact left there in mid-August 1933 for Manchuria. The German consul at Mukden was told of Ott's impending arrival at Kwantung Army HQ for a month's visit. Ott was reported to have arrived at Tsitsihar on 16 August accompanied by the head of the Heiho special service unit (*tokumu kikan*) and had given a bland interview to the press. In late October, Ott had asked for an early recall, but was urged to stay in Tokyo until the new German ambassador, Herbert von Dirksen, arrived there by sea on 16 December. There is no proof of their meeting, but it would be quite consistent with Ott's return to Berlin via Siberia by 12 January 1934. He met up in Moscow with Colonel Hartmann and knew he was nominated as military attaché in Tokyo. It is quite likely, therefore, that he was apprised by von Dirksen of meetings with Defence Minister von Blomberg and Hitler on 17 and 18 August 1933, when von Dirksen was told by Hitler that he was being sent to Tokyo 'to bring about a deepening and expansion of German–Japanese relations'.[33]

The embassy was informed of Ott's appointment on 4 January 1934 and a series of briefings was arranged for him in Berlin between 19 January and 17 February. On 28 January, Colonel Hartmann in Moscow had met the

retired Colonel Heins – a close aide of General von Seeckt – who had been invited by Chiang Kai-shek to replace General Wetzell as chief adviser. Heins was encouraged by Hartmann to make contact with Ott when he reached Berlin, in order to obtain an updated briefing of the situation in China.[34] Before he left for Japan, Ott was ordered by the Defence Ministry to contact Wetzell at Nanking after he reached Shanghai on 10 April. But von Dirksen intervened and urged that the meeting take place in private at Shanghai as he feared that 'Ott's outstanding position here until now would be gravely impaired' in view of the fact that the military mission was 'regarded by the Japanese military with the greatest mistrust'.[35]

The news of Ott's appointment was warmly received by the Japanese General Staff at a meeting between von Dirksen and General Ueda Kankichi, the Vice-Chief, in early March. Ueda was strongly in favour of offensive operations against the USSR and was in command of the Kwantung army at the time of its major border conflicts with the Red Army at Changkufeng Hill in 1938 and at Khalkhin-Gol (Nomonhan) in 1939. Ott's extremely influential status until 1933 and his personal contacts with Hitler and other leading figures in the Nazi Party undoubtedly impressed the Japanese army, but also ensured that he would have been well placed to provide it with authentic background both about the Red Army and about the German role in supplying arms to the Chinese Nationalists.[36] Ott also appears to have assumed that his previous status gave him a wide degree of licence in interpreting his role in Tokyo, as he failed to submit any of his written reports to the Foreign Ministry prior to 1935 in accordance with the regulations for attachés in diplomatic missions abroad.[37]

In the summer of 1935, a General Staff officer who spoke Russian and had served for several years on the Soviet desk in the military intelligence division, Captain Erwin Scholl, was sent to Tokyo as Ott's assistant and provided with an Enigma cypher machine with the express purpose of exchanging intelligence with the Japanese General Staff about the USSR. Scholl had been an officer in the regiment to which Sorge had been attached during the First World War and thus fortuitously strengthened existing friendly contacts with senior members of the German embassy, some of whom had agreed to give him references for journalistic accreditation and membership of the Nazi Party. An internal inquiry in the German Foreign Ministry in April 1942 pointed directly to Scholl and Ott as the principal sources of confidential information being obtained by Sorge and this was reinforced by Sorge's own testimony to his Japanese interrogators.[38]

As was confirmed after the war by Max Clausen, the radio operator of the 'Ramsay Group' in Japan, Sorge had a high personal regard for the German naval attaché in Tokyo, Commander (later Admiral) Paul Wenneker, with whom he had lodged many of his personal papers prior to his arrest in October 1941. He evidently regarded Wenneker as someone who was unsympathetic to the Nazis and did his best to convince the interrogators that he had had particular difficulty in obtaining any information from Wenneker. That this was wholly false has been confirmed not only by his widow and private secretary, but also by Wenneker's own statements in a top-secret cypher cable to the German navy Chief-of-Staff dated 27 July 1942.[39] It has also been claimed by East German sources that Sorge managed to persuade Captain Joachim Lietzmann, German naval attaché in Tokyo from 1937 to 1940, to let him read his war diary entries for the period from 1939 to 1940 and that he obtained a copy of Naval Code A, the main hand system used for radio traffic by naval attachés prior to the introduction of the Enigma DJ system in operation from January 1940 to June 1942.[40]

During his first tour of duty in Tokyo, from December 1933 to June 1937, Wenneker went unaccompanied following divorce from his first wife, and by all accounts led a rather free bachelor existence with separate accom-modation in the suburbs away from the embassy. Wenneker made friends with Sorge – a fellow-bachelor with a penchant for alcohol, women and socialising – often attending dinner parties, diplomatic receptions and other social occasions. The rather strait-laced wife of Ambassador von Dirksen was sent by her husband to take refuge at Wenneker's house during the February 1936 Incident when the area round the German embassy (now occupied by the National Diet Library) was under the control of the army rebels, and surprised an embarrassed Wenneker entertaining a young Japanese woman in his house. On another occasion, Wenneker was out on the town and drove his car and two female passengers straight into Tokyo Bay. The press also got hold of the story that Wenneker had paid a night-club owner to free a young hostess from the contract between the club owner and the girl's family, but he was able to enlist the assistance of the British assistant naval attaché and the Navy Minister's adjutant and get the story suppressed.[41] Somehow or other, these stories got back to Erich Raeder, the commander-in-chief of the German navy, who insisted that Wenneker get married for a second time before he was allowed to return for his second tour of duty in Tokyo in February 1940.

Wenneker – who had spent most of the First World War as a British prisoner after the battle of the Dogger Bank – shared the anti-British feelings of both Raeder and his successor, Doenitz, who was a witness at Wenneker's second marriage and subsequently attended his funeral in 1979, having shared quarters at Wilhelmshaven with him in 1938–9 when he was captain of the armoured cruiser *Deutschland*. Raeder resented Hitler's support for the Anglo-German Naval Treaty of June 1935 and pressed for the con-tinuation of the offensive against the British Isles in preference to Hitler's obsession with Operation *Barbarossa*, a line loyally followed by Wenneker.

Wenneker became aware of Japanese concern about Anglo-German co-operation in 1935 and was taken into the confidence of the Japanese navy about its ambitions in the south in the autumn of that year – after he had secretly photographed a report on Anglo-Japanese naval relations since 1922 (lent to him by the British naval attaché, Captain Vivian) and indicated to his Japanese contacts that it viewed the Japanese navy as 'second-class'. In May 1936, Wenneker produced a detailed report on the role of the Japanese navy in the February Incident, highlighting the deep rivalry and potential conflict that existed between the Japanese army and navy in matters of domestic politics.[42] In the course of the summer of 1936, following Japan's withdrawal from the London Naval Conference, Wenneker was also briefed at length and most explicitly by the pro-German chief of staff of the Combined Fleet, Admiral Nomura Naokuni, about the fundamental opposition of the Japanese navy to the anti-Soviet policy of the Japanese General Staff and Nomura later confirmed that the Navy had sanctioned the Anti-Comintern Pact with Germany only after it had received assurances from the Army that it was intended as a purely defensive arrangement.[43]

The Soviet embassy in Tokyo made it clear to the German embassy that it was aware of the text of the Secret Annexe to the Pact even before it had been passed on by the German Foreign Ministry. The defection of Walter Krivitsky to Britain in 1937 indicated that the Red Army General Staff had succeeded in penetrating the *Abwehr* and in obtaining full details of the secret efforts of General Ōshima Hiroshi, the Japanese military attaché in Berlin, to persuade the Germans to join in a staff agreement with the Japanese army against the USSR based on an existing convention between the Japanese and Polish General Staffs.[44] At the end of 1936, the head of the *Abwehr*, Admiral Canaris, discovered that unaccompanied diplomatic bags passing through the Soviet Union were being opened and secretly resealed by the Soviet security authorities. Warnings were passed to Japan to follow the German example of organising military couriers to carry diplomatic pouches between Berlin and Tokyo and to submit reports on their observation of military targets along the Trans-Siberian Railway. Subsequent evidence of Soviet knowledge of Japanese activities convinced the German Foreign Ministry that the USSR was reading Japanese diplomatic messages in the course of 1937, and appropriate warnings were passed on. Post-war confirmation that Soviet agents were obtaining access to Japanese code materials prior to 1945 was later obtained from the wife of Soviet defector Petrov, who revealed to the Australian security service that she had worked as a Japanese translator in the KGB central decryption agency in Moscow during the Second World War.[45] The USSR was ideally placed to intercept German or Japanese cable and wireless traffic between Europe and the Far East, especially after the outbreak of war in 1939, but resolution of codes was made easier by secret photography of code materials by means of break-ins and by employing listening devices in official and private residences of diplomatic and military personnel. The techniques were most effectively used from the autumn of 1941, when all foreign diplomats were forcibly moved from Moscow to already prepared premises at Kuibyshev. No firm evidence about Soviet capacity to read German or Japanese machine cyphers has so far been confirmed, though there is the possibility of the leakage of material from Bletchley Park via the Soviet agents planted in MI 5 and MI 6.

The 'Ramsay Group' in Japan, however, functioned throughout the period 1933–41 with varying access to Sorge's sources in the German embassy and to the contacts of the Japanese agents in the ring to the Konoe administration and the Japanese army. This was certainly of considerable assistance during the Sino-Japanese War after July 1937 and during the border incidents of 1938–9, when information from Japanese policymakers and Soviet defectors was of assistance in the timing of the offensives of the Red Army in August 1938 and in May and August 1939. The strong resistance of the Japanese Navy Ministry to the strengthening of the Axis alliance was confirmed along with the Navy's conviction that Britain was the key factor in prolonging Chinese resistance. Captain Lietzmann's continuing contacts with Admiral Nomura and officers in the Naval Staff and Navy Ministry, following the Soviet–German Non-Aggression Pact, corroborated the sense of betrayal about Hitler's deal with Stalin felt within the Japanese army – especially among the most ardently anti-Soviet officers. But the contacts paradoxically provided encouragement in Berlin in the form of the welcome given by the Japanese navy to German accommodation with the USSR through indications of greater willingness on the part of the Army to concentrate on ending the war in China and of providing greater support for the Navy's economic goals in South-East Asia – with their risk of conflict with Britain, France, the Netherlands and the USA. Stalin's accommodation with Hitler temporarily lessened the risk of a German attack in the east through a diversion of German warmaking capabilities westward. But the bloody nose given to the Japanese army in Outer Mongolia discouraged its appetite for a two-front assault on Soviet territory and stimulated the possibility of greater willingness to reach an accommodation with the USSR and to divert Japanese expansionism more firmly to a southward course.

Given the dearth and destruction of much of the evidence regarding Stalin's thoughts on the threat of Germany and Japan combining against the USSR, any assessment of the real nature of the threat is bound to be full of imponderables. Certainly, there were plenty of statements reiterating Soviet determination not to yield an inch of territory without a fight. The purges of the

Red armed forces undoubtedly did create a great deal of ambiguity about the credibility of such statements. Given the absence of a common frontier between Germany and the USSR prior to the subjugation of Poland, there was a sense in which a Soviet–Japanese showdown may have been an inevitability as opposed to some kind of rational choice, though knocking out the weaker ally is a logical move if one is uncertain of the capabilities of one's own side. No doubt, Stalin played his hand with great skill, delaying the knock-out blows with superb timing shortly before the onset of winter in order to minimise or eliminate the likelihood of counter-attack. On the other hand, it demonstrates a preference for reliance on the natural elements rather than on the fallibility of interpretation of any intelligence gathered.

Given the consistency and forcefulness of the determination of the Japanese navy leaders to veto any major conflict with the USSR, it is possible to argue that the strategic threat was low regardless of Stalin's actions. Strong pressure was exerted by the Navy and its allies on the central Japanese army authorities to deny tank and aircraft support and reinforcements to the 6th Army in order to eliminate the possibility of a wider conflict. There is no doubting the credibility of Soviet determination to defend every inch of territory so far as the Japanese were concerned. It had much less of an impact on Hitler in Europe, since concern about the Finnish–Soviet conflict and its ambiguous impact obscured the significance of the decisive defeat of the Japanese in the Far East. A prime Japanese casualty in Europe had been General Ōshima, who was withdrawn from Berlin at the end of 1939 and not replaced with an alternative Japanese confidant as able as himself to bend Hitler's ear or even provide an authentic account of events. The humiliation was largely kept from the general public in Japan, but it had a significant effect in swelling the numbers of Japanese who mistrusted Hitler and in convincing many people within and close to the army and the radical nationalist groups at home of the correctness of the navy's long-held contention that the costs of a northern strategy substantially outweighed any economic or territorial benefits that might accrue from military victory over the Russians.[46]

In the aftermath of the Russo-Japanese War, it was frequently claimed by Ōkuma Shigenobu that it had been the Japanese repulse of Tsarist expansionism in Asia that had forced the Russian leadership to refocus their attention on the Balkan problem and spared Japan the ill-effects of the First World War. There would appear to be a similar phenomenon attending Stalin's confrontation in Outer Mongolia in decisively impelling the Japanese leadership to shift their expansionist urges from North-East to South-East Asia, except that it appears to have had virtually no impact on Hitler's long-term aims in the east save to ensure that *Barbarossa* was postponed by a further two years. Hitler's comments about the USSR after August 1939 are full of rueful regret and resentment, and Matsuoka's adviser, Shiratori Toshio, hit the mark precisely in a discussion with Admiral Wenneker on 16 August 1940:

> An understanding, whether it be a non-aggression pact or whatever, is the pre-condition for any positive move to be taken against any third party. However, he regarded it as off the mark to believe that any such understanding could last for long, just as he was moved to see the understanding between Germany and Russia as of only short duration.[47]

DICHOTOMIES OF STRATEGIC RATIONALE

An important component of the Japanese navy's strategic thinking about the North-versus-South argument lay in contentions about the profitability of war. Japanese experience of expansionism after 1868 had been significantly shaped by the fact that winning wars under the old imperialist rules entitled the victor to the spoils of war, normally at the expense of the loser. For everyone in the imperialist system, however, a clear distinction had come to be made between the short victorious war and the war of attrition, and the European experience tended to be one where attrition and loss had predominated. In the Japanese case, the balance of profit and loss had been more even. But navy leaders tended to be more influenced by the dangers of attrition and the need for caution. They could point to the low or negative return, particularly in past deadly quarrels with the Russians and the drain currently being suffered in those with the Chinese; they had had fights with other Europeans – such as the Germans and Austrians in China and the Pacific – dismissed by German observers as an example of peripheral, colonial warfare. Experience of fighting alongside or observing European and American military performance had largely been a matter of judging how to come out on the winning side.

There was much discussion of Japan at the crossroads and of choices that would have fateful consequences, not least because 1940 marked a notional 2,500 years of the Imperial system as well as the more immediate dilemmas posed by the changes taking place in the European balance of power. Even before the European war broke out, the Italians had been able – on the basis of intercepted British communications – to predict to their German and Japanese colleagues that an Axis combination would force Britain to make hard choices about which areas of Imperial defence would be given priority. They felt confident that all the colonial areas in South-East and East Asia, including Singapore and the Philippines, would be extremely difficult to defend in the event of war in Europe.[48] The image of the effete aristocrat and the soft plutocrat readily floated across the propagandists' imagination and contrasted sharply with that of the hardened proletarian automata regimented by pitiless dogmatists.

Certainly, the pattern of prioritisation in Japanese strategy towards the USSR had been one of repeated postponement of an 'inevitable' showdown throughout the 1930s, reinforced by the reverses that had occurred whenever action on the ground had been attempted. The ultranationalist groups, which in the early 1930s had clamoured most for war with Russia and had experienced tough repression by the police and judicial system, came to terms with the social and economic disciplines imposed by the needs of the war in China and became far more concerned with anti-Western than anti-Soviet agitation by the late 1930s. These agitators and assassins were effectively used by the military bureaucrats as populist organisers of public demonstrations and publicists, as bully-boys to silence opposition and, with the prospect of US embargoes after July 1939, were increasingly employed as procurers of goods and manpower at home and abroad, by any means of enforcement, to service the demands of the war economy and enrich themselves in the process.[49]

The Italian intervention in the war was widely viewed as ill-judged opportunism, and the Japanese were conscious that the image of 'corpse-stripper', which might also be attached to them if they moved too precipitately, would be an 'abhorrent' one. As Matsuoka put it on his tour of Europe in the spring of 1941, the image of the man who entered the tiger's lair to steal its cubs was infinitely preferable for Japan. Nevertheless, the German victories in western Europe unquestionably exercised a major influence over Japanese thinking. Most attention under the post-war historical orthodoxy has been paid to the impact of the fall of France on the role of the Japanese army and its efforts to regain the political initiative at home. What has not been adequately understood is how far the Japanese navy was impressed by the earlier events in Norway, when the tenfold British naval superiority on paper had been frustrated and beaten by local German air superiority.[50] Close study of this convinced both the Fleet and the Naval Staff that a maximisation of Japanese land-based and carrier-based air power would mean that they need no longer fear the US Pacific Fleet, even if it were superior on paper. The surrender of France and the entry of Italy into the war indicated the decreased likelihood of Britain being able to mount offensive fleet operations from Singapore. This was substantially corroborated by the Germans' hand-over to the Japanese on 8 December 1940 of an intercepted British Chiefs-of-Staff memorandum on British options in the event of a Japanese entry into the war.[51]

The Japanese ambassador in London, Shigemitsu Mamoru, tried to commend a more cautious middle-of-the-road rationale, suggesting in August 1940 – on the basis of his observations of closer Anglo-American relations and of the territorial gains made by the USSR without any firm commitment to Germany – that Soviet policy should serve as the ideal role-model for Japan and that Japan should resist the demands for adhesion to the Tripartite Pact.[52] German pressure on Japan called for tokens of commitment as justification for sharing the colonial spoils of war, for behind the charade of Hitler's gleeful dance of victory at Compiègne lay a clear note of resentment that the Japanese, as well as the Russians, Italians and Americans, would profit from German commitment of blood and iron. The timing of the signature of the Tripartite Pact with the Franco-Japanese accord on Indo-China was Matsuoka's token gesture of reciprocity: in practice, however, the Japanese navy's opposition to the Pact was waived principally by virtue of the Army's agreement that funds would be made available to implement the completion of the Fleet's offensive air capabilities.[53]

In order to protect his personal position within the Nazi hierarchy, von Ribbentrop had been prepared to secure Japanese adhesion almost at any price. It was an invitation for the Japanese to set down their own agenda of demands, the most important of which was that Japan would unilaterally decide whether and under what conditions it would enter the war. There was almost no concession whatever to the concept of reciprocal obligations in their alliance with Germany and Italy (not so dissimilar to the post-war alliance with the USA. It is hardly surprising in such circumstances that there was such a limited basis for mutual trust and positive collaboration. Hitler's peace overtures to Britain and the earlier volte-face in his dealings with Stalin provoked suspicion that Japan ran the risk of being left to face the music alone against Britain and the USA at the whim of a dictator.[54] Contrary to what was believed in London and Washington, Japan saw itself as far from dependent on Germany. The German victories convinced the Japanese navy that it could wage a successful war against the United States provided that it retained independent control over its own resources and that the broad parameters of the new international balance of power were sustained.

While there were some – such as Shiratori and Matsuoka – who suspected strongly that the accommodation would not last for long, the bulk of the Japanese establishment felt there was plenty of room within the wide spectrum of thinking for naïvety to co-exist quite happily with the arrogance and cynicism emerging at this time – when the air was riven by triumphant cries about a 'redivision of the world' and a variety of 'New Orders'. Japanese demands for German support in the transfer of advanced technologies and resources could be given lip-service when stated as a general concept, but their actual delivery proved to be a far more difficult task than perhaps anyone could have foreseen. Closely bound up with it was the Japanese demand for German support in the matter of persuading or deterring the Soviet Union from 'interfering' in East Asian and Pacific affairs.

Out of touch with the rationale of the factions in the Japanese army as a result of Ōshima's removal from the scene, Hitler's conclusions about the triumph in western Europe mirrored the superconfidence of the Japanese navy. Throughout the 1930s Hitler had accepted the rationale of the Japanese army officers, who had made the Nazi leadership a target of influence, that a joint German–Japanese assault on the Soviet Union would be sufficient to eliminate Bolshevism. This had been denied by his General Staff and the denial was reiterated by Colonel Ott in conversation with Hitler during the autumn army manoeuvres in 1936, by which time Britain (and later Poland in an approach organised by Admiral Canaris at Ōshima's suggestion) had rejected 'a crusade against any ideology'.[55] Ott and Hitler agreed to differ about the value of a military alliance with Japan, arguing that only time would tell, and Ott received instructions subsequently to urge the Japanese to keep their sword in its sheath until such time as they were strong enough to use it.[56] Hitler read a detailed report from Ott's successor, Colonel Gerhard Matzky, about the difficulties encountered in persuading the Japanese to enter into an unrestricted alliance with Germany against the USSR and Britain. Matzky concluded that the Japanese probably felt that they did not absolutely need to conclude an alliance with anyone since they tended to prefer to attain their objectives by their own independent efforts.[57] Not surprisingly, Hitler had already made up his mind to do without Japanese or Italian assistance and go it alone. There appears to be no record subsequently of Hitler expressing any disappointment or regrets about the lack of Japanese support.

His decision in the summer of 1940 to attack the USSR involved no consultation whatever with the Japanese, even though they had direct experience of conflict on a large scale with the Red Army and Air Force. The ease and scale of the German victories in the West had provided the most convincing background of all of likely German prowess against the Soviet Union.

As Hitler later remarked to Ōshima, he recalled personal anecdotal evidence about the ease with which his Brownshirts had put superior numbers of German Communists to flight.[58] Even later, Ribbentrop recounted to Ōshima how Hitler had resisted the entreaties of his colleagues and advisers about the danger of suffering the same fate as Napoleon by saying that there was every risk that the nation would grow fat and soft if he shirked his responsibility while he retained his vigour.[59] His resentment at the Japanese not being prepared to pull their weight and the effrontery of their demands for German technology in what was tantamount to 'an intellectual sell-out', together with the long time-lag between his 'irrevocable' determination to attack the Soviet Union and to open hostilities, all contributed to not apprising the Japanese of his decision even during the presence of Foreign Minister Matsuoka in Europe in March – April 1941. At the conclusion of the visit, a circular to the German armed forces reported that Matsuoka had indicated that there was still a degree of opposition to be overcome in domestic politics in Japan to the highest degree of co-operation with the Axis states and noted that

> Matsuoka clearly had a special interest in ascertaining what view was held in Germany about Soviet Russia. The following alternatives were commended to him in making such a judgment:
> a) If the Soviet Union behaved itself, then everything would actually be fine; but, if on the other hand,
> b) it behaved badly, it must be 'neutralised'.
> From outward appearances, Matsuoka is supposed to have given no sign of having taken in the full meaning of b). But people who know him, especially the German ambassador in Tokyo, Ott, estimate that Matsuoka is too sly a character for that to be doubted.[60]

Given that for months rumours had been circulating in Moscow and other capitals about the massing of German troops in the east, the decision to delay briefing Germany's allies greatly assisted Admiral Canaris and the *Abwehr* to carry out their brief of maximising confusion about the direction of the main offensive.[61] Japanese military attachés in Europe, meeting in Berlin at this time, all favoured the likelihood of a descent on the British Isles, except for the military attaché in Stockholm, General Onodera, who was working closely with the representatives of the Polish General Staff there responsible for liaison with the Home Army in occupied Poland.[62]

Ott, who accompanied Matsuoka to Europe, was apprised of Operation *Barbarossa* by the new German military attaché in Tokyo, Colonel Kretschmer, who had scrutinised Soviet issues in the 1920s and who remained in touch with his predecessor, General Matzky, now head of the Intelligence Division of the General Staff.[63] Sorge obtained information from Colonel Scholl, who passed through Tokyo on his way to a new posting as military attaché in Thailand from 1 June, and from military couriers as well as from his embassy contacts, who included the Gestapo attachés, Huber and Meisinger.[64] But as everyone now knows, Stalin's chief of military intelligence fed Stalin's assumptions about the irrationality of an attack, while both Churchill and Roosevelt similarly convinced themselves and each other of the irrationality of a Japanese attack.[65]

FROM DICHOTOMY TO DIVERGENCE

Stalin's handling of the international crisis of 1939, combined with the threat of US economic sanctions, helped stimulate greater convergence of views between the Japanese navy leadership (which was virtually solidly united in opposition to war with the USSR) and the groupings in the Japanese army concerned about the trends in the conduct of operations in China. Since the Sino-Soviet Non-Aggression Pact of 1937, the USSR had been the main provider of aid and volunteers to China.[66] The navy groups with the greatest interest in a convergence of Army – Navy policy on China were to be found on the staff of the 2nd and 3rd Fleets, of the Naval Air Inspectorate and of the Japanese Naval Mission in Shanghai (headed by Admiral Nomura Naokuni, who had briefed the German naval attaché in Tokyo, Captain Joachim Lietzmann, on the value of German intercession on behalf of a *rapprochement* between Japan and the USSR). The Japanese Naval Staff specialist on China, Commander Fujii Shigeru, was chosen by the Navy to accompany Foreign Minister Matsuoka to Europe to keep an eye on him and to ensure that he would seek a culmination to the negotiations for a non-aggression pact or some other suitable means of achieving *détente* with Stalin *en route* through Moscow on his way to and from Europe.[67]

Largely as a result of Lietzmann's reporting, Ribbentrop and the Armed Forces High Command in Berlin (OKW) had been pursuing the notion of encouraging the USSR to support the war against Britain and France, suggesting that the USSR seek to expand its interests and influence over Iraq and Iran (at British expense and despite Hitler's reservations). The move, however, did nothing to divert the USSR from taking advantage of Hitler's back being turned in the west by demanding the cession of Bessarabia by Romania – the main source of German crude oil imports – in addition to all the other territorial changes in eastern Europe that Germany had already conceded in existing secret agreements. When the build-up of German forces in the Balkans was becoming clearer in February 1941, the Soviet Military Attaché in Belgrade confirmed that the USSR would tolerate any German offensive into Greece and Turkey, aimed at occupying Iraq.[68]

Soviet–Japanese negotiations, aimed initially at settling the problems arising out of the Nomonhan battles, moved rather fitfully forward because of the need to negotiate fisheries and trade questions, as well as the matter of a non-aggression pact. The initiative for determining the scope and momentum of these discussions lay firmly with Moscow, although the German defeat of France also took the Russians by surprise. Matsuoka was able to capitalise on the new strategic situation by seeking to use German support in the context of the signature of the Tripartite Pact to put pressure on China to reach a secret peace agreement and on the USSR to reduce or eliminate Soviet support for China. Molotov promised to sort out difficulties with Japan and Italy only after sorting out German–Soviet problems. Ribbentrop proposed an arrangement under which the USSR would be linked to the Axis by means of protocols, drafts of which were prepared in advance of Molotov's visit to Berlin in mid-November 1940.[69] Like the Japanese protocols for British adhesion to the Anti-Comintern Pact in 1936, the German proposals were dropped in the face of Hitler's determination to have no further truck with the Soviet Union beyond squeezing it as hard as possible in order to extract the maximum demands for the supply of foodstuffs, fuel and raw materials required for further pursuit of the war.

The Soviet evasion of any commitment to help liquidate the British empire was compounded by a similar vagueness in the Japanese response to German demands for a Japanese seizure of Singapore, by US Lend-Lease measures and the re-election of Roosevelt and by Italian reverses in Greece and Egypt. It was hoped that Matsuoka might come to Berlin with concrete operational proposals. But when he arrived in Berlin, Ambassador Ott reported to Ribbentrop that the discussions he had attended with General Sugiyama Gen (the Japanese army chief of staff) and Admiral Kondō Nobutake (the Navy vice-chief of staff) before he left Tokyo indicated the likelihood of preparations for war in the south being completed by the end of May 1941. Matsuoka, however, emphasised that freedom in the rear from Soviet pressure was the decisive question for Japan and linked it to the early dispatch of an economic mission to Japan under Helmut Wohlthat.[70] The German side noted that Matsuoka had set aside a week for a further stay in Moscow in pursuit of a diplomatic compromise, following an extremely critical speech by Molotov on 29 March in which he denounced Japan's temporising and lack of will about the signature of a non-aggression pact. The Soviet demands included the retrocession of south Sakhalin and the Kurile Islands in return for a non-aggression pact, demands which were completely unacceptable. The alternative of a neutrality pact in return for the ending of economic concessions on north Sakhalin, which had previously been rejected by the Russians, was pursued, but the decision not to tie it to any counter-demands of the Japanese – the result of a personal intervention by Stalin – attracted considerable comment.[71]

Through the use of heavy hints the Germans had tried to dissuade the Japanese from pursuing these options, but in an atmosphere where no one believed anyone else, it is scarcely surprising that the power of truth had become a long-outmoded concept in all societies. Following a discussion with Admiral Kondō, Admiral Wenneker reported, that the agreement had been particularly welcomed by the Japanese navy, which has always actively supported it, as a clarification of the position with the Soviet Union has long been the primary and most significant precondition for any operation against the South. People are struck particularly by the fact that the Russians have not named their price to Japan so far. People have pointed mainly to the major German successes in the Balkans and the German troops assembled along the Russian frontiers as the explanation for the unwonted Russian willingness to be accommodating. At some later date they must anticipate Russian counter-demands.[72]

The Japanese army's hopes for any commitment by the Russians to a reduction in aid to the Chinese were, however, little affected until the German attack on the Soviet Union. Subsequent interrogation of Soviet officers employed as advisers in China showed that approximately 300 were employed at divisional level or as pilots and air support staff in the period shortly before the agreement. Their mission was defined as part of a strategy of 'weakening the Japanese and in so doing divert their attention away from the [Soviet] Far East'.[73] Efforts to employ the Germans, who still retained a diplomatic mission at Chungking, to threaten a recognition of Wang Ching-wei unless Chiang proved more accommodating at secret Sino-Japanese peace talks proved fruitless. According to Admiral Toyoda Teijirō, the Navy vice-minister, the Japanese initiative for peace had already broken down well before the end of 1940 as a result of the hardening in relations between Japan and the USA, especially since the Tripartite Pact.

The movement of Soviet forces from Central Asia to Europe during 1941 appears to have been influenced to some degree by the neutrality pact with Japan rather than by the intelligence reports of people such as Dr Sorge. Force levels in the Far East in the areas assigned to the 1st and 2nd Red Banner Armies were maintained at a high level throughout 1941 because, as German interrogations of Soviet captured personnel showed, Soviet strategy in the event of a Japanese intervention was geared to an offensive drive against the north Manchurian salient because of the need to prevent the principal supply route, the Trans-Siberian rail link, from being overrun.[74]

When questioned about Japanese intentions by Colonel Kretschmer in May 1941, Japanese General Staff officers indicated that they still saw the conclusion of the war in China as important to them prior to undertaking any new tasks. Asked if a US entry into the war against Germany would result in an immediate acceptance of the obligation to declare war, Colonel Akita Hiroshi hedged by saying that Japan would recognise its obligation in principle and was prepared for attacks on Singapore and Manila, but was not yet ready to open hostilities immediately. He said that if a German–Soviet war occurred and provoked a US entry into the war, then preparations for attacking Vladivostock and Blagoveshchensk would be made in addition to Singapore and Manila.[75]

The response from the Japanese navy, however, to similar questions from Admiral Wenneker pertaining to US moves to protect convoys across the North Atlantic and the increased likelihood of conflict, was much less positive on 10 June. Wenneker reported that the attitude of senior navy officers was that, if a *casus belli* occurred, Japan would consult with its allies, but no one felt any need for an immediate entry into the war unless it was clearly in Japan's interest. While the Navy was prepared for war, there was concern that any attack on Singapore would automatically drag the USA into what could only be a protracted war. It was also claimed that the Army was not ready for a war in the south and that it had decided not to participate in any Soviet–German conflict for the foreseeable future.[78] This exchange followed receipt of the news from Ambassador Ōshima about his briefing by Hitler on the impending outbreak of the German–Soviet war, news about which had been streaming in from Europe for many weeks.

Hitler's choice of timing when breaking the news of the impending attack on the USSR to Ambassador Ōshima on 3 June 1941 was particularly inopportune from the Japanese point of view. Army and Navy had been actively co-ordinating their policy aimed at maximising peaceful penetration of South-East Asia since the end of 1940, in the expectation that Germany would undertake landing operations in the British Isles some time in the spring or early summer of 1941.[77] Matsuoka's argument that the Army and Navy would be ready for operations against Singapore by May was geared to a stable international environment and the Neutrality Pact seemed to have secured stability in Soviet relations with Japan. For their ally to threaten to pull the rug from under their feet at a time when their horizon seemed unprecedently clear was extremely unsettling. Hitler's argument was that Germany was doing Japan a favour: his attack would provide the Japanese with security in the rear far more reliably than could be achieved by diplomatic means. Instead of being grateful, however, the Japanese navy in particular complained that 'in the event of such a conflict, one of the fundamental principles on which the Three Powers' Pact was based will disappear'.[78] Since the Navy had managed to take the Army with it on the path towards an encirclement of China by beginning to close down Anglo-American access to China from the south and by moving closer to obtaining alternative sources of economic and technological supply to the Anglo-American capitalist system, the German plans effectively instituted a major divergence of interest between the two countries.

Economic and Technological Culs-de-Sac

Much attention has been paid to the economic causes of the Pacific War and the emphasis on the full-scale boycott and embargo policies adopted by the United States and its allies against Japan in July 1941. Most of that emphasis has been concentrated on the denial of fuel and raw materials. Relatively little has been said about Japanese access to advanced technology. Closer examination of this indicates that US advanced technologies had been selectively and deliberately withheld from Japan and other countries for a very long time indeed. If we look at a technological system that was to play a key role in the Japanese offensives against the western powers, namely the aircraft-carrier, we can see that the US already tried to put pressure on Britain in the early 1920s to deny these skills to the Japanese navy.[79] In the early efforts at Anglo-German *rapprochement* in the 1930s, the German navy had repeatedly requested access to British aircraft-carriers without success. Knowledge of this came to Japanese attention in late 1934 or early 1935, and the Japanese navy – concerned lest Anglo-German *rapprochement* interfere with Japanese hopes for the growth of conflict in Europe – agreed to provide Germany with access to the technology in the course of 1935.[80] By 1940, the most advanced aerial torpedoes in the world had been developed in Japan, and access to the technology was supplied to Germany in 1941 in the hope that it would be used to reduce the imbalance in naval power between Britain and the European Axis and ensure that Britain would be unable to dispatch substantial numbers of capital ships to the Singapore base.[81]

Russia had been a significant market for Japan prior to 1918 when intervention in Siberia and the ideological opposition to the spread of communism had frustrated efforts to develop the tightly controlled market in the USSR and contributed to mutual mistrust. The USSR, on the other hand, became a highly important market for German heavy industrial goods and military technology in the inter-war period. Even when Hitler ordered a drastic reduction in trade after 1933, influential groups in both countries continued to do business under cover and frequently hankered for the restoration of the previous relationship. Trade with the USSR eased the economic pressures that Germany experienced at the hands of the French and their allies in the 1920s and during the Great Depression. Hitler's desire for an autarkic economic system imposed restrictions that made it extremely difficult to regulate Germany's relations with the other major economies in the international system, which contributed substantially to the hand-to-mouth financing of its national economy and to subsequent resort to conflict with its neighbours and temporary relief through the seizure of their assets. Even the defeat of France was a mixed economic blessing as Germany had to find ways of obtaining resources from outside the European economy it controlled, in order to keep the whole functioning.

The economic resources of European Russia provided a convenient supply on Germany's doorstep, and transit of goods through the USSR was valuable for providing access to markets in China, the Americas and South-East Asia restricted by Allied controls over the world's oceans. The Japanese economy was even more constrained by the paucity of its domestic economic resources and its dependence on overseas markets. The Japanese military aspired to controlling China as a means of achieving an autarkic system, but never possessed the scale of capital for investment to achieve this, even if the Chinese had proved much more compliant with Japanese wishes. From 1939, the prospect of independent prosperity was dimmed even further by wartime restrictions on world trade and US threats to existing access to US-controlled resources. The impediments to German domination of Europe were seen by Hitler as increasingly dependent on seizing the resources of the USSR, while the impediments to Japanese domination of East Asia were seen as increasingly dependent on seizing the remainder of China and South-East Asia. But these aggressive seizures indirectly or directly threatened the interests and security of the USA. Whereas the German economy was sufficiently mature to find substitutes for many goods through technological adaptation, this was far less the case for the Japanese economy. Skills and resources that could have been forthcoming from the USA to promote technological adaptation, however, were likely to be completely denied by continued threats to US interests and territory, and the only possible alternative source lay in Germany – to which access would be possible only overland via the USSR. Although, for Germany, control of Soviet territory would provide access to a range of essential materials – such as natural rubber and tin, less easily obtained elsewhere – Japan absolutely needed to find vital access to German mass-production techniques and machine-tools (seen as the key bottleneck in the Japanese economy in 1941) and a whole range of advanced technology, weapons systems and processes via Soviet territory.[82]

So far as the Japanese navy was concerned, the bulk of the raw materials essential for the Japanese war economy could be obtained in East and South-East Asia and not on Soviet territory. Close examination of the Soviet Asian area had shown that the short-term economic prospects were far from ideal and that the physical, capital and manpower costs of seizing and holding the area were likely to be insuperable.[83] If Japan moved northward, there was every likelihood that the Red Air Force would be in an ideal position to bomb the main centres of Japanese industrial production and be reinforced easily from North America. By contrast, seizure of the Philippines and the

European colonies in South-East Asia would increase the distance between Japan and the principal territories and bases of its enemies.

Japanese Assessments of German Strategy

Although many in the Army, not least General Okamoto Kiyomoto, the head of military intelligence, believed Hitler's claims that the USSR could be subdued in a matter of weeks rather than years, others in the Army were sceptical.[84] It was also strongly denied by the Navy. When Hitler's argument about providing Japan with total security in the rear was put to Captain Mitsunobu Tōyō, the Japanese naval attaché in Rome, soon after the outbreak of war in the east, he expressed deep scepticism to his German colleague, Captain Löwisch, on 25 June and 1 July. He argued that even if German forces succeeded in occupying Moscow and destroying the military production capabilities in European Russia, the Soviet authorities had prepared their defences in depth beyond the Urals and such losses would 'not deliver a fatal blow'. Rather, the German forces would face the kind of experience met in the interior of China by the Japanese army which now faced 'in a vast and barely accessible hinterland an enemy which will resort to the means of guerrilla warfare which tie down vast numbers of one's own troops without being able to bring about a decisive military victory'.[85] The mobilisation and reinforcement of the Kwantung army that had followed the opening of the German attack on the USSR (*Kantōkuen*) led to substantial increases in the number of Soviet forces stationed along the Manchurian and Mongolian frontiers, with women and children being withdrawn from the frontier areas behind the many fortified lines constructed since the early 1930s.[86] Mitsunobu observed on 10 July: 'While the Russians had organised substantial troop transfers from Siberia to the Russian western front prior to the outbreak of the German–Russian war, such troop movements were no longer being observed after the outbreak of war. Russian forces in Siberia would be held in the Far East against Japan.'[87]

While the Japanese army's reactions demonstrate quite clearly a willingness to exploit the situation to its advantage, what comes across most clearly in the contemporary statements of Japanese navy personnel abroad in the first half of 1941 is their anxiety about the predictability of the outcome of whatever German moves would be made in the European war before they were in a position to launch their own attacks. In late 1940, the US Pacific Fleet units had been observed mainly refitting in West Coast bases and this posed no threat of US intervention. By the time they returned to Hawaii, the Japanese navy leadership believed that the US would provide maximum assistance to Britain short of their own involvement in the war. But all the talk of German landing operations against the British Isles or the possibility of seizure of the Suez Canal in the summer months betrayed deep worries that that could induce the USA to intervene in the war against the European Axis, something that the Japanese Navy feared as 'premature' and unwanted from their point of view. They wanted an even and balanced set of conditions in relations with both the USA and USSR so that the move southward would develop smoothly and not disturb the equilibrium of Navy–Army planning.

If one looks only at the development of Japanese army policy in the first six months leading up to the decision to occupy southern Indo-China – a decision ratified at the Imperial Conference on 2 July 1941 – and does not examine the parallel Navy policymaking, it is easy to fail to spot that the divergence between the north and the south in Japanese strategy was fatefully sealed in favour of the south in the period between 13 April and 6 June.[88] This was precisely the period during which Hitler observed silence about his true intentions in the east and the tilt in favour of navy priorities ensured that economic necessities would prevail over ideological preferences, whereas in Hitler's case both coincided. By 10 June, Admiral Wenneker was able to confirm this on the basis of conversations with various middle-ranking officers in key positions in the Naval Staff and Navy Ministry: 'Contrary to previous reports, the Japanese Army will not take part in a German–Russian conflict for the foreseeable future because it is evidently not prepared for this. The Navy approves such a decision.'[89]

Scepticism about Hitler's true intentions continued within the Army even after the Hitler – Ōshima meeting on 3 June, and Matsuoka only made his play – ending in his isolation and resignation – after Ribbentrop sought to intervene in favour of a Japanese commitment to a joint strategy directed at the USSR. There is no indication that Hitler really shared such an initiative. At his meeting with Ōshima on 14 July, Hitler argued that both Russia and the Anglo-American states would be enemies of both Germany and Japan and that they should seek to eliminate them together. 'He is saying this,' Hitler added, 'not because he needs support. He can wage this struggle alone. But he is thinking of the future of Japan. The moment when we defeat Russia will also be fateful for Japan.'[90] Hitler's confidence in going it alone at this stage knew no bounds. European Russia was expected to collapse within six weeks. He believed that, if Moscow fell, the rest of the USSR would collapse, but he was prepared to pursue the surviving Soviet forces beyond the Urals and into Siberia, anticipating a last stand in the region of Omsk. In conclusion, he expressed a readiness to take a lead in the struggle against the USA, if necessary, but ended by arguing that, if Germany and Japan worked hand in hand to crush the USSR, they would keep America out of the war.

By 23 August at a meeting with Ribbentrop, Ōshima observed that Japan had made preparations for both a northward and a southward advance simultaneously, but would not (as in the summer of 1939) be able to mount offensives in both directions simultaneously. Ribbentrop was content with the thrust of this argument, but wanted the Japanese to reverse the existing strategic priorities from south to north. By this date, when it was clear that Hitler's timetable was wildly optimistic, Ribbentrop had introduced the idea that it might be 1942 before Russia was eliminated and Hitler's own view had veered towards hoping for Japanese intervention before the winter.[91] His preference, nevertheless, appears to have been for the Japanese to keep everyone uncertain of their real intentions, as it helped force the Russians to tie down substantial resources in the Far East that might otherwise be released to their western front, as well as operating as a deterrent to US intervention against Germany while the conflict in the east remained unresolved. Only after the Japanese were committed to war with the USA was Hitler prepared to sanction the transfer of advanced technologies desired by the Japanese armed forces.[92]

The view expressed by Admiral Wenneker in late 1940 that a Japanese entry into the war would be more advantageous than disadvantageous for Germany – on the grounds that Japan would have to bear the main burden of a Japanese entry and that Germany was to all intents and purposes at war with the USA already – may not necessarily have been shared by Hitler at that date.[93] But it was certainly shared by Hitler a year later, not least as a result of the impact of Operation *Barbarossa* on the United States. Captain Mitsunobu had expressed his view on 10 July about the conflict that 'since 22 June the probability of an early American entry into the war had increased' and mentioned that Japanese intelligence gathered in the US mainland pointed to the conclusion that 'the entry of the USA into the war must be expected in a few months' time'.[94]

This hardening of US attitudes was also noted – though welcomed – in Britain by the Joint Intelligence Committee (JIC) which had set up an Axis Planning Section in March 1941, following agreements at a joint Anglo-American conference on an exchange of intelligence. Whereas assistance short of war had been noted in January, by July it was evident that the USA had become convinced that the German attack on the Soviet Union was a decisive turning-point in the war, encouraging the USA to believe that an Axis defeat was inevitable. Reports reached the navy in Japan that the USA was 'said to be making preparations for the war to last two years'.[95] Shortly before the outbreak of the Pacific War, it was confirmed in information leaked to the press by the US air force that plans had been drawn up after the Roosevelt – Churchill meeting at Argentia in August 1941 for US landing operations against the European mainland. The assumption appears to have been made at this early stage that the Japanese also realised that the German move in the east was likely to prove disastrous and consequently that caution would prevail in Japanese counsels and would deter any precipitate move by the Japanese. It was also believed that Japanese actions were largely dependent on German capabilities, but it was not until some months later – in November 1941 – that a study of the intercepted Japanese diplomatic decrypts convinced Allied analysts that Hitler's failure to convince the Japanese to reverse their strategic priorities meant that they would pursue their own independent goals.[98] The realisation that the Japanese were intent on continuing their advance southward, however, still obscured – and probably helped to obscure – the fact that the southward drive was contingent on a successful surprise attack in an easterly direction by the Japanese Combined Fleet. The disappearance of main fleet units from British monitoring of radio tracking in the middle of November, which was also picked up by the US navy, was brought to US notice by means of a letter from the chairman of the JIC, Victor Cavendish-Bentinck, contrary to claims in recent years that Churchill deliberately withheld knowledge of an attack on Pearl Harbor from Roosevelt.[97] By the end of November 1941, intercepts of Japanese diplomatic exchanges with Berlin indicated Japanese intentions to enter the war against the USA, as well as Britain, and German preparedness to support Japan no matter what the *casus belli* by means of a no-separate-peace agreement.

The long-drawn-out effort to deter the USA from intervening by means of the diplomatic negotiations in Washington was a last-gasp effort to prevent the major powers in the Far East from uniting against Japan. The Japanese navy had realised from long operational planning that the USA was the key country capable of unifying opposition to Japanese expansionist plans. But the Japanese navy had argued – on the basis of the experiences of war in Europe from the summer of 1940 – that it need no longer be constrained by its thinking (since 1907) of a defensive posture in the face of US fleet superiority, especially as the European Axis effectively eliminated British offensive capabilities in the Far East.

The main problem in the strategic equation in the Pacific was to seek to prevent a Soviet – American united opposition to Japan, the threat of which first arose in 1934 at the time of their normalisation of diplomatic relations. The existence of sizeable Soviet bomber forces in Far Eastern bases, together with their possible reinforcement by US bombers via the North Pacific, constituted a not inconsiderable danger to the Japanese home islands. Even after signing the Neutrality Pact, but especially after the German attack, worries were expressed by Japanese navy planners about the unification of these offensive forces and co-operation between submarines of the Soviet Pacific Fleet and of the US Asiatic Fleet in interdicting seaborne communications with the Asian mainland. The denuding of the defences of the homeland through a dispatch of the Combined Fleet to Hawaii and of the 2nd Fleet to the Gulf of Siam – because of the need to maximise the offensive capabilities of naval strike forces – posed a major risk. The choice of December for the outbreak of hostilities was designed to minimise the risks of any Soviet invitation to lease air and naval bases along the Japan Sea coast to the USA, but coincided exactly with weather conditions that enabled Stalin to organise transfers and exchanges of equipment and units between Europe and the Far East with minimum risk of Japanese intervention.[98]

CONCLUSIONS

An important test of the effectiveness of any combination of forces ranged against the Soviet Union lay in the willingness of the parties to commit themselves to simultaneous co-ordination of capabilities in Europe and the Far East, whether such capabilities were directed at attacking or defending against the USSR. The Japanese had been disappointed that any willingness on the part of the French and Poles to co-operate closely against the USSR in the 1920s was almost totally dissipated by 1931. This encouraged the move towards a *rapprochement* with the Nazi Party in 1932, which was sustained in subsequent years by the knowledge that the Franco-Soviet Mutual Security Pact excluded the Far East. Anglo-Soviet negotiations in 1939 saw no advance in this direction at a time when the USSR and Britain were under more immediate armed threat from Japan than from Germany. After the German attack in June 1941, the JIC in Britain put forward proposals for the establishment of intelligence collection facilities at Vladivostok, and the US gave indications of a willingness to intervene in support of the USSR against Japan at the time of the *Kantōkuen* build-up in Manchuria. However, the Soviet Union gave no indication of a willingness to allow Allied forces on its territory, especially not in the Far East, beyond the facilitation of measures to import raw materials and aircraft. The import of arms and military equipment was reserved strictly to the import routes through the Arctic and the Persian Gulf to ensure that no provocation would be offered to Japan.

Knowledge of the unlikelihood of Soviet – American military collaboration against Japan was retrieved by Japan not only via bilateral diplomatic channels, but also through the interception and decryption of parts of US State Department radio traffic between Washington and Moscow by the 9th Section of the Japanese Naval Staff in the late autumn of 1941.[99] How far there was active secret collusion between Japan and the USSR, however, may only be obtainable from former Soviet archive sources, yet to be disclosed. It is certainly the case that repeated claims made by Admiral Wenneker in August and October 1941 that Japan would definitely not attack the USSR were leaked back to the Soviet Union by Dr Sorge and the 'Ramsay Group' prior to their arrests in mid-October. There was a naval *kenpei* group assigned to the German embassy for security purposes at this date, and on 4 November Captain Maeda Tadashi of the Naval Staff informed Admiral Wenneker of suspicions about leaks of information from the office of the German Naval Attaché in Tokyo.[100] Maeda gave a reassurance that the content of his numerous meetings with Wenneker since early October did not appear to have been leaked to the British Intelligence Service, as was the case with two non-German employees of the *Abwehr*'s War Organisation at Shanghai. It is far from clear, however, if such a statement ruled out – perhaps deliberate – leaks of information to the Soviet Union, especially as the raid on the premises of Max Clausen, Dr Sorge's radio operator, yielded coded text and corresponding clear-language messages that could readily confirm indications of Japan's real intentions.[101] Understandably, there would have been concern to avoid discussion in the documentation generated by the police and prosecutors involved in the subsequent trials about the most secret aspects of the case, such as telephone surveillance, bugging devices and decryption at the time. The accessible Japanese and US records, however, do not give much indication of these secret aspects and it is not at all clear what has been withheld by US agencies, let alone what was withheld from US agencies by the Japanese, not least because the case was deliberately politicised by the US Occupation authorities in 1947 in order to influence the attitudes of the Congress and the media towards the USSR.[102]

Soviet and East German agencies, in turn, sought to politicise the activities of Richard Sorge and Ozaki Hotsumi and their associates for their own purposes from 1964 onward. The claim was frequently made that information from Sorge's group enabled the Soviet Union to transfer forces from the Far East to European Russia and help prevent the fall of Moscow, but the weight of evidence tends to refute this. Evidence from Japanese sources, for example, suggests that significant transfers occurred in the spring and early summer of 1941. While there is evidence from German sources that some Central Asian troops began arriving in the Tikhvin section of the frontline in early September, the main Red Banner armies in the Far East were placed on maximum alert from August onward in positions designed for *offensive* operations against any Japanese intervention. In the winter of 1941, many units were sent from the frontline to re-form in the Far East in exchange for fresh divisions when the Siberian winter virtually ensured that the Japanese could not launch attacks. It was probably only in the winter of 1942–3 that trained manpower was diverted in large numbers to the Stalingrad front. It led Ribbentrop to complain bitterly to the Japanese about letting the Russians off the hook. On 8 March 1943, we have one of the few clear statements of Hitler's attitude toward his Japanese allies. When discussing the military situation in the Far East, Hitler remarked particularly on Japanese secretiveness:

> The *Führer* continued that if there was really anything in the wind, we would never hear of it. If they drew attention to the fact that they had an operation on in the South, he would sooner believe that they were up to something in the North rather than in the South. He had said to the Foreign Secretary: 'My dear Ribbentrop, they will operate when and as they please!' As long as they noticed that the Russians were withdrawing forces, they would say with Asiatic cunning, 'Let him bleed'. But as soon as they noticed that the Front was becoming stabilised over here, and that reinforcements were being sent to the East, one would see how quickly they toed the line and how soon they were there.[103]

Ribbentrop functioned primarily as an intermediary between Hitler and Ōshima in matters connected with Japan and was not really capable of providing either independent or accurate knowledge about Japanese policy. He relied far too heavily on the partisan views of Ōshima, who skilfully manipulated Ribbentrop as a means of influencing Hitler. However, Hitler was also receiving his own private information, garnered by the Security Service (SD) and the *Forschungsamt* from electronic surveillance of the Japanese embassy and its communications, which indicated that Ōshima was not always fully briefed by Tokyo. He also tended to represent the viewpoint of the Japanese army and was viewed with mistrust by the Japanese navy and the *Gaimushō*. The operational feats of the Japanese navy genuinely astonished Hitler. But there are many signs in surviving records that Japanese navy officials in Berlin continued to complain that the significance of the Navy, with an alleged control of 80 per cent of Japanese heavy industry, was still being underrated by foreign observers because they continued to be duped by the pretensions of Japanese army representatives even after Pearl Harbor.[104]

This low profile, however, served to protect Japanese navy personnel in post-war relations with the US Occupation since US study of relations with Germany was intensified in the period between the end of the war in Europe and the end of the war in the Pacific for operational purposes and continued in the context of the war crimes tribunals, not least because so much of the surviving Japanese archives was deliberately destroyed prior to the arrival of US forces. It helped, too, that General Willoughby, MacArthur's intelligence chief, spoke fluent German and could converse directly with General Staff specialists who had spent time on duty in Berlin. The navy historians could consequently observe a discreet silence about their Russian policies and play up the confusing complexities of factional rivalries between those who thought the USA could be deterred and those who were convinced from an early stage of the need to pursue an offensive strategy against the United States. Even less attention was paid to how the Japanese navy sought to persuade the German leaders from 24 October 1941 that their Russian policy had failed and that they ought to make peace with the USSR through Japanese mediation in order to concentrate the combined Axis war effort against the western powers. The high profile of the Army as an antagonist of the USSR, on the other hand, was successfully transplanted from the alliance with Germany to the prejudices of MacArthur and his 'lovable fascist', Willoughby, who regaled US public opinion with tales of Red conspiracy every bit as blood-curdling as those about a fascist conspiracy with which J. Edgar Hoover had fed the Congressional Committees on Un-American Activities. It provided the window of opportunity for the discredited political right in Japan and Germany to persuade the United States taxpayer to shoulder the burdens of the Cold War, but while joining fulsomely in the anti-Soviet rhetoric, restoring their shattered national fortunes throughout four decades of superpower gridlock.

Notes

AA	Foreign Ministry (Germany)
CAB	Cabinet Office papers (UK)
CIC	Counter-Intelligence Corps (US)
COS	Chiefs-of-Staff (UK)
DMI	Director of Military Intelligence (UK)
DNI	Director of Naval Intelligence (UK)
GRU	Directorate of Military Intelligence (USSR)
IPS	International Prosecution Section, Tokyo Tribunal
JIC	Joint Intelligence Sub-Committee (UK)
KGB	Directorate of Security (USSR)

OGPU   Directorate of Security (USSR)
OKH   High Command of the Army (Germany)
OKL   High Command of the Air Force (Germany)
OKM   High Command of the Navy (Germany)
OKW   High Command of the Armed Forces (Germany)
OSS   Office of Strategic Services (USA)
RKM   Ministry of War (Germany)
SD   Security Service (Germany)
SIS   Secret Intelligence Service, MI6 (UK)
SOE   Secret Operations Executive (UK)
USNR   United States Naval Reserve

1. 'Fifty Years After: The Pacific War Re-examined', Lake Yamanaka, Japan, 14–17 November 1991. The author is grateful to the International House, Tokyo for its invitation to participate as a commentator, as well as to the Japan Foundation Endowment, the British Academy, the Japan Society for the Promotion of Science and the Canon Europe Foundation for support of the research in this chapter. In line with Japanese practice, the Japanese family name is given first, followed by the given name.

2. See B. N. Slavinsky, 'The Soviet Occupation of the Kurile Islands and the Plans for the Capture of Northern Hokkaidō', *Japan Forum*, 5, no. 1, Apr. 1993, pp. 95–114, which is based primarily on the Central Naval Archive of the Soviet Ministry of Defence. The official Japanese account is in Bōeichō, Bōei Kenshujō, *Senshi Sōsho*, vol. 44 (*Kita-Higashi Hōmen Rikugun Sakusen – 2*) (Asagumo Shinbun-sha, Tokyo, 1971).

3. See Jonathan Steele, 'Japanese Graves Hold Last Secret of Stalin's Gulag', *The Guardian*, 10 Aug. 1993.

4. See *Senshi Sōsho*, vol. 52 (*Rikugun Kōkū no Gumbi to Unyō – 1*) 1967, pp. 30–110 and maps 1–2 for background information on the Siberian Expedition. Captain Malcolm D. Kennedy, in charge of the Japan desk in the War Office (MI 2c) from April 1921, recorded in his diary contacts with Major R. B. Denny who had organised the supply of arms and funds to the Ataman Semeonov in 1918. Denny had been awarded the OBE for this work, 'but never boasted about it!' *Kennedy Diary*, vol. 2, pt 9, pp. 19–21 (University of Sheffield Library). Subsequently Semeonov was taken over by the Japanese and reports of atrocities became rife after the Nikolaevsk massacre. In 1941, proposals for a reciprocal evacuation of civilians between the UK and Japan in the event of war were put forward by the Foreign Office via the chairman of the Joint Intelligence Sub-Committee, Victor 'Bill' Cavendish-Bentinck, 7th Duke of Portland. See Public Record Office, Kew: Minutes of the JIC, 31st Meeting, 7 Nov. 1941, CAB 81/88.

5. *Senshi Sōsho*, vol. 8 (*Daihonei, Rikugun-bu – 1*) 1967; vol. 27 (*Kantōgun – 1: Tai-So Gunbi, Nomonhan Jiken*) 1969; vol. 53 (*Manshū Hōmen Rikugun Kōkū Sakusen*) 1972; A. D. Coox, *Nomonhan* (Stanford UP, Stanford, Calif., 1985; *Istoria Velikoi Otechestvennoi Voini Sovetskogo Soyuza SSR* (Voenizdat, Moscow, 1960) vol. I, pp. 231ff.

6. See R. J. C. Butow, *Tojo and the Coming of War* (Princeton UP, Princeton, NJ, 1961).

7. Author's correspondence and discussions with Captain Roger Pineau USNR (retd), Washington DC, December 1989.

8. One example comes in the handling of the interrogation of Admiral Kondō Nobu-take, former vice-chief of the Naval Staff and commander-in-chief, 2nd Fleet, as active a supporter of the alliance with Germany as Ōshima had been. Interrogators who spoke to him put no pressure on him and told him he would not be prosecuted, but he kept very silent indeed about his political role prior to his fleet appointment in September 1941. Navy Captain Ōtani Inaho, who had played an important role in navy procurements in China and had worked closely with the notorious ultranationalist Kodoma Yoshio, was arrested on charges of larceny in February 1946, but was not prosecuted. His diary clearly indicated his involvement in pro-tecting the interests of former navy personnel and careful monitoring of the activities of the US navy in occupied Japan. A case was instituted which looked into the history of navy corruption, but again no prosecutions followed from it. Kodama and Sasagawa Ryōichi, who had both opened up close links with the Navy after 1940 and were widely reckoned to be the two individuals who had profited most from the war, had contacts with Admiral Yamagata, head of the Navy Air Force Office, and Admiral ōnishi Takejirō, deputy Minister of Munitions, as well as with Admiral Yamamoto Isoroku, the Fleet commander-in-chief. National Archives, Washington DC, Record Group 319/IRR Files (hereafter abbreviated to NAWRG).

9. B. van Poelgeest, 'The Netherlands and the Tokyo Tribunal', *Japan Forum*, 4, no. 1, Apr. 1992, p. 89; A. Cassese and B. V. A. Röling, *The Tokyo Trial and Beyond* (Polity Press, Oxford, 1993).

10. The USSR contingent attached to the IPS was among the last to arrive in Tokyo and the name of General Umezu Yoshijirō was the last added to the list of defendants at its insistence. IPS Exhibits 835–8 contain Soviet records of interrogations or affidavits of Japanese personnel captured in Manchuria or Korea and more detailed documentation can be seen in NAWRG 331, Allied Operational & Occupation Headquarters, World War II, which show an increasing tendency after 1945 to be more concerned about the ideological reliability of informants than about the content of their information.

11. Ibid. for materials on the Yokohama, Manila, Shanghai and other US-organised trials. Soviet trials relating to the Far East were held at Khabarovsk in December 1949. For details of British trials in SE Asia, see the compilation by Dr R. J. Pritchard, *The British War Crimes Trials in the Far East, 1946–1948*, 21 vols (Garland Publ. Inc., New York, forthcoming).

12. General Arisue was the first person to welcome General MacArthur at Atsugi Airfield on 2 September 1945. He served as head of the Intelligence Division of the General Staff in the years 1943–5 and actively organised a group of advisers for General MacArthur during the Korean War period. See Arisue Seizō, *Za · Shin-chūgun: Arisue Kikanchō no shuki* (Fuyō Shobō, Tokyo, 1984).

13. Report by 441st CIC Detachment, 25 Apr. 1952. NAW/RG 319/IRR File XA509530. The author is grateful to General Arisue, General Sugita Ichiji, Lieutenant-General Miki Hideo and Major-General Onodera for information provided in interviews and correspondence between 1986 and 1989, as well as to former Administrative Vice-Minister Hōgen Shinsaku, one of the late General Tatsumi's executors.

14. See J. Chapman, 'Commander Ross RN and the Ending of Anglo-Japanese Friend-ship', *International Studies*, 1985/III STICERD/LSE, (London) pp. 34–56. The 4th Division of the Red Army General Staff (GRU) had penetrated the *Abwehr* and reports on Ōshima's negotiations with Canaris, Ribbentrop and von Blomberg for a secret staff agreement were being passed on to Krivitsky in Amsterdam. But as Krivitsky's organisation was being kept under surveillance by the SIS, an offer was made to him to defect which he accepted. He was given a new identity and a refuge in Huddersfield for a year before moving on to France and the United States. Lord Gladwyn (Jebb), interview with NHK TV, Feb. 1987.

15. Ushiba was 1st Secretary and Furuuchi 3rd Secretary in the Japanese embassy in Berlin during World War II. Ushiba's brother was compromised by association with Ozaki Hotsumi, a key informant in the 'Ramsay Group' of the GRU in Japan, headed by Dr Richard Sorge. Ushiba was subsequently head of the Economic Department and Administrative Vice-Minister in the *Gaimushō*. Furuuchi ran unsuccessfully as a candidate for the Diet in 1966.

16. See particularly the case of General Ishii Shirō and his colleagues in the chemical and biological weapons testing activities of Units 100 and 731, the results of which were largely kept from the Soviet Union as a result of the intervention of the War Department in Washington. See P. Williams and D. Wallace, *Unit 731* (Hodder & Stoughton, London, 1989).

17. A series of monographs was prepared by the Demobilisation Bureaux in Tokyo for the Military History Section at Headquarters, US Armed Forces in the Far East. Holdings were moved in 1952 to the Department of the Army in Washington DC and eventually transferred to the Library of Congress. In the 1960s, all Japanese Army and Navy documentation in US hands was returned to Tokyo and from 1967 the Defence Agency in Tokyo began publishing the definitive *Senshi Sōsho* series of monographs cited in n. 2 above. For a contemporary commentary on the preliminary deliberations about the series, see the memorandum prepared for the UK Cabinet Office by Colonel G. C. Wards, former British assistant military attaché in Tokyo: Wards Papers, Imperial War Museum, London.

    In charge of the compilation of earlier monographs relating to the history of the Japanese navy was Rear-Admiral Tomioka Sadatoshi, who appears to have fallen out with the official historians in the Defence Agency because it had become dominated by former army personnel. He then set up a private naval historical institute, the *Shiryō Chōsa-kai*, which continues to be run by former naval officers in Tokyo.

18. A detailed analysis of the Incident was compiled by the German Naval Attaché in Tokyo for the War Ministry in Berlin, in which he revealed that fleet units, marines and ground attack aircraft had been mobilised at Shibaura, Osaka and Yokosuka by the Navy, which demanded that the Army clean up its act or the Navy would strike at the mutineers unilaterally. See Wenneker memorandum, 'Haltung der Japanischen Marine während und nach den Februar-Ereignissen', in secret report *B. Nr. 230/36g* of 6 May 1936 in Reichskriegsministerium hereafter RKM, Marine-Archiv, M Att: 'Attaché-Berichte Tokio, 1936', vol. 1 (Original in the Militär-Geschichtliches Forschungsamt (hereafter MGFA), Freiburg-am-Breisgau; microfilm copies at the Ministry of Defence, London and National Archives. Washington DC.) This was compiled mainly from information provided by officers in the Navy Ministry and the Combined Fleet. It confirmed earlier contentions that the Japanese navy wanted defensive measures in the north and expansionism in the south, theoretically by peaceful diplomatic means. But Wenneker insisted that the Japanese navy wanted to eliminate economic dependence on the western powers and he 'expects such an expansion *by force* definitely to take place at the moment when Britain is seriously tied down by a conflict in Europe'.

19. See Sakai Tetsuya, 'Nihon Gaikō ni okeru Sorenkan hensen', *Kokka Gakkai Zasshi*, 97, nos 3–4, 1984. Soviet diplomatic reports from Tokyo referred to Army – Navy rivalries and access to leading members of the Russo-Japanese Society in Tokyo (Gotō Shimpei, a former home minister and advocate of an alliance of Japan, the USSR and Germany in the 1920s; Admiral Saitō Makoto, prime minister from 1932 to 1935; Admiral Katō Kanji, a former chief of Naval Staff and naval attaché in Russia). See *Dokumenty vneshnei politiki SSR* (National Diet Library, Moscow, 1965–1970) vols 10–16; *Saitō Makoto Kankei: bunsho, mokuroku* (Kokuritsu Kokkai Toshokan, Tokyo 1967).

Captain Wenneker reported a tour of Japanese fleet vessels in the course of June 1936 and evidence of major changes in Japanese naval policy from conversations with fleet officers, especially the chief of staff, Rear-Admiral Nomura Naokuni. These indicated that Britain had now become a significant target as a future opponent for the first time in operational planning and that the Navy would not be taken in by British efforts to encourage Japanese–Soviet conflict: 'the Navy would regard a war with Russia as a national disaster.' Wenneker report *B. Nr. 237/36g* of 26 June 1936, seen by Grand-Admiral Raeder and War Minister von Blomberg in RKM, Marineleitung, M Att: 'Attaché-Berichte Tokio, 1936', vol. 1.

20. The scale of Soviet armaments and plans for future expansion became a steadily more worrying factor in Japanese army and navy calculations and this was even more clearly spelled out in Germany as a result of German involvement in the provision of military and aviation equipment to the Soviet armed forces. As the two countries did not share a mutual border, there was less immediate concern on the part of the German army. But German aviation circles became greatly alarmed and the unpalatable facts about the huge scale of production greatly outstripping maximum German production in World War I and the capacity to project Soviet airpower offensively unhindered by land frontiers could be ignored even less as a result of the devastating effects of the Great Depression on the German aviation industry, especially as it had been a known target of Soviet espionage since 1928. See Felmy top-secret note of 28 October 1931 enclosing a memorandum from the President of the National Association of the German Aircraft Industry (Rear-Admiral Lahs) of 19 August to the Defence Minister on the desperate need for government support, confirmed as accurate by General von Mittelberger. Felmy note *In 1 Nr. 1098/31 III geh. Kdos* of 23 Nov. 1931 enclosed a detailed report from a German engineer, Tschersich, on the booming state of the Soviet aviation industry, which he wanted kept absolutely confidential, as he feared reprisals if the Soviet secret police learned about it. MGFA, Freiburg, RH12-1, vol. 105, pp. 196–211 and 156–94.

21. Because of Japanese army support for Poland and France against the Soviet Republic in 1919 and German support for the Bolsheviks against the western powers, there had been no return to the former collaboration between the German and Japanese armies. Japanese military and naval missions had been sent to Berlin in 1919 and attaché posts created, but no German attachés were appointed until the end of 1932. There had been secondments of military officers to friendly countries, which accelerated from 1928, but not with Japan as it was feared that it could alienate the Chinese, with whom an increasing intimacy developed from 1927 onward. Three Japanese army officers were finally allowed to be seconded to German army units in 1931 and for the first time since 1914, the Intelligence Section of the General Staff compiled a manual on the Japanese army: see Fischer note *T3 III/Ia 100/31* of 15 Jan. 1931 and Bamler memorandum *T3 III 469/30g* of 4 July 1930 in Auswärtiges Amt, Bonn (hereafter AA), Abteilung IV Ostasien, Akte Po. 13: 'Militärische Angelegenheiten in Japan', vol. 2, Jan. 1927 – Nov. 1932.

22. Reporting on the plans for the reform of the Japanese army, the German *chargé* in Tokyo, Otto von Erdmannsdorff, stated that the press had contained details of the Army's opposition to any cuts in its budget prior to the opening of the Disarmament Conference in Geneva. The Army called for increases of 60 and 30 per cent in air power and war material respectively in view of the fact that Russia had one million and China 1.5 million men under arms. The suggestion was also made that

Japan should put forward a proposal at the Conference to release Germany from the obligations under Article 160 of the Treaty of Versailles. In view of the continuous Soviet spending on economic and military preparations, Germany

must have a strong army in order to help keep Russia in check in the west, especially in view of the fact that the military capability of Poland must be regarded as slight.
Foreign Minister Shidehara reassured the French and Belgian ambassadors that there would be no such support from the *Gaimushō*. See von Erdmannsdorff report J. No. 1657 of 28 July 1931, relayed to the German Defence Ministry on 27 Aug.: ibid.

23. The German industrialist, Fritz von Thyssen, head of the Vereinigte Stahlwerke conglomerate, provided funds to Ferdinand Heye – who had headed a small company in Manchuria in the 1920s that allegedly engaged in the illegal opium trade before going bust – as a lobbyist. Heye approached Goering, the leading Nazi in the *Reichstag*, in late 1931 with proposals for expanding German trade in North-East Asia in collaboration with Japanese interests. Thyssen's companies apparently had been heavily involved in barter arrangements under which arms and industrial products were exchanged for the very substantial Manchurian exports of soya beans to Germany, which were routed via a holding company in Denmark. The Japanese takeover torpedoed these arrangements and Heye lobbied the Japanese embassy for the sale of items such as Zeppelins via Goering and Rosenberg.

    The Nazis were the only party in Germany which openly endorsed the Japanese invasion of Manchuria and took sides against the Chinese. Rosenberg's colleague, Schickedanz, met Japanese Ambassador Obata Yukichi in the spring of 1932 and explained Nazi aspirations in the Ukraine. The much-expanded bureau of the Japanese military attaché in Berlin was full of ultranationalist hotheads who complained that Obata was failing to advocate the Japanese case properly and forced his recall. Thyssen and other industrialists were constantly pressed to make contributions to Nazi electoral funding and there are indications that Hitler was receiving funds from Japanese sources.

24. The assistant military attaché in Berlin, Major Okamoto Kiyomoto (1894–1945), was reported to be in close touch with ex-servicemen's associations and right-wing parties, including the Nazis. The Soviet minister in Berlin, Alexandrovskii, claimed that White Russian organisations in Europe were recruiting *émigrés* to serve with the Ataman Semeonov and adverts appeared in the press in Berlin for recruits. The popular press picked up such an appeal in Nazi circles with a reference to 'SA Gendarmes in China', on 2 May 1932 and the attention of Ambassador von Dirksen was drawn to this in Moscow by Litvinov, particularly referring to the suggestion that negotiations were being conducted between the Nazi Party and the Japanese embassy in Berlin. This was subsequently denied by Okamoto. AA, Abteilung IV Ostasien, Akte Po. 3: 'Politische Beziehungen zwischen Japan und Rußland', vols. 6–7.

    While the Nazi Party in Manchuria was the first to be formed in the Far East (1931), a number of prominent Nazis had been recruited on the recommendations of Goering to the German military advisory mission in China following the death of Colonel Max Bauer in April 1929. One of these advisers was a pilot named Fritz Moellenhoff, who had served as an artillery spotter for Chiang Kai-shek's forces on the Lunghai front in the anti-Communist encirclement campaign in 1930 and who subsequently went on to Manchuria to volunteer his services to the Ataman Semeonov and was contacted in Shanghai by Dr Sorge. It has been claimed that Sorge succeeded in obtaining details of the code-book employed by the military advisers for communication between the Nanking HQ and the front. See Karl Mader, *Dr. Sorge-Report* (Militär-Verlag, East Berlin, 1984) pp. 93 ff.

25. Lieutenant Bamler, who had been the desk officer responsible for compiling the General Staff handbook on the Japanese army in 1930, was transferred subsequently to *Abwehr IIIf*. A long-standing contact of counter-intelligence in Berlin was Dr

Friedrich Hack, a Japanese-speaker whose links with the Japanese armed forces stretched back to 1919 and who was involved as a middleman in the sale of Heinkel aircraft until 1936. He is credited with introducing General Ōshima to Joachim von Ribbentrop in 1935. See J. Chapman, 'A Dance on Eggs: Intelligence and the "Anti-Comintern" ', *Journal of Contemporary History*, 22, No. 2, Apr. 1987, pp. 334 ff. After 1945 Bamler pursued his military career with the East German army.

26. Bamler – Czibulinski telephone conversation of 8 April, 1932. On 15 April, Bamler sent a map showing the disposition of Soviet and Japanese forces in the Far East, asking for information on the location of specific divisions. See AA, Abt. IV OA, Akte Po. 3: 'Politische Beziehungen zwischen Japan und Rußland', vol. 7. Czibulinski was a reserve officer who had served as a diplomat in Japan and was at this time China desk expert in the Foreign Ministry in Berlin. Shortly after this, the General Staff issued a study on the Soviet–Japanese confrontation, which concluded that war was unlikely as 'any relatively calm appraisal of the situation indicates that no vital interests are at stake on either side'. On 9 May 1932, Bamler received information from Colonel Banzai Heihachirō, the Japanese military attaché in Berlin, about the transfer of Soviet units to the Far East and relayed it to the Army and Navy commands in *Abw. IIIf Nr. 214/5.32g*, which appears to mark the opening of a regular exchange of military intelligence between the two countries. It was followed up by exchanges of views with Japanese military attachés in Moscow and with the central authorities in Tokyo after German attachés were appointed in 1933.

The German Naval Command had maintained correspondence with a network of agents in the Far East during the 1920s, but this had been discontinued in 1929. Members of the military advisory mission in China maintained correspondence with serving officers who travelled to Shanghai via Siberia, and a small number of top-secret reports from unidentified correspondents sent to China were circulated by the *Abwehr* to the chiefs of staff. *Abw. 3/32 GKds* of 9 Jan. 1932 contains an extract from a letter sent from Harbin on 11 December 1931 and retailing information on the conflict in Manchuria and rumours of coming conflicts between Japan and its neighbours. *Abw. 60/32 GKds* of 18 Apr. 1932 relays information from Shanghai about the fighting there and contains an eye-witness account of atrocities against unarmed Chinese civilians in the Shanghai Racecourse by Japanese officers and men.

27. German Foreign Ministry instruction *IIF 40* of 12 Jan. 1933 to Tokyo, in: AA, Büro RM: 'Militärwesen', vol. 3, 1933–5. Ambassador Voretzsch in Tokyo, who spoke scathingly in his reports about the appearance of a variety of mania among the Japanese military which he termed 'megalomania Japonica', showed little interest in encouraging invitations from the Japanese General Staff to participate in man' uvres. When told to prepare for the posting of a naval attaché to Tokyo, Voretzsch passed on the view of other naval attachés that 'in view of the complete secrecy maintained by the Japanese about all matters of any interest, the material accumulated by the attaché during his stay is likely to be practically nil'. The Foreign Ministry declined to pass on a copy of this report to the Defence Ministry because of its 'pontificatory form'.

28. Negotiations between the German Defence and Foreign Ministries over the regulations to be observed by attachés took place between December 1932 and February 1933. Ott was involved in arranging briefings by the *Abwehr* of the first of the new attachés in early March 1933, after which he was replaced by Alfred Jodl. See Ott statement of 15 Nov. 1945 to Andrew B. Puskas of the OSS, sent to the CIC in Tokyo on 29 Jan. 1946. Ott revealed that the suggestion about Manchuria came from his wife in an off-the-record answer to questions from Lieutenant-Commander J. D. Shea on 18 Feb. 1946: see NAW/RG 331, Case File No. 324/Serial 106, and Serial 9, pp. 19–20.

29. See memorandum by 1st Lieutenant G. R. Splane jun. of the US Army Signal Corps of 13 Apr. 1946. The *Abwehr* contacts are not named, but are stated to be individuals who 'actively intrigued against Ott while he was German Ambassador to Japan', but appear to be two journalists, Ivar Lissner and Werner Crome, who suffered at the hands of the Japanese military police (*kenpei*). They claimed that Helma Ott had been married to an architect, Ernst May, who was a Communist city councillor in Frankfurt-am-Main and who divorced her and then left for Moscow. Ibid., Serial 61. Mader, *Dr. Sorge-Report* p. 140 states that Ott married her in 1921 and that she was the daughter of a lawyer, Dr. Robert Bodewig.

30. Marie-Therese von Hammerstein-Equord is referred to in correspondence between the police attaché in Tokyo, Meisinger, and the Gestapo in 1942–3 as the eldest daughter of General von Hammerstein. According to Gestapo central files she had been a member of the German Communist Party, employing the cover name of 'Maria Stein' and connected to the Soviet assistant military attaché in Berlin. She and her husband, Jochem Paasche, who was allegedly half-Jewish, had lived in Tokyo since November 1935 and were suspected of being Soviet intelligence operatives. AA, Inland IIg: 'Ostasien – Deutsche Agenten', vol. 1, 1941–2, p. 105.

31. Mader, *Dr. Sorge-Report*, p. 140, basing it on Sergei M. Golikov, who had evidently made a rendezvous with Sorge in Berlin in the Spring of 1933.

32. Ott had proposed to go to Nanking to make contact with the advisory mission, but was ordered to have a more discreet meeting in Shanghai instead. See AA, Abt. IV OA, Po. 13: 'Militärische Angelegenheiten Japans', vol. 3, 1932–5.

33. Ott left Nagoya in early August 1933 and Sorge arrived in Tokyo from Canada in September. It is possible that this is the result of confusion of Richard Sorge with Wolfgang Sorge, who was a journalist for the Scherl press in Manchuria and Japan at this period. See Splane memorandum (n. 29) and F. W. Deakin and G. R. Storry, *The Case of Richard Sorge* (Chatto & Windus, London, 1966) p. 138. The latter do, however, point to Sorge having a letter of introduction from Dr Zeller of the *Tägliche Rundschau* to Ott. Sorge initially stayed at the Sanno Hotel, where Ott is recorded as being a guest in October 1933, but Ott himself gave 1934 as the date when he first got to know Sorge.

     Ott's contacts with the Kwantung army in AugustSeptember 1933 included dealings with Japanese undercover agencies and could scarcely have avoided discussion of the Soviet military threat. Ott was certainly in contact with the *Abwehr* on his return to Berlin in early January 1934 and his report on his experiences in Manchuria and Japan, no longer extant, would have been widely circulated within the Defence Ministry. He was invited by Defence Minister von Blomberg to give a 20-minute report to Hitler prior to his departure for Tokyo as military attaché-designate. Von Dirksen, as ambassador in Moscow, had made friends with his Japanese colleague, Hirota KŌki, on instructions from Berlin. His stepmother was an acolyte of Hitler and had ambitions for von Dirksen to be appointed foreign minister. As with Ott, von Dirksen was introduced to Hitler by von Blomberg and von Neurath and urged by Hitler to develop closer relations with Japan with a view to eventual co-operation against the USSR. Ott – Shea interview (note 28 above), pp. 21–4, which suggests that Hitler had read Ott's report closely. Von Dirksen's letter of 4 Feb. 1934 to State-Secretary von Bülow records Hitler's oral instructions and Hitler's encouragement of efforts to negotiate economic advantages in return for the recognition of Manchukuo: AA, Geheim Akten Abt. IV OA: 'Mandschurei: Anerkennungsfrage', 1933–6. The Defence Ministry advised Ott to try to remain in Tokyo until von Dirksen arrived by sea on 16 December.

34. Hartmann (Moscow) *B. Nr. 4/34* of 31 Jan. 1934, in AA Geheim Akten, Abt. II F-M: 'Militär-Attaché Moskau (auch Kowno)', vol. 2, 1934. There was concern in the Foreign and Defence Ministries in Berlin about complaints arising in China and

the USSR about rumours of a German–Japanese *entente*, which threatened the preferential position of German trade and industry in China. Because of his close identity with the 'von Schleicher clique', Ott was viewed with deep suspicion by von Seeckt and his circle and von Seeckt did everything he could to discourage Ott from pursuing efforts by the Japanese General Staff to use the advisory mission in Nanking as a channel of pressure on Chiang Kai-shek.

35. AA, Abt. II F-M; Akte M6: 'Verhandlungen über die Entsendung von Militär- und Marine-Attachés', 1932–5; 'Militär-Attaché Tokio', 1933–6.

36. Ott visited Manchuria next in October 1934 and attended Japanese army man' uvres but so little of his reporting for 1934 survives in the archives that we are unsure how far an exchange of intelligence about the USSR had progressed. He was particularly active in promoting trade in industrial goods and arms to Manchuria in 1934 and 1935 during major trade missions to the Far East.

37. The Foreign Ministry in Berlin complained that it had had no copies of any reports by Ott during his first year in Tokyo, despite the service regulations stipulating that reports of a military-political variety should pass through the hands of the head of mission and be copied to the Foreign Ministry. See Frohwein letter *zu II M 720* of 23 May 1935 to Counsellor Noebel in Tokyo: AA, Geheim Akten, Abt. II F-M: 'Militär-Attaché Tokio'. Noebel and Ott had defended an interpretation of practice in the Tokyo embassy that was deemed unacceptable and the Defence Ministry had supplied a selection of out-of-date reports for Foreign Ministry files. However, these were among records that were partially burned at the end of the war and rescued documents show burning at the edges. The main files were in the *Heeresarchiv* at Potsdam and everything dating from before 1940 was evidently destroyed by Allied bombing in 1943. Some departmental files which contain occasional references to military information about Japan survive, including observations about intelligence-gathering by the Japanese army in countries on the Soviet periphery.

38. Captain Scholl arrived in Tokyo at the end of June 1935 and submitted to Ott a summary of the observations he had made in the course of his trip by rail across Siberia. This was incorporated in Ott report *B. Nr. G 124* of 5 July 1935, when Ott reported the good effect that the German announcement of rearmament had had on the Japanese army, which thought that it would have a major impact on the Red Army and would exercise a restraining influence on it in the event of a Soviet–Japanese conflict. In early August, he reported an unaccustomed openness on the part of Colonel Wakamatsu, the General Staff desk specialist on Germany, in matters of foreign policy. By the end of October General Ōshima, military attaché in Berlin since the spring of 1934, had submitted the draft of a staff agreement directed against the USSR to Canaris and von Blomberg. Shortly beforehand, Ott proposed that the Japanese army be invited to provide data about the Red Army and support for the German trade mission in return for extensive Japanese visits to German industry and military establishments.

Ōshima and the Army raised objections in 1938 and 1940 to the promotion of Scholl as military attaché in succession to Ott and Matzky, claiming he was too vain and too clever by half, according to Ōshima in conversation with Ribbentrop in 1942 and to post-war statements by Major-General Kretschmer. AA, Büro RAM, Handakten von Loesch: 'Japan', 1936–43, Items J/50–J/52; von Weizsäcker memorandum of 4 Apr. 1942, where the most damaging evidence about Ott and Scholl was supplied by Secretary of Legation Karl Otto Braun (b.1910), in AA, Büro RAM, 'Dr. Richard Sorge', 1942; Kretschmer interrogation, NAW/RG 331, Case File 324; *Gendai-shi ShiryŌ*, vols. 1–3 (*Zoruge Jihen*) (Misuzu ShobŌ, Tokyo, 1962).

39. Author's interviews and correspondence with the late Frau Irma Wenneker and Fräulein Ingeborg Krag. Admiral Wenneker sent a top-secret cable, *Nr. 11/42 Chefs.* of 27 July 1942, that was intercepted by the Allies, in which he mentioned that he

and Ambassador Ott had been closely linked to Sorge and that it had led to Japanese mistrust of them. Unfortunately only an abstract of the content of the cable is given in translation and a continuation of the signal was not processed by the US navy. NAW/RG 457, Series SRLG, p. 0297. Clausen statements to CIC on 5 Dec. 1945 in RG 319/IRR File XA50243.

40. This is asserted by Mader, *Dr. Sorge-Report* p. 326, but with no evidence to back it up.

41. Author's interviews with the late Rear-Admiral George C. Ross, British assistant naval attaché in Tokyo, 1934–6, who showed the author copies of dinner menus with the signatures of von Dirksen, Wenneker, Ott and Sorge.

42. A summary of Vivian's translated report may be seen in: Oberkommando der Kriegsmarine (OKM), M-IV-1: 'Attaché- und Auslandsangelegenheiten', 1934–6, pp. 211–34. In the same file is a memorandum by Admiral Canaris, *Chef Abwehr Nr. 30/35 g. Kdos* of 12 Nov. 1935, to Grand-Admiral Raeder relaying news from General Ōshima that the Japanese navy delegation to the London Naval Disarmament Conference would be passing through Berlin on its way to London at the end of the month. Its members would be glad, he said, to meet Raeder and Ribbentrop for wide-ranging general discussions and to make up for the fact that Admiral Yamamoto Isoroku had been dissuaded from showing a similar openness when he visited Berlin on his way from London to Tokyo in late January 1935. Attached to the memorandum are handwritten notes relating to the subjects for discussion with the delegates at a dinner at Raeder's house in Staaken. The head of the navy delegation, Admiral Nagano Osami, called on Wenneker before he left Tokyo and reiterated his determination not to yield at any price to Anglo-American demands for the maintenance of existing naval construction ratios.

Nagano subsequently became Navy Minister and set up the Hasegawa committee which laid down guidelines for the new southward policy. The Nagano visit proved to be far more significant for the development of Japanese strategy than the Anti-Comintern policy line pursued by Ōshima, which has received far greater attention in the literature. The Anti-Comintern line was correctly interpreted by Soviet spokesmen as 'dust in the eyes' of the western powers, as it was a deliberate smokescreen framed by Canaris as a policy of deception (*Politik der Irreführung*) intended to disguise Hitler's efforts to sidestep Franco-Soviet encirclement and gain access to the world economy via Italy and Spain. This was precisely the role assigned to the *Abwehr* in the planning for *Barbarossa* when guidelines for deception of the enemy were issued to Canaris in *OKWWFSt/Abt. L. (I op) Nr. 44142/41 g. Kdos. Chefs* of 15 Feb. 1941 in OKM, 1. Skl, Akte V, 5, Bd. 1: 'Barbarossa-Weisungen des OKW und Zeittafel', 1940–1. The Japanese were able to confirm that the Franco-Soviet Pact did not apply to the Far East and actively sought to reinforce German efforts to encourage US isolationism and concentrate expansionist efforts on centralsouth China.

43. Wenneker *B. Nr. 265/36g* of 1 Dec. 1936 to Grand-Admiral Raeder confirmed opinion in the Navy that a war with the Soviet Union would be ruinous even if the Russians were defeated. OKM, M Att: 'Attaché-Berichte Tokio, 1936'.

44. The staff agreement proposed by Ōshima was discussed with Canaris, von Blomberg and Wakamatsu, but rejected in its existing form pending discussions in Tokyo by Ōshima during his leave in the winter of 1936–7. The *Abwehr* was aware – from the decryption of Japanese diplomatic traffic in Europe – of efforts by Yoshida Shigeru (the Japanese ambassador in London to persuade the British to join in the proposed Anti-Comintern Pact and by Shiratori (the Minister in Stockholm) to urge the Poles and the Germans to get together against the USSR. The Germans had known since June 1934 of arrangements whereby space had been created within the Polish General Staff building in Warsaw for Japanese army officers to collate

attaché and agent reports from all over Europe relating to the USSR. Canaris had been busily forging links with the Hungarian, Italian, Lithuanian and Finnish General Staffs since he was appointed head of the *Abwehr* in January 1935 and the approach from Ōshima fitted nicely into his schemes. What has not been published until now is the fact that Canaris also made an approach for closer co-operation with the Polish military intelligence service on 5 April 1936 via Ambassador Lipski in Berlin, co-ordinated with pressure from Ōshima and Sawada, the new Japanese military attaché in Warsaw. See AA, Geheim Akten, Abt. II F-M: 'Militär-Attaché Warschau', vols 1–2, 1933–6 and *Geheim Akten, Abt. IV Polen, Akte Po. 15: 'Agenten- und Spionagewesen, Austauschverhandlungen', 1932–6.* Wakamatsu was told that the secret agreement with Poland would be void if Japan and Germany became close allies: NAW/RG 319/IRR.

45. Mrs Petrov began work on cryptanalysis with the GRU from the beginning of 1933 and transferred to the *Spets-Otdel* of the OGPU in June 1934. Until 1942, she worked in the Japanese Sub-Section, specialising in the processing of Japanese diplomatic telegrams. Her section sent instructions to intelligence agents in the field to lay hands on any code material available: 'working in the Japanese sub-section, I knew that certain codes were being secured through agents'. Australian Archives, Canberra, CRS A6283/XR1/14, pp. 1–5. The author is grateful to James Barros, Toronto University, for this information.

Mader, *Dr. Sorge-Report*, refers to the bugging of the German embassy in Warsaw by members of the Polish Communist Party, with whom Sorge had contacts in the summer of 1936 on the way to Berlin. Among the visitors to the embassy was General Uborevich, who asked Major Kinzel on 29 January 1936: 'what kind of an alliance do you have with Japan against us?' Uborevich then went on to say that it was his dearest wish to call on War Minister von Blomberg on his way back from Paris. Whether such talks were intercepted and used in connection with the subsequent purges by Stalin remains to be clarified.

46. After Nomonhan, General Ueda was replaced by Umezu. Attention was also paid to the impact of the ending of normal trade relations by the USA, not only direct with Japan, but also in major procurement centres such as Shanghai. Although a major reason for the scale of the Japanese defeat had been a deliberate withholding of reinforcements and equipment from the 6th Army by the central authorities, the latter had also been made painfully aware of technological backwardness in equipment and firepower in artillery, tanks and aircraft. The War Ministry set up its own trading company, *Shōwa Tsūshō KK*, to procure raw materials in China or South-East Asia and technical equipment from Europe and elsewhere, independently of the long-established trading companies with close Navy connections. See Yamamoto Tsuneo, *Ahen to taihō: Rikugun Shōwa Tsūshō no shichi nen* (PMC Shuppan, Tokyo, 1985); Inoue Dendō, *Maboroshi no taikigyō: Shōwa Tsūshō* (Kokusai Jōhōsha, Tokyo, 1983); and J. W. M. Chapman (ed.), *The Price of Admiralty* (Saltire House Publications, Ripe, E. Sussex, 1982–9) vol. II, pp. 500–1.

47. Ibid. vol. I, pp. 179–82.

48. The Italians intercepted an exchange between the British China Fleet and the 1st Sea Lord on Imperial defence and relayed copies to Berlin. A close watch on fleet movements in the Far East was kept by the *B-Dienst* during Anglo-Japanese tension. A signal of protest at the boarding of the liner *Ranpura* off Hong Kong was deciphered. The incident formed part of the growing pressure on Britain by the faction in the Navy headed by Admiral Nagano, supported by Admirals Oyokawa Kojirō, Kondō Nobutake and Nomura Naokuni, and linked to the retired Admirals Katō Kanji and Suetsugu Nobumasa, who pressed for an alliance with the European Axis. The open-ended alliance formula was ferociously opposed by Navy Vice-Minister Yamamoto Isoroku because of the unacceptability of the risk of a war on

all fronts when the Fleet's preparations for war were far from complete, especially against the USA, the primary enemy for Yamamoto.

49. See NAW/RG 319/IRR Files on Kodama Yoshio and Sasagawa Ryōichi. Both men had been deeply involved in the right-wing plots and assassinations in the early 1930s, but were imprisoned in the crackdown on the ultranationalists up to 1937. They then involved themselves with Army and Foreign Ministry covert organisations in China rather than in domestic politics. Britain was regarded as the prime obstacle to a settlement of the China 'Incident' and the ultranationalists received official approval organising anti-British demonstrations in 1939 and after the boarding of the *Asama Maru* in January 1940. Sasagawa already had a personal fortune by 1939 and funded much of the agitation with the apparent assistance of elements of organised crime (*bōryokudan*). Kodama, who had had informal contacts with Sasagawa's organisation in the early 1930s joined forces with Sasagawa by early 1941 and participated in subsequent anti-British and anti-American agitation. Sasagawa offered his support to Fleet Admiral Yamamoto in the course of that year, while Kodama was the owner of a pistol used in the attempted assassination in August 1941 of Baron Hiranuma, a former premier who supported confrontation with the Soviet Union.

Both made huge fortunes from supplying the Army and Navy and were arrested as war crimes suspects in 1945, but the charges were reduced when they proved co-operative in making charges against Tōjō and generals in the War Ministry stick. Three years in detention, it was hoped, would prevent them from exercising any influence over the establishment of democratic structures, but in fact both were actively working to fund the activities of the Liberal Party, headed by Hatoyama Ichirō, who replaced Yoshida as premier following the founding of the Liberal Democratic Party in 1954. Kodama had developed links with the dominant crime syndicates in the Kantō area and was appointed agent for the Lockheed company in Japan, giving him both physical and financial muscle over the ruling party's factions. The pattern of corruption that was established after 1937 was briefly dented by the Occupation but prevailed over the political system from 1954 until now. Cf. the obituary of Tanaka Kaknei in *The Guardian*, 17 Dec. 1993.

50. Statements by Admirals Kondō and Yamagata to Admiral Wenneker: Chapman (ed.) *The Price of Admiralty*, vol. I, pp. 124, 128–9 and 162. A paper by Hata Ikuhiko, 'Admiral Yamamoto's Surprise Attack and the Japanese Navy's War Strategy', Pacific War Conference, Imperial War Museum, London, 5–6 December 1991, p. 14, citing a paper by Ōmae Toshikazu of 1956, speaks of a sudden, drastic downward revision in the ratio of Japan's estimated naval strength from 5:10 to 7:10 by the Operations Division of the Naval Staff in 1940. The Japanese navy was not informed until 1944 that the successes of the German armed forces in Scandinavia were directly related to the ability of the Germans to read British Naval, Administrative and Interdepartmental Codes, which had given clear advance warnings about the departure of the Home Fleet for Norwegian waters. Further information had been gleaned from code seizures at British diplomatic and consular buildings in Denmark, Norway and the Netherlands. *B-Dienst* war diary; postwar statements by Hitler's Naval Adjutant, Commander von Puttkamer; and JIC memorandum of 45th Meeting, 14 June 1940, Item 2: PRO/CAB 81/87.

51. See Chapman (ed.), *The Price of Admiralty*, vol. II, pp. 332–8 and 513–14. The intelligence triggered pressure on Japan to intervene against British and Dutch territories in South-East Asia and, in turn, hastened closer Anglo-American collaboration in the intelligence field against Japan. Details of the loss of Cabinet, War Office, SIS, Air Ministry and Admiralty papers seem to be missing from JIC Sub-Committee minutes released in 1993, but more light is shed on Anglo-American intelligence collaboration following meetings in Washington and Singapore and the

establishment of an Axis Planning Section in March 1941: PRO/CAB 81/88. The author is grateful for further information from Sir Julian Ridsdale, who was a GS03 in DMI/MI 2c in the War Office at this period and helped service the JIC, as well as from Lady Ridsdale, who was secretary to Admiral Godfrey, DNI.

52. On Shigemitsu, see I. H. Nish (ed.), 'Shigemitsu Studies', *International Studies*, 1990/II STICERD/LSE, (London). A number of reports originating from Shigemitsu and the naval attaché bureau in London were passed on to the Germans by Captain Mitsunobu Tōyō, Japanese naval attaché in Rome in 1940–1: see OKM, M Att Rom, Akte BS I SN Gkds: 'Feindnachrichten', Sept. 1939 – Mar. 1942. Rome was an important centre for communications intelligence as enemy signals were extensively monitored and deciphered in direct exchanges with German signals agencies under arrangements dating back to the end of 1933.

53. Sustained pressure was brought to bear on Navy Minister Yoshida, who was forced to resign shortly before the signature of the Pact, particularly by the First Committee made up of key Naval Staff and Navy Ministry officers. On 13 September 1940, Admiral Wenneker was informed by Captain Kojima of the Naval Staff that 'lately, to his knowledge, a change has also come about in the views of the Fleet Commander-in-Chief, Yamamoto, who until now has always adopted a pro-Anglo-Saxon attitude'. This was confirmed a week later in a hint by Admiral Suetsugu 'that a substantial change in attitude had taken place within the Navy toward the Axis following the change of ministers, and that the treaty now being negotiated would certainly not be sabotaged by the Navy'. Wenneker gave most of the credit for the change to the efforts of Kondō, but post-war records place a great deal of importance on army budget concessions to the Navy in swinging acceptance. Once the dust settled, Wenneker recorded:

> As previously reported, the final resistance to the consummation of the alliance came from the Navy, which sought to deny that it had any prospects of success, i.e. of the possibility of keeping America out of the war, and kept on being mesmerised by achieving some kind of understanding with America, or some other sort of compromise. Once it was finally recognised, rather late in the day, that no improvement in relations with America could be achieved under any circumstances, and that in fact everything pointed to exactly the opposite conclusion, namely that there would soon be a complete break in relations, and that, furthermore, Japan would also be a loser in the event of a German defeat, because she was getting in the way of Anglo-Saxon interests, and, finally, that Japan would also benefit from a German victory, there was a sudden change in opinion. Added to that was the hope that the Pact could possibly also lead to an improvement in relations with Russia – relations that were always regarded and demanded as a basis for any orientation toward the South on the Navy's part.

See Chapman (ed.), *The Price of Admiralty*, vol. II, pp. 264, 270 and 287; *Senshi Sōsho*, vol. 91 (*Daihonei Kaigunbu: Rengō Kantai – 1, Kaisen made*) 1975, pp. 410 ff.; Bōei-chō, Bōei Senshi-shitsu, 'Fujii Nisshi', entry for 29 Sept. 1940. Army operational planning in the south was initially dictated by the requirements of the China campaign, while the Navy was especially worried that too rapid a military expansion in Indo-China and Thailand would precipitate a premature US reaction. Events in East and South-East Asia could be controlled quite effectively if Army and Navy maintained a united front. But there was concern that, even if the terms of the Tripartite Pact gave Japan great flexibility, there was still the possibility that a German landing in Britain or the capture of the Suez Canal or the outbreak of a German–Soviet conflict or direct US–German clashes in the Atlantic could precipitate a US entry into the war before the Navy was ready to launch strategic surprise attacks.

54. Every time there were rumours of an Anglo-German truce or *rapprochement*, there

was apprehension and suspicion among the Japanese. Efforts were made on the British side to put such rumours about in the fortnight before the outbreak of the Pacific War, but by then it was much too late to have a significant impact on the course of events. Stalin, for his part, also used such tactics to put pressure on the western powers to gain concessions or support by waving the threat of a truce with Germany. See Chapman (ed.), *The Price of Admiralty*, vol. IV, pp. 729 and 735.

55. The consistent advice of the German armed forces to Hitler had sought to warn him of the technological backwardness of the Japanese army and the general vulnerability of the Japanese economy to foreign pressures. In a memorandum of 16 May 1936, the General Staff pointed to the likelihood that any closer link with Japan would earn Germany the enmity of Britain and the USA, an argument that the Weimar Government had accepted on the advice of Canaris after a trip to Japan in 1924. It was reinforced by expert opinion on the strength of the Soviet economy and the armed forces up to the time of Stalin's purges, which were almost certainly in part the result of disinformation or distortion of continuing covert contacts with Red Army officers such as General Uborevich. See NAW/RG 319/IRR File on Ott; RKM Abt. Ausland, 'Akte Stein, GKdos. Japan und Sonstiges', 1935–8.

56. In 1946, Ott recalled instructions that he had received after a meeting with Hitler in February 1934, when in fact they were given to him after meeting Hitler at the autumn manLuvres of 1936. These ordered him to try to ensure that 'the Japanese sword was made as sharp as possible, but be kept in its sheath'. Top-secret memorandum by Colonel von Tippelskirch of 31 March 1937 to General von Fritsch on Ott's subsequent discussions in Tokyo: ibid. Ott's suggestion that Germany would have to supply substantial technical support to Japan was emphatically rejected by von Fritsch on the ground that there were insufficient trained officers available. Basically, however, von Fritsch – a disciple of von Seeckt (and opponent of Ott and the 'Schleicher clique') – believed in the greater potential and profitability of relations with China and accepted the current advice of von Falkenhausen that any link with Japan could only ever be a 'platonic' one.

57. Matzky B. Nr. 31/39g. *Kdos* of 3 July 1939, 'Die Haltung der japanischen Armee in der Bündnisfrage'; *Gendai-shi shiryō*, vol. 10 (*Nitchū sensō, III.*) (Misuzu Shobō, Tokyo, 1963) pt 3 on the strengthening of the Anti-Comintern Pact.

58. Hewel memorandum *Füh. 42/41 g. Rs* on the meeting between Hitler and Ōshima on 15 July 1941 in: AA, BRAM: 'Handakten von Loesch. Japan, Geheime Reichssachen', 1936–44, Item J/35.

59. In his discussion on 19 May 1943 at Fuschl with Ōshima and Major-General Okamoto (the head of an Imperial delegation, who had come to explain the developments in the war in the Pacific), Ribbentrop recalled the situation after the fall of France and how Hitler had decided to press ahead with the attack on the USSR, despite the opposition of German business circles and how Japan should steel itself to do the same. Ibid., Item J/63.

60. Bürkner memorandum *OKWAusl. III Org. Nr. 127/41 g. Kdos. Chefs.* of 10 Apr. 1941 in: Oberkommando der Luftwaffe (OKL), Genst. d. Lw., 8. Abteilung: 'Matsuoka-Besuch', 1941. The summary was circulated to the three services and appears not to have been published until now.

61. The reasons for Hitler's decision of 5 March 1941 to conceal the intention to attack the USSR from the Japanese are complex. Partly it stems from a need to keep the enemy powers in suspense, especially after April 1941, when troop concentrations in the east could no longer be explained away easily. The enemy states could be expected to believe that Germany's principal allies would be authentically informed about major German intentions. But as they were not informed until June, they contributed significantly to the general confusion generated by leaks about *Unternehmen Albion* and by the exaggeration of the importance of preparations for operations in the Balkans and North Africa. The decision not to inform the Italians and Japanese prematurely was undoubtedly affected also by Keitel's directive of 3

April 1941 announcing that the opening of *Barbarossa* would be delayed by at least four weeks, together with reports from August and December 1940 about the compromising of Italian codes and of the Japanese diplomatic code employed in Tokyo – Washington communications.

62. General Onodera was contacted by Major Michał Rybikowski, a Polish General Staff officer who escaped from occupied Poland and was appointed to head the covert organisation 'Anna' in Sweden by the 6th Section of the General Staff in London. Both worked closely together until 1944, even though the relationship was known to the German authorities. Other Polish agents were employed in the Legation of Manchukuo in Berlin, but they were uncovered as a result of an Italian tip-off and the reading of parts of Polish and British cypher communications and arrested in July 1941. Polish communications were also carried with the assistance of Japanese couriers (with the help of Third Secretary Furuuchi) to Rome and Tokyo to be forwarded by the Polish military attaché, Colonel Levittoux. Two Polish cryptanalysts continued to work on Soviet communications for the Kwantung army throughout the war, even after the closure of the Polish mission in Japan and a Polish declaration of war. Author's interviews with the late General Onodera and correspondence with the late Colonel Rybikowski and Polish files in the *Studium Polski Podziemnej*, London.

The Japanese military attaché in Berlin, General Okamoto, returned home at the end of March 1941 to take up the post of head of military intelligence, confidently predicting that Germany would invade the British Isles. See *Senshi Sōsho*, vol. 20 (*Daihonei Rikugunbu* – 2) 1968, p. 218.

63. NAW/RG 331/File 324, interrogation of General Kretschmer; RG 319/IRR File on Ott; author's correspondence with Kretschmer and Matzky interview.

64. Sorge made contact with Major Nedtwig, who was subsequently drowned while returning home in the blockade-runner *Spreewald* which was accidentally sunk by U-333 in the central Atlantic. According to Meisinger, who arrived in Tokyo in the company of a former mistress of Himmler in March 1941, his predecessor Huber held receipts of monies paid by him to Sorge. According to the German journalist, Werner Crome, Sorge warned him and his colleagues that the outcome of the German–Soviet conflict was likely to be quite different from their initial expectations. OKM, M Att: 'Blockadebrecher', vol. 1, 1941–2, p. 325; NAW/RG 319/Meisinger File; author's correspondence and interviews with Crome.

65. See John Erickson, *The Road to Stalingrad* (Panther Books, London, 1975) pp. 128–9 and J. Chapman, 'Richard Sorge i voina na Tikhom Okeane', *Problemi Dalnego Vostoka*, no. 6, 1991, pp. 122–35 and 'Shinjuwan chokumae no Sangoku Dōmei awai de no chōhō katsudō kyōryoku', *Gunji Shigaku*, 27, nos 2–3, Dec. 1991, pp. 181–207.

66. This was recognised particularly by the Japanese army leadership, which came round gradually to support the idea of bringing the USSR into the Axis camp after the German–Soviet Non-Aggression Pact as a means of persuading the Russians to reduce their support of China and hasten a Sino-Japanese peace. This argument has been advanced by a younger historian in the Defence Agency, Hatano Sumio, 'Dokuso Fukashin Jōyaku to Nihon Doitsu', in Gunji Shigaku-kai (eds.), *Dai-Ni Taisen: Hassei to Kakudai* (Kinseisha, Tokyo, 1990).

67. Captain Joachim Lietzmann, German naval attaché in Tokyo until February 1940, was contacted regularly by middle-ranking naval officers such as Shiba Katsuo of the Navy Ministry and Yokoi Tadao and Captain Yoshida of the Naval Staff about the need to pursue Japanese–Soviet *rapprochement* as a way of isolating Britain in China. Yoshida, who had served on the staff of the Combined Fleet under Vice-Admiral Nomura Naokuni – who made a point of meeting Lietzmann informally while on leave from Shanghai – was particularly emphatic about the view that Britain was the No. 1 enemy. All omitted, however, to make any comment on any role of the USA in the matter. Chapman (ed.) *The Price of Admiralty*, vol. I, pp. 18–19.

Lietzmann's efforts were sustained by his successor, Admiral Wenneker, whose subsequent reports indicated very slow steps on the way to promoting *détente* with the Soviet Union, even though he was at pains to bring the two sides together at receptions in the German embassy throughout 1940. Before Ott left for Europe in the company of Matsuoka, he had discussions with Army Chief of Staff Sugiyama and Navy Vice-Chief Kondō on 4 and 5 March 1941. Wenneker had a private meeting with Kondō later, on 8 March, and came away with the strong impression that 'Japanese willingness to take the offensive had suffered a number of reverses in comparison with six months ago'. Highlighted in the conversation was Kondō's concern about US operations from the Philippines if these were by-passed by a Japanese southward advance. Ibid. vol. II, pp. 538–9. A draft policy statement prepared by the *Gaimushō* in advance of Matsuoka's departure for Europe called for a British defeat and US neutrality: see *Taiheiyō sensō e no michi*, vol. 5 (*Sangoku Dōmei, Ni-So churitsu jōyaku*) (Asahi Shimbun-sha, Tokyo, 1962) pp. 280–2.

68. AA, VAAbOKH, Etzdorf Handakten: 'Aufzeichnungen', 15 Feb. 1941. Subsequently Molotov complained about it being a breach of the security arrangements proposed during his Berlin visit.

69. Ibid., 3 Dec. 1940 referred to a published agreement, together with two secret protocols concerned with Soviet–Japanese relations. Molotov demanded that Japan renounce claims to rights on north Sakhalin.

70. Wohlthat, who had been a senior official of the Economics Ministry and the Four-Year Plan, was recommended to Ribbentrop to head the German delegation to Tokyo and negotiate an economic treaty with Japan. Wohlthat prepared a preliminary report on the German negotiating position in memorandum W.1769 of 25 Mar. 1941 before departing for Tokyo. AA, St. S.: 'Japan', vol. 3, 1941.

71. See Bidder memorandum *e. o. Pol VIII 2287/41g* of 9 May 1941 to Under-Secretary Woermann in the German Foreign Ministry, who noted that the initiative on the neutrality pact had always rested with the Russians. AA, Pol Abt., Akte Po. 23 A g OA, vol. 1: 'Krieg zwischen Deutschland, England, Frankreich und Polen', 1940–1. Matsuoka resisted pressure from the Army to resort to naked force to settle the Thai – French border dispute, arguing at an audience with the Emperor that that would only alarm the USA unnecessarily, a position that suited the Navy moderates, who had happily accepted a draft policy outline on the issue on 30 January. Before the treaty with the USSR was secured, however, the Navy produced an outline of the principles to be enforced in relation to the south (*tai-Nanpō shisaku yōkō*), which was finally accepted on 17 April 1941. This identified the advance southward as a matter of life or death for Japan and emphasised preparedness to resort to force if no other means could be found, depending on developments in the European war and in Japan's diplomatic relations with the USSR, even at the risk of war with the USA and its friends. *Senshi Sōsho*, vol. 101 (*Daihonei Kaigunbu: Dai Tō-A Sensō Kaisen Keii – 2*) 1979, pp. 169–209.

In Britain, the Joint Intelligence Sub-Committee noted that 'the USSR, with the European war drawing closer to her territory, was ready to welcome the Japanese overtures, though purely in her own interests', but drew comfort from 'the absence of any reference to Soviet support to China'. JIC(41)155 of 15 Apr. 1941 to Chiefs of Staff, PRO/CAB 81/101.

72. Wenneker B. Nr. 279/41 g. Kdos of 17 Apr. 1941 to Navy High Command: Chapman (ed.), *The Price of Admiralty*, vol. II, pp. 545–6.

73. Interrogation of Lieutenant-Colonel V. N. Shkharabidze, military adviser attached to the Chinese 19th Army Group during operations against the Japanese 33rd and 34th Divisions until February 1941. He estimated that some 300 advisers and pilots had been seconded to China during 1940–1. *Stab Walli Tgb. Nr. 3673/41g* of 28

Oct. 1941 to General Staff in: OKH, Genst. d. H., Abt. Fr. Heere West (V), Akte 7 China: 'Wehrmacht, Gliederungen', 1940–2.

74. During the mobilisation measures for reinforcing the Kwantung army (*Kantōkuen*) in July and August 1941, Russian families and installations had been withdrawn to Siberia from the Primorie District. From interrogations of captured Soviet officers in October 1941, there was evidently some apprehension about the possibility that an offensive might be launched if Japanese forces successfully completed their missions in the south and that such an attack might hasten a Soviet collapse: OKH/*Genst. d. H./Abt. Fr. H. Ost Nr. 1025/42 gKdos* of 25 Apr. 1942.

The JIC in Britain estimated that Japanese forces in Manchuria would remain considerably inferior to the Red Army even after reinforcement was completed in September: JIC(41)320 of 11 Aug. 1941, 'Simultaneous Move by Japan against Siberia and Thailand'. A further paper of 13 August for the Chiefs of Staff on Japanese air power expressed the view that more modern aircraft would be required for defence against Soviet air attacks and that older models would be reserved for the south: JIC(41)327 in CAB 81/103. At its 19th Meeting on 26 June 1941, the chairman stated that the Foreign Office 'attached great importance to the despatch of British officers to the Soviet armed forces in the Far East'. This appears to have been predicated on the belief that there might be a Soviet collapse in Europe and that a liaison mission in Siberia was 'probably our only hope of ensuring that the Trans-Siberian Railway would remain cut if the Russian Far Eastern Army continued in the war against Germany': CAB 81/88.

75. Kretschmer had been instructed to contact General Okamoto, head of military intelligence, lately returned from Berlin. Okamoto's assessment of the chances of a Soviet–German war, even after Hitler had broached it to Ōshima, was given as 6:4 against, but when war did break out, he accepted Hitler's highly optimistic assessment that the Bolshevik regime would fall apart in weeks. Having previously accepted equally enthusiastically that Germany would successfully carry out a landing in the British Isles, Okamoto's views did not weigh heavily even with his colleagues. See Kretschmer cypher *Tel. Nr. 47/41 gKdos* of 23 May 1941, apparently routed via a direct wireless link set up in the German embassy at this date: OKH Genst. d. H., O Qu IV, Attachéabteilung: 'Chefsachen, Bd. 1941'.

76. This statement is consistent with the Japanese navy's insistence that the policy towards the south adopted on 17 April should have priority over any demands from within the Army for intervention in the north (cf. n. 71 above). Wenneker *Tel. Nr. 474/41 gKdos* of 10 June 1941 to Navy High Command: Chapman (ed.), *The Price of Admiralty*, vol. III, pp. 462–3. The decision to open negotiations with the USA was predicated on a hope that the USA might be induced into a position of neutrality, but when it became clear that the USA was negotiating on behalf of its friends as well, the position of the hawks within the Navy was vindicated. The reaction of the USA to the Soviet–German conflict and its threatening tone about the possibility of Japanese intervention in Siberia made it increasingly clear that, whichever move Japan might make, the opposition of the USA would have to be overcome. *Senshi Sōsho*, vol. 101, pp. 230 ff (see n. 71 above).

77. The German authorities found themselves being relentlessly pressed from the Japanese side to provide them with clues about the timing of operations in the British Isles. If there had been a serious likelihood of landing operations, there would have been grave anxiety on the part of the Japanese navy, as that could have triggered a (premature) US entry into the war. The advice coming from the Japanese embassy in London, however, was that there were only two other ways that Britain could be defeated: either the Royal Navy would have to be decimated in the eastern Atlantic or weakened by diversion of major fleet units to the Mediterranean. In

other words, the likelihood of protracted war remained substantial, though the Japanese did seek to assist by making available aerial torpedo technology. See Löwisch (Rome) *B. Nr. Gkds. 1088/41* of 27 June 1941 to the Navy High Command in: OKM, M Att: 'Italien-Land', Bd. 3, 1941–2.

78. Wenneker report of 10 June 1941: n. 76 above. The German initiative was not welcomed by the Japanese navy. It again destabilised the global situation and threatened to accelerate a (premature) US entry into the war. There was concern lest there be active military collaboration between the USSR and the Anglo-American powers against Japan.

79. As a result of the very strong financial position acquired by the USA in the First World War, it was able to put strong pressure on Britain and the Dominions to end the alliance links with Japan in 1921. Direct insights into this can be found in the diary of Captain Malcolm Kennedy, a member of the Japan desk in the War Office in London (MI 2c), who had served on secondment with the Japanese army at the end of the war and argued that the USA had 'a wholly unwarranted fear that it [the Alliance Treaty] contained secret clauses posing a threat to the US'. They opposed the dispatch of an official air/naval mission under the Master of Semphill to Japan, but because it was a response to the dispatch of an earlier French air mission to the Japanese army, the mission went ahead as an 'unofficial' one. The Japanese military attaché in London subsequently warned Kennedy in December 1921 that the British were in for a let-down if they believed that dropping the Japanese alliance would result in any easing of war debts to the USA. Kennedy warned that the Japanese would turn to the Germans or the Russians. *Kennedy Diary*, vol. 2, Pt. 9 (Sheffield University Library).

80. A naval technology exchange had been organised between Germany and Japan in the early 1920s, but this was put largely in cold storage from 1924 because of Germany's need for US investment and trade credits. The Japanese armed forces, nevertheless, continued to second large numbers of technical specialists to Berlin throughout the 1920s and a fairly brisk trade was conducted, especially in the aviation field. With the relaxation of the Versailles restrictions on offensive weapons acquisition, the German navy was anxious to get hold of as much advanced know-how and equipment as it could and made approaches to all the leading navies. Approaches to Britain aroused no enthusiasm at a time when public opinion feared a future surprise mass air attack by Germany, comparable to Japan's surprise attack on Port Arthur in 1904. By contrast, however, the Japanese and German navies rediscovered mutual advantages after 1933. The Germans obtained important economic orders for air and naval equipment from Japan at a time when there was a serious trade deficit and dangerously heavy capital outflows, while the Japanese navy supplied details of aircraft-carrier construction and operation denied to the Germans by the British. The Japanese naval attaché in London, Captain Oka Takazumi, is credited with the initial suggestion for a 3:1 Anglo-German naval building ratio and informed an Abwehr contact over dinner at the Nippon Club in London that 'war with Britain in about ten years was a virtually obvious pre-condition' for a Japanese alliance with China and the exclusion of all foreigners. See *Abwehr Va 3541/34g* of 16 Aug. 1934: OKM, Abt. MND: 'Flottenkonferenz 1935'.

81. Löwisch (Rome) *B. Nr. Gkds 225/41* of 4 Feb. 1941 on a talk with Mitsunobu following a visit to Berlin for discussions with Admiral Nomura Naokuni: OKM, M Att: 'Italien, Land', vol. 2, 1940–1.

82. The abrogation of the US – Japan trade treaty in July 1939 marked the starting-point for a serious threat of economic denial and both the armed forces and firms began to expand contacts in Germany, Switzerland and Sweden. Ayukawa

Yoshisuke (1882–1967), the head of the Manchurian Heavy Industrial Development Co. and founder of the Nissan conglomerate, revisited Germany at this date and expressed his astonishment at the expansion of mass production methods in Germany since his last visit. Japanese military and naval missions arriving in Europe in early 1941 presented huge lists of demands for equipment and know-how that were described as equivalent to an 'intellectual sell-out'. Japan was placed on the same level of priority as the USSR so long as it remained unclear that Japan would definitely enter the war against the US, with a proviso that that would change in the autumn once the USSR had been eliminated from the war. Hitler's policy response was to say that Germany had little to offer Japan because Germany faced pressure from the USA and could not supply war materials on an *ad hoc* basis but would accept rubber supplies in exchange for equipment at a later date. See Thomas directive *OKW/Wi-Rü-Amt/Wi VIIa Nr. 193/41 g. Kdos* of 21 Feb. 1941: OKM, 1. Sk1. IIIa: 'Japan-Kommission', 1941.

The Soviet authorities did all in their power before June 1941 to prevent any military equipment or machine-tools for war production being carried on the Trans–Siberian Railway in order to minimise the risk of a German–Japanese assault on their country. By contrast, raw materials such as rubber from the Far East which was vital to the German war effort, were not controlled: 'Kurze Übersicht der Wehrwirtschaft Japans' in *OKWWi-Rü-AmtWi VIc Nr. 2071/41g* of 18 Mar. 1941.

83. Initial British intelligence estimates of the economic value of conquered Soviet territory to Germany suggested that 'no economic advantages could be got from war with Russia until a long time after occupation had taken place'. 'German Strategy in 1941', JIC(41)138 of 7 Apr. 1941: PRO/CAB 81/101. This was revised in 'German Intentions against the USSR', JIC(41)218 of 18 May 1941 to indicate that there would be 'initial economic losses' and that 'some months would have to elapse before she could draw a dividend'. Germany could not fight a long war without obtaining greater economic help from Russia, whether by agreement or war: 'the advantages, therefore, to Germany of concluding an agreement with the USSR are overwhelming'. PRO/CAB 81/102.

Briefed by Admiral Fuchs about the need to obtain materials for the German war economy before he left Berlin for the Far East in January 1940, Admiral Wenneker explored the possibilities for trade between Japan and Europe via the Northern Sea Route. In his first long private conversation with Admiral Kondō, the vice-chief of naval staff, he was assured that the Japanese navy had 'reached the conclusion that eastern Siberia is hardly in a position to supply any worthwhile quantities of exportable goods'. Chapman (ed.), *The Price of Admiralty*, vol. I, p. 113.

84. Okamoto left for Tokyo prior to the return of the head of the Japanese Military Mission to Germany, General Yamashita Hōbun, whose report was submitted on 7 July 1941, less than a week after the fatal decision to occupy bases in southern Indo-China. Coming on top of Yamashita's earlier experience of reports on the role of the Red Air Force in the Nomonhan débâcle when he had been head of the Army Air Inspectorate, his report recommended that Japan avoid war with *any* of the more technologically advanced armies for as long as possible: see Bōei-chō, Senshi-shitsu, 'Yamashita Shisatsudan Hōkoku,' (Gunji Gyōsei Sonota 87).

85. See Löwisch (Rome) *B. Nr. Gkds 1088/41* of 27 June 1941 to OKM and OKW and the German Foreign Ministry in OKM, M Att: 'Italien-Land', vol. 2, 1941–2.

86. There was a substantial disparity between German and Japanese estimates of the strength of the 1st and 2nd Red Banner Armies in the Far East, especially prior to the opening of *Barbarossa* and before more reliable figures could be calculated on the basis of captured documentation. Even after that, the tentative German assessment of 455,000 men provided in April 1942 to the Operations Section of the

General Staff, which prepared outlines of two major offensives that could be undertaken by the Japanese army in the directions of Vladivostok and Lake Baikal, was significantly below the Japanese estimate of 600,000 men.

87. Löwisch (Rome) *B. Nr. Gkds 1158/41* of 10 July 1941: OKM, M Att: 'Italien-Land', vol. 2, 1941–2. The Kwantung army employed large numbers of Koreans as agents in the Soviet Far East, and the special service agency (*tokumu kikan*) in Hsinking, headed by Major-General Yanagida Genzō, supplied information and facilities for a small group of *Abwehr I* contacts, led by German journalist Ivar Lissner from 1941 to 1943. Colonel Yamamoto Bin, head of a covert operations group in Berlin and subsequent head of the *Nakano Gakkō*, offered Japanese assistance in mounting sabotage operations from Manchuria and Turkey to Colonel Erwin Lahousen (*Abwehr II*) after the outbreak of the German–Soviet war: see Lahousen memoranda *Abw. II Nr. 1465/41 g.Kdos* of 4 July 1941 and *Abwehr II LA Nr 990/42 g.Kdos* of 1 May 1942.

88. Alvin Coox, 'The Pacific War', in P. Duus (ed.), *The Cambridge History of Japan* (Cambridge UP, London, 1989), vol. 6, pp. 326–8 employs the official Japanese army history accounts for the period up to the end of June 1941 and thereafter turns to the navy histories. An earlier essay, Michael Barnhart, 'Japanese Intelligence before the Second World War', in Ernest R. May (ed.), *Knowing One's Enemy* (Princeton UP, Princeton, NJ, 1984) pp. 424–55 employed the *Daihonei Rikugunbu* volumes as principal source and ignored the *Daihonei Kaigunbu* volumes entirely. He argues (p. 441) that, although the navy had been the proponents of a southward advance throughout the inter-war era, it was the army that had 'pressed for executing its first steps in the summer of 1940'. Despite mentioning the formal acceptance of the southward policy in August 1936, Barnhart gives no weight to the view that the navy's interventions at Shanghai in 1932 and 1937 were specifically designed to counter the initiatives of the army in Manchuria and north China and draw important elements of the army – especially the War Ministry – away from the General Staff's obsession with the idea of a pre-emptive war against the USSR. The *Daihonei Kaigunbu* volumes were among the last to appear to be sure, but it is particularly important to look at the parallel navy and army accounts for the period up to the fateful Imperial Conference of 2 July 1941, when the balance tipped decisively in favour of priority for the southward operations.

89. Wenneker *Tel. Nr. 474/41 g.Kdos* to Berlin. This was reiterated in *Tel. Nr. 645/41 g.Kdos* on 22 Aug. and *Tel. Nr. 678/41 gKdos* on 30 Aug., which confirmed the reappointment of Yamamoto Isoroku as Combined Fleet commander-in-chief two months ahead of the normal time for naval appointments. Chapman (ed.), *The Price of Admiralty*, vol. III, pp. 462–4, 487–8 and 491–2. Naval attachés abroad appear not to have received clarification until late September, and Wenneker was briefed on the impasse in Japan – US negotiations at noon on 6 October, with the clear recognition that Manila could not be bypassed and that, therefore, there would be war with the USA.

90. Ambassador Ott cabled the German Foreign Ministry in Tel. No. 1069 of 28 June to enquire if the instructions given to him in Berlin in April – to give priority to southern operations – still held good or not. Ribbentrop replied in Tel. No. 916 of 28 June that he had met with Ōshima and had agreed on Ōshima's working to influence his government to intervene at the earliest moment in the Soviet–German war. AA St. S.: 'Japan', vol. 3, 1941; Handakten von Loesch, Item J/35.

In response to a request for guidance from the British Commanders-in-Chief Far East and China on 23 June, the Joint Intelligence Committee dispatched a cable to Singapore on 25 June to say that there had not been any indications so far of Japan's attitude. But it was thought that Japan would be inclined to abstain from intervention against the USSR and probably to opt for 'intensified pressure on Indo-

China for bases and facilities'. It reported 'strong pressure by Germans to secure Japanese assistance against Russia' according to Ambassador Craigie. It was estimated that the Red armed forces in the Far East would be able to hold out for at least six months in any event, although the Chiefs of Staff made it clear that 'no alliance with Russia has been suggested nor would one be likely to be accepted'. JIC(41)261 of 25 June 1941 in: PRO/CAB 81/103.

91. AA, Handakten von Loesch, Item J/36.

92. Wenneker B. Nr. 553/40 g.Kdos of 22 Nov. 1940 to Admiral Schniewind, chief of staff, German Naval War Staff: Chapman (ed.), *The Price of Admiralty*, vol. II, pp. 511–13.

93. Löwisch B. Nr. Gkds 1158/41 of 10 July 1941: see n. 87 above.

94. For example, even though the Yamashita Mission had been given a demonstration of radar-controlled anti-aircraft guns early in 1941, it was not until after the rapid progress of Yamashita's forces in Malaya that Hitler agreed to give the Japanese army access to the technology. Even then, difficulties with transport resulted in delays in delivering the equipment until 1943. See Bōei Daigakkō, 'Nihon oyobi doitsu ni okeru rēdā kaihatsu', *Kagaku gijutsu gunjishi* (National Defence Academy, Yokosuka, 1990) pp. 64–8.

95. The JIC papers released in 1993 point to alarm in London about a serious possibility of a Japanese intervention in Malaya when the Joint Planning Staff asked the JIC on 4 January 1941 to prepare a paper as a matter of urgency on 'Sea, Land and Air Forces which Japan Might Make for an Attack on Malaya'. JIC(41)8: PRO/CAB 81/99. This paper was seen as a reappraisal of the scale of forces that Japan could muster compared to the position discussed in the Chiefs of Staff Far East Appreciation of 15 Aug. 1940, COS(40)592. This last paper, it should be noted, was one that had fallen into German hands when it was retrieved, together with a large haul of secret papers and code-books from the liner *Automedon*, destined for the Commander-in-Chief, Far East, the Commander-in-Chief, China and intelligence officers at Hong Kong and Shanghai. It has never been admitted – either in official histories or in records so far released to the Public Record Office – just how extensive and damaging these losses really were for the defence of the realm. The Cabinet Office has denied that memoranda of Dec. 1940 and Jan. 1941 withheld from the JIC records are of any reference, although the late Sir John Colville, one of Churchill's private secretaries at this time, stated in writing his belief in the existence of a bureaucratic cover-up of the *Automedon* loses. cf. PRO/HN3/HN715/HN716 for related extracts from selective intercepts sent to Churchill by Brigadair Menzins. We know from other evidence that at least one of the lost code-books, which reached Berlin on 1 January 1941, was passed on to German and Italian units in the Mediterranean and that loss appears to have been directly connected with the ambush of Force H in the western Mediterranean, resulting in serious damage to the aircraft-carrier HMS *Illustrious* and the loss of the cruiser HMS *Southampton* in mid-January.

An inquiry was set up into that disaster, but it also appears to have led to the establishment of an Inter-Service Cypher Security Board under the chairmanship of Admiral John Godfrey (DNI), who submitted a progress report at the 26th Meeting of the Sub-Committee on 16 September 1941. He drew attention to the need for civilian departments to become more 'cypher conscious', especially the Dominions, Colonial and India Offices. But he also drew attention to the fact that 'there was a grave danger of compromising cyphers in cases where a number of departments made identical signals'. This was particularly risky in the case of instructions from the Chiefs of Staff to commands abroad when an identical signal in Naval Cypher could enable the enemy to read the War Office Cypher, if one of these signals fell into enemy hands and it was recommended that there should be a shift to one-time tables for such important signals. JIC(41)361 of 9 Sept. 1941, PRO/CAB 81/104.

This general prescription, however, did not mention any specific cases in the report, but earlier papers, such as JIC(41)221 of 24 May 1941 drew specific attention to 'Action to Counter Pro-Axis Activities in the Far East' which had led the JIC to focus on the problems of security there. The Committee 'had a discussion on the matter of leakage of certain most secret information' and 'it was agreed that this leakage in all probability occurred in Singapore'. The JIC papers relating to the specific details of this leakage have been withheld so that it would appear that the initial loss of papers and codes sent from Liverpool to Singapore in September 1940 'by safe hand' dealt extremely severe and long-lasting damage to British security throughout 1941. There are also signs of Japanese interception of communications between Indo-China and Singapore and clear evidence of the insecurity of codes and cyphers employed by the US State Department, several of which were variously intercepted and decrypted by agencies in all three Axis states. The most serious of these was the Japanese navy's decryption of wireless traffic between Washington and the US embassy in Moscow, which confirmed the lack of co-operation between the USA and the USSR in the Far East and destroyed the credibility of British attempts to bluff the Japanese into accepting circulated, misleading rumours about the USA and Soviet Union being willing to work together to carry out air attacks on the Japanese homeland should Japan move southward: see Chapman (ed.), *The Price of Admiralty*, vol. IV, pp. 675–6 and JIC(41)284 of 14 July 1941 in PRO/CAB 81/103.

96. *Kennedy Diary*, vol. 37, entry for 5 Nov. 1941. Kennedy was Japan desk officer in the Political Section of GC and CS at Bletchley Park (PID). What Kennedy appears not to have learned, however, was the fact than an initiative had been put forward via the Japanese navy on the morning of 24 October 1941 to learn if there was any interest in a Soviet–German truce or peace and if Japan could pay any useful role as a mediator. This message was relayed by Admiral Wenneker to Ambassador Ott, but it is by no means clear if it was passed on to Berlin or if any reply were forthcoming. Chapman (ed.), *The Price of Admiralty*, vol. IV, pp. 688–9. But it was only the first of a whole series of suggestions and proposals to be put forward by the Japanese navy and subsequently supported by the Army, which received negative replies from Hitler but which German Foreign Ministry officials recognised made Japan a very important player in any end-game negotiations that might have ensued. For further discussion of these moves after 1941, see Gerhard Krebs, 'Japanische Vermittlungsversuche im deutsch – sowjetischen Krieg, 1941–1945', in J. Kreiner and R. Mathias (eds), *Deutschland – Japan in der Zwischenkriegszeit* (Bouvier Verlag, Bonn, 1990) pp. 239–88. Evidence from intercepted Japanese navy signals decrypted after the war indicate that the Japanese naval attaché in Washington, Captain Yamaguchi Tamon, wired Admiral Oka on 21 August 1941 with the rather naïve suggestion that Japan offer mediation on conditions that would prevent the USSR from accepting Anglo-American aid and would guarantee both the supply of raw materials to Germany and maintenance of the rail link between Japan and Germany. NAW/RG 457/SRH-406, 'Pre-Pearl Harbor Japanese Naval Dispatches', pp. 128–9.

97. The JIC in Britain produced a series of estimates of the Japanese order of battle and capabilities through the second half of 1941. A constant factor in all of these was the assumption that 'the main fleet is likely to remain based in Japanese waters'. PRO/CAB 81/105. However, radio monitoring in Britain and the USA began losing track of the movements of Combined Fleet units from the middle of November and radio silence was imposed on the strike force from 26 November. Sir Julian Ridsdale has confirmed to the author that this was brought to Washington's notice by the JIC, and corroboration of US navy monitoring of this can be found in NAW/RG 457/SRH-406. The British Chiefs of Staff received an accurate appraisal of the likely

Japanese army strategy in Malaya from 1 May 1941 onward by way of a 'landing near the frontier on the east coast of the Kra Peninsula in conjunction with landings at suitable points on the east coast of Malaya, the whole developing into a southward move on Singapore'. It was argued that this 'would not be an easy operation in the face of strong British naval and air forces'. See 'Future Strategy of Japan', JIC(41)175, PRO/CAB 81/102.

98. Weather patterns were a much more reliable basis for operational planning, even though not wholly predictable. December was favourable for landings and offensive movements in South-East Asia, but also favourable defensively for both Japan and the USSR in North-East Asia. For a German discussion of the military and military-political significance of the Soviet Far East, see *OKWAbwehr I M F/O Nr. 1865/6.42g* of 22 June 1942 in: OKM, 1. Sk1., Akte X, 5: '*Meldungen und Berichte aus Tokio*,' 1941-3, pp. 227 ff.

99. For material on Japanese signals-monitoring and decryption capabilities, see Miyau-chi Kanya, *Niitakayama nobore 1208: Nihon Kaigun no angō* (Rokkoshi-shuppan, Tokyo, 1975) and Samejima Sunao, *Motogunreibu tsūshin kachō no kaiso* (Shin-kōsha, Tokyo, 1981) especially chapter 4. The insecurity of US State Department wireless traffic was cited by the JIC in Britain as one of the reasons for exercising caution in relaying most secret information via US channels or details of SIS and SOE operations: JIC 39th and 40th Meetings on 23 and 30 Dec. 1941, PRO/CAB 81/88. For a copy of a decrypted signal from Washington to Moscow, supplied by the Japanese Naval Staff on 15 October 1941, see Chapman (ed.), *The Price of Admiralty*, vol. IV, pp. 675-6.

100. On 3 November 1941, Captain Maeda Tadashi of the Naval Staff informed Admiral Wenneker that the decision had been taken for war with America by the end of the year and regardless of the outcome of the Soviet–German war. Ibid. pp. 700-2. Orders for Sorge's arrest appear to have been given on 15 October, but delayed until the following day because of the presence of a foreign female visitor in the evening, allegedly Mrs Ott. The War Diary of the Navy Minister's Secretariat, dating from 1 October 1941, records that a naval *kenpei* group was assigned to security duties at German embassy premises. But there is no indication of security levels being raised, although it would seem to have been a likely step after Maeda's appointment at the beginning of October, with his brother as head of the Naval Intelligence Division. Bōei-chō, Senshi Shitsu, 'Kaigun Daijin Kambō Nisshi' (1941-5).

101. The report by the public prosecutor, compiled in March 1942, argues that the Sorge group was tracked down by regular police methods and progressive incrimination of other group members. However, a regular watch of radio and cable traffic was conducted by police, diplomatic and military authorities. The Naval Staff did not scrutinise German traffic until the end of 1940 and was in a position to assess the degree of cypher security, but no doubt supplemented the work of the *kenpei* with its own counter-espionage group (*bōchō*) in the 11th Section in the Signals Division, also headed for a time by Admiral Maeda. Telephones in Tokyo had been tapped and recorded on wax disks at least since the mid-1930s and the employees of the German Naval Attaché's Bureau would have been kept under surveillance.

An unregistered transmitter in the German embassy had been monitored by the authorities since May 1941, according to the General Staff, so it should have been possible from traffic analysis to work out a pattern of exchanges between the Vladivostok and Tokyo areas and to pinpoint, even roughly, the location of Clausen's transmitter. Since December 1940, collaboration with German Army Signals in monitoring Soviet radio traffic and about decryption had been initiated in Berlin by General Okamoto. After the outbreak of the Soviet–German war, Japanese officers had also received Soviet radio and code materials in August and September

1941. Even if there had been no decryption success before the arrests, the seizure of coding data made a recovery of the intercepted traffic and its content feasible.

102. See e.g. Deakin and Storry, *The Case of Richard Sorge*, pp. 329 ff. on the US ramifications of the Sorge Affair. The US dossier on Kawai Teikichi, described as a 'Sorge remnant', involved co-operation between Kawai and senior members of the MacArthur staff. Kawai was pressed to give information on Agnes Smedley and Günther Stein in particular: NAW/RG 319/IRR Files, declassified on 3 August 1990.

103. Fragments from stenographic records of daily situation reports (*Lagebesprechungen*) at Hitler's field headquarters at Vinnitsa, translated by the UK Air Ministry. The comments are dated 5 March 1943 and appear to have been prompted by Jodl, who had to hand a compilation of the Japanese order of battle derived from the military attaché in Tokyo and a projection of figures for April 1943. The documents used for the briefing survive in files of the Armed Forces Command Staff (*OKWWFSt*) and bear a note stating that 'it is particularly striking how meagre are the number of units facing the Soviet Union'. *Amt Ausland/Abwehr Nr. 0061/43 g.Kdos I A 5., 2. Ang.* of 27 Feb. 1943 in: OKW, WFSt, VO Ausland Ic: 'Fernost, Indien, Japan, China', 1943–4.

104. See the comments of Sakai Naoe, a civilian member of the staff of the Bureau of the Japanese Naval Attaché in Berlin since 1920 who thereby had perhaps the most comprehensive knowledge of relations with Germany of any Japanese, in a memorandum by Dr Brücher (*OKW/Wi Ausl. VIc*) of 8 Dec. 1942. OKW, Wi-Rü-Amt, Wehrwirtschaftsabteilung, Ausland VIc, Akte 3 i 39/Japan: 'Mappe Sakai/Jap. Marine', 1942–3.

Chapter 9

Moscow 1941

The Turning-Point

KLAUS REINHARDT

Early in 1942 – when Germany's Eastern Theatre Army, despite all setbacks, had survived the crisis of the battle before Moscow and the subsequent winter battles, and when Germany had also succeeded in increasing the output of the armament industry by reorganising it – the Third Reich appeared to be capable of successfully continuing the war, although the battle for Moscow had been lost. It appeared that it was only the defeat in the Battle for Stalingrad which initiated the turn of the tide. Today, however, this interpretation does not stand up to critical analysis based on the extensive source material now available.

This chapter intends to demonstrate that Hitler's plans – and therefore the prospects for a successful outcome of the war for Germany – had probably already failed in October 1941, and certainly so at the start of the Russian counter-offensive in the battle for Moscow in December 1941. The principle of the *Blitzkrieg*, which was aimed at a quick victory over the Soviet Union by a campaign to be concluded before the winter of 1941, could no longer be maintained. The increasing scarcity of labour, which imposed considerable restrictions in both the military and the armament fields, could not be made good satisfactorily. Also, not only hopes of compensating for raw material shortages in Germany itself by a rapid capture and utilisation of Russian raw material sources had failed, but also those of enabling Germany to become economically self-sufficient from the Anglo-Saxon naval powers. Thus, early in 1942, Hitler was in a situation which no longer permitted him to pursue his far-flung objectives. The advance to Stalingrad and the Caucasus in the summer and autumn of 1942 was nothing but a final, desperate attempt to regain the initiative, though, even if it had been successful, it would not have brought about a favorable outcome for Germany.

First, it is necessary to analyse the objectives which Hitler associated with the Russian campaign in general and with the thrust on Moscow in particular. Thereafter, it has to be determined when he realised that his concept developed in the fall of 1940 could not be carried through as expected, and when, how and to what effect he modified that concept. In addition, the effects of the defeat in the military field and also in the areas of both defence economy and politics will have to be examined.

<h2>HITLER'S 'IMPROVISED WAR PLAN'</h2>

The basis for the strategic and operational planning of the eastern campaign was the opinion maintained by Hitler and almost all the German military that the Soviet Union could be defeated in a *Blitzfeldzug* of a few months' duration. In view of Hitler's overall estimate of the situation, which deemed it possible that the USA would enter the war in 1942, it was felt that the Soviet Union had to be so defeated.[1] Thus, without further deliberation, this estimate presupposed that the German forces would succeed in defeating the Red Army west of the Dnepr – Drina line, and that afterwards the Russian would not have adequate *matériel* reserves to offer consistent and effective resistance. A widespread opinion at that time was that the required operations would be more a matter of marches and organisation of supply than of eliminating or neutralising Soviet armies.

What was to be done if a decisive victory west of the Dnepr – Drina line could not be achieved was a problem which was left unanswered, even during the planning phase in January 1941. The German Army High Command (OKH), overrating its own capabilities, simply thought that a different outcome was unworthy of further consideration.[2]

Thus, early in 1941, the OKH did not voice reservations against a war in the east because the operations were considered too difficult, but rather because the assessment of Britain's capabilities had changed considerably compared to the estimates of July 1940 and because the Army General Staff had realised the danger of war on two fronts. Serious differences between Hitler and the OKH, however, did not arise in this phase. Initial deployment was continued and, in addition to military preparations, preparations for the achievement of political, racial and military-economic objectives for an eastern empire were initiated, beginning in March 1941.[3] Although there had been disagreements between Hitler and the OKH about the main thrust for the campaign, their differences were not resolved because both sides anticipated a rapid and easy success. The OKH's basic idea was a thrust by Army Group Centre towards Moscow – which was deemed certain to result in a decisive military success – whereas Hitler, who emphasised the military-economic aspects, planned initial thrusts on both flanks in order to launch a double envelopment east of Moscow once the Donets Basin in the south and Leningrad in the north had been reached.[4]

This *Blitzfeldzug* against the Soviet Union was to provide security for the 'Grossdeutsche Reich' with regard to space and raw materials, so that the Reich – now a continental empire, invulnerable to blockade, with coherent territory and economically self-sufficient – would be in a position successfully to conduct a long war against the Anglo-Saxon powers, in particular the USA. From the viewpoints of economics and power-politics, this first step was to form the basis for the second stage of Hitler's *Weltblitzkrieg*. The latter included extensive operations against the Middle East, individual thrusts as far as Afghanistan and north-west Africa, as well as the occupation of the Azores.[5]

It is important to remember especially when considering armament industries – that the beginning of the Russian campaign coincided with preparations for the accomplishment of the second stage of Hitler's general programme, which aimed at establishing Germany as a world power. These preparations were reflected in the order of 14 July 1941 reorganising armament efforts,[6] in Directive No. 32 for the 'preparations for the time after Operation *Barbarossa*',[7] and in a series of orders to withdraw some of the major mechanised and motorised units from the eastern front as early as August to re-equip them for new operations – 'after Operation *Barbarossa*' – which were to start as early as the fall of 1941.[8]

Details of operational planning provided for a complete resumption of the 'siege of Britain' by the Navy and the air force after the end of the eastern campaign, and the preparation of an assault landing in Britain.[9] In addition, planning envisaged 'the closing of the western approach to the Mediterranean by the neutralisation of Gibraltar', an operation which 'might already have to be conducted during the closing phase of the operations in the east'. The *Schwerpunkt* of Army operations, however, was

> the continuation of the battle against the British position in the Mediterranean and the Middle East by a concentric attack
> a. from Libya through Egypt,
> b. from Bulgaria through Turkey against Suez,
> c. and – if necessary – from Transcaucasia against Iraq (possibly Iran).

During this second phase, Britain was finally to be 'forced' to make peace and, in close co-operation with Japan, the USA was to be included to maintain its neutrality. Within the framework of operations necessary to achieve his aims, Hitler hoped to be able to raise Germany to the position of a 'world power' capable of successfully conducting war against any other power.

This planning not only shows how certain Germany was of success, but demonstrates first and foremost the functional importance of the Russian campaign within Hitler's overall strategy at that time. In addition, it reveals to what extent the destiny of Hitler-Germany was dependent on the successful conduct of this campaign.

On the other hand, it also demonstrates all the more strikingly the almost incredible, yet fatal underestimation of the Soviet Union and, as a consequence, the careless planning of Operation *Barbarossa*.

THE FAILURE OF THE FIRST PHASE

At first, however, the optimists appeared to be right. When, after successful border battles and rapid thrusts in depth – in particular on both sides of the Pripet Marshes and in the area of Army Group North towards Leningrad – there were indications of a serious crisis within the Red Army early in July, Halder, chief of the Army General Staff, wrote in his diary, 'It is certainly no exaggeration if I assert that the campaign against Russia was won within 14 days.'[10] One day later, Hitler said, 'I always try to put myself in the enemy's shoes. He has virtually lost this war already. It is of great importance to us that we have destroyed the Russian tank and air forces at the very beginning. The Russians are not in a position to replace them.'[11]

However, even in the second half of July, this optimism began to change into scepticism. Halder realised that 'the Russian colossus had been underestimated'. Although originally he had expected 200 Russian divisions, the section 'Fremde Heere Ost' within the OKH now counted 360 divisions. It is true that they were poorly equipped, but as soon as the Germans had destroyed a dozen of them the Russians produced another dozen.[12]

An OKW memorandum of 27 August 1941 also reflected some doubt as to whether it would be possible to defeat the Soviet Union that year, but it had to be achieved at all costs.[13] It stated: 'If this aim is not achieved in 1941, the continuation of the eastern campaign will have first priority in 1942.' Only after eliminating Russia as a power factor could the campaigns in the Atlantic and the Mediterranean be started at full strength.

During the remaining months of the fall of 1941, Hitler's military decisions in the east were directed by his determination to accomplish his programme in 1941, despite considerably more sceptical forecasts. This determination was certainly based on his awareness of the consequences which the failure of this *Blitzfeldzug* would have on his overall strategy.

When the expected rapid success did not occur, the different assessment of priorities between Hitler and the OKH came into the open for the first time and resulted in a serious command crisis and a crisis of confidence.

The raw material problem – which became more and more critical in the Reich and forced cuts in armament programmes as early as July 1941 – was the main reason why Hitler did not continue the attack in the centre beyond Smolensk[14] but initiated a thrust in the direction of Kiev and the Crimea in the south, as well as sealing off Leningrad in the north.[15]

Although, after the successful encirclement battle near Kiev, he considered the capture of the Crimea and the Donets Basin only as a question of time, he was forced to realise that the USSR had not collapsed but had concentrated the remaining bulk of its army in front of Moscow. If, therefore, Hitler still wanted to achieve his aim in the east in 1941 so that he could then concentrate on the war in the west early in 1942, he had to employ all his forces in order to defeat the Red Army and to seize Moscow – exactly in accordance with the original idea of the OKH. Thus, on 6 September, the order for Operation *Taifun* (the attack on Moscow) was given.[16]

OPERATION TAIFUN

The concept for the attack on Moscow was based on a large-scale double envelopment of Red Army forces deployed in the area east of Smolensk.[17] Strong flanks, forming the *Schwerpunkt* and separated from the armoured elements, would penetrate and encircle enemy forces near Vyazma, once the two flanks had wheeled inwards and locked. As the preparations for the offensive took almost the whole month of September, Army Group Centre and its subordinate commands had sufficient time to plan this new operation in detail and to test its validity by means of map exercises. In September, Field-Marshal von Bock, commanding general Army Group Centre, decided to attack on both sides of Smolensk not only with two armoured main thrusts – as originally planned – but with an additional third, Panzer Group 2, extracted from the battle of Kiev and brought up from the south. This third armoured thrust was allocated far-reaching objectives to the east, a fact which made it apparent that the plan aimed at an extensive pursuit towards Moscow after the end of the battles of encirclement.[18]

THE PREPARATIONS

At the end of September, preparations in the personnel and *matériel* sectors had brought Army Group Centre to an overall strength of just under 2 million men.[19] Army Group Centre was organised into three Army High

Commands and three Panzer Groups, having at their disposal a total of 78 divisions.[20] Field-Marshal Kesselring's 2nd Air Fleet,[21] consisting of Air Corps II and VIII as well as the AA Corps of 4th Air Fleet, was ordered to provide air support. The German High Command was convinced that this huge force under the command of Field-Marshal von Bock was, in spite of some deficiencies, capable of bringing this 'decisive and critical operation against Army Group Timoshenko employed west of Moscow to a successful end by the beginning of the winter', thereby ending the entire campaign. These forces were reinforced by the last two armoured divisions of the OKH reserve, so that the OKH had deprived itself of all its available reserve forces.[22]

The fact that as late as 6 September Hitler wanted to have the attack on Moscow fixed for the first third of September clearly reveals to what extent he had already come under the pressure of time. However, because of the military requirement to concentrate and regroup forces, the beginning of the offensive was not possible before early October. Although Hitler was prepared to agree to the reinforcement of Army Group Centre from the neighbouring Army Group, he was still unwilling to postpone his planning for 'the time after *Barbarossa*'. This was clearly demonstrated when he forbade replacing the high losses of the Panzer Groups with tanks, motor vehicles and guns scheduled for the later operations. In spite of his concentration of forces on Moscow, Hitler adhered to the dual concept of his military plans, i.e. the destruction of the Soviet Union and the simultaneous preparation for operations 'after Operation *Barbarossa*' in the matériel field.[23]

He still hoped to destroy the USSR in a last gigantic effort and then to turn at once to the next operation in his programme.

THE DEFENSIVE ACTIONS OF THE RUSSIANS

The Russian command, however, was determined to prevent a German advance towards Moscow and to bring it to a halt by defending from a well-prepared system of defences along the Vyazma–Bryansk line. To do this, the Bryansk Front – under the command of Colonel-General A. I. Eremenko – had occupied positions between Putivalya and Frolovka on the eastern bank of the Desna River at the beginning of the operations.[24] Adjacent in the north were two armies of the Reserve Front[25] and those of the West Front under the command of Colonel-General I. S. Konev.[26] They conducted defensive operations along the Elnya–Lake Seliger line. Behind the West Front, the Reserve Front was employed as second echelon under the command of Marshal S. M. Budenny.[27] His forces held the Spas–Demensk–Ostaškov line. The Russian forces had at their disposal a total of 83 rifle divisions,[28] 2 motorised rifle divisions, 1 armoured division, 9 cavalry divisions and 13 armoured brigades,[29] totalling 1,250,000 men,[30] 849 tanks,[31] approximately 11,500[32] guns and mortars as well as 936 aircraft.[33] The main thrust of these forces was along the Smolensk–Moscow highway and in the area of Bryansk where the main thrusts of German forces were expected. The well-prepared defensive positions of the Russian divisions and the defensive lines prepared in their rear between Vyazma and Gzatsk and around Mozaysk, to be occupied if the German forces achieved penetration and to prevent a further attack on Moscow, should clearly have shown to the Commanding General of Army Group Centre that the distance of approximately 350 km. to Moscow was not to be negotiated easily.

THE FIRST PHASE OF OPERATION TAIFUN

After Panzer Group 2 had started the attack on 29 September 1941 it was followed by the bulk of Army Group Centre on 2 October. These forces were to conduct 'the last great decisive battle of this year' which by Hitler's order was 'to destroy the enemy ... in a powerful final blow ...'[34]

These operations seemed to have hit the enemy forces unexpectedly. Initially, they were so successful that the German command once more felt reassured in its policy of staking everything on one card. It thought that after the battles of encirclement near Vyazma and Bryansk, in which a major part of the three Russian fronts had been encircled and destroyed, the war in the east had definitely been won.[35]

On 7 October, Field-Marshal von Brauchitsch, commander-in-chief of the Army, had been flown into the Army Group Centre Headquarters in order to discuss with von Bock the immediate pursuit of the defeated opponent.[36] Three days later, when Stalin ordered General Zhukov to leave Leningrad and come to Moscow, and charged him with the command of all forces west of the Russian capital and the organisation of the new defensive line, Reichspressechef Dietrich announced that the Soviet Union 'was finished militarily'.[37] On 11 October, the headline on the front page of the Völkischer Beobachter read 'Stalin's armies have vanished from the earth!'[39]

Because of these enormous successes, Hitler ordered Army Group Centre, which up to that time had been limited in the encirclement of Moscow, to undertake still further objectives. These objectives were extended to Vologda in the north to encircle the enemy in front of Army Group North and to establish contact with the Finns, and up to Voronezh in the south in order to establish closer contact with Army Group South.[39]

This new allocation of effort, resisted in vain by von Bock, resulted in an excentric splitting-up of the armoured elements and consequently in a decisive weakening of units which might have successfully conducted a rapid pursuit towards Moscow. There was also the resistance offered by the Russians which intensified in the second half of October; consequently the attacker suffered unexpectedly heavy losses. Furthermore, supply difficulties increased and the climatic conditions had not been taken into account early enough. These factors resulted in the discontinuation of the attack during the last ten days of October, and this was officially approved by von Bock on 1 November.[40]

THE CONFERENCE OF THE EASTERN ARMY CHIEF OF STAFF
IN ORSHA ON 13 NOVEMBER

At that time, the advance had also stopped on the other sectors of the front in Russia – except on the Crimea. During the first few days of November, the German command considered whether and how the operations against the Soviet Union could be continued.

Halder ordered the Chiefs of Staff of the Army Groups, Armies and Panzer Groups of the Eastern Front to Orsha on 13 November. He wanted to consult with the commanders of the field forces as to how operations should be continued in Russia, i.e. whether to continue offensive operations or whether to go over to defensive operations until spring 1942.[41] The Chiefs of Staff of Army Groups North and South, as well as the Commanding Generals of the Armies of Army Group Centre, were convinced that it would be absurd to continue offensive operations.[42] As reasons they gave: weaknesses in the personnel and *matériel* fields, the enormous supply difficulties and the imminent winter together with the considerable resistance still being offered by the Russian forces. They advocated a withdrawal of German forces back to the start-line positions of the October offensive, and even to positions as far back as the borders of the Reich.

This concept, which clearly acknowledged the failure of the campaign plan, stood in direct contradiction to the concept of the OKH and von Bock. They held that one ought not to give up so close to reaching one's objective, but put everything at stake once more.[43]

These considerations may have been based largely on experiences from the First World War – especially on the end of the battle of the Marne – but what was even more important was that Hitler, too, wanted to strike and defeat Moscow in a second thrust despite the failure of the first.

Not only did he not approve of the negative estimate of the situation made by some of his generals but, in spite of it, he even extended the objectives for the operations of 1941 to include Maikop, Stalingrad, Voronezh, Gorkii and Vologda. The unrealistic nature of these objectives had been recognised during the Orsha conference, but nevertheless the plans were not changed.[44]

Hitler dismissed reports about the activation of new Russian armies in the Ural Mountains and Volga River areas, remarking that this was impossible even if only because the necessary armament technology was not available. However, the fact is that, from the middle of October to early in December, the Soviet Union was building up eleven new armies.[45] In addition, the USSR was able to make good most of the severe losses of the front troops already in combat by activating new forces and by redeploying troops from the Far East, Siberia and the Caucasus.[46]

Thus, while the Stavka moved fresh forces up to the front, five divisions of the German eastern front, including four divisions from the area of Army Group Centre,[47] were withdrawn, relocated to the west and re-equipped to allow their deployment as armoured units for operations 'after Operation *Barbarossa*. Hitler also believed that the situation along the eastern front permitted the withdrawal of elements of the 2nd Air Fleet in order to redeploy them in the Mediterranean area.[49]

It is extraordinary that in this context Hitler now made use of OKH arguments which he had rejected earlier: as a result of Russian centralism, the Soviet system would collapse immediately if Moscow had been seized, because the Russian traffic and communication network would then be neutralised or in German hands and then command by Stalin would no longer be possible. Opposing arguments by General of the Infantry Thomas, Chief of the War Economy and Armaments Office, were dismissed as 'too optimistic for the Soviets'.[49] He had warned the High Command against such considerations and pointed out in a memorandum as early as October that, even if the Donets Basin, Stalingrad, Voronezh, Moscow, Gorkij and Leningrad could be seized by German troops, the Russians would still remain viable as a result of their potential remaining in the Ural area and therefore able to continue war.[50] Thomas's study, in which he pointed out that the Anglo-Saxons were in a position to compensate for most of the losses suffered by the Red Army until the middle of 1942, was not taken seriously.[51] Because the hope that Russia would surrender after the defeat of Moscow was Hitler's last chance to bring this war to a successful end according to his concept, he clung to the hope and consistently tried to enforce his concept.

THE FINAL FAILURE OF THE OFFENSIVE IN THE EAST

After a pause of almost three weeks for resupply, offensive operations of Army Group Centre were started again on 15 November, only to come to a definite standstill early in December. The Russians had made such successful use of the pause that the attacking forces did not achieve any decisive penetration. Although elements of the German forces approached up to within approximately 30 km. of the Russian capital, they had to discontinue their offensive as a result of exhaustion.

On 5 December, the Russians started their counter-attack, which hit the German troops lying unprotected in open terrain, smashed their line and produced an almost fatal crisis. These operations by the Red Army destroyed Army Group Centre as an attacking force. Elements of Army Group Centre were forced to withdraw up to 250 km. by the end of January.[52]

Army Groups North and South, too, had passed their 'climax' early in December. Army Group South suffered a defeat of dire consequences near Rostov in the closing days of November and had to stop its offensive operations. Army Group North, which had succeeded in seizing the important junction of Tikhvin by a thrust towards Vologda, from 13 November onwards was conducting defensive operations in this area against severe Russian counter-attacks, and the Army was forced to abandon Tikhvin on 7 December.[53] This denoted the end of the offensive operations by Army Group North too.

MILITARY CONSEQUENCES

The losses suffered during the forced disengagement from the offensive in the east and during subsequent defensive battles could not be replaced in the years to come – as figures illustrate.

By 31 January 1942, the casualties of the Eastern Theatre Army had amounted to a total of 917,985 men, including 28,935 officers.[54] Army Group Centre alone was short of 396,000 men at that time,[55] while the casualties of the air force reached a total of 18,098 men in the eastern theatre. In spite of increasing replacements in the ensuing months, the vacancies in the Eastern Army could not be filled even approximately. An OKW study on 'the defence strength of the *Wehrmacht* early in 1942' stated that 'full replacement of the casualties sustained in the winter ... was impossible.[56]

Reserves were no longer available. Available personnel could only be assigned as replacements to Army Group South, because in 1942 this Army group would have to bear the brunt of operations. To withdraw more workers from industry and to allot them to the *Wehrmacht* was impossible, because German industry would then have collapsed. Early in April, the industrial war economy alone expected a total labour requirement of 1.4 million by July 1942, 900,000 of which could probably not be made available.[57] The weakness of the German Reich, which did not have at its disposal adequate manpower to sustain a lasting war, had now been clearly revealed.

In addition to the personnel losses and the moral effects of the defeat on the Eastern Theatre Army – especially on the commands and staffs from division upwards – the losses of *matériel* and equipment had increased by leaps and bounds. Eastern Theatre Army had started the Russian campaign with 3,580 tanks. In the middle of November 1941, the losses of tanks and self-propelled assault guns amounted to 2,090, and by the end of January 1942 had jumped up to 4,241.[58] The sixteen Panzer divisions employed in Russia reported a total strength of only 140 combat-ready tanks on 30 March 1942.[59]

Also, the mobility of the Army was limited primarily by the tremendous loss of motor vehicles. Of the approximately 500,000 motor vehicles available at the beginning of the campaign, 77,000 had already been lost at the middle of November. Another 250,000 had to be repaired.[60] The heavy losses of horses, which had reached almost 207,000 by the end of January 1942, must be added to these figures.[61]

But it was not only the mobility of the Eastern Theatre Army that had decreased; the operational readiness of troops themselves had also been reduced by the heavy losses in weapons and equipment, especially the losses in small arms and machine guns, heavy weapons and guns. As early as the middle of January, the OKH was forced to announce that losses of heavy weapons and guns in particular could not be replaced any more 'because BdE does not presently have any stock'.[62]

In the status report of 30 March on the combat effectiveness of all divisions deployed in the eastern theatre, the OKH stated that only eight of the 162 divisions deployed along the eastern front were completely combat-ready for the offensive operations to come. Three divisions required a short period of rehabilitation, 47 divisions had only a limited capacity for offensive operations, and the majority of the divisions could only be employed for defensive tasks at best.[63]

The aircraft losses of Eastern Theatre Air Forces, which at the beginning of the Russian campaign had had about 1,800 aircraft, increased to a total number of 6,894, including 5,102 total losses at the end of January. From the middle of January, the air forces reported that their losses in the Eastern Theatre could no longer be replaced since the supply agencies had no more first-line planes available at the end of January.[64]

CONSEQUENCES WITH REGARD TO DEFENCE ECONOMY

The defeat in the battle for Moscow was a fatal set-back, not only in the purely military field but also in the field of the armaments industry. Hitler's

Blitzkriegkonzept envisaged the defeat of individual opponents in quick, lightning campaigns, not letting them develop their own economic power. According to the concept current at the time, the *Blitzkrieg* campaign against the Soviet Union seemed to have been adequately stockpiled and sufficiently prepared. After initial successes in the east, therefore, and as early as 14 July 1941, Hitler issued an order to change the armament policy in support of the second phase of his plan, i.e. to establish the air forces main effort, as well as, the submarines, and the armoured forces. The armament order of 14 July put a stop to all other armament programmes and brought disastrous consequences late in 1941. Thus, during the actual Russian campaign, the priority for German armaments was placed on a programme to be initiated only after the end of Operation *Barbarossa*. However, already in mid-August, it was evident that the 'Extended Air Force Programme' planned at that time was not feasible.[65] Under this programme aircraft production was to be doubled and to amount to 2,400 aircraft. Primarily, it was labour which was inadequate, although as many as 3 million foreign workers from 27 nations were working in Germany at this time.[66] For the same reasons, an increase in tank production to 900 tanks per month was not possible. Therefore, for the time being, tank production was reduced to 600 tanks per month. In reality, however, hardly 50 per cent of this figure was reached. The average number of tanks produced was 250 per month in 1941 and only 350 per month in 1942.

Very soon, the economic limits of armament production became apparent, i.e. lack of labour and raw materials – in particular iron, steel, aluminium, copper and mineral oil. Originally, this lack of raw materials was to have been balanced by the exploitation of Russian raw materials. However, the latter could not support the German armament effort adequately.

The German High Command hoped to be able to make up for the lack of labour by employing Russian prisoners of war. Nevertheless, the labour problem for 1941 could not even be solved by these measures. Originally, Germany had expected to be able to release approximately 300,000 soldiers by disbanding the bulk of the divisions after the victory over the Soviet Union late in 1941 and to reintegrate them into defence production. From November, the defence industry was confronted not only with giving up hope of getting the expected 300,000 workers, but also with having to detach a considerable labour force as soldiers for the east front.

The consequences of these shortages were severe. In a memorandum on the armaments situation in the Army, the OKH stated on 5 November that even if all the main raw materials allotted to the Army were diverted exclusively to support the 14 July 1941 programme for the production of tanks and anti-tank guns, not more than 25–30 per cent of these programmes would be feasible.[67] One week later, the air force, too, came to the conclusion that the required aircraft programme could not be met for lack of labour and raw materials.[69] Thus, the prerequisites for operations after Operation *Barbarossa* in the field of defence economy had already become questionable as early as November, without even taking into account the actual losses incurred during the Russian campaign.

In December, the worsening of the military situation on the eastern front forced the full-scale continuation and, compared to former times, even an intensification of armament efforts for the Army. These had previously been stopped, especially in the field of ammunition, in order to compensate for losses.

Because of the disastrous situation in the defence economy, Colonel-General Fromm, commanding general of the Reserve Army, stated on 25 November that a peace had to be concluded soon.[69] Fromm, who was able to assess clearly both available personnel replacements and conditions actually prevailing in the field of armaments, could not but realise that the *Wehrmacht* was close to collapsing if it continued to conduct the war as it had so far. Dr Todt, Hitler's Minister for Armaments and Ammunition, reported to his *Führer* on 29 November that the conclusion of the war in favour of Germany was possible only by political means: 'The war was already lost as far as military operations and the defence economy were concerned.'[70] Hitler's question how actually to bring about the conclusion of war, could not however, be answered by Todt.

Summarising all armaments measures taken, Thomas stated on 23 December 1941 that war requirements exceeded by far available capacities, and that therefore drastic reorganisation had to be undertaken.[71]

Hitler ordered the reorganisation of armament production on 10 January 1942 because even he now felt compelled to shift the main production effort in armaments immediately and quite clearly to the Army.[72] Thus, Hitler had to bury his plans for the second phase in order to be able to commit the latter's planned forces to the eastern front and to adapt further defence production to meet the requirements of the Eastern Theatre. The system of the *Blitzkriegwirtschaft*, which Hitler had tried to stick to as long as possible and the success of which was critical for the success or failure of his programme, was altered to become a long-term system of economic warfare.

In spite of energetic measures taken by Albert Speer, the new Minister for Armaments and Ammunition, the well-known calamity – shortage of qualified labour and raw materials – was not remedied as quickly and effectively as was essential in the following months.

POLITICAL CONSEQUENCES

What conclusions did Hitler draw from this situation? On 19 November, he pointed out in a discussion with Halder that a total defeat of Russia was no

longer possible. He even expected that a negotiated peace might still come
about because 'the two opposing groups could not destroy each other'.[73]
The further course of the campaign and the political developments made
him become even more sceptical during the ensuing days about his former
expectations of victory.

On 27 November, he told Scavenius, the Danish Foreign Minister, that
the German people ought to perish and be destroyed by another power if
they were not sufficiently strong and willing to make sacrifices.[74] This statement clearly showed that Hitler had realised that the war in the east according to his original concept was no longer feasible, and that the conduct of
the war had shifted from the purely military level to the level of moral and
economic endurance. In other words, a long-term war was beginning to
develop.

Apart from his realisation of the military situation and of the disastrous
situation in the defence economy, Hitler had become absolutely certain by
the middle of November that war against the USA would be unavoidable in
the foreseeable future. Already in the first few days of November, the German
Naval Attaché in Tokyo had reported that 'the endeavour of Japan to convert
America towards an insight and understanding for the situation of Japan
has failed entirely ... The Japanese Government has virtually decided to go
to war against America. Operations in the south will probably be started as
early as this year.'[75]

Shortly afterwards, Herr Ott, German ambassador in Tokyo, reported
details of Japanese offensive operation plans and their objectives.[76] Thus
Hitler, although he had tried to postpone the armed conflict with the USA,
was drawn into a new war by the attitude of Japan and by his adherence to
the arrangements of the 'Three-Power Alliance', but without having finished
the eastern campaign and without being prepared and equipped for such a
war in any way. He had slipped into a war against the USA without having
established those prerequisites which he himself had demanded again and
again. Since Hitler had started this war with the objective that 'Germany
will be world power or it will not exist at all'[77] and as he stuck to this idea –
as the discussion with Scavenius shows – he did not see a way of getting out
of this dilemma even after he had realised that victory could no longer be
achieved. This may account for the fact that, although he had agreed to the
course of action taken by Japan, Hitler did not want the war against the USA
to be initiated at a time so unfavourable for his own plans. Included in his
concept might certainly have been the idea that America would have to split
up its forces in a 'Two-Ocean-War' and, therefore, would not be in the
immediate position to throw all its forces against Germany and help Great
Britain rapidly. Hitler had hoped to delay the appearance of the USA on the

European continent by Japan's entry into the war, and perhaps to regain the initiative against the USSR.[78]

Hitler had accepted the war against the USA without having any plans to show how this armed conflict could be conducted in reality.[79] He knew that his war plan had failed and all hope of a military victory had already been lost before he declared war against America. Therefore, the hopelessness of the new overall strategic situation did not result in a new concept for the war plan, which still remained based on the theory of the *Blitzkrieg*. His former idea, which provided for a constant alternation between a *Blitzfeldzug* and a 'strategical pause', had finally failed. Thus, Hitler no longer saw a way of adequately opposing the superior economic potential of the nations united in the war against Germany, nor of being able to balance in future the unfavourable power ratio by dealing the first surprise blow.

CONCLUSIONS

The Russian counter-offensive, coupled with the heavy German casualties and the lack of personnel and *matériel* reserves, were among the principal factors that caused not only the loss of one battle but ultimately the *Blitzkrieg* in the east and thus Hitler's overall strategy devised in 1940. Another major factor was the shortage of raw materials, which neither permitted a considerable increase of armament production to replenish diminished stockpiles, let alone an increase in potential. When, on the day the Japanese attack on Pearl Harbor caused America's entry into the war and thus the actual expansion of the war into a world war, Hitler declared war on the USA, this decision was not made deliberately but meant nothing but 'a seizing of the bull by the horns'. It was a gesture designed to conceal that the initiative for all subsequent strategic decisions of major importance had gone over to the enemy.

As Colonel-General Jodl, Chef des Wehrmachtführungsstabes, stated in 1945, Hitler was fully aware, that 'when the disaster of the winter 1941–2 occurred ... from this climax early in 1942 on, victory could no longer be forced through'.[90] And from this, he concluded with resignation, 'Earlier than anybody else in the world, Hitler suspected and knew that the war was lost.'[91] Thus, all subsequent measures taken by the German High Command were in fact only desperate efforts to adapt the armaments industry, economy and *Wehrmacht* to a long drawn-out war against the Soviet Union on the one hand and against the Anglo-Saxon powers on the other. From then on, the question was no longer how to win the war but how long Germany would be able to resist the enemy's personnel and *matériel* forces.

Notes

1. For details see A. Hillgruber, *Hitler's Strategie: Politik mit Kriegsführung 1940* (Frankfurt a. M., 1965) pp. 207ff.
2. Cf. Tagebuchnotizen Generalfeldmarschall Fedor von Bock, dated 31 Jan. 1941, in Bundesarchiv – Militärarchiv, Freiburg im Breisgau, N 22/9, cited hereafter as BA – MA: Tagebuch Bock.
3. Hitler explained these essential points in the discussion on 30 Apr. 1941 with the military commanders. See H. Greiner, *Die oberste Wehrmachtführung 1939–1943* (Wiesbaden, 1951) pp. 307 ff. See also 'Richtlinien auf Sondergebieten zur Weisung Nr. 21' (Operation *Barbarossa*), printed in W. Hubatsch, *Hitler's Weisungen für Kriegsführung 1939–1945* (Frankfurt a. M., 1965) pp. 88 ff., cited hereafter as *Weisungen*.
4. See the discussion between Hitler and the chief of the Army General Staff, Colonel-General Halder, dated 5 Dec. 1940 in F. Halder, *Kriegstagebuch: Tägliche Aufzeignungen des Chefs des Generalstabes des Heeres*, vol. 2 (*Von der geplanten Landung in England bis zum Begim des Ostfeldzuges 1.7.1940–21.6.1941*, compiled by H-A. Jacobsen (Stuttgart, 1963), cited hereafter as *KTB Halder 2*. See also *Kriegstagebuch des Oberkommandos der Wehrmacht* (Wehrmachtführungsstab), vol. I, 1 Aug. 1940–31 Dec. 1941, compiled and annotated by H-A. Jacobsen (Frankfurt a. M., 1965) p. 203, cited hereafter as *KTB OKW I*.
5. Cf. Directive No. 32 'Vorbereitung für die Zeit nach Barbarossa', dated 11 June 1941, in Hubatsch, *Weisungen*, pp. 129 ff.
6. Printed in Hubatsch, *Weisungen*, pp. 136 ff.
7. Ibid., note 5.
8. Details of this planning in OKH Org. Abt. (I), doc. no. 507/41 gKdosChefs, dated 7 Apr. 41, briefing paper (*Vortragsnotiz*) 'Welche Forderungen sind an die Organisation des Heeres nach der militärischen Niederlage Gesamt-Europas zu stellen?', in BA – MA: RH 15/V170.
9. For the draft operational documents covering the 'Zeit nach Barbarossa' see Oberquartiermeister I of the General Staff of the Army, doc. no. 430/41, gKdosChefs, dated 3 July 41, file Paulus, in BA – MA: H 3/1, p. 2047/15 f.
10. See F. Halder, *Kriegstagebuch: Tägliche Aufzeichnungen des Chefs des Generalstabes des Heeres*, vol. 3 (*Der Russlandfeldzug bis zum Marsch nach Stalingrad* (23 June 1941 – 24 Sept. 43), compiled by H-A. Jacobsen (Stuttgart, 1964) p. 38, entry for 3 July 1941, cited hereafter as *KTB* Halder 3.
11. See *KTB OKW I*, p. 1020, entry dated 4 July 1941.
12. See *KTB* Halder 3, p. 170, entry dated 11 Aug. 1941.
13. Published in *Akten zur Deutschen Auswärtigen Politik 1918–1941*. In the Archives of the Foreign office, ser. D 1937–1941, vol. XIII/1 (*Die Kriegsjahre* (23 June – 14 Sept. 1941) (Göttingen, 1970) doc. no. 265, pp. 345 ff., cited hereafter as *ADAP* D XIII. See also *KTB* Halder 3, p. 226.
14. See BA – MA: Tagebuch Bock, entry dated 12 Aug. 1941.
15. For the greatest detail concerning Hitler's 'Studie' of 22 Aug. 1941 in response to the OKH (Oberkommando des Heeres: Army High Command) for the further development of operations (Fortführung der Operationen), see *KTB OKW I*, p. 1063.
16. The attack on Moscow was ordered on 6 Sept. 1941 by Directive No. 35 and given the code-name 'Taifun' (Typhoon) from 19 Sept. 1941. See Hubatsch, *Weisungen*, p. 153 and pp. 150 ff.
17. For details see BA – MA: Tagebuch Bock, entry dated 2 Sept. 1941.
18. For details see *Das Deutsche Reich und der Zweite Weltkrieg*, vol. 4 (*Der Angriff auf die Sowjetunion*), published by the Militärgeschichtlichen Forschungsamt (Stuttgart, 1983) pp. 569 ff.

19. *Kriegstagebuch der Heeresgruppe Mitte*, no. 1, Oct. 1941, enclosure p. 48 (2 Oct. 1941), in BA – MA: III/H 371/4, enclosure B, cited hereafter as *KTB HGr Mitte* B.

20. Specifically 46 infantry divisions, 1 cavalry division, 14 Panzer divisions, 8 motorised infantry divisions, 6 security divisions, 1 SS cavalry brigade.

21. See Hubatsch, *Weisungen*, p. 152, entry dated 6 Sept. 1941.

22. Ibid.

23. See *KTB* Halder 3, p. 53.

24. See *Geschichte des Grossen Vaterländischen Krieges der Sowjetunion* (in Moscow, Institute of Marxism-Leninism, Central Committee CPSU) vol. 2 (*Die Abwehr des worthbrüchigen überfalls des faschistischen Deutschlands auf die Sowjetunion: Die Schaffung der Voraussetzungen für den grundlegenden Umschwung im Kriege*) (East Berlin, 1963) p. 281, cited hereafter as *Geschichte* 2.

25. The particular armies involved here were the 43rd Army (Sobennikov in command) and the 24th Army (Rakutin in command) of the Reserve Front.

26. The Soviet Western Front comprised the 20th Army (Yersakov in command), 16th Army (Rokossovskii in command), 19th Army (Lukin in command), 20th Army (Khomenko in command), 29th Army (Maslennikov in command) and the 22nd Army (Yushkevich in command).

27. In addition to the Soviet armies mentioned in note 25 above, the Soviet 33rd Army (Onuprienko in command), the 49th Army (Zakharkin in command), the 32nd Army (Vyshnevskii in command) and the 31st Army (commander Dolmatov) also belonged to the Reserve Front.

28. Details from 'Dokumenty i materialy. Moskovskaya bitva v tsifrakh' in *Voenno-istoricheskii zhurnal*, no. 1, 1967, p. 70, note 3, cited hereafter as 'Dokumenty'.

29. 'Dokumenty', table 2, p. 71.

30. Ibid.

31. Ibid.

32. Ibid.

33. 'Dokumenty', table 3, p. 72.

34. Tagesbefehl Hitlers dated 2 Jan. 1941, printed in M. Domarus, *Hitler: Reden und Proklamation*, vol. 2 (*Untergang* (1939–1945) (Würzburg, 1963) pp. 1756 ff.

35. See *KTB HGr Mitte* B, entry dated 19 Oct. 1941.

36. Discussion dated 7 Oct. 1941 concerning 'Einleitung der Operation gegen Moskau', see *KTB HGr Mitte* B, p. 126.

37. O. Dietrich, *12 Jahre mit Hitler* (Munich, 1955) p. 101.

38. Quoted in W. Boelcke (ed.), *Wollt Ihr den totalen Krieg? Die geheimen Goebbels-Konferenzen 1939–1943* (Stuttgart, 1967) p. 189.

39. See 'Befehl für die Fortsetzung der Operationen', Oberkommando der HGr. Mitte Ia, doc. no. 1960/41 gKdosChefs, dated 14 Oct. 1941, in *KTB HGr Mitte* B, p. 236.

40. BA – MA: Tagebuch Bock, entry dated 1 Nov. 1941.

41. See *KTB* Halder 3, p. 276.

42. *KTB* Halder 3, p. 281.

43. Chef GenSt AOK 6, Az.7, doc. no. 2692/41 gKdos, dated 15 Nov. 1941, with respect to the exchange: Besprechung in Orscha, dated 13 Nov. 1941. See also AOK 6, Führungsabteilung, Anlagen zum KTB, no. 9, p. 1215c. In BA–MA: 16 027/5.

44. *KTB HGr Mitte* B entry dated 15 Nov. 1941. See also *KTB* Halder 3, p. 295.

45. Cf. *Geschichte* 2, p. 308 and p. 325.

46. See 'Dokumenty', table 1, p. 70.

47. The formations under discussion were VIII AK (VIII Corps) with the 28th and 8th Infantry Division, the 5th and 15th Infantry Division, as well as the 1st Cavalry Division. See *KTB HGr Mitte* B, p. 282.

48. See Hitler's letter to Mussolini, dated 29 Oct. 1941, printed in *ADAP* D XIII, document no. 433, pp. 584 ff.

49. Der Chef des Wehrwirtschafts- und Rüstungsamtes im OKW, doc. no. 3208/41 gKdos Wi, dated 2 Oct. 1941, file Thomas, in BA – MA: Wi ID 73, pp. 41 ff.

50. VerbStd OKW/RüAmt beim Reichsmarschall, dated 31 Oct. 1941, file Nagel, in BA – MA: W 01-B/27.

51. Der Chef des Wehrwirtschafts- und Rüstungsamtes im OKW, doc. no. 3409/41 gKdos, dated 22 Oct. 41, file Thomas, in BA – MA: Wi ID 73.

52. For details see K. Reinhardt, *Die Wende vor Moskau: Das Scheitern der Strategie Hitlers im Winter 1941/42* (Stuttgart, 1972) pp. 197 ff.

53. *KTB* Halder 3, p. 332 and p. 334.

54. Breakdown of figures in Anlg. 1 zu OKH / GenStH / GenQu / Abt. I Qu 2 / III, doc. no. 720/42, dated 5 Feb. 42, see BA – MA: III W 805/8, pt. 1, p. 88.

55. Details of losses in *KTB HGr Mitte B, passim.*

56. See OKW 'Wehrkraft der Wehrmacht im Frühjahr 1942', dated 6 July 42, file Warlimont, printed in H-A. Jacobsen, *Der Zweite Weltkrieg in Chronik und Dokumentaten* (Darmstad, 1962) p. 309.

57. See OKW / WiRüAmt Stab Z/SRL, doc. no. 1016/42 gKdos, dated 11 Apr. 42, in BA – MA: W 01-8/56, Bl. pp. 75 ff.

58. See OKH /GenStH / Abt. I/ Qu 2 (III), doc. no. I/720/42 gKdos, dated 5 Feb. 42, in BA – MA: III W 805/8, pt. 2, p. 75.

59. See Jacobsen, *Der Zweite Weltkrieg*, p. 690.

60. See above, note 58.

61. Ibid.

62. Ibid.

63. See Jacobsen, *Der Zweite Weltkrieg*, p. 690.

64. See Der Befehlshaber der Luftwaffe, GenSt GenQu 6, Abt. doc. no. 908/42 gKdos (I A), dated 4 Feb. 42, in BA – MA: III W 805/8, pt. I, Bl.62.

65. See OKW / WiRüAmt Stab Z / SR doc. no. 2667/41 gKdos, dated 11 Aug. 41, in BA – MA: W 01/8/5, pp. 36 ff.

66. Figures according to E. L. Homze, *Foreign Labour in Nazi Germany* (Princeton, NJ, 1967) p. 68.

67. See OKH/HWA doc. no. 2550/41 gKdos Wa Stab Ib, Denkschrift 'Die rüstungswirtschaftliche Lage des Heeres', file Leeb, in BA – MA: H 15/23.

68. See Der Reichsminister der Luftfahrt und OBdL, GL/A-Pl, dated 10 Nov. 41, file Milch, in BA – MA: III W 803.

69. See *KTB* Halder 3, p. 309.

70. See *Militärgeschichtliche Mitteilungen*, no. 1, 1969, p. 89.

71. See WiRüAmt/Rü (II a) doc. no. 4010/41 gKdos, dated 23 Oct. 41, file Thomas, in H. Thomas, *Geschichte der deutschen Wehr- und Rüstungswirtschaft (1918–1943/45)* (Boppard a. R., 1966) pp. 470 ff.

72. See *KTB OKW* I, pp. 1265 ff.

73. See *KTB* Halder 3, pp. 296 ff.

74. See A. Hillgruber, *Staatsmänner und Diplomaten bei Hitler: Vertrauliche Aufzeichnungen über die Unterredungen mit Vertretern des Auslandes*, vol. 1 (1939–1941) (Frankfurt a. M., 1967) doc. no. 91, p. 657.

75. See Kriegstagebuch der Seekriegsleitung, 1. Abteilung, pt. A. Nov. 1941, dated 6 Nov. 41, in BA – MA: III M1000/27.

76. See *ADAP* D XIII, doc. no. 486, p. 658.

77. See A. Hitler, *Mein Kampf*, 608–612 edn (Munich, 1941) p. 742.

78. See *KTB* Halder 3, p. 296.

79. Cf. W. Warlimont, *Im Hauptquartier des deutschen Wehrmacht 1939–1945* (Frankfurt a. M., 1963) p. 217.

80. See *KTB OKW* I, p. 1503.

81. See P. E. Schramm, *Hitler als militärischer Führer* (Frankfurt a. M. and Bonn, 1965) p. 154.

Part 3
Conflict, Compromise, Cost

Introduction

The Soviet–German war was hideous beyond all imagining. It was befouled by and drenched in criminality. The German troops who launched the invasion of the Soviet Union were both exhorted and encouraged to act with the maximum cruelty against the Red Army and the civilian population, with the *Wehrmacht* freed from the accepted constraints of law, whether military or civilian. Soldierly honour and the conventions of front-line comradeship were not merely abandoned but subverted through a relentless portrayal of the enemy's inhumanity which demanded a barbarous response. While this will remain a residual horror, perhaps the true legacy of Operation *Barbarossa* is its role in the debate which has been generated both in Germany and in what was the Soviet Union, now Russia, over the responsibility and the accountability for this monstrous behaviour. The impassioned debate concerns the existence (or the absence) of a crucial difference between the nature of the Nazi and the Soviet regimes and the policies each pursued. For those who would argue for the uniqueness of Nazism and its depravity, there were others who cited the existence of the 'Gulag Archipelago', chronicled by Alexander Solzhenitsyn as providing an early Soviet model for the subsequent Nazi death camps. Did not Bolshevik 'class murder' precede Nazi 'racial murder'?

Much of this ground has been trampled by the so-called *Historikerstreit*, the great debate of the historians, in Germany. In the former Soviet Union, dissidents – at the risk of their liberty if not their lives – investigated the relationship between Nazi Germany and Stalinist Russia, concluding in many cases – after reviewing the Holocaust and the Great Terror – that one regime was the moral equivalent of the other, that the barbed wire which whipped in the wind of the Siberian taiga was indistinguishable from that spanning Auschwitz. But this perspective had more to do with criticising the Soviet regime than conveying specific historical accuracy. Andrei Sakharov – the most celebrated of Soviet dissidents – at first embraced this argument about the relativism of the two regimes, but on reflection concluded that the Soviet victory over Nazi Germany in 1945 was preferable to the triumph of Nazism.

With respect to the German army and the Russian campaign, Professor Dr Klaus-J. Müller is most immediately concerned with investigating the breakdown of all restraint on behaviour in a process which was not traditional 'normal brutality' associated with warfare. Nazi indoctrination alone cannot supply the answer, rather it is necessary to point to the witches' brew of anti-Semitism, anti-Slavism and anti-Bolshevism, and explanation which pre-dates the Nazi period and identifies long-term influences working on important, indeed key figures in the German officer corps and the German high command.

In this emotionally charged and highly complex undertaking to come to terms with the past, facing up to the implications of wartime collaboration with the enemy has proved to be a prolonged and distressing affair, nowhere illustrated more starkly than in the former Soviet Union where millions were involved. What occurred was clearly more than limited, corrupt self-serving accommodation with the occupying power. From the mass of more than 5 million Soviet prisoners, of whom at least 3 million were to die from German maltreatment or outright execution, Lieutenant-General Andrei Vlasov formed an anti-Stalinist 'Russian Liberation Army', established with German assistance, albeit lukewarm. In 1942, General Vlasov was commander of the 2nd Shock Army in the north-west, an army encircled by the Germans. Vlasov himself was made prisoner and turned himself over to the German side. Since then, he has become a name to conjure with, a figure not only of fascination but also of retrospective approval for his anti-Stalinist stance. Though some, mindful of what allegiance to the Nazi occupiers implied, still execrate him as a foul traitor. Dr Kudryashov now uses hitherto highly secret Soviet files to explore what was known to Soviet authorities during the war of the scope, scale and significance of Soviet collaboration with the Germans, not simply passive collaboration but the deliberate defection of a sizeable segment of the populace, involving many nationalities.

In that pitiless war, with Soviet partisans fighting their fellow-citizens and battling their German masters – the latter responding with unrestrained ferocity – casualties could not be counted. At long last, a start has been made on full reckoning of the human and *matériel* losses incurred by the Soviet Union in the course of the Great Patriotic War. Taking into account both direct and indirect losses, there seems to be general agreement that the figure stands at some 47 million. Yet there is more work to be done, work which will continue for many years – listing the dead and locating the missing – work in which the Russian authorities have invited the co-operation and participation of foreign scholars and experts who might have access to or knowledge of relevant archives and records. It is a doleful task, though one intended as an act of national remembrance.

Chapter 10

The Brutalisation of Warfare, Nazi Crimes and the *Wehrmacht*

KLAUS-JÜRGEN MÜLLER

This chapter raises several important questions. First, there is the question of whether and to what extent criminal directives were executed; secondly, to what extent the *Wehrmacht* was involved in this affair; and finally, how the officer corps or single officers reacted to the orders, and how their attitudes can be explained.[1]

First of all, one has to emphasise that – so far as these criminal orders and directives and their implementation are concerned – the point in question is *not* that of 'normal brutality' which happened during almost all military conflicts of our century, as in the massacres of Nanking (1937), Oradour and Tulle (1944), Freudenstadt and Sétif (1945), Deir Jassin (1948) and My Lai (1968), or when the Red Army invaded Germany's eastern provinces (1945) or during the French Algerian War (1954–62). Even so, these appalling incidents do reflect the increasing brutalisation of modern warfare.[2]

Equally, we are not specifically dealing with guerrilla warfare or anti-terrorist operations in which the rules of international law of war have often been neglected. But what distinguishes the criminal acts under review here from this kind of 'normal brutalisation' is the very fact that the war against Soviet Russia was deliberately conceived by Nazi Germany's highest political and military authorities, and was actually waged as a war of extermination and oppression. Not only were special forces such as the SS and Security Police Units involved in its execution, but also the regular army made an active contribution to war brutalities.

On the other hand, it is quite obvious that, during the war in Russia, acts of 'normal brutalisation' happened, and that the war of extermination contributed to increasing this kind of brutaliation. This can be seen by the phenomenon of the so-called 'war of scorched earth', which both sides regarded as strategically necessary, but to which the German army in Russia resorted much less reluctantly than it would have done elsewhere in western European countries. However, at the very end of the war, Hitler – determined not to spare his own nation the scorched-earth strategy – ordered the total destruction of Germany's infrastructure.

Moreover, the war of extermination against Soviet Russia produced a type of guerrilla warfare that tended to increase normal brutalisation, against which the German army responded with unrestrained measures of anti-guerrilla repression. To the soldiers, ideologically conditioned as they were, this guerrilla fighting seemed to confirm the propaganda arguments – 'Russian Bolsheviks are sub-human beings' – put forward to their political and military superiors in order to justify the issued criminal directives and orders.

On the one hand it is clear that there was a certain interdependency of 'normal brutalisation' and ideologically motivated warfare; on the other, however, the latter phenomenon presents considerable methodological difficulties, as reflected in some recent analysis.[3]

In response to the questions raised at the beginning of this chapter, we have to admit that we are encountering equally serious methodological problems.

First, as regards the employment of the criminal directives,[4] we are still lacking precise and comprehensive quantitative studies covering the whole eastern front during the period of the war.

However, so far as Soviet POWs are concerned, we can rely on well-based informative studies – such as Streit's *Keine Kameraden* – which show that four out of five Soviet POWs died of starvation, maltreatment or execution. The 'Directive regarding the Behaviour of German Troops in Russia', issued by the *Wehrmacht* High Command (OKW) on 15 May 1941, referred to Bolshevism as the 'deadly enemy of the Reich', and ordered 'ruthless measures against Bolshevist agitators, guerrillas and Jews'. It obviously contributed considerably to reducing traditional restraints in dealing with POWs. The identification of 'Bolshevists', 'guerrillas' and 'Jews' is supposed to have produced the same results regarding prisoner mishandling.

As to the execution of political commissioners of the Red Army and other categories of POWs singled out for liquidation, broadly based quantitative analyses are not yet available. There is sufficient evidence, though, that the results of the directives in question were horrible. Recently published studies suggest that about half a million people were killed by special 'Einsatzgruppen' during the first five months of the campaign.

How many political commissioners and other 'politically suspected' POWs were executed by combat units or other units of the regular army, immediately after their capture or in the DULAGs (POW transit camp) cannot be ascertained correctly. However, many sources show, beyond any doubt, that army units not only co-operated with the Special Units of the Security Service (SD) and the Security Police by transferring the specified categories of POWs to the SD/Police Einsatzgruppen for 'special treatment', but in some cases also tried to improve the implementation of the directives.[5]

On the other hand, there were also officers who tried to prevent the executions in their own divisions. We know only of a single case – that of General von Arnim, 17th Panzer Division – where the Commissar Directive was not implemented. For good reasons, one may assume that the application of the directives varied widely, but available sources suggest that generally they were 'correctly' executed by the great majority of the army units, at least during the first six months of the campaign.

From late August 1941, however, initiatives were taken by some officers commanding combat units to get the 'Kommissar-Befehl' cancelled because of the negative effects it produced. The Army's High Command (OKH) supported these initiatives, but the OKW, not to mention Hitler, turned them down. It is significant that these initiatives came at a moment when the German army's advance in Russia began to slow down owing to increasingly stiffer Soviet resistance. Soviet troops were obviously less ready to give up, knowing what treatment they – and particularly their political officers – could expect after being captured.

Taking into account the difficulty in interpreting the relevant sources, one nevertheless, gets the impression that during the last three months of 1941 there was an indirect controversy on the implementation of the directives between certain German generals serving at the eastern front. On the one hand, there was General Schmidt's memorandum of 18 September 1941 – favouring the cancellation of the 'Commissioners Directive' – as well as Fieldmarshal von Bock's initiative of 5 November 1941 – raising objections against transferring certain categories of POWs to the Einsatzgruppen, and particularly emphasising the fact that the Army's responsibility towards POWs could not be shared with other authorities.

Some weeks later, Fieldmarshals von Reichenau and von Manstein and Colonel-General Hoepner – all prominent Army commanders – issued Orders of the Day, which attracted a certain notoriety. In these orders, they tried to justify the war of extermination, demanding that every soldier readily accept 'ruthless, but justified measures to be taken against Jewish sub-human gangsters'.

Admittedly, it is difficult to interpret these Orders of the Day. One may conclude that they were intended to be an answer to the above-mentioned initiatives of cancelling the criminal directives. But were they only destined to brush aside opposition against these directives or even to intensify relevant actions and attitudes? Or may they also be taken as a reaction against soldiers' reluctance to implementing the directives?

Other sources are equally difficult to interpret. Colonel von Gersdorff's report, submitted to the Commander-in-Chief of the 4th Army in December 1941, referred to the fact that the execution of Jews, prisoners and political commissioners of the Red Army was almost generally rejected by the officer corps, and that it was regarded as being contrary to the honour of the German army. Despite those strong words, the question is, however, how representative they are for the majority of officers and soldiers.

It is equally difficult to ascertain whether official demands, made by commanding officers, to withdraw the so-called 'Kommissar-Befehl' were simply motivated by practical purposes, as they pretended, or whether tactical arguments were put forward because ethical arguments were regarded as useless in the eyes of the *Führer*.

Another question is how Germany's military élite reacted to these directives and how its reactions can be interpreted.

First of all, it is a sad truth that neither Hitler's speeches to his generals nor the directives issued by the OKW caused any official or outspoken protest from the Army's High Command. On the contrary, the highest Army authorities reacted like subordinate functionaries by obediently transforming Hitler's general directives into precise orders.

However, acts of individual protest within the ranks of the High Command against such orders have been recorded. In this respect, a controversy between Admiral Canaris, Chief of Intelligence of the *Wehrmacht*, and Fieldmarshal Keitel, Head of OKW, is significant: Canaris, in a statement of 8 September 1941, protested against an OKW Directive which openly referred to a possible mass execution of Soviet POWs. Keitel turned Canaris' intervention down, stating in a marginal note that the Admiral's scruples reflected 'traditional ideas of gentlemanlike warfare; but this war is an ideological war of extermination; I, therefore, approve and authorise the measures stipulated in this directive.'

The controversy obviously highlights the very fact that in those days two entirely different ideas about the nature of warfare and of the military ideal coexisted in the German officer corps: one ideal was represented by Canaris, who was still conditioned by the traditional values of European military élites, whereas Keitel's attitude was definitely determined by the new model of the ideologically motivated soldier. To the Admiral, war was still a military conflict between armies and nations; to the Fieldmarshal, war had become an all-out struggle between irreconcilably antagonistic ideologies and their protagonists.

It is difficult to quantify the number of representatives of either attitude within the Army. In this respect, we have to take into account the fact that, owing to the precipitated rearmament of the *Wehrmacht* in the 1930s and the increasing ideological indoctrination, the homogeneity of the officer corps had been disintegrating with all the weakening effects on the traditional code of values.

Some figures are significant: in 1935 the Army had approximately 3,800 officers; in 1938, however, the number had jumped to almost 22,000; and in December 1941 it enveloped more than 35,000 professional officers. If one adds to these figures those of reserve officers, the result is even more stunning: in 1939 there were more than 38,000 reserve officers and in 1944 more than 125,000. In 1943, the total officer corps numbered close to 250,000. It is clear that traditional attitudes and the traditional code of values must have been severely affected by such gigantic increases in personnel. Restraints in behaviour, hitherto determined by traditional values and socially enforced conformity, were likely to have dissolved among an increasing number of officers.[6]

There is another aspect which must be taken into account. Recent research on barbarisation of warfare on the eastern front makes the point that Nazi indoctrination played a major role in the younger officers' accepting and obeying criminal orders. The problem, however, is that the extent and intensity of the indoctrination's effect cannot really be assessed. Simply taking for granted that all officers who had passed their A-level exams between 1936 and 1940 and who had been members of the Hitler Youth were indiscriminately subjected to Nazi indoctrination seems to underestimate the complex situation in Hitler's Germany in so far as its indoctrination and effects are concerned, given the considerable diversity and variety of factors determining social attitudes and behaviour. Moreover, this approach seems even more inadequate as higher officers who had spent their formative years in the Wilhelminian empire and in the Weimar period were also involved in what we call the 'criminal orders'-issue.

Nazi indoctrination cannot be held solely accountable for the behaviour of those participating in criminal behavior. For even generals well known for their traditionally ethical standards, as well as some of those who later actively participated in the 1944 plot against Hitler, were – to a certain extent, at least – involved in the war of extermination in Russia.

Some authors try to explain the involvement of so many German officers and soldiers in Hitler's war of extermination through a lack of character and a perverted sense of absolute obedience. These factors certainly have to be taken into account. But, as it is impossible to assess the effects of personal shortcomings, this kind of explanation is not very convincing from a methodological point of view.

Another, more general approach to the problem is that of mentality: there was a general feeling among German soldiers of being culturally superior.

Basically, this had nothing to do with the Nazi ideology of *Herren-menschentum*, although, in a way, it was close to it. At any rate, it resulted in a certain temptation of neglecting traditional rules of warfare. Being confronted with an enemy who was regarded as culturally inferior, one tends not to treat him as an opponent of equal rights. Colonial wars provide ample proof of this psychological mechanism and of the consequences of warfare brutalisation by dehumanising the enemy.

There are indications that this kind of mental mechanism was also at work when the German army was confronted with eastern European people and their special civilisation. For example, Major General Felber, an officer born in 1889, wrote in his personal war diary during the Polish campaign: 'Civil population here more than lousy. Most of them Jews. We'll be happy if we don't have them here any longer.' And the famous Panzer leader, General Geyr von Schweppenburg, a convinced anti-Nazi officer, reported in his diary the following incident: 'Wlodowa, a disgusting Jewish town. They show indications of undisciplined behaviour. Opinion is aired that looting the Jews is allowed. A series of court-martial proceedings are quickly restoring discipline.'[7]

This brings us closer to the origins of an evolution that, eventually, brought Germany's military élite to accepting criminal directives which it certainly would not have executed had they been issued in a war against western European armies (although criminal directives with regard to the treatment of Italian soldiers remaining loyal to their king after Italy's surrender have also been accepted without protest and widely implemented).[8]

Recent research has shown that 'there was a substantial ideological agreement between Hitler and the officer corps'. This does not mean that these officers were particularly indoctrinated by genuine Nazi ideas; but there were some elements of Nazi ideology which were shared by Germany's traditional élites and, to a certain extent, by other social strata.

First of all, there was an anti-Semitism which, in fact, was not much reflected but fairly widespread. It was not so much a racial factor, but rather a strange mixture of xenophobia, Christian prejudices and cultural arrogance combined with political scapegoatism.

There was also a sort of anti-Slavism, familiar but not exclusively limited to Prussian Protestant upperclasses. This was another strange mixture of cultural and religious feelings of diversity, of political dominance and of unconscious anxiety caused by the imagined nightmare of the Slavic masses steamrolling towards the German west. All this had become ideologically virulent since before the First World War by the increasing antagonism of both pan-Slavism and pan-Germanism.

Finally, there was a militant anti-Bolshevism which, since the German revolution of 1918, and together with the idea of German hegemony in central Europe, had become the most influential element of political thought in Germany's traditional élites, shared even by those members who deliberately kept their distance from Nazism.

Since the Russian revolution of 1917 and the revolutionary waves which in its wake swept over Europe, Bolshevism had become the absolute enemy, particularly to those officers who were still imbibed with traditional values and ideals of old pre-revolutionary Europe. To them, Bolshevism was not only challenging their own social and political position but, above all, was the very negation, the antithesis to all their political, social and moral values.

Bolshevism was perceived as a deadly enemy which not only needed to be defeated in a traditional way, but also had to be completely and totally exterminated. Traditional standards of fighting were no longer feasible against this sort of enemy. No quarter could be given in a fight between good and evil, this was the rule of fighting which had already developed during the conflicts of revolutionary Germany throughout the years 1918–20.

Militant anti-Bolshevism, therefore, had the tendency of neglecting traditional codes of value in peace and war. This can be demonstrated by the example of those officers who – on the one hand – protested against killing POWs or abstained from executing collective reprisals against the population, but who – on the other hand – confirmed the directives destined to liquidate 'Bolshevist commissioners, Jews and Komsomolets'.

To most of these officers, Hitler's war on Soviet Russia was as much a repetition of Hindenburg's and Ludendorff's Grand Strategy of 1917–18 as it was a continuation of the antirevolutionary fight against the absolute evil of Russian Bolshevism which was – in their view – responsible for Germany's breakdown in 1918, for the demoralisation of the German army and for all the post-war turmoil of the early 1920s. Given the general anti-semitic feelings, Hitler's identification of Bolshevism and Jews was thus digested without much reflection. In this respect, the officers' perception of the enemy was, to a large extent, identical with Hitler's ideologically motivated perception. Here we have all the elements which might provide a fairly convincing explanation of the Army's involvement in inhuman warfare in Russia.

Seen in a larger historical perspective, the Army's participation in Hitler's war of extermination may be taken as an indicator of the deep changes to which the military had been exposed in an era of new ideologies, social and political turmoil and fundamental changes in the nature of war.

In the war against the Soviet Union, the *Wehrmacht* came close to the point where the traditional, military soldier showed a tendency of being transformed into the prototype of an ideologically motivated political warrior which was intentionally created by the Waffen-SS. Bernd Wegner has shown this in his brilliant thesis.[9]

Thus, the German military was not only integrated into Hitler's policy of extermination, but at the same moment it undertook a kind of self-transformation: on the one hand, it was the structural pressure exerted by the Nazi system that, to a certain extent, determined their actions in Russia; on the other hand, however, these actions sprang from a political mentality which was substantially formed by traditional elements and, predominantly, through the experience of revolution. The Army's involvement in Hitler's war of extermination had exogenous as well as endogenous origins/causes. This happened in a transitory phase in which 'modern' phenomena – like that under review here – and more traditional reactions co-existed: there was the Army's involvement in Hitler's war; but there was also the military's rebellion against its dictator – involvement as well as resistance. This gives evidence of what is often called 'die Gleichzeitigkeit des Ungleichzeitigen' (the simultaneity of differences).

Notes

1. Cf. the relevant literature *inter alia*: Jürgen Foerster's contribution to Horst Boog et al., *Das Dritte Reich und der Zweite Weltkrieg*, vol. 4 (*Der Angriff auf die Sowjetunion*) (Deutsche Verlags-Anstalt, Stuttgart, 1983); Bernd Wegner (ed.), *Zwei Wege nach Moskau: Vom Hitler – Stalin-Pakt zum 'Unternehmen Barbarossa'* (Beck, Munich; 1991); Christian Streit, *Keine Kameraden: Die Wehrmacht und die sowjetischen Kriegsgefangenen 1941–1945* (Deutsche Verlags-Anstalt, Stuttgart, 1978); Helmut Krausnick and H. H. Wilhelm, *Die Truppe des Weltanschauungskrieges: Die Einsatzgruppen der Sicherheitspolizei und des SD 1938–1942* (Deutsche Verlags-Anstalt, Stuttgart, 1981).
2. Cf. Immanuel Geiss, 'Massaker in der Weltgeschichte: Ein Versuch über die Grenzen der Menschlichkeit', in Uwe Backes et al. (eds), *Die Schatten der Vergangenheit: Impulse zur Historisierung des Nationalsozialismus* (Propylaen, Frankfurt a. M. and Berlin, 1990).
3. Cf. Omer Bartov's books: *The Eastern Front 1941–1945: German Troops and the Barbarisation of Warfare* (MacMillan, London and New York, 1985) and *Hitler's Army: Soldiers, Nazis and War in the Third Reich* (OUP, Oxford and New York, 1991). A more differentiated view in his articles: 'Soldiers, Nazis and War in the Third Reich', in *Journal of Mod. Hist.*, 63, 1991, pp. 44–60 and 'Von unten betrachtet: Überleben, Zusammenhalt und Brutalität an der Ostfront', in Wegner, *Zwei Wege*, pp. 326–44.
4. Cf. Hans-Adolf Jacobsen, 'Kommissarbefehl und Massenexekutionen sowjetischer Kriegsgefangener', in Hans Buchheim et al. (eds), *Anatomie des SS-Staates*, vol. II (Rombach, Olten and Freiburg i. Br., 1965) and Foerster, p. 1030 ff. (see note 1) giving the results of recent research.
5. Cf. Jacobsen, 'Kommissarbefehl' document 42 and Foerster, p. 1060 ff. (see note 1).
6. Cf. Bernhard R. Kroener, 'Die personellen Ressourcen des Dritten Reiches', in *Das Deutsche Reich und der Zweite Weltkrieg*, vol. 5/1 (Deutsche Verlags-Anstalt, Stuttgart, 1988) pp. 693–990, and Kroener, 'Auf dem Wege zu einer nationalsozialistischen "Volksarmee": Die soziale Öffnung des Heeresoffizierkorps im Zweiten Weltkrieg', in Martin Broszat et al. (eds), *Von Stalingrad zur Währungsreform, zur Sozialgeschichte des Umbruches in Deutschland* (Beck, Munich,

1988) pp. 651–82; cf. also Kroener, 'Squaring the Circle: Blitzkrieg Strategy and Manpower Shortage, 1939–1942', in Wilhelm Deist (ed.), *The German Military in the Age of Total War* (Berg, Leaminton Spa, 1985) pp. 282–303.

7. Quoted in Klaus-Jürgen Müller, *Armee und Drittes Reich 1933–1939* (Schöningh, Paderborn, 1987) p. 191, documents 54 and 55.

8. Cf. Gerhard Schreiber, *Die italienischen Militärinternierten im deutschen Machtbereich 1943–1945, verraten, verachtet, vergessen* (Oldenbourg, Munich, 1990).

9. Bernd Wegner, *The Waffen-SS: Organization, Ideology and Function*, (Blackwell, Oxford, 1990).

Chapter 11

The Hidden Dimension

Wartime Collaboration in the Soviet Union

SERGEI KUDRYASHOV

Literature about collaboration in Europe during the Second World War is certainly extensive. French historiography, in particular, has devoted much attention to this theme; English, German, Italian and Norwegian historiography continues to show a strong interest in it, owing, to the wartime history of these countries. Experience of foreign researchers is most useful in studying that phenomenon on Soviet territory, as it offers the opportunity to compare the scale of collaboration in different countries, trace the evolution in the policy of occupying forces, reveal its characteristics, specifics and so on.[1]

The history of the Second World War shows that all countries which had been occupied by the Germans and their allies have been forced to look at the question of collaboration. The Soviet Union is no exception.

The term 'collaboration' is not widely used in western historiography when referring to the territories of the Soviet Union. In Soviet literature, at least until the beginning of the 1990s, it was never even mentioned. A significant number of foreign researchers devoted a great deal of their attention to the military and political aspects of collaboration by the Soviet population with the German military and civil government, and were inclined to regard such co-operation not as collaboration, but as a movement for 'liberation'. At the same time, they often borrowed – rather uncritically – the terminology used during the war: 'Liberation Movement of the Peoples of Russia' (ODNR), 'Committee for Liberation of the Peoples of Russia' (KONR), 'Russian Liberation Army' (ROA), 'Russian Liberation People's Army' (RONA) and so on. It stands to reason that just because the participants of those 'movements' and 'armies' called themselves 'liberators', it does not mean that they were exactly that. It is the duty of historians to research, then prove or disprove. However, strong ideological prejudices hindered both western and Soviet authors. If we were to consider all forms of collaboration with the German authorities as opposition to Stalinism, or as the beginning of the liberation struggle against Bolshevism, then one could conclude that the phenomenon of collaboration had no place on Soviet territory. This argument not only politicises, but also distorts the true historical picture. One obvious example is the work of the German historian Joachim Hoffman, recognised as an authority in the field of studies on military formations of various nationalities inhabiting the USSR.[2] Hoffman's undoubted achievement was that he systematised and researched a mass of previously unknown documents, but his overall opinions are biased. They display the spirit of the cold war. Hostility to Bolshevism, and perhaps to Russia as a whole, blinded Hoffman. Nowhere does he admit to the occurrence of treason during the Soviet–German war. For him, only the 'freedom movements' existed. Unjustifiably, he regards all prisoners of war as potential enemies of the system, and he accepts Vlasov's anti-Stalinist propaganda at face value. In this, Hoffman maximises the use of any information which might be said to present collaboration in a favourable light.[3]

Soviet historiography also fell victim to a one-sided representation. Uniformly used definitions like 'traitors', 'turn-coats', 'occupiers accomplices', 'anti-Soviet elements', and so on, cover only a part of the entire scene, and in no way offer a total explanation. Many citizens – women with children, juveniles – who worked as hired hands in the German administration do not fall into that committed collaborationist category.

After August 1991 and the break-up of the USSR, the leaders of the three republics felt that there was no basis for talking about a unified Soviet history. Each historiography (Russian, Ukrainian, Belorussian) took off independently, following the road of nationalist history. One could only but welcome that process, had it not been for one very obvious fact in the present political situation. The monopoly of socialist ideas has been replaced by a monopoly of nationalist ideas, and a very powerful tendency has emerged, whereby almost any enemy of the Soviet regime is depicted as a martyr and fighter for 'freedom of the fatherland'. The concept of 'patriotism' is misrepresented, and numerous politicians – followed by historians – seek to justify the individuals who collaborated with the German fascist authorities (government) during the war. This is especially noticeable in the Baltic States and in the Ukraine, where the political rehabilitation of the collaborators has, in fact, been completed, even though this has not been officially declared yet. Nevertheless, even President Kravchuk of the Ukraine considered it laudable to admit that as a child he helped the *banderovtsi*[4]–the armed Bandera nationalists.

No political leaning in which a historian strives – in the first instance – to prove something, rather than to examine it through study, can ever lead to worthwhile scientific results. If one's starting-point is anti-communism, then much of Soviet Russia's history, on the whole, cannot be explained, especially when dealing with the war period. Proclaiming Vlasov and his adherents 'patriots and liberators of Russia' obliges one to agree with the possibility that Nazi Germany was involved in a war of 'liberation'. And from there it is only a short step to the endeavour to prove that fascist aggression was preventive in nature.

Departure from the methodological blind alley of the politically ster-eotyped opinion lies, manifestly, only in the recognition of the contra-dictions that exist in social developments. Otherwise it would be very difficult, on the one hand, to rise above the level of Hoffmann and others who look for evidence of 'friendship' between the Germans and the Soviet people during the war, and, on the other, to avoid the confines of a simplified concept prevalent in the Soviet boastful historiography, which labels all dissenters 'traitors' and 'falsifiers'.

One accepts that every historian is a free agent where his sympathies and antipathies are concerned. But the logic of historical research demands concrete objective conclusions, which can be arrived at only on the basis of multidimensional analysis, by using a maximum number of sources.

The bitter nature of both the military and the ideological conflict and Nazi policy throughout the occupied territories of the USSR greatly influenced Soviet collaboration. With the recent release of the most secret papers from the more accessible Russian archives, it is possible to study wartime col-laboration by comparing the documents of the combatant countries. This chapter wishes to examine the history of collaboration in the first year of the war, with emphasis on the RSFSR (Russian Republic) territory. Having taken the term collaboration to mean co-operation of the population with the occupying authorities, I have considered it expedient to single out three basic forms of collaboration: military, political and economic.

When studying collaboration in the military sphere, a researcher's first concern is the terminology, which was well formulated in the German vocabulary. German documents mention the following categories: *Frei-willige, Hilfswillige, Ordnung Hilfspolizei, Schutzmannschaft, Ver-trauensleute (V-Leute), Ordnungsdienst (Odi)* and *Gema*.

Freiwillige was the most commonly used term, the literal translation mean-ing 'volunteer'. However, as a rule, this was the term used for those who fought in the German ranks on all fronts.

Hilfswillige (shortened to *Hiwi*) meant 'voluntary helper' and was the name used for individuals who belonged to the local population or were prisoners of war. They were employed for non-combatant duties in the German army.

The *Ordnung Hilfspolizei* was the external auxiliary police, recruited from the representatives of the local population, to perform the functions of the police in the occupied territory. By Himmler's order of 6 November 1941, the *Ordnung Hilfspolizei* was renamed *Schutzmannschaft* (shortened to *Schuma*), which could be translated as 'security commands'. *Schuma* was subordinate to the SS.

Functions similar to *Schuma*'s were performed by the security service or *Ordnungsdienst* (shortened to *Odi*), but this was attached to the military commands and was subordinated to them.

Gema was the universally adopted term during the war for *Gemeinde* (community, city/town council). This term covered individuals from the local population who by order of local government performed the functions of the police during vital periods. As a rule, *Gema* was employed in the regions of partisans' activities.

The concept *V-Leute* (secret service, agents) was used by the *Abwehr* for individuals within the *Abwehr* command who were left behind on Soviet territory in order to reconnoitre and act as saboteurs.[5]

Despite this diversity of terminology, what stands out is the fact that all these terms denote persons performing auxiliary and police functions within the German army or administration. To a great extent, it reflects the nature of military collaboration on the eastern front.

Since Hitler's plan was to effect a quick victory in the war with the USSR, there was no need to consider the possibility of military collaboration with the vanquished peoples of the Soviet Union. In addition, this kind of thought went against Nazi ideology, according to which *Untermenschen* were not allowed to aspire to equality. 'Only a German has a right to carry arms', said the Führer time and again. However, after the stunning successes of the first few weeks of the war, events on the eastern front ceased to follow the scenario of the German General Staff. Staunch resistance of the Red Army and the vast expanse of space inexorably swallowed up the forces of the German army. Already in August 1941 it was clear that the war would drag on and that there would be no *Blitzkrieg*. These circumstances compelled the German command to think about creating military units consisting of prisoners of war and the local population of recruiting age. In December 1941 Hitler officially agreed that such legions should be created from the non-Slav population. And so the Turkestan, Armenian, Azerbaijan, Georgian and north Caucasus legions were formed, as well as the legion of Volga Tartars and field battalions of Crimean Tartars. Apart from these, there were some smaller units of combatants from other nationalities (Kalmyks and others) active in the German forces.

It is important to stress that all these nationalist units were included in the *Wehrmacht* structure, and that they had no independence. Recruitment was carried out both on a voluntary and compulsory basis. Command rank was always allotted to a German. Had the commander not been German, he could not have given an order to a German soldier. Fighting efficiency of the legions was low, and desertion reached 10 per cent in some of them. I have been unable to find any documents, either in the German or the Soviet archives, in which there was even a mention about the high combat quality of the legions. It was therefore not by accident that in 1943 the German command began to dispatch the legions to the west, where it used them mainly as security units or to fight partisans.

But what about the Slavs? It is well known that throughout the whole war, Hitler was against the establishment of Slav military units, and especially Russian ones. Strictly speaking, at the beginning of the war, 'Russian' very often encompassed all the Slav population in the occupied zone, and only gradually did the gradation come into effect. The Ukrainians benefited most from the German authorities, which very likely could be explained by taking into account the economic role that the Nazis assigned to the Ukraine. A powerful method, used to win over the population, was the practice of freeing the prisoners of war on the basis of their nationality. And so, in the period between 22 June 1941 and 31 January 1942 – according to the *Wehrmacht* statistics – a total of 280,108 men were freed. Out of these, there were 270,095 Ukrainians and not a single Russian. One can suggest that a few Russians may have managed to pass for Ukrainians, but a fact is a fact – within the inventory of the freed men, there is no mention of Russians.[6]

By a strange coincidence, the Nazis did not regard Cossacks as Slavs. For that reason formation of Cossack units proceeded more easily. One of the first attempts relates to the autumn of 1941. According to Count Hans Rittberg, on 28 October 1941 he was summoned by the commander of the Rear Services units Army Group Center, General Schenkendorf, and was introduced to the former major in the Red Army, Kononov, who had surrendered during the battle of Smolensk. Schenkendorf told Kononov that he was appointing him as commander of the Cossacks squadron, which was to be formed in the city of Mogilev from the Soviet prisoners of war. Schenkendorf said that the squadron had been earmarked to carry out operations against the partisans, and for punitive functions against the population which supported the partisans. Rittberg was designated the representative of the German command attached to Kononov. Later, when interrogated and asked who was the real commander of the squadron, Rittberg replied: 'I commanded Kononov, and Kononov commanded the squadron.' It is worth noting that the squadron was composed not only of Cossacks, but also of Russians.[7]

In spite of the Reich's top-leadership's feeling of repugnance at the idea of forming Russian military units, commanders of the German military units took the responsibility upon themselves and permitted the formation of such units. It is true that for the first year of the war (but also subsequently), I have uncovered no information about any nationalist unit which was continually in action on the front, and which had not been used for punitive, police or security purpose. It is hard to say who takes the prize for organising the first Russian units. Possibly it was B. A. Smyslovskii (alias Hol'mston, alias von Regenau), who with the approval of the 16th German Army Command formed the first Russian foreign-educational battalion in July 1941. Amongst the bigger units it is possible that the Russian Corps was one of the first. It was launched in Serbia in September 1941.[8]

Perhaps the greatest attention should be paid to the units that were formed without participation of the *émigrés*. That is why we shall dwell a while on the antecedents of the formation which latterly became the 'Kaminski Brigade'.

. After the German occupation of the Brasov region of the Orlov *Oblast* in October 1941, one of the local inhabitants from Lokot' (a small town), Voskoboinikov, actively began to help the Germans. According to the data from the Special People's Commissariat for Internal Affairs (NKVD) section, Voskoboinikov Konstantin Pavlovich (alias Ivan Lashkov, alias engineer Zemlia) was born in 1895 in the village Smela in the Kiev *Oblast*. Prior to the revolution he obtained a law degree from Moscow University, and after the revolution he graduated in electrical engineering at the Institute of Moscow. During the Soviet rule he suffered repression by the NKVD. He was exiled and served his sentence. Before the beginning of the war he was a lecturer at Lokot' Forestry Polytechnic.

On 17 October 1941, the German command appointed Voskoboinikov as burgomaster of the Lokot' *volost* (smallest administrative division in Tsarist Russia); and as his deputy, Bronislav Kaminski, a 37-year-old Pole, who at the onset of war worked as an engineer at the Lokot' spirits factory. In 1937 Kaminski had been tried and exiled from Leningrad to the small town of Lokot'. In November 1941, Voskoboinikov and Kaminski established a press and began to publish an anti-Soviet newspaper *The People's Voice*. Already in December, having obtained an agreement from the German command, leaders of Lokot' government began to create voluntary police units from former servicemen of the Red Army and inhabitants of neighbouring regions who were of call-up age.[9]

In principle, there was nothing extraordinary in this. Nearly always did the Germans find men ready to co-operate. In many regions, therefore, the Germans tended to form police units from the local population. But the difference lies in the fact that on the territory governed by Lokot' rule, these actions were combined with a powerful political propaganda, carried out by the local leadership.

The whole body of currently known documents attests that nearly to the end of the war, German Government in the east was very guarded in relation to political collaboration. Those who entered into political collaboration were required to demonstrate total loyalty. Not by accident did the Germans painstakingly control Vlasov's actions, checking and editing his speeches and appeals. At one time they even transported the captive general around the Russian villages where he addressed the peasants. But when Vlasov took the liberty to talk about an equal partnership with Germany and about the future existence of an independent Russia, his trips were quickly terminated. The same thing happened to the Organisation of Ukrainian Nationalists (OUN) in the Ukraine. At first, OUN members were used very actively. From their ranks, organs of the local government were formed, police, and so on. But when the *Ountsi* (members of the OUN) began to aim for independence and to initiate their own policies, the German command broke up their organisation and arrested Stepan Bandera, a Ukrainian nationalist. The OUN was forced underground and, in actual fact, fought on two fronts until the end of the war.

Under such prevailing attitudes of the occupying forces, existence of any political organisation with its own programme deserves serious attention. It was this kind of party – named People's Socialist Party of Russia (NSPR) – that Voskoboinikov together with Kaminski tried to establish, by publishing a special manifesto on 25 November 1941. Another name for the party was *Viking* or *Vitiaz'* ('Knight'), no doubt owing to the organisers' thoughts of the association with the ancient past, when 'knights, supported by the Russian people, created the Russian state'. The banner of the party was proclaimed to be a white background with the image of St George and the George cross in the top left corner of the flag. The manifesto announced that the People's Socialist Party was founded in the 'underground of Siberian concentration camps', and that it had taken upon itself the responsibility to establish a government which would ensure calm and order and all the conditions necessary for the world's labour to flourish. The party programme contained twelve points. Only one point, which speaks of 'merciless annihilation of the Jews and former commissars', points to the connection between this party and the Nazis. All the other clauses of the programme were aimed at 'total destruction of the communist and *kolkhoz* system within Russia'. The manifesto was intended to grant the peasants the use of all the arable land in perpetuity, with the right to lease it and to exchange their plots, but without the right to sell. Every Russian citizen was guaranteed a personal plot with rights of inheritance and exchange, but also without the right to sell it. Advancing the slogan of free development of private initiative, the party endorsed government ownership of forests, mineral wealth, railways, large factories and plants. Important and significant political points of the programme were those which proclaimed amnesty to all Komsomol members, ordinary members of the Communist Party, who 'had not been stained by insulting the people', and also other communists, who took arms in order to 'overthrow the Stalinist regime'. As distinct from Vlasov's declarations, constantly seeking friendship with Germany, the NSPR limited itself to bold 'greetings to the courageous German people'.[10]

According to our data, the NSPR was the only party in occupied Russia that existed not only on paper. It possessed its own press, and printed pamphlets and the newspaper *The People's Voice*. Several party cells were created, and these undertook recruitment. The centre of the NSPR was in Lokot'. A special garrison of around 200 men was responsible for its security. Support for people's everyday needs, anti-*kolkhoz* propaganda and the promise to divide and allot all the land found response among the peasants. Influence of the party grew, and this caused a great deal of disquiet in the Soviet state. Partisans received an order to destroy the centre of the party and its leadership.

On 8 January 1942, Voskoboinikov was killed by the partisans. With the death of its founder, the NSPR ceased its activities. Kaminski, having been appointed as an *ober*-burgomaster of Lokot' administration, was more interested in fighting the partisans than in promoting the political ideals of the *Vitiaz'* party. In July 1942, the commanding officer of the 2nd German Panzer Army, Lieutenant-General Schmidt, singled out 'the work' of Kaminski in a report and he reorganised Lokot' local government, making it a regional government and incorporating into it eight additional districts. At the same time, Kaminski was granted the rank of *Kombrig* (brigadier), and he began to form a so-called People's Army from the volunteer police units. This subsequently became known as the Kaminski Brigade. According to the data of Soviet counter-espionage, in January 1943 fifteen battalions were formed, numbering 12,000–15,000 men. In the main, the Brigade was used by the German command for combat with the partisans. Only during the period of advance of Red Army Central Front units did the Kaminski Brigade, together with the German and Hungarian units, take part in defensive actions (February – March 1943).[11] In 1944, the Brigade took part in suppressing the Warsaw rising. After this, Kaminski disappeared without trace. The most widely held version is that Kaminski was shot by the Germans because of his obduracy, but there is no reliable documentary proof.

What was the total number of military-collaborator formations? The answer to this question has worried many a historian for a long time. But to give an accurate account is still hardly possible. Documents, both on the German and the Soviet side, are extremely contradictory, especially about the early years of the war. The figure of one million men, frequently quoted in western historiography, requires an explanation. The fact is that foreign authors include all *Hiwis* in this number, and this is not totally correct. One cannot count *Hiwis* as conscious fighters against the USSR. There is a vast difference between working in auxiliary units and participating in armed combat. Therefore, one should differentiate between active and passive military collaboration. Taking this approach, even if one consciously accepts the highest number, the quota of armed military collaborators could not exceed 250,000–300,000 men.

But the economic or civilian collaboration is the hardest to study. Sometimes it is very complex, and at other times it is almost impossible, to delineate the border between ordinary co-operation with the occupying forces and actual collaboration. However, the so-called civilian collaboration was most widely spread, and potentially and factually it fuelled all other forms of collaboration. Even taking into account the complexity of that aspect, one can talk about collaboration only when one discusses the actual participation of the representatives of the local population in effecting the government on the occupied territory. The scale of such collaboration was closely linked to the occupying policy of the enemy.

The majority of Soviet people saw fascists' actions as meaning: murder of peaceful citizens, universal pillage, terror and suppression. Many documents confirm that this was indeed so, but it was not always like that. Since, in the front-line regions, the leadership of government consisted of German commanders, the character of the relations with the local population depended entirely on the qualities of the command. A proportion of the German officer corps understood very well the necessity for collaboration with the population. Witness the order of the 11th German Army of 30 August 1941, which demanded that the commanding officers carry out a determined fight against pillage and looting, especially in the case of the units of the rear. The instruction issued by the 11th Panzer Division said: 'Every case of looting and destruction of domestic enterprises is most strictly forbidden. Important industrial and agricultural businesses are to be occupied as quickly as is possible and secured against sabotage. Whenever possible, leave the workers in their own workplaces.'[12] In his order, the Commander of the 4th Army, General Heinrici, stated: 'The civil population that has been freed from the Bolshevik rule enjoys the protection of the German armed forces. This is an important political and domestic duty.... Incorrect, unjust and unlawful treatment of Russian people in the occupied regions, whether prisoners of war or peaceful population, can easily make new enemies from citizens previously well disposed towards us. Yet we need the trust, friendliness and co-operation of these people in military, economic and political relations. In this country, one cannot succeed by the superiority of the German arms alone. In this fight we need the help of our better customs and conduct, greater humanity of the German soldier and lawfulness.'[13]

As regards large-scale terror against peaceful citizens, it is necessary to investigate those cases which were a response to partisan activities. Hundreds of books have been written about the partisan war in the USSR, but the fact that this war cost the USSR one million human lives is never mentioned. Everywhere, the Germans introduced the system of hostage-taking. As a rule, for the killing of one German soldier or representative of the German administration, the first 100 local inhabitants caught – including children and old men – were shot. Savage cruelty indeed, but was it always imperative to provoke the Germans to it? One of thousands of bulletins by the NKVD to the leadership of the country reports that 'in the small village of Novyi Gorodok, outside the city of Dnepropetrovsk, three militiamen, hiding in the house of a local Communist, killed three German officers. As a response to this terrorist act, by the order of the German command, over 300 inhabitants of Novyi Gorodok were shot.'[14] Nobody is disputing that the militiamen were heroes. But who asked the local population whether they wished to be sacrificed? Is it possible to rejoice and reward such terrorist actions? Alas, few thought about it. Stalin's leadership sacrificed human lives lavishly: the country was big; there were plenty of people.

Partisans themselves frequently pushed the local population into collaboration with the Germans. Many peasants feared the partisans more than they feared the occupiers. It is time to disabuse ourselves of the myth of a do-gooding people's avenger. This was a savage war. As of necessity, the partisans themselves indulged in expropriation (they plundered) and took any required specialist labour by force. In addition, in several places combat troops of the NKVD were active, and their job was not only to inflict casualties on the enemy, but also to carry out repression of the 'unreliable' villages.[15]

In the eastern territories, two Reichskommissariats were created: Ukraine and Ostland. The latter included Belorussia and the Baltic Republics. The occupied territories of the Russian Republic did not have a unified administration. There was no unified system of governing in regions or cities. However, the organisation of government in the Ukraine, Belorussia and the Republic of Russia was similar. Every big region was subdivided into counties, and these in turn were divided into districts (*volosti*) and village communes (*uyezds*). It is very noticeable that the Germans wished to use pre-revolutionary administrative divisions and terminology. Local representatives were never appointed above county level. German forces also made an effort to appoint Germans as heads of the county or district, but that rule was not mandatory. In some instances, Germans renamed the former Soviet *oblast* into *guberniia* (as with Orlovskaia). Each county encompassed 20–30 districts (up to 10 in the Russian Federal Republic), with a population of between 50,000 and 250,000. Also, larger towns with a population of 100,000 were added on to counties or districts. A district consisted of village communes (*uyezds* or *volosts*). There were no big differences between these territorial divisions. Each *uyezd* or *volost* could contain up to fifteen villages. Beginning with the *uyezd*, the commune or yet again the *volost*, the district, the occupying forces appointed only individuals from the local population in posts of authority. As a rule, the head of a *uyezd* or *volost* was a burgomaster; and of villages and other smaller population centres, an elder or a headman. In addition to enforcing the orders of the higher civil administration, the burgomaster had to submit to the military field command of his district. Political reliability of burgomasters was verified by the field gendarmerie or Gestapo. No man could become a burgomaster merely by chance. The fact that the local population could address the German authorities only via burgomasters added great weight to the latter's authority.[16]

At the head of a city was a commandant and, as a rule, he was German. Under his authority were the Gestapo, gendarmerie, police, civil authority and church community. The local population made up the civil and police authority. City control was in the hands of the city head. Each authority consisted of 8–9 sections: housing, municipal, commercial, finance, transport, highways, industrial, sanitation and public catering.[17]

Both village and city population were meticulously registered. It is worth noting that the basic document which served as an identity card remained the Soviet passport. Burgomasters and elders were obliged to submit to the German command a nominal roll of the local population. In addition, they were personally responsible for the reliability of all people whom they entered on the roll. Those who were not entered were sent into the concentration camps for civilian prisoners of war or labour columns attached to the army rear services. The local population wishing to remain at home (and this was the majority) immediately had to demonstrate its loyalty.

The jurisdiction of civil authority did not extend to the front-line districts. Here all authority belonged to the German military command. The front-line belt was divided into two zones. In the second zone, not only movement was prohibited, but also any appearance on the street after twilight. There, going to the fields was done only in the presence of a German soldiers' convoy. In the first zone, immediately adjacent to the front, the whole population was compulsorily evacuated to the rear and accommodated into special camps. Any local inhabitant who entered the first zone could be shot forthwith without any explanation. It is ludicrous that Soviet war films sometimes show front-line districts where scouts meet peasants on their carts or drink tea in some village.[18]

The Germans restored only small workshops and handicraft enterprises to their former owners. So, many peasants, dispossessed during the 1930s, began returning to their places of birth, where they were permitted to repossess their former mills, creameries and so on. However, the German authorities categorically forbade division of *kolkhoz* land, livestock and property. In order to complete the harvesting and autumn sowing in 1941 as quickly as possible, the Germans aimed to preserve the collective form of running village economy, while at the same time they took very little notice of the wishes of the peasants – who wanted to be masters of their own households. Masses of documents provide evidence that the peasants harboured no great love for Stalinist *kolkhoz*. On the contrary, they were for ever hoping that these were just about to be disbanded. This is why the Germans announced that in the near future they would definitely liquidate *kolkhozy*, but that for the present they were simply renaming them 'public or communal enterprises', promising every peasant who distinguished himself a part of the harvest and an augmented piece of land adjoining his household. Tilling of land, sowing and harvesting in these public enterprises were performed jointly. As a rule, all able-bodied went into the field. Calculation of the amount of work was done in man-hours, to which were added points dependent on the strenuousness of the work. The land department of the German commandant's office allotted everybody's sowing task and determined how much each person had to surrender from his harvest. Once the stocks of seeds had been topped up and fodder had been rendered, the rest was divided amongst the workers according to man-days or according to how many dependants a family had. The amount of bread distributed varied sharply from region to region and depended also on the harvest. For example, in the Zaporozh *Oblast*, for one day's work the ration varied from 0.5 to 2.5 kg., elsewhere from 10 to 15 kg. per person. In some places, parts of the *kolkhoz* were organised into *gromadas* and given a piece of land, livestock and draught animals according to *desiatidvorka* (every 10 households). In the majority of public village enterprises and in the *gromadas* (*desiatidvorka*), it was permitted to rent land on the condition that it had to be under total cultivation and that tilling of it was the responsibility of the tenant. In the autumn of 1941, the Germans began actively to augment peasants' personal plots in many regions, bringing them up to 1–1.5 hectares. As an incentive, in the Dnepropetrovsk general district, the Germans granted additional plots to 2,716 households. In practice, there were individual households in every occupied region, but these were not widespread.[19]

One has to admit that – although not everywhere – the Germans did succeed in regulating village production and managed to rouse peasants' interest in co-operation with the German government. In all those places where the supernumerary administration was maintained, partisan movements experienced serious difficulties or were totally absent.

In order to entice the city population to work, the Germans established a differential scale of pay on the principle of the higher the education, the greater the wage. The middle wage of the qualified worker stood at 400 roubles per month. For the white-collar workers the following scale applied: mechanics, draughtsmen and similar – 400 roubles; bookkeepers – 500; white-collar workers in responsible posts – 650; managers and specialists – 900; managers of businesses – 1,200–1,500 roubles per month. Salaries varied from region to region, but this kind of correlation was maintained in all the occupied territories. It has to be pointed out that this rule did not apply to the Jewish workers.[20]

At first, the German Government did not forget to regulate the trade and food supplies. But when it became obvious that the war would drag on, the situation changed, and the authorities began to support private initiative in commerce. In the majority of occupied regions, at the end of the autumn of 1941 and the beginning of winter, private cafés and snack bars appeared. In order to open one's 'business', one had to obtain a licence. Competition was quite strong, since the licence provided substantial privileges – the owner of a licence could not be recruited for compulsory labour, and he could not be sent to Germany. In several larger towns, the Germans formed special free canteens that could be attended by invalids and families with many children. Food in these canteens was meagre – only soup, and no bread.[21]

Thus, circumstances led the civilian population to co-operate with the German forces. Under these conditions, crossing the line from neutral participation to closer co-operation was very easy. To a certain degree, economic collaboration was unavoidable, and sometimes even mandatory. The Germans, for example, frequently suggested to the peasants·that they themselves should elect the elder, assuming that they would choose someone who held the greatest authority among them. The latter would make it simpler for the Germans to procure the execution of their orders. However, the elder also gained definite opportunities for the protection of his fellow villagers. This kind of an intermediary was simply indispensable. That is why, if there was no volunteer or the peasants did not select somebody, the Germans would compulsorily appoint an elder, at the same time making his family and relatives hostages.

Preliminary analysis of documents allows us to establish that civilian collaboration was general. Practically in every inhabited location, the Germans found men who voluntarily or under orders co-operated with them. It is necessary to examine to what degree this was conditioned by previous Soviet policy, as it was by no means always only those dissatisfied with the Soviet Government, the dispossessed, criminals and such who co-operated with the German administration. On acquaintance with documents, one is struck by a factor which was previously unmentionable, namely that the Germans were able to attract previous Communists to collaborate with them, even those who prior to the war had been part of the Soviet leadership. In every inhabited locality, all Communists were instructed that it was obligatory for them to report and register. It is remarkable how strictly the occupying forces adhered to the policy of using those Communists who relinquished their party membership for administrative duties. Let us look at just one example from the Kalinskaia Oblast. The former people's judge of the central district of the *Oblast*, A. V. Sergeeva, member of the Communist Party from 1927, went to work for the Gestapo. In the Staritski District, the party organisation of the Staritski flax mill, headed by the secretary and including the whole staff, worked in the mill which had been restored by the Germans. Candidate member of the party from that organisation, technical director Khrustaleva, was elevated by the Germans to become the director of the enterprise and during the retreat she fled together with the Germans. Forewoman of the knitted-goods factory in the city of Kalinin, A. K. Iakovleva, also a member of the party, reported for registration, was appointed director of the factory and launched production. The German administration deliberately used several former Communists – since they knew their people' – in the cities, in the capacity of non-commissioned police officers. In numerous places, the Germans did not replace the presidents of the *kolkhoz*, but converted them into elders. One can quote many similar facts from other districts in the country as examples. Collaboration of a proportion of communists with the enemy serves as a clear proof to what degree the Party was demoralised and damaged by Stalin's pre-war policy. In actual fact, the activity of many party organisations had been reduced to functions of control and punishment. Disregarding ideological considerations, the occupiers were ready to use the experience and standing of self-renounced communists.[22]

In practice, the fight against collaboration in the Soviet Union has not been studied by historiography. It is evident that the bogey of the 'fifth column' was ever present in the policy of Stalin's leadership. Therefore, when at the beginning of the war favourable conditions for the 'fifth column' appeared, feverish activities took place to fight both the imaginary and the real enemy in Soviet ranks. Preventive measures were: widespread pressure through the mass-information network, kindling of hatred towards the enemy, propaganda stress on the horrors of the German regime; and evocation of ancient values – patriotism of the Russian people, figures from the heroic past, and the use of the church to the same end; also, if there was a threat of retreat, those in prisons and camps would be evacuated; and Communists were forbidden to remain on occupied territory without the party organisation's permission. Manifestations of measures taken in the straight fight were: terrorist acts against persons who collaborated; when retreating, shooting the 'unreliable' individuals, those that NKVD – NKGB (People's Commissariat for State Security) deemed liable to act suspiciously close to sabotage; bombing the camps of the prisoners of war, especially in the initial stage of the war; repression against families and relatives of collaborators; spreading rumours was regarded as a criminal act, as was keeping of German pamphlets; spreading information for public consumption in occupied territory, namely that the fatherland forgives those who cease to collaborate with the enemy. Soviet documents support the claim that the effectiveness of such measures was quite high, but even so the Soviet system was not without defects. Many Red Army soldiers, who managed to escape from the encirclement, returned to their native towns and villages. Partisans regarded them as traitors and frequently shot them. This led to 'those not returning to the Red Army' themselves uniting, taking up arms, and fighting the partisans. All the Germans had to do was to organise them.[23] In some places, local leadership directly provoked the higher command into waging preventive terror. For example, in the autumn of 1942, in a memorandum of the Saratov *Oblast* Committee of the Communist Party, it was stated: 'With the approach of the front to the Saratov *Oblast*, enemy action has noticeably increased, carried out by the remaining Germans who had not been the subject of the Presidium of the Supreme Soviet of the USSR order about resettlement of Germans living in the city of Engel's and other districts of the former German republic (women married to Russian men). It was only in a narrow circle of those closest to them that they expressed their feelings about "communism" which had evicted their fellow countrymen.' Even the style of this document is worthy noting for its total absence of any concrete facts.[24]

Analysis of NKVD–NKGB reports, special dispatches from the intelligence directorate of the NKVD and the General Staff demonstrate that these organs reduced co-operation of the population with the occupying forces, as a rule, to 'activities of the *kulak* (dispossessed peasant) and bandit elements.' It is interesting that nobody who submitted these reports ever thought why there were so many *kulaks* all of a sudden in a socialist country. However, the methods that the Germans used when recruiting Soviet citizens have been studied very closely. The greater part of the examination records is devoted to elucidating these very questions.

In the months before the battle of Stalingrad, amnestying and freeing

600,000 Soviet men who had been locked up around the middle of May 1942 played a role in preventing collaboration. This was not noised abroad, but people did know about it, and saw in it a certain act of patriotic justice. Only a narrow circle of individuals was in possession of factual information. The system took its toll, all the same. During that period (from July 1941 to June 1942), 862,760 men were convicted of varying periods of imprisonment.[25]

The subject of collaboration needs lengthy research and a large amount of various documents needs to be looked at. The level of current knowledge allows us to conclude that it was the military actions and the failure of *Barbarossa* which compelled the Germans to consider the issue of collaboration with the local population, especially in the Slav regions. However, in many cases they missed both the right moment and the initiative.

How the Germans reacted to voluntary co-operation of the population differed significantly according to particular regions. Collaboration in military and political spheres was consciously kept strictly controlled by the German command. Civil collaboration was widespread. To some degree it was obligatory, but it could assume far less inoffensive forms and then develop into active military-political collaboration.

Notes

1. See: H. Amouroux, *La grande histoire des Français sous l'occupation*, vols I–III (Paris, 1977–8); J. P. Azema, *La collaboration, 1940–1944* (Paris, 1975); D. Brandes, *Die Tschechen unter deutschen Protektorat*, Vol. 1–2. (Munich and Vienna, 1969, 1975); G. Hirschfeld, *Fremdherrschaft und Kollaboration: Die Niederlände unter deutscher Besätzung 1940–1945* (Stuttgart, 1984); D. Littlejohn, *The Patriotic Traitors: A History of Collaboration in German-Occupied Europe 1940–1945* (London, 1972); A. Milward, *The New Order and the French Economy* (Oxford, 1970); Id., *The Fascist Economy in Norway* (Oxford, 1972); W. Rings, *Life with the Enemy: Collaboration and Resistance in Hitler's Europe 1939–1945* (NY, 1982).
2. J. Hoffman, *Deutsche und Kalmyken 1942–1945* (Freiburg, 1981); Id., *Die Geschichte der Wlassow-Armee* (Freiburg, 1986).
3. J. Hoffman, *History of the Vlasov Army* (Paris, 1990) pp. 3–6 (transl. from German).
4. See *Komsomol'skaya pravda*, 26 Jan. 1993, p. 2.
5. Bundesarchiv-Militärarchiv, Freiburg (BA-MA), RH 22/67, pp. 36–57.
6. BA-MA, WiID/33, p. 94.
7. From the testimony of Count Hans Aurel Rittberg, interrogated by the Ukrainian NKVD Novosibirsk *Oblast*, 6 Feb. 8 Mar. and 13 July 1946, in *Rodina*, No. 2, 1993, p. 73.
8. BA-MA, MSg 123/3, pp. 70–1.
9. Report written by L. Tsanav, chief of the NKVD Special Section of the Central Front, to L. P. Beria, about the Kaminski Brigade, Mar. 1943 (author's archive).
10. The original manifesto is kept in the KGB archives. The manuscript copy is held in the Russian Centre for Custody and Research of Documents of the Most Recent History (RTsKhIDNI), f. 17, Op. 125, D. 94, pp. 35–6.

11. See: Memorandum (Report) about the 'Kaminski Brigade' (note 9 above), pp. 2–6.
12. RTsKhIDNI – former Central Party Archive, f1117, Op. 122255, D. 52 1.4, p. 4.
13. RTsKhIDNI, Archive 17, Inventory 125, File 94, pp. 38–9.
14. Ibid., File 52, p. 113.
15. From the reports of the chief of the 1st (Intelligence) Directorate of the NKVD, L. Fitin, RTsKhIDNI, Arch. 17, Coll. 121, File 235, pp. 3–8.
16. Memorandum in the TsK VKP(b) about organisation of administration and the regime on occupied territory, RTsKhIDNI, Arch. 17, Coll. 121, File 235, pp. 3–8.
17. Ibid. p. 9.
18. Ibid. p. 12 and pp. 14–15.
19. Ibid. pp. 16–21.
20. Ibid. pp. 37–8.
21. Ibid. pp. 46–8.
22. RTsKhIDNI, Arch. 17, Coll. 122, File 20, p. 21, pp. 45–8, pp. 75–9 and pp. 107–8; Coll. 125, File 52, p. 102 and 111.
23. RTsKhIDNI, Arch. 17, Coll. 125, File 52, pp. 71–2.
24. RTsKhIDNI, Arch. 17, Coll. 122, File 19, p. 23.
25. As calculated in the memorandum of the public prosecutor of the USSR. RTsKhIDNI, Arch. 17, Coll. 121, File 157, p. 112.

Above: Lieutenant-General
Vlasov with German officers at
Za Rodinu newspaper, 1943.

Lieutenant-General Vlasov and
Goebbels meet, 1944.

Above: Trial of the
'Vlasovites', Moscow, 1946.

Killed in action, Belorussia,
1944.

The human cost . . .

Chapter 12

Soviet War Losses

Calculations and Controversies

JOHN ERICKSON

There is an earlier observation which seems to be singularly pertinent to an inquiry of this nature. It reads quite succinctly: 'Any exhaustive inquiry into the vital statistics of Russia during the years of the War is greatly impeded by the unsatisfactory condition of the available material.' This is no newly minted addition to present confusions and controversies but rather one taken from *The Cost of the War to Russia*, published as part of the Carnegie Endowment for International Peace.[1] In spite of its disclaimer, these are models of works on war losses, and can still serve to furnish lessons in methodology to which both Russian and Western scholars might attend. As one of the titles suggests, it is not merely a question of assembling data and statistical material (though that is important in its own right, difficult as it is to manage), but equally a matter of assessing 'social cost' and examining the social dimension of the war effort and consequent losses.

Approaching the latter aspect even in the most rudimentary form demands that some estimate or evaluation should be made of the nature or essence of a particular war, which in this instance is the Soviet–German war or the 'Great Patriotic War of the Soviet Union 1941–5'. This was far more than a series of battlefield encounters, protracted and gruelling as they proved to be. In German terms, it was nothing less than a *Vernichtungskampf*, a war of annihilation and a war of racial extermination, a *Rassenkampf* directed against the 'Jew–Bolshevik' enemy in particular and the Slav *Untermensch*, the sub-human in general. The rules of warfare and the standards of soldierly conduct were not only suspended but dissolved in *die Einschränkung der Kriegsgerichtsbarkeit*, the dissolution of responsibility before the law. Let loose upon Jew, Bolshevik, prisoners and populace were the killer squads of the *Einsatzkommandos*. The shape of things to come, and which indeed came to pass, had been accurately predicted in an earlier age by Friedrich

Engels when he espied a future war of 'universal ensavagement' with its consequent 'barbarisation', chronicled in part by Omer Bartov in his study of three German divisions on the eastern front, 12th Infantry, 18th *Panzer* and *Grossdeutschland*.[2] But here was a mere segment, a particle of that giant military encounter between Nazi Germany and the Soviet Union, one which kept the Red Army operationally committed for 88 per cent of 1,418 days of warfare, grappling with something in the order of 65 – 70 percent of the total field strength of the *Wehrmacht*. The same Red Army was committed to 9 campaigns, involving 7 substantial defensive operations and 160 offensive operations, destroying or disabling in the process 607 Axis divisions.

To concentrate on the battlefields alone is, however, to miss yet another key dimension of this struggle: the war which Stalin waged on his own people. Witness, for example, the proscription of Soviet prisoners of war and their families with the infamous Order No. 227, the semi-legality of wartime government, the illegal 'militarisation' of sections of labour, the deportation of suspect nationalities, the *GULAG* enslavement, the secret, intensive, barbaric war for control of the resistance movement with the treacheries and tragedies of partisan warfare. It follows that 'simple arithmetic' can never account for either 'loss' or 'cost' or even approach a comprehension of the 'social size' of this war. The conflagration engulfed Stalin's warfare state, one paradoxically and tragically lacking an effective, working war machine, which might have fended off, or at least diminished, those grievous initial disasters in the summer of 1941.

THE CONGLOMERATE OF NUMBERS

There has been no shortage of numbers, gross numbers, to account for human losses in the Soviet Union. Much of it has been 'simple arithmetic', *prostaya arifmetika*, creating in its wake much political mischief and no small degree of public anguish. Little was done to distinguish between direct and indirect loss and to indicate what time-scale the 'loss figure' was intended to cover. Until very recently, the census figures for 1939 were not publicly available, which certainly impeded any closer analysis of population changes over time. Estimates dealing with 'direct loss', intended to include the armed forces as well as partisans and civilians lost through enemy action, varied between 26 and 27 million, while a figure of 22 million battle casualties and 24 million civilian dead had been advanced as a 'global' figure, though this seemed to combine (or confuse) direct and indirect losses.

The first post-war figure for Soviet losses, 7 million, was produced by Stalin in February 1946, no doubt intended to be accepted as a 'global' figure though this was a most conservative estimate of battlefield loss. The much-touted and oft-quoted figure of 'in excess of 20 million' for *both* military and civilian losses was announced by Khrushchev and widely employed by both Soviet and Western commentators in the 1960s. This seems to have been 'plucked out of the air' in an act of political convenience. Two decades later, the *Encyclopedia of the Great Patriotic War 1941–1945* hardly advanced the cause of exactitude and clarification by simply reasserting the figure of 'upwards of 20 million Soviet citizens – *part of them* civilians who perished in the Hitlerite death camps, from Fascist brutalities, illness, hunger'.[3]

To displace this arbitrary figure of '20 million plus' has proved to be difficult and not without a great deal of controversy. For example, in an estimate of 'global loss' for the Soviet Union and computing both direct and indirect loses, L. E. Polyakov in his brochure *Tsena pobedy, Demograficheskii aspekt* adduces the figure of 46 million, from which he subtracts 26 million as a figure for 'indirect loss', thus arriving at 20 million for battlefield/war loss.[4] This figure for 'global loss' is worth further closer examination, for there is something of a consensus about that loss figure in the order of 47–50 million. Thanks to the recent publication of the hitherto secret figures for the 1939 census, there is a certain vindication of Professor I. Kurganov's earlier work, published in *Argumenty i Fakty*. Publication of the 1939 census figures gives a baseline of 197.1 million for the population of the Soviet Union in the period immediately preceding the war. Given natural population growth, without the intervention of war, and using an officially accepted coefficient of 1.7 growth, we could anticipate a population level of 212.5 million in 1946, whereas it was only 168.5 million. In 1950, it had climbed only slowly to 178.5 million. Professor Kurganov strikes out boldly for an *absolute loss* figure of 44 million, compounding both direct and indirect losses, including battle casualties, civilian casualties (hunger, disease, enemy action, enemy atrocities), civilian losses (concentration camps), emigration (refugees, defectors) and allowing for 'natural loss' due to wartime diminution of the birth rate.[5]

V. I. Kozlov approached the problem from a somewhat different angle, having first looked at morbidity, infant mortality and natural growth rates for 1940.[6] He argues that allowing for estimates of annual natural growth rates, without war, the population by the beginning of 1946 should have reached a total of 212–25 million and 225–30 million by the beginning of 1950. But in 1946, unofficial figures put the figure for the population at 167 million; and in 1950 at 178.5 million. Thus, over the wartime period and including the first four post-war years, the 'population deficit' was in the order of some 45–8 million. Applying an even smaller growth coefficient but using the 1940 and 1946 baselines, Polyakov arrives at a deficit of 46 million, a figure not dissimilar to A. Ya. Kvasha's estimate of 48–50 million.[7] A mean figure of some 48 million seems to be generally accepted as 'global loss', which, put in other terms and over time, signifies a deficit in the order of 23 per cent in Soviet human resources, compounded of actual wartime loss, the wartime 'birth deficit' (set by some at 10 million 'not born' babies), together with the lower post-war birth rate due to the 'male deficit' and drastic alterations in the age-specific sex-ratios. A particular and stark reminder of what this has meant for Soviet women is furnished in a study by Barbara Anderson and Brian Silver with their analysis of the 'war-widow cohort' and the 'war bride cohort', the latter paradoxically and tragically including an appreciable percentage of women who never were and never would be brides.[8]

This question of indirect loss (I prefer the term consequential loss) and its social effects is one which will require some further comment, but it is impossible to ignore the controversy which continues to rage over the question of direct wartime loss. Colonel Pronko has defined 'direct human loss' as 'that total number of Soviet servicemen and civilians killed as a result of military actions and their immediate aftermath, such as death from injuries, concussion, hunger etc.'. Such direct losses were incurred over the period from 22 June 1941 to mid-September 1945 (the conclusion of Soviet operations in the Far East), but Colonel Pronko adds what he calls a 'demographic aftermath' to include serving soldiers and civilians from the war zones succumbing to war wounds, injuries and nervous ailments. This 'aftermath' is indeed a problem in its own right, by no means confined to Russia, and making its presence felt far and wide almost half a century later. British prisoners of war, held by the Japanese, still suffer – uncompensated, infirm – their own 'aftermath'.

BATTLEFIELD LOSS: MEN, WOMEN AND MACHINES

Over the past few years various figures have appeared relating to Red Army losses for the period 1941–5. This sparked off not only a 'numbers game' but also a furious controversy over the ratio of Soviet losses to those of the German army. In the April 1990 issue of the *Military Bulletin*, Major Viktor Gobarev asserted in his paper on 'facts and figures' of the Soviet–German war that 'in the course of the entire war, losses of Soviet troops in practically any major operation were greater than those of the enemy'.[9] This politically loaded theme of inordinate (and unnecessary) loss rapidly became the subject of some elementary and even bizarre arithmetic, ranging from a 'loss ratio' unfavourable to the Red Army of 7:1 to 4:1 or 3.5:1. Suffice it so say that this added little to our knowledge of battlefield losses even as it begged the question of how these losses had been sustained: by which arms, in what types of operations – offensive, defensive, breakthrough, operations in built-up areas – by theatre, duration and so on. Such discussions also displayed a rather scant knowledge of how the *Wehrmacht* calculated and presented German losses, so that much of the discussion of 'loss ratios' was for all practical purposes worthless.

It was not until the spring of 1990 that some of the mystery was at long last dispelled, when Army General Moiseyev, then chief of the Soviet General Staff, reported on the work of two official commissions: one dealing with human loss, the other with losses in *matériel*. Human losses for 'the war', including the Far Eastern campaign in 1945, and including categories of killed in action (KIA), missing in action (MIA), prisoners of war who did not return, those who died of wounds, illness, accident or suicide amounted to 8,668,400. (What is not differentiated in this total is a figure for women combatants.) Losses by arm and service are shown in Table 12.1.
Other casualties owing to wounds, shell-shock, frost-bite and those taken sick amounted to approximately 18 million (with the proviso that here was possibly a certain amount of double-counting where a serviceman may have been wounded several times – there is one recorded case of a soldier wounded seven times and each time returning to his unit).[10]

These figures are not greatly at variance with those furnished by B. V. Sokolov, namely 8.5 million battle casualties (those killed in action), though he adds a figure of 2.5 million for those who died of wounds.[11] However, he goes on to cite a ratio of three wounded to every man killed in action, and a mortality rate of 10 per cent for the wounded. This 3:1 ratio gives a total figure of some 25 million casualties from the total mobilised manpower pool of 30.6 million (one-third of the male population). Now, thanks to the release of the latest figures, it is possible to be much more specific than Sokolov (though he was not too far off the mark), a process begun by Colonel-General G. F. Krivosheyev, previously chief of the Mobilisation-Organisation Directorate of the Soviet General Staff. General Krivosheyev, in his articles in *Voenno-istoricheskii zhurnal*, provided the figure of 27 million for 'direct loss', that is, loss due to enemy action, servicemen killed in

TABLE 12.1: Overall Soviet combat losses

Army and Navy	8,509,300
Internal troops	97,700
Frontier troops	61,400

action or succumbing to wounds, deaths from hunger and disease, casualties among partisans and *podpol'shchiki* (underground resistance fighters), Soviet civilians killed by bombing or artillery fire, Soviet prisoners of war, and the *aktivisty* (Party and *Komsomol* members) shot or done to death in concentration camps.[12] General Krivosheyev supplies the same total loss figure for the Red Army plus internal troops and frontier troops as General Moiseyev but that overall figure did *not* include either 939,709 men listed as missing in action in the early catastrophic days of the war but re-enlisted once Soviet troops recovered occupied territory. Nor did it take into account 1,836,000 prisoners of war returned from captivity – in all, 2,775,700 men. Medical casualties amounted to 18,344,148 (wounded/shell-shocked 15,205,692, sick 3,047,675, frost-bite victims 90,880). General Krivosheyev makes some provision for 'double-counting' the wounded and battle casualties but emphasises that the relationship of killed to wounded varied greatly throughout the war – in 1941 4:1, in 1942 almost 3:2, in 1943 a reversal of the ratios to 2:3, in 1944–5 in the breakthrough and pursuit operations a greater proportion of wounded, fewer fatalities.[13]

One of the key elements in General Krivosheyev's presentations was his analysis of loss rates in relation to three periods of the war (see Table 12.2). This, of course, gives a greater total figure for total loss in killed and missing than that supplied by General Moiseyev, but the discrepancy is removed by taking account of 'missing manpower' recovered after 1943 in liberated territory. The Red Army at once set field *voenkomats* to register and induct men in the liberated areas for military service. For many men this was a double induction, having been first mobilised in June – July 1941, after which they 'disappeared' into the German-occupied rear, often escaping from encirclement and thus posted 'missing'. Here was also a manpower

TABLE 12.2: Soviet losses by wartime operational periods

Period	Loss
June 1941–Nov. 1942	+11 million (including non-combat loss) 6.1 million killed/missing +5 million wounded
1943 (13 months)	8,586,200 total casualties +2,500 killed in action
1944–45	9,892,000 total casualties 2.5 million killed/missing

mass who had been given a machine-pistol and a handful of rations and were set to fight against some very determined German troops fighting desperate rearguard actions. Partisan units in the rear joined up with the advancing Red Army and more women appeared in front-line units, more than 20,000 serving with the 2nd Belorussian Front, 22,000 fighting in the offensive operation to break the siege of Leningrad. The Soviet navy mustered at least 25,000 women, while 41 per cent of the Red Army's doctors and 43 per cent of its front-line medical personnel were women, working under heavy fire and up front with the rifle battalions, often caught up in hand-to-hand fighting. After 1942 the *Komsomol* sent no less than 247,551 young women to the front with a further 85,921 assigned to support roles in the military districts.[14]

It comes as no surprise to learn that rifle troops suffered the heaviest losses, particularly in the 28-month period from 1943–5. Old soldiers will recall that brutal adage: 'the artillery is for killing, the infantry for dying'. General Krivosheyev's figures clearly reflect this. During the period 1943–5, casualty figures reached 16,859,000 of which 4,028,000 accounted for those killed or missing in action and 12,831,000 for battle casualties. The rifle troops, the infantry battalions, regiments and divisions suffered no less than 86 per cent of this loss, the armoured forces 6 per cent, artillery 2.2 per cent and the air force 0.29 per cent.

With the recent publication of *Grif sekretnosti snyat*, a massive statistical compilation, we have at last a very substantial body of data dealing with Soviet losses (this volume covers the period from 1918 to 1989, giving a total loss figure of 9,763,326 killed and missing, 29,878,153 wounded or disabled).[15] Chapter III covers the loss tabulations for the period 1941–5 with a breakdown of losses for all the operations of the Red Army (defensive and offensive) beginning with the defensive operations in the Baltic States (22 June – 9 July 1941).

Before delving into this mass of statistics, it is useful to examine the data presented in a table published in *Krasnaya Zvezda*, the Russian army newspaper, on 22 June 1993 (see Table 12.3).

The figure for total loss – 11,444,100 – must be adjusted downwards, since 1,836,000 prisoners of war returned to the Soviet Union and 939,700 men previously accounted missing or prisoners were inducted in liberated territories – 2,775,700 men in all. Thus, the total loss properly adjusted becomes 8,668,400 (11,444,100 minus 2,775,700).

One section of the data is devoted to losses in the Soviet officer corps. Comparing Red Army officer losses with those of the Tsarist Army in the First World War, the latter lost 72,000 officers (14.6 per cent of the officer

---

TABLE 12.3: Soviet mobilised manpower and war loss, 1941–45

1941	4,826,900 (army and fleet strength)
	2,900,000 men in the frontier military districts
	74,900 men in other Defence Ministry bodies
1945	12,839,800 (army and fleet strength)
	11,390,600 in unit service
	1,046,000 men recovering in hospital
	403,200 in civilian agencies coming under Defence Ministry aegis

Total wartime inducted manpower (with a deduction for 'double induction'): 29,574,900 (including 767,600 men already inducted for military service at the beginning of the war)

Total mobilised manpower for service with the Army, Navy and other agencies (including the peacetime cadre force): 34,476,700 men

Discharged/released manpower from the Army and Navy:
  21,636,900
  3,798,200 demobilised/released on leave because of wounds/disability
  2,576,000 invalided out
  3,614,600 assigned to industry, air defence, etc.
  1,425,000 to man NKVD troops and agencies
  994,300 men convicted
  442,700 men punished by posting to penal units, *shtrafnie podrazdelenii*
  436,000 imprisoned
  206,000 discharged for various reasons
  212,400 not apprehended as deserters, missing from troop trains, missing without trace in internal military districts

Total loss (according to front-line figures):
  11,444,100
  6,885,1000 killed in action, died of wounds, accident victims, suicides
  4,559,000 missing in action, prisoners of war

---

corps) while the comparable figure for the Red Army was 35 per cent. The total loss figure for all command staff, including political officers, was 1,023,093 (losses in the officer corps for 1941 amounted to 233,316).[16]

'Command and political staff' bore the brunt of the losses, their casualties amounting to 90 per cent of their strength. Combat officer loss in the Red Army amounted to 973,260 or 95.13 per cent of the total casualty figure for officers. Infantry officers suffered more than half of that total (569,794 or 58.54 per cent). Armoured troops lost 47,105 officers, the artillery 94,189 (4.84 per cent and 9.68 per cent respectively of the total loss). The air force lost 39,104 officers (3.82 per cent) and the Navy 10,729 (1.05 per cent). Splitting up the total loss figure, 631,008 officers were killed in action, 392,085 missing in action or taken prisoner, with the heaviest losses – more than 50 per cent – incurred in the first period of the war, 1941–2.[17]

Losses among senior officers amounted to 421 generals and admirals (killed in action, missing, incapacitated or lost for 'other reasons' – execution by firing squad). Major-generals, the bulk of them promoted in 1940 as Stalin refilled ranks previously purged, lost most heavily – 344. Seven rear-admirals and 59 lieutenant-generals came next, followed by 2 vice-admirals, 4 colonel-generals and 4 full generals. The death of Marshal Shaposhnikov accounted for the sole death at this most senior level.[18] More than 50 Soviet senior officers were taken prisoner by the Germans, though only a handful chose to collaborate (Vlasov being the most prominent of this group).[19] Going further down the ranks, the Red Army lost 2,502 colonels, 4,887 lieutenant-colonels, 19,404 majors, 71,738 captains, 168,229 senior lieutenants, 353,000 lieutenants, 279,967 junior lieutenants and 122,905 men carrying out officer duties without official officer rank.[20]

The mass of statistical information in the Krivosheyev volume is enormous and obviously a great deal of time will have to be expended to extract this information. For the purposes of this chapter perhaps the most economical approach, yet one combining an illustrative aspect, is to take the analysis which covers specific Red Army operations and supplies key figures, killed in action, medical casualties and the combined total (see Table 12.4).[21]

In dissecting these figures there is clearly a relationship between 'duration of operations' and loss figures, as well as the strength of the Soviet force, the nature of its support, competence of command and indeed a whole range of factors which require detailed analysis. Several 'fronts', in one guise or another, lasted throughout a lengthy period of the war. The battered, bruised western front, ripped to pieces by the German army in 1941, finally disappeared in 1944, to be replaced by a multi-front organisation. The Leningrad front fought on as an entity from August 1941 to May 1945, recording a total of 1,353 operational days. The same test can be supplied to various Red Army formations, such as the 1st Shock Army, which enjoyed only thirty-six days out of the line during the entire war. In looking at loss figures it is pertinent to point out that once the Red Army seized the strategic initiative after the titanic battle of Kursk in 1943, the nature of Soviet operations changed with the advance of multiple fronts westward. It has been the habit of Soviet commentators to light upon casualty figures to demonstrate a heedless leadership which inflicted unnecessary losses in the field, some of these discussions bordering on the frantically propagandistic and polemical. It was left to a Swiss army colonel, Fritz Stoeckli, to approach this question in a more methodical and methodological manner. Colonel Stoeckli approaches Soviet loss rates by examining typologies of operations and actions.

Though it may appear to be overly clinical in approaching such a brutal

TABLE 12.4: Soviet losses in operations, June 1941–Sept. 1945

Red Army operation	Killed in action	Medical casualties	Combined total
Baltic defensive operation 22 June–9 July 1941	75,202	13,284	(88,486)
Belorussian defensive operation 22 June–9 July 1941	341,073	76,717	(417,790)
W. Ukrain defensive operation 22 June–6 July 1941	172,323	69,271	(241,594)
Polyarnoe/Karelia defensive operation 29 June–10 Oct. 1941	67,265	68,448	(135,713)
Kiev defensive operation 7 July–26 Sept. 1941	616,304	84,240	(700,544)
Leningrad defensive operation 10 July–30 Sept. 1941	214,078	130,848	(344,926)
Smolensk battle 10 July–10 Sept. 1941	486,171	273,803	(759,974)
Donbass–Rostov defensive operation 29 Sept.–16 Nov. 1941	143,313	17,263	(160,576)
Moscow defensive operation 30 Sept.–5 Dec. 1941	514,338	143,941	(658,279)
Tikhvin offensive operation 10 Nov.–30 Dec. 1941	17,924	30,977	(48,901)
Rostov counter-offensive operation 17 Nov.–2 Dec. 1941	15,264	17,847	(33,111)
Moscow strategic offensive 5 Dec. 1941–7 Jan. 1942	139,586	231,369	(370,955)
Kerch–Feodosiya amphibious landing 25 Dec. 1941–Jan. 1942	32,453	9,482	(41,935)
Rzhev–Vyazma offensive operation 8 Jan.–20 Apr. 1942	272,320	504,569	(776,889)
Voronezh–Voroshilovgrad defensive operation 28 June–24 July 1942	370,552	197,825	(586,834)
Stalingrad defensive operation 17 July–18 Nov. 1942	323,856	319,986	(643,842)
N. Caucasus defensive operation 25 July–31 Dec. 1942	192,791	181,120	(373,911)
Stalingrad offensive operation 19 Nov. 1942–2 Feb. 1943	154,885	330,892	(485,777)
N. Caucasus offensive operation 'DON' 1 Jan.–4 Feb. 1943	69,627	84,912	(154,539)
Leningrad de-blockading operation 'ISKRA' 12–30 Jan. 1943	33,940	81,142	(115,082)
Voronezh–Kharkov offensive operation 13 Jan.–3 Mar. 1943	55,475	98,086	(153,561)
Kharkov defensive operation 4–25 Mar. 1943	45,219	41,250	(86,469)
Kursk defensive operation 5–23 July 1943	70,330	107,517	(177,847)

TABLE 12.4: *continued*

Red Army operation	Killed in action	Medical casualties	Combined total
Orel offensive operation 12 July–18 Aug. 1943	112,529	317,361	(429,890)
Belgorod–Kharkov offensive operation 3–23 Aug. 1943	71,611	183,955	(255,566)
Smolensk offensive operation 7 Aug.–2 Oct. 1943	107,645	343,821	(451,466)
Donbass offensive operation 13 Aug.–22 Sept. 1943	661,166	207,356	(273,522)
Chernigov–Poltava offensive operation 26 Aug.–30 Sept. 1943	102,957	324,995	(427,952)
Novorossisk–Taman offensive operation 10 Sept.–9 Oct. 1943	14,564	50,946	(65,510)
Lower Dnieper offensive operation 26 Sept.–20 Dec. 1943	173,201	581,191	(754,392)
Kiev offensive operation 3–13 Nov. 1943	6,491	24,078	(30,569)
Liberation W. Ukraine 24 Dec. 1943–17 Apr. 1944	270,198	839,330	(1,109,528)
Leningrad–Novgorod offensive operation 14 Jan.–1 Mar. 1944	76,686	237,267	(313,953)
Crimean offensive operation 8 Apr.–12 May 1994	17,754	67,065	(84,819)
Vyborg–Petrozavodsk offensive operation 10 June–9 Aug. 1944	32,674	72,701	(96,375)
Belorussian strategic offensive 23 June–29 Aug. 1944	178,507	587,308	(765,815)
(1st Polish Army)	1,533	3,540	(5,073)
Lvov–Sandomir offensive operation 13 July–29 Aug. 1944	65,001	224,295	(289,296)
Jassy–Kishinev offensive operation 20–9 Aug. 1944	13,197	53,933	(67,130)
E. Carpathian offensive operation 8 Sept.–28 Oct. 1944	26,843	99,368	(126,211)
(1st Czechoslovak Corps)	1,630	4,069	(5,699)
Baltic offensive operation 14 Sept.–24 Nov. 1944	61,468	218,622	(280,090)
Belgrade offensive operation 28 Sept.–20 Oct. 1944	4,350	14,488	(18,838)
Petsamo–Kirkenes offensive operation 7–29 Oct. 1944	6,048	15,149	(21,233)
Budapest offensive operation 29 Oct. 1944–13 Feb. 1945	80,026	240,056	(320,082)
Vistula–Oder offensive operation 12 Jan.–3 Feb. 1945	43,251	149,874	(193,125)
W. Carpathian offensive operation 12 Jan.–18 Feb. 1945	16,337	62,651	(78,988)

TABLE 12.4: *continued*

Red Army operation	Killed in action	Medical casualties	Combined total
E. Prussia offensive operation 13 Jan.–25 Apr. 1945	126,464	458,314	(584,778)
Vienna offensive operation 16 Mar.–15 Apr. 1945	38,661	129,279	(167,940)
Berlin offensive operation 16 Apr.–8 May 1945	78,291	274,184	(352,475)
Prague offensive operation 6–11 May 1945	11,165	38,083	(49,348)
Far Eastern offensive operations 9 Aug.–2 Sept. 1945	12,031	24,425	(36,456)

subject as battlefield loss, it is important to have a corrective to the somewhat inflammatory views which have been expressed over this subject. Colonel Stoeckli makes an important distinction between loss figures and loss ratios at the operational and the tactical level. The difference is indeed marked and relates to what the Colonel derives as 'efficiencies', which he adduces by setting the Soviet casualty level against the strength of the opposing German forces. He also takes into account the observations of Ye. I. Smirnov's *Voina i meditsina*[22] in discussing casualty rates in the breakthrough phase (lasting between two and four days): Soviet losses in wounded alone here could be as high as 2 per cent per day at *army level*, though this conformed to planning predictions. Since Soviet forces in the later stages of the war enjoyed superiority in tanks and artillery and a 3:1 superiority in manpower, German efficiency at the *tactical* level was pronounced (expressed as 5–7 Soviet casualties per day for every 100 German defenders). In Soviet offensive operations in the later stages of the war, Soviet success involved a casualty rate which equalled 25–30 per cent of *enemy strength*. German 'efficiency' in inflicting casualties (killed and wounded) was by such estimates in the order of 1.5:1 (sobering enough but a far cry from the more furiously hysterical assessments of Soviet ineptitude and profligacy).[23] A recent Russian account, using gross figures, arrives at a figure of 1.6:1 Soviet casualties for every German casualty, but for some reason these figures did not take account of returned Soviet prisoners of war when reporting 'total losses'.[24] In fact, one of the 'adjustments' made to these figures, adding non-German combatants and their losses to the German figure and this time subtracting the figure for returned Soviet prisoners from the Soviet loss figure, brings what is called the 'dynamics of combatant losses' virtually to unity or a fraction over it.

The analysis of Soviet battlefield techniques and operations is too vast a subject to broach and in the event it has been encompassed by a multitude of volumes.[25] In general terms, there can be no doubt that in most instances Soviet divisions (whose strength and organisation varied enormously) were over-tasked and under-manned. Looking at patterns – or typologies – over time, there is a marked contrast between German and Soviet practice. Soviet tactical handling was too often wasteful, to the point of profligate, but virtually any price was paid to attain operational success. On the other hand, German tactical brilliance and effectiveness inflicted brutal losses, but this alone did not guarantee operational success. Yet another criticism levelled at Soviet wartime performance is that the Red Army doctrine was itself defective. However, once the requisite 'armament norms' were reached – as they were by 1943 – the doctrine proved to be both sound and innovative. Much confusion has been brought about by the temptation to compare 'like with like'. At the beginning of the war, the Soviet rifle division with enormous variations in strength represented the equivalent of one-third of a fully manned German infantry division. Only towards the end of the war was anything approaching 'parity' reached. Throughout the war the *Wehrmacht* retained a conspicuous edge in mobile formations, numbers notwith-standing, the German tank and mechanised infantry formations. A Red Army tank/mechanised corps was roughly the equivalent of a German *Panzer/Panzergrenadier* division. In 1942 the Red Army possessed less than a dozen of these corps, but after 1943 these corps tripled in numbers and no less than six tank armies were raised (with two more reportedly in reserve).

Initial loss, on a catastrophic scale, in the years 1941–2 clearly had a serious effect on combat effectiveness. The 'mob of riflemen' of the 1941 rifle division, facing crack German divisions, took time to evolve, for example bringing in more mortars and a gradual increase in artillery for direct fire. Between June 1941 and June 1943 almost one-third of 670 Soviet rifle divisions had been destroyed. After Stalingrad, Soviet divisions with greater heavy weapons support still maintained a large number of men 'right up front', thus inviting heavy casualties, but a form of 'compensation' was afforded by equipping the Soviet infantryman with more automatic weapons, sub-machine guns and machine pistols.

The wartime 'learning curve' of the Soviet tank forces was cruel and costly. The greatest struggle was to shift the balance between the mass of infantry and mobile forces. To hold off a German advance in 1941–2, in the absence of adequate artillery support, the only answer had to be perforce an infantry mass. The key rested with the organisation of Red Army mobile forces, and balancing infantry with armour. The Germans destroyed almost all of the cumbersome, ill-trained mechanised formations in 1941. After that débâcle, brigades were all that remained of a decimated tank force, but as Soviet industry produced more tanks, so the tank corps reappeared (the equivalent of the German *Panzer* division). Those early corps took on infantry as 23 percent of their establishment, as well as 240 tanks, but organic artillery was lacking, forcing reliance on independent artillery brigades and even 'tank-busting' *shturmovik* aircraft for fire-support. That weakness brought heavy losses if faced by a defence effectively deploying its artillery resources; frontal assault was hazardous, outflanking was not always possible, waiting on further infantry and fire-support to draw up meant the tanks stopping dead (and literally staying that way).

In his major study of Soviet tank operations, *Tankovyi udar*, Army General Radzievskii made precisely that point: losses inflicted on Soviet armour by German artillery ranged from 58 to 94.8 per cent. Air strikes accounted for up to 17 per cent of losses; anti-tank mines 14 per cent; and in 1944 the *Faustpatrone* (the German 'bazooka') and hollow-charge munitions inflicted losses ranging from 30 to 80 per cent. Tank losses in built-up areas were particularly heavy; for example, in January 1943 the Third Tank Army committed 378 of its tanks in the battle for Kharkov and emerged with only 98.[26] Colonel-General Krivosheyev has supplied figures for total wartime tank losses: 20,500 in 1941, 15,100 in 1942, 23,500 in 1943, 23,700 in 1944 and 13,700 in 1945.[27]

Lest this discussion appears to rely too heavily on Soviet sources, it is useful to run a rapid 'cross-check' with wartime German military reports. The German files *Panzer-Verluste Ost* compiled by *Fremde Heere Ost (IIc)*, in a report for 26 January 1944 summarising *Feindliche Panzer-Verluste 1941–1943*, tabulated troop after-action 'reported losses' with confirmed loss. The figure for Soviet tank losses in 1941 was 22,000 (with only the smallest discrepancy between the two figures, 246). For 1942 the figure of actual loss was 16,200 (compared to a 'reported loss' of 21,367). In 1943 actual loss was 17,300 (as opposed to a 'reported loss' of 34,659!). For the period 1941–3, German intelligence arrived at a figure of 55,300 Soviet tanks destroyed (compared to a 'reported loss' of 78,272, much of it attributed to 20–50 per cent double-counting).

Using gross figures and applying a comparative Soviet–German 'loss ratio' have been interpreted to the disadvantage of the Red Army in anything ranging from 4:1 to 10:1. Though the Red Army was not very efficient, it was efficient enough at the operational level, if wasteful and frequently profligate at the tactical level. Any estimate of this nature demands the most careful qualification, but by way of generalised assessment and taking some account of the variations and vagaries, if German 'effectiveness' was unity – 1 – then comparable Soviet performance fluctuated widely (even wildly) between 0.4 and 0.8. But what precisely constitutes 'efficiency' (or effectiveness) is open to the widest questioning and requires a much closer investigation of the data assembled by General Krivosheyev and others. What cannot easily be countenanced is to resort to simple 'statistical' explanations for the military eventualities and outcomes of the eastern front.

This heated and passionate discussion on the part of Russian analysts and commentators – as regards the Soviet–German 'loss ratio' – has been complicated if not actually obfuscated by calculations of German losses on the eastern front. 'German strength' needs a certain qualification, for to the tally of German casualties must be added the toll exacted of the Italian, Hungarian, Finnish, Romanian and Slovak units. The Romanians incurred the heaviest losses of men, paying twice: first for their participation in the German invasion and then after 1944 when Romania changed sides and fought alongside the Red Army.

Though there is considerable doubt about the exact figures for losses in the 'satellite armies', numbers are in the region of half a million for the Romanians, 350,000 for the Hungarians, and 90,000 for the Finns and Italians. A number of Soviet sources settled for a figure of 'about a million' for losses in the 'satellite armies' and thus arrived at a 'total loss' figure for German – Axis forces of 7,051,000 (6,046,000 German losses plus 1,005,000 'satellite' losses).[28] To the Red Army casualty list should also be added the figures for those national units fighting with the Red Army, numbering 47,000: 13,900 Poles, up to 11,000 in the Czechoslovak Corps, up to 15,000 Romanians and 7,000 Bulgarians. There is also the problem of collaboration which tends to confuse the issue of 'German manpower'. At least one quarter of the German manpower on the eastern front was supplied by about one million Soviet citizens, many recruited to fight with the *Ostlegionen* or to provide rear security or support (often of a dangerous kind) with the *Hiwis* (Hilfswillige). At one point after 1943, the German *Ostheer* incorporated a greater cross-section of Soviet nationalities than the Red Army: Central Asians, Caucasians, Volga and Crimean Tartars, Ukrainian guards and national units from the Baltic States. No less than 78 battalions from camps in Poland and the Ukraine were assigned to the German army, plus the Independent Turkic Division and the Kalmyk Cossack Corps, not to mention SS units, East Turkic and Caucasian, all part of the SS *Waffenverband*.[29] By 1944 three Baltic *Waffen* SS divisions were fighting alongside the German army against the Red Army, and continued to do so until the end of the war. Among other 'armies' were the men of the 'Russian Liberation Army' (the ROA), the Vlasov army,[30] the anti-Soviet 'Ukrainian Revolutionary Army' (UPA), a whole array of renegade battalions and regiments, recruits to the German *Polizei-divisionen*, and the notorious

Kaminsky Brigade raised to fight Soviet partisans. To whom should casualty figures be attributed, Germans or Russians, if indeed there was ever any way of arriving at such a figure?

There are obvious anomalies in the figures, not so much deliberate distortions as ambiguities. However, there is one glaring omission which demands correction. Among the 'total mobilised manpower' were 800,000 women, of whom 490,235 were assigned for active service with the Red Army and the Navy. No casualty figures have been presented for women combatants. The Krivosheyev volume remarks laconically: 'Many of them did not return from the war'.[31] Of an anguishing subject, perhaps the most agonising is the fate of Soviet prisoners of war and slave labour in Germany. Once again the question of numbers looms extremely large. Colonel-General Krivosheyev fixes 4,559,000 as the most likely realistic figure for Soviet personnel taken prisoner or missing in action, though German army figures quoted by Colonel Eliseyev and Lieutenant-Colonel Mikhalev set the total of Soviet prisoners of war on 1 February 1945 at 5,734,580, with the proviso that this larger number may be due to the inclusion of partisans and even civilians made prisoners by German army units. The Red Army prisoners of war suffered an unbelievably ghastly martyrdom; a comparison has been made with the Holocaust, for deaths among Soviet prisoners and death by shooting, starvation, gassing and inhuman treatment amounted to some 3,300,000. This hideous saga has been most exhaustively treated in Christian Streit's monumental study, *Keine Kameraden* (excerpts from which have been only recently published in the Russian military press). The estimates (and they are largely estimates) of Soviet prisoners of war who perished in captivity range from 1,900,000 to 3,600,000.[32] What can be established with some degree of certainty, based on the figures for repatriated Soviet citizens (military and civilian), is that by 1 January 1953 5,500,000 individuals had returned to the Soviet Union, of which only 1,836,562 were former prisoners of war: 250,000 ex-prisoners elected not to return to the Soviet Union.[33]

One of the murkiest and most disturbing questions is the relationship between 'casualties' and 'combatants'. In the German Army Group Centre report *ObKdo Abt. Ic/A.O.* on prisoners and captured weapons, issued on 1 April 1943 and covering the period 21–31 March 1943, is entered a tally of 2,466 prisoners with an explanatory note '*davon 452 Banditen erschossen*', the execution of '452 bandits'. These '*Banditen*' were presumably Soviet partisans, suspected partisans or people suspected of lending aid and comfort to the partisans, victims of what the German command chose to call the *Bandenkrieg*. The diversion of German resources to *Bandenkrieg* was considerable, as was the Soviet investment in the partisan movement. By the summer of 1942 the numerical strength of Soviet partisans had grown appreciably, from 30,000 to some 150,000, the bulk in Belorussia and neighbouring areas. At the beginning of 1943, German reports mentioned a figure of 200,000 for the strength of Soviet partisans, finally arriving at a total of 400–500,000. Soviet sources cited a figure of 360,000 armed partisans in Belorussia and 220,000 in the Ukraine.[34]

This was a savage war within a brutal war, knowing no frontiers either legal or moral. In May 1943, to take but one example of a German anti-partisan operation, *Zigeunerbaron* involved German, Hungarian and Russian defector units assigned to clear areas south of Bryansk of an estimated partisan force 3,000 strong. All civilians unfit for military service were to be evacuated from the area. All men between the ages of 15 and 56 were classified as 'prisoners of war'. Any Red Army soldiers, Party members or Jews were to be used as guides to clear minefields. Villages would be burned to the ground. The net result of the operation was the capture of 1,568 'prisoners', 1,584 killed, 15,812 civilians left homeless, the roofs over their heads burned, deprived of bare necessities.[35]

The probability of ever establishing loss figures for Soviet partisans is remote. Colonel-General Krivosheyev's volume cites one tiny example and a few minute figures, but this merely illuminates the scale of the problem. One indication of what might be involved is demonstrated by the work of Major-General Shomody who has literally 'walked the ground' in Belorussia, recording in his *Marshrutami narodnoi slavy* hitherto unidentified graves and locations of partisan operations and actions.[36] To whatever figure one might arrive at must be added the great swathe of 'the missing', forced into servitude as hapless *Ostarbeiter* or dragged off as handmaidens to the German *Hausfrau*, or yet again the population of the unimaginably ghastly death camps. Researchers such as E. A. Brodskii have made herculean efforts to uncover not only figures but individual fates of this 'lost dimension' in studies such as *Oni nie propali bez vesti*. In the terrible empire of the *Konzentrationslage*, only the Jews and Red Army prisoners fought back, but even the German mania for rigid bureaucratic book-keeping of the toll of the dead does not disclose what losses ensued.[37] More numbers loom up in the ghastly, ghostly world of the dead and the dying. Some numbers were of a frightful scale, like the 1,900,000 Jews trapped by the German attack on Russia and then done to death, the 'massacre of the innocents' – when badly armed, untrained 'militia units', the *narodnoe opolchenie*, were sent into action against crack Nazi fighting troops in 1941 – or the 800 firemen in besieged Leningrad, dead from starvation in a city which lost 900,000 of its inhabitants, 65,000 from the shells of the German long-range siege guns.

Yet another twist to this controversy over 'loss ratios', one which is an indirect commentary on the scale of human loss, has been the disclosure of Soviet battlefield losses in weapons and equipment, a subject which became the centre of yet more furious altercation. Soviet figures affirm the destruction of 607 enemy divisions (including 100 'satellite' divisions) on the eastern front, together with 48,000 tanks, 167,000 guns and 77,000 aircraft (57,000 owing directly to Soviet action). Comparable Soviet losses included 15,500,000 infantry weapons, 96,500 tanks and self-propelled (assault) guns, 317,500 guns and mortars and 106,400 aircraft (46,100 lost to direct enemy action). This colossal list includes 351,000 lorries, 75,100 radio sets, 10,000 items of combat engineering (pontoons, scrapers, graders ...), 24 million gas-masks and 31,068 pieces of chemical warfare equipment. The Soviet navy lost 1,014 warships of all classes (314 large surface ships among them); the figure disclosed for losses in submarines is 102. Colonel-General Krivosheyev's volume provides detailed information on Soviet wartime weapons systems followed by a breakdown for each year of the war for losses in main weapons (small arms, tanks, aircraft, warships) as well as items of military equipment.

The figures for tank losses over each wartime year are especially illuminating. In 1941, out of a tank-park of 22,600, the Red Army lost 20,500 (72.7 per cent of all tanks available, front-line or in production). At the beginning of 1942 the tank-park stood at 7,700 machines, boosted by increasing production to 35,000 machines with the loss of 15,000 (42.1 percent of total strength). In the year of giant tank battles, including the huge encounter at Kursk in 1943, the Red Army lost more than half of its machines, 51.5 per cent, 22,400 out of 43,500 tanks produced or available. After 1942, the introduction and production of self-propelled (SP) guns substantially alters the loss profiles. The Red Army began 1944 with 21,100 tanks and 3,300 SP guns, losing 16,900 tanks (40 percent of the park) and 6,800 SP guns, some 40 per cent of those finally produced. The final year of the war saw the Red Army with a combined force of 35,500 tanks and SP guns (25,400 tanks and 10,100 guns), losing 8,500 tanks and 5,000 assault guns. Out of a total wartime production of tanks, 108,700, the Red Army lost 83,500 machines (76.8 per cent of the available park) and 13,000 SP guns (56.3 per cent of the 23,100 guns produced). From a total of 131,700 tanks and guns produced, the battlefield loss was 73.3 per cent, 96,500 units.[38]

SOCIAL LOSS, SOCIAL COST

What precisely constitutes the 'social size' or the 'social dimension' of a war, in particular a war of this magnitude? It is relatively easy to measure the 'destructive dimension'. In the case of the Soviet Union this amounted to 30 per cent of the national wealth, 23 per cent as a 'population deficit', some

679 billion roubles at 1941 prices, a catastrophic urban population loss. In what was left of Stalingrad only 12.2 per cent of the population remained, while in Voronezh only 19.8 per cent remained. The result of such decimation was the persistence of a cruel male/female imbalance. The land lost 46,000 tractors to seizure and 18,000 combined harvesters in the RSFSR (the Russian Republic) alone, cattle were seized, 23,000 schools razed, 1,800,000 inhabitants wiped out in 19 administrative districts, 2,400,000 from 17 districts taken for forced labour in Germany, and the land stripped of its manpower – leaving old men and women, or youths, to act as draught animals and drag ploughs. During the war, natural population growth virtually ceased. In terms of the Soviet war economy – men, money, guns – the country was pillaged for resources and duly emptied of them. By 1942 wartime mobilisation meant that more than 50 per cent of all Soviet assets were committed for war.

Labour conditions were horrendous in the process of turning out thousands of tanks and guns. A juvenile labour force was taught rudimentary skills and was augmented once again by the aged and the pensionable, living off scanty canteen rations. When exhaustion overcame workers, as it did from overwork and malnutrition, there was a brief night of rest, the *nochnye sanatorii* and infusion of special rations, the so-called *stakhanovskie obedy*. The cost of the huge industrial migration, the uprooting of whole factories and transplanting them in the eastern hinterland, has never been calculated. What is evident is the unimaginable social deprivation, a work-force living in earth dug-outs, lacking all heating in a Siberian winter, with miserable rations and draconian work disciplines.

Categorising social loss is a demanding task, one to which Soviet historians paid less than assiduous attention, save with honourable exceptions such as A. V. Mitrofanova on the working class, M. S. Zinich on social conditions and social welfare in wartime, and Yu. V. Arutyunyan on the peasantry. In pursuit of the 'heroic myth', too many Soviet historians missed the heroic reality, much of it humdrum but none the less of heroic proportions. Of Soviet women at war there is a vast amount to be learned; Valentina Galagan's *Ratnyi podvig zhenshchin* is useful but we have yet to see a full-scale, documented study of the keepers of the home-fires, conscripted as anti-tank ditch diggers, munitions workers, air raid wardens, locomotive drivers and telegraphists, working in the illegally militarised rail and communications systems – subject to military law.[39] A pitiable dimension of social loss and deprivation lies behind the figure of those 350,000 orphans, dependent on charitable family adoption for shelter and care, or a whole generation of the young deprived of anything but the most rudimentary 'three R's' education under German occupation.

Who, in the final analysis, made war on whom? The exactions of the German army are now a matter of record, going far beyond the accepted usages of war, grim though those are. Yet as slave trains clanked westwards into Germany, so also did they rumble eastward into the Soviet interior as the GULAG continued to fill up throughout the war, and inflict its own losses through punishment and pestilence: 100,997 in 1941, 248,877 in 1942, 166,967 in 1943, almost 70,000 in 1944 and 43,848 in 1945.[40] What is all the more extraordinary is that the slave camps continued to turn out munitions of war, often surpassing the production 'norms' of factories beyond the camps. While it would be an exaggeration to say that Stalin's wartime regime made war on its own people, with mass deportations and draconian punishments both at home and in the front-line, it is hard to see where the line might be drawn. This was a regime which could callously abandon its own people, and yet demand of them inordinate sacrifice. It was not the institutions of the regime which assured survival – for it was those very institutions and practices which prejudiced it so gravely – but the popular exercise of self-discipline, devotion to duty, responsiveness to firm leadership when manifested and a deep attachment to true patriotism.

The controversy over Soviet wartime losses will take time to subside, if indeed it is ever stilled. The search for greater accuracy and comprehensiveness will continue. For this, Russian analysts and historians are anxious to enlist the aid of foreign specialists with access to yet more records. But the controversy is not of itself so very important when it is used only for polemical or overtly political propagandistic purposes. The compilation of loss can be made to mean everything and nothing. It should above all commemorate the memory of the individual as well as the scale of the national sacrifice. It is for these reasons that the proposed Russian national Book of Remembrance, *Kniga pamyati*, should be properly conceived and scrupulously, generously executed, vast and reverential in its embrace.

Notes

1. S. Kohn and A. F. Meyendorff, *The Cost of the War to Russia: The Vital Statistics of European Russia during the World War 1914–1917* (Yale Univ. Press, New Haven, Conn., 1932) (Howard Fertig Reprint, New York, 1973); id., *The Social Cost of the War*, p. 3.
2. For this particular study, see Omer Bartov, *The Eastern Front, 1941–1945: German Troops and the Barbarisation of Warfare* (Macmillan, London, 1985). For a somewhat wider review of the German army, also Omer Bartov, *Hitler's Army: Soldiers, Nazis, and War in the Third Reich* (OUP, New York and Oxford, 1991).
3. M. M. Kozlov (ed.), *Veklikaya Otchestvennaya voina 1941–1945: Entsiklopediya* (Voenizdat, Moscow, 1985) p. 23.
4. L. E. Polyakov, *Tsena pobedy: Demografīcheskii aspekt* (Finansy i statistika, Moscow, 1985) *passim*.

5. For a detailed analysis of the 1939 census, see V. S. Kozhurin, O chislennosti nase-leniya SSSR nakanune Velikoi Otechestvennoi voiny', *Voenno-istoricheskii zhurnal* (hereafter *ViZh*), no. 2, 1991, pp. 21–6: the Russian journal *Argumenty i Fakty* reprinted the analysis of I. Kurganov, 'the Soviet *émigré* writer', in 1990 (no. 13). V. S. Kozhurin also refers to the work of I. Kurganov.

6. V. I. Kozlov, 'O lyudskikh poteryakh Sovetskovo Soyuza v Velikoi Otechestvennoi voine 1941–1945 godov', *Istoriya SSSR*, no. 2, 1989, pp. 132–8, which includes a critical review of earlier demographic/loss studies. On manpower/equipment losses and 'loss ratios', see also B. V. Sokolov, 'O sootnoshenii poter v ludyakh i boevoi tekhnike na sovetsko – germanskom fronte v khode Velikoi Otechestvennoi voiny', *Voprosy istorii*, no. 9, 1988, pp. 58–64. The Special Issue of the *Military Bulletin* (APN; Moscow English-language edition) April, 1990 printed Colonel Pronko's paper 'Counting Soviet Losses in World War II', pp. 11–15.

7. A. Ya. Kvasha, *Sovetskaya kultura*, 3 Sept. 1988.

8. For details and figures, see Barbara A. Anderson and Brian D. Silver, 'Demographic Consequences of World War II on the Non-Russian Nationalities of the USSR', in Susan J. Linz (ed.), *The Impact of World War II on the Soviet Union* (Rowman and Allanheld, Totowa, NJ, 1985) pp. 207–42.

9. Victor Gobarev, 'War on the Soviet–German Front – Facts and Figures', *Military Bulletin*, nos 7–8, Apr. 1990, pp. 6–11.

10. On 23 June 1992, the conservative newspaper *Sovetskaya Rossiya* published a com-prehensive report on the personalities and the work of the commission (established in April 1988) studying and verifying documents and data on Soviet war losses. It affirmed, among other things, that the officially accepted figure for the ratio of losses was 1.3:1, comparing Soviet and German losses. A general discussion and disclosure of the loss figures for men and equipment was presented in an exchange between the editor of *ViZh*, Major-General V. Filatov, and the then chief of the General Staff Army, General M. A. Moiseyev, in 'Tsena pobedy', *ViZh*, no. 3, 1990, pp. 14–16. These were 'round figures', though they do not differ widely from subsequent, more detailed studies.

11. B. V. Sokolov, 'O sootnoshenii poter v lyudyakh i boevoi tekhnike na sovetsko-germanskom fronte v khode Velikoi Otechestvennoi voiny', *Voprosy istorii*, no. 9, 1988, pp. 56–64.

12. Colonel-General G. F. Krivosheyev began a more detailed examination of loss figures in two articles published in 1991: 'V pervykh srazheniyakh', *ViZh*, no. 2, 1991, pp. 10–16 and 'Tsena osvoboditel'noi missii', *ViZh*, no. 3, 1991, pp. 48–51. These articles deal with the two main periods of the war, 1941–3 and 1944–5 and compress a great deal of data into a few pages, illustrated with pie charts and tables.

13. A detailed analysis of the 'structure of losses' is presented in the form of eleven graphs (plus text and tables) in Lieutenant-Colonel S. N. Mikhalev's, 'Boevye poteri storon v strategicheskikh nastupatel'nykh operatsiyakh Sovetskoi Armii 1941–1945 gg.', *ViZh*, no. 11, 1991, pp. 11–18. This also covers the numbers of prisoners taken by the Red Army as well as enemy losses (graphs 7–10). For the purposes of transferring data to graphs, Colonel Mikhalev has divided the war into six periods (excluding the Far Eastern campaign). The total for prisoners taken by the Red Army on the Soviet–German front is cited as 4,078,100 but a Soviet General Staff figure also quoted is somewhat higher, 4,541,900; see also V. P. Galitskii on prisoners of war taken by the Red Army in *ViZh*, no. 9, 1990, pp. 39–46.

14. It is extremely difficult to obtain data on the losses of Soviet women or even on the numbers of women serving in the Soviet forces; these figures are taken from the appendix in V. Ya. Galagan, *Ratnyi podvig zhenshchin v gody Velikoi Ote-chestvennoi voiny* (Vysshaya Shkola, Kiev, 1986).

15. G. F. Krivosheyev (ed.), *Grif sekretnosti snyat: Poteri vooruzhennykh sil SSSR*

v voinakh, boevykh deistviyakh i voennykh konfliktakh (Voenizdat, Moscow, 1993).

16. On losses in the officer corps, see G. F. Krivosheyev, *Grif sekretnosti snyat* (hereafter *Grif*), pp. 314–21, with three tables for officer losses in the Red Army, air force and Navy, analysing losses at each level of command (losses were heaviest among the lowest, front-line level: 434,510 infantry section commanders, 18,464 pilots, 1,861 naval officers serving with the naval infantry). The particular figures for officer losses in 1941 are taken from P. N. Knyshevskii (ed.), *Skrytaya pravda voiny: 1941 god. Neizvestnye dokumenty* ('Russkaya kniga', Moscow, 1992) pp. 342–3. This is followed by a list of those senior officers shot in 1941 and those taken prisoner.

17. See Table 80 and Table 81 in Krivosheyev, *Grif*, pp. 316–17.

18. Krivosheyev, *Grif*, pp. 320–1. *ViZh* is now publishing names and photographs (where available) of senior officers down to divisional commanders killed in action, missing or executed, under the title 'Otdali zhizn za Rodinu'.

19. Michael Parrish of Indiana University is preparing a major study of the fate of senior Soviet officers during the war. On the captured Red Army generals, see Michael Parrish, 'Soviet Generals in German Captivity: A Biographical Enquiry', *Survey*, June 1982, pp. 66–85. A Soviet version is supplied by I. I. Kuznetsov, 'Generaly 1940 goda', *ViZh*, no. 10, 1988, pp. 29–37.

20. Krivosheyev, *Grif*, p. 315 (also comparing the figures with those for officer losses in the Russian Imperial Army).

21. Derived from the tabulation in Krivosheyev, *Grif*, pp. 162–223. This is followed by loss tabulation for selected front offensive operations divided by the three separate periods of the war (1941–2, 1942–3 and 1944–5).

22. See Ye. I. Smirnov (wartime chief of the Main Medical Administration of the Red Army), *Voina i voennaya meditsina* ('Meditsina', Moscow, 1979).

23. Fritz Stoeckli (Swiss army reserve colonel), 'Wartime Casualty Rates: Soviet and German Loss Rates during the Second World War. The Price of Victory', *Journal of Soviet Military Studies*, 3, Dec. 1990, pp. 645–51.

24. See the discussion in Sokolov, *Voprosy istorii*, no. 9, 1988, pp. 56–64, on comparative loss rates.

25. Among these many studies, the most reliable work might be identified as Colonel David M. Glantz's *Soviet Military Operational Art: In Pursuit of Deep Battle* (Frank Cass, London, 1991), with detailed tables and extensive notes.

26. This is a major work by Army General A. I. Radzievskii, *Tankovyi udar* (Voenizdat, Moscow, 1977), see figures pp. 218–20. For further details of tank operations, see I. M. Anan'ev, *Tankovye armii v nastuplenie* (Voenizdat, Moscow, 1988).

27. G. F. Krivosheyev, *Grif.*, table, pp. 357–8.

28. V. V. Gurkin and O. G. Gurkov, 'Tsena agressii', *ViZh*, no. 9, 1989, pp. 33–41. It is noteworthy for its frank admission that 'during the whole period from 1942 to 1945 more than a million Soviet servicemen were active on the side of the Hitlerites' (p. 37).

29. For a detailed analysis of German policy, see Joachim Hoffmann, *Kaukasien 1942/43: Das deutsche und die Orientvölker der Sowjetunion* (Rombach Verlag, Freiburg, 1991) and id., *Die Ostlegionen 1941–1943: Turkotataren, Kaukasien und Wolgafinnen im deutschen Heer* (Rombach Verlag, Freiburg, 1986). See also Alex Alexiev, *Soviet Nationalities in German Wartime Strategy, 1941–1945.* (RAND Corp. Santa Monica R-2772-NA Aug. 1982.)

30. Joachim Hoffmann published a history of the Vlasov army in 1986: *Die Geschichte der Wlassow-Armee* (Rombach Verlag, Freiburg, 1986). See also Catherine Andreyev, *Vlasov and the Russian Liberation Movement: Soviet Reality and Emigré Theories* (CUP, Cambridge, 1987). Much more material on Vlasov and the *Vlasovshchina*– including the interrogation of Vlasov after he was handed back to the Soviet Union – has recently been published in the Russian press.

31. Krivosheyev, *Grif*, p. 329.

32. See Christian Streit, *Keine Kameraden: Die Wehrmacht und die sowjetischen Kriegsgefangenen 1941–1945*, 2nd edn (Dietz Verlag, Bonn, 1991). See also the discussion on losses in Colonel Eliseyev's, 'Tak skol'ko zhe lyudei my poteryali v voine?', *ViZh*, nos 6–7, 1992, pp. 31–4.

33. On Soviet personnel repatriated, see V. Zemskov, 'K voprosy o repatriatsii sovetskikh grazhdan 1944–1951 gody', *Istoriya SSSR*, no. 4, 1990, pp. 26–41, which uses the reports of the official Soviet Repatriation Commission. By using the *lower* official German figure for Soviet prisoners of war and the *lower* (or conservative) official Soviet figure for prisoner-repatriates – 5,245,882 and 2,000,735 respectively – this gives the figure of 3,245,147 'missing' Soviet prisoners (dead or unaccounted for).

34. See 'Die "Partisanenfront" ', ch. 10 in Erich Hesse, *Der sowjetrussische Partisanenkrieg 1941 bis 1944 im Spiegel deutscher Kampfanweisungen und Befehle* (Musterschmidt Verlag, Göttingen, 1969) pp. 190–9 for figures taken from wartime German military reports; for Soviet figures, see Alexander Werth, *Russia at War 1941–1945* (Barrie & Rockliff, London, 1964) pt. 6, ch. XI, 'Partisans in the Soviet–German War', pp. 710–26.

35. The captured German Military Documents (GMDs: US National Archives) contain a huge mass of documentation on German operations on the eastern front and intelligence on the Red Army (*Fremde Heere Ost* records). There are daily/weekly/monthly/annual compilations of Soviet losses in men and equipment (*Gefangene u. Beute*). The report quoted here is from *Heeresgruppe Mitte* (*ObKdo Ic/A.O.*) under *Gefangene u. Beute* for 1 Apr. 1943. The summary of *Gefangene u. Beute* for the period covering 22 June 1941–31 Mar. 1943 (prisoners taken, equipment destroyed or captured by Army Group Centre) gives 2,169,248 prisoners taken and 19,228 tanks, 1,400 aircraft and 15,853 field guns destroyed or captured.

36. G. F. Krivosheyev, *Grif*, p. 328 for a mention of partisan losses. Also V. K. Shomody, *Marshrutami narodnoi slavy* (Voenizdat, Moscow, 1989) *passim*.

37. On Jewish and Red Army resistance in the death camps, see Reuben Ainsztein, *Jewish Resistance in Nazi-Occupied Eastern Europe* (Paul Elek, London, 1974). On Soviet resistance in the camps, see N. M. Lemeshchuk, *Nie skloniv golovy* (Polit. Lit. Ukrainy, Kiev, 1986). See also E. A. Brodskii, *Vo imya pobedy nad fashizmom*: *Antifashistskaya bor'ba sovetskikh lyudei v gitlerovskoi germanii (1941–1945)* (Nauka, Moscow, 1970); id., *Oni nie propali bez vesti. Nie slomlenye fashistskoi nievoli* (Mysl, Moscow, 1987).

38. Krivosheyev, *Grif*, Table 96, pp. 351–65. See also Krivosheyev, 'Voina broni i motorov', *ViZh*, no. 4, 1991, pp. 36–41.

39. V. Ya. Galagan, *Ratnyi podvig zhenshchin*, deals mainly with women in front-line service (see note 14 above). For details of women and the Soviet home front, see J. Erickson, 'Soviet Women at War', in John Garrard and Carol Garrard (eds), *World War 2 and the Soviet People* (St Martin's Press, London, 1993) pp. 50–76.

40. See the discussion 'GULAG v gody Velikoi Otechestvennoi voiny', in *ViZh*, no. 1, 1991, pp. 14–24.

Notes on the Contributors

PROFESSOR DUŠAN BIBER, Institut za novejšo zgodovina Ljubljana, Slovenia, joined the Yugoslav Resistance in 1941. He was a war correspondent with the Yugoslav National Army, 1941–5, was President of the Yugoslav National Committee. Vice-President of the International Committee for the History of the Second World War.

PROFESSOR JOHN CHAPMAN, University of Sussex, is a leading British scholar in Japanese history and politics, and author of a both four-volume work *The Price Admiralty: The War Diary of the German Naval Attache in Japan, 1939–1943*, and *Japan's Quest for Comprehensive Security*. He is also the editor of *Japan Forum* (The International Journal of Japanese Studies).

PROFESSOR DAVID DILKS is Vice Chancellor of the University of Hull, and co-editor with Christopher Andrew of *The Missing Dimension: Governments and Intelligence Communities in the Twentieth Century*.

PROFESSOR JOHN ERICKSON is Director of Defence Studies at the University of Edinburgh, and author of works on the Red Army and Soviet military history, as well as the forthcoming *Blood, Bread and Steel*, a wartime social history of the USSR.

PROFESSOR GABRIEL GORODETSKY is Director of the Cummings Center for Russian and East European Studies at Tel Aviv University, Israel. He is Academic Advisor to the Israeli Defence Forces Staff College, and author of *Sir Stafford Cripps' Mission to Moscow, 1940–1942*.

PROFESSOR SIR HARRY F. HINSLEY, Professor Emeritus of the History of International Relations at the University of Cambridge, is author of the four-volume work *British Intelligence in the Second World War*, as well as a recent historical memoir of the wartime code-breaking work at Bletchley.

DR SERGEI KUDRYASHOV is a Moscow researcher and historian associated with the literary-historical journal *RODINA*.

PROFESSOR DR A. MERTSALOV, Guards Colonel (Ret.), was a participant in the Battles of Moscow, Stalingrad and Kursk. He specialises in German military historiography, and his publications include *Istoriya i Stalinizm* and *Dovol'no o voine?*.

LIEUTENANT-GENERAL (AVIATION) (RET.) STEPAN A. MIKOYAN is the son of Anastasas Ivanovich Mikoyan, the Soviet Deputy Prime Minister, wartime member of the Politburo, and close associate of Stalin. Stepan Mikoyan graduated as a fighter-pilot in 1941, becoming a military pilot during the Second World War, and a military test-pilot and commandant of military test-pilots, 1951–78. He became Deputy General Director of the design bureau for 'MOLNIYA', responsible for flight testing and crew ergonomics.

KLAUS-JÜRGEN MÜLLER, Professor of Modern and Contemporary History, University of the *Bundeswehr* and University of Hamburg, is author of several works, including *Das Heer und Hitler: Armee und nationalsozialistisches Regime, 1933–1940.*

LIEUTENANT-GENERAL DR KLAUS REINHARDT, Commanding General *Bundeswehr* III Corps, is author of *Moscow: The Turning Point?* (English edition).

COLONEL-GENERAL DMITRI VOLKOGONOV, adviser to President Boris Yeltsin, is author of *Stalin: Triumph and Tragedy*, translated from the original four-volume Russian work.

DR GEOFFREY T. WADDINGTON, University of Leeds, is currently working on a biography of Ribbentrop.

INDEX

Endnotes and references not indexed. Military commanders accorded last rank.

A-20 Boston, US bomber, 130
A-54 intelligence agent, 46, 47, 53, 67
Abwehr, 46, 158, 162, 181
Adamić, Louis, 39
Administration, German-occupied Russia, 247, 248
Afghanistan, 209
Africa, 9, 13, 209
Agriculture, 249, 250
AI, *see* Air Intelligence
Air Force Engineering Academy, Soviet, 124
Air Force Flight Test Institute, Soviet, 124
Air Forces, German, *see* Fliegerkorps (German Air Corps)
Air Intelligence, 48, 55, 63
Airacobra, US fighter aircraft, 130
Akita, Hiroshi, Colonel, 172
Ammunition Factory No. 80, 84
Amnesties, 252, 253
An den Soldaten der Ostfront (June 1941), 84
Anderson, Barbara, Dr, 258
Andric, Ivo, Dr, 36
Ansel, Walter, 40
Anti-Comintern Pact, 10, 14 162, 171
Anti-Semitism, 145, 235
Argumenty i Fakty, 257
Arisue, Seizō, Lt. General, 154
Armaments industry (German), 216, 217, 218, 219
Armstrong, Hamilton Fish, 39
Armies
  German: Army Group B, 62; Army Group Centre, 208, 211, 212, 213, 215, 216, 270; Army Group East, 46; Army Group North, 210, 213, 214, 216; Army Group South, 213, 214, 216; Panzer Group 2, 211, 213; 2nd Army, 63; 4th Army, 232, 246; 12th Army, 61, 62; 16th Army, 243
  Japanese: 6th Army, 164, 166, 176
  Soviet: 3rd Army, 83, 89; 4th Army, 83, 89,

90; 5th Army, 83; 6th Army, 83; 7th Army, 83; 8th Army, 83; 10th Army, 83, 90; 12th Army, 83; 13th Army, 83, 90; 14th Army, 83; 16th Army, 84; 19th Army, 84; 22nd Army, 84; 23rd Army, 83; 26th Army, 83, 87; 31st Army, 84; 33rd Army, 147; 43rd Army, 147; 1st Shock, 263; 3rd Tank, 268
Arnim, Hans-Jürgen von, 231
Arutyunyan, Yu.V., Professor, 273
Asiatic Fleet, US, 180
Attolico, Bernardo, Ambassador, 17
Auchinleck, Sir Claude, Field Marshal, 114
Australia, 9
Axis Planning Section (JIC), 178
Azores, 209

B-25 Mitchell, US bomber, 130
Bagramyan, I. Kh., Marshal, 129
Baltic Special Military District, 80, 83, 84, 85, 86, 87
Baltic States, 1940 occupation of, 19
Bandenkrieg, 270
Bandera, Stepan, 244
Banzai, Heihachirō, Colonel, 159
Barbarossa, Operation Barbarossa, planning, preparation, 3, 22, 26–7, 34, 38, 40, 44, 45, 46, 48–9, 52, 54, 60–3, 67–8, 70–1, 80–1, 84, 102, 208, 209, 230, 255
Barbarossa directive, 18 December 1940, 48
Bartov, Omer, 256
Battle of the Atlantic, 64
Battleaxe, 102
Bear Island, 112, 113
Beaverbrook, Lord, 108, 110, 116, 117, 131
Beloff, Max, Professor, 39
Berezhkov, Valentin, 7, 28
Berghof conference, 31 July 1940, 20
Beria, L. P., 127
Bernstorff, Count Sigismund, 37

Bernstorff, Albert, 37
Bessarabia, 1940 occupation of, 19
Bismarck, Otto von, 26, 28
Bletchley Park, 163
Blokhin, Colonel, 81
Blomberg, Werner von, Field Marshal, 159
Bock, Fedor von, Field Marshal, 211, 212, 213, 214, 231
Bonnet, Georges, 12,
Brauchitsch, Walther von, Field Marshal, 10, 39, 213
British Empire, 8, 24, 28
British Military Mission (Moscow), 98
Brodskii, E. A., 271
Budenny, S. M., Marshal, 212
Bukovina, 19,
Bulgaria, 19, 23, 24, 25, 26, 48, 52, 209
Buran, Soviet Space Shuttle, 124
Burrows, Montagu Brocas, Lt. General, 98
Bush, George, US President, 150
Butt, US diplomat, 131
Butler, Rohan, Professor, 39

Cadogan, Sir Alexander, 105
Canaris, Wilhelm, Admiral, 37, 162, 168, 169, 232
Carnegie Endowment for International Peace, 255
Caucasus, 50, 59, 60, 69
Cavallero, Count, 11
Cavendish-Bentinck, Victor, 179
Chamberlain, Neville, 138
Chiang Kai-shek, Generalissimo, 157, 160, 172
Chicago Daily News, 49
Chief of the Imperial General Staff, 51, 61
Chief War Correspondent, German, 70
Chiefs of Staff, British, 43, 47, 58, 61, 69, 70, 72, 101, 102, 103, 105, 106, 107, 108, 109, 110, 111, 112, 113, 114, 115, 116, 117, 166
China, 9, 105
Chinese Communist Party, 156
Christie, Malcolm, Group Captain, 9
Churchill, Winston Spencer, 4, 36, 43, 44, 45, 50, 55, 56, 72, 76, 102, 104, 105, 106, 108, 109, 111, 113, 114, 115, 116, 117, 118, 125, 126, 137, 139, 169, 179
Ciano, Galeazzo, Count, 16, 17, 18, 25
CIC, *see* Counter-Intelligence Corps
CIGS, *see* Chief of the Imperial General Staff
Clausen, Max, 160, 181
Clausewitz, Carl von, 134
Code and Cypher School, 53
Combined Fleet, Japanese, 179, 180
Comfort women, Korean, 151
Comintern, 138
Commander-in-Chief, High Command, German Army troops, Romania, 67

Committee for Liberation of the Peoples of Russia (KONR), 238
Communist Party, defection from, 251; Manifesto of, 138
Comrade Stalin's Visitor's Book, 89
Congressional Committees on Un-American Activities, 183
Conservative Party Central Office, 154
Control Commision, 77
Cossacks, 242
Coulondre, Robert, French Ambassador, 12
Counter-Intelligence Corps, 152, 153, 158
Crete, 69
Creveld, Martin van, 40
Crimean Tartars, 241
Cripps, Sir Stafford, 34, 43, 44, 45, 50, 51, 57, 58, 69, 71, 72, 97, 107, 108, 109, 110, 113, 116, 117
Czechoslovakia, 8, 10

Dalton, Hugh, 39, 106
Data on Examining Experience of Operations, Soviet Report, 147
Deception measures, German, 54
Defence Committee, British, 50, 103, 110
Dekanozov, Vladimir, 7, 86
Deutsches Nachrichten Buro (DNB), 9
Dietrich, Reichspressechef, 213
Dill, Sir John, Field Marshal, 57, 106, 110
Directive No. 18, 22
Directive No. 21, 26, 77
Directive No. 32, 209
Director of Combined Operations, 106
Director of Military Intelligence, 44, 52, 53, 54, 61
Dirksen, Herbert von, 159, 160
Dixon, Mr, 38
DMI, *see* Director of Military Intelligence
DNB, *see* Deutsches Nachrichten Buro
Donovan, William, US Colonel, 37

Eden, Sir Anthony (Lord Avon), 34, 35, 36, 58, 69, 70, 102, 103, 104, 109, 111, 112, 115, 154
Egypt, 53, 60, 69, 118, 209
Einsatzgruppen, 231
Eliseyev, Colonel, 270
Encyclopedia of the Great Patriotic War 1941–1945, Soviet, 257
Engel, Major, 40
Engels, Friedrich, 134, 139, 256
Enigma, decrypts, 56, 58, 62, 63, 64, 66, 67, 68, 70, 72, 160, 161
Eremenko, A. I., Marshal, 212
Extended Air Force Programme, German, 218

Fall-B, Contingency B, 62, 67
Feindliche Panzer-Verluste 1941–1943, 268
Felber, Major General, 234

Felix, 54
Finland, 19, 21, 23, 24, 25, 26, 45, 46, 48,
    56, 64, 70
Flakkorps: I, 62, 63, 67; II, 62, 63, 67
Flakregiment 'Hermann Goering', 62
Fliegerführer Baltic, 67
Fliegerkorps (German Air Corps): II, 61, 62,
    67, 212; IV, 62, 67, 71; V, 61, 67; VIII,
    61, 62, 67, 212
Fomini, E. M., 89
Forced labour, 273
Foreign Office, British, 12, 43, 50, 72
Forschungsamt, 182
Fortier, Louis J., US Colonel, 37
France, 8, 17
Franco, Francisco, General, 22
Franco–Japanese Accord (Indo–China), 167
Franco–Soviet Mutual Security Pact, 180
Franco–Soviet Pact, 12
Free Town, 55
Freiwillige, 240
Fremde Heere Ost, 46, 210, 268
Frentsel, J. J., 81
Fromm, Friedrich, Colonel General, 219
Fujii, Shigeru, Commander, 170
Furuuchi, Hiroo, 154

Gaimushō, 15, 154, 157, 159, 182
Galagan, V., 273
Gavrilović, Milan, Dr, 34, 35, 36
GC and CS, see Government Code and Cypher
    School
Gema (Gemeinde), 241
General Staff, German, 10, 59, 60, 59, 158,
    208
General Staff
    Hungarian, 53
    Japanese, 15, 152, 153, 155, 157, 160, 162
    Polish, 162, 169
    Soviet, 84, 87, 89, 143, 145, 146, 162, 252,
        259
    US, 113
George II, King of the Hellenes, 36
German Air Force, 49, 52, 54, 55, 61, 62, 64,
    66, 67, 68, 69, 70
German Air Force Enigma, see Enigma,
    decrypts
German Army, 45, 47, 49, 52, 78–9, 102,
    211–20, 230–7, 267, 269
German Strategy 1941, JIC paper, 59
German–Russian Treaties, August–September
    1939, 19
German–Soviet Boundary and Friendship
    Treaty (28 September 1939), 76
Germany, passim
Gersdorff, Rudolf, Colonel, 231
GKO, see State Defence Committee
Gobarev, V., Major, 258
Goebbels, Joseph, Dr, 83

Goering, Hermann, Reichsmarshal, 12, 67
Golikov, F. I., Marshal, 112, 113, 115, 131
Government Code and Cypher School, 53, 63,
    66, 67, 68, 69, 71, 154
Grand Strategy (London HMSO), 39
Great Britain, passim
Greater East Asian Sphere, 23
Greater East Asian War (Dai Tōa Sensō), 151
Greece, 23, 48, 55, 57
Grif sekretnosti snyat, 148, 261
Grigor'ev, A. A., 89
Gulag, Soviet prison camps, 274
Gulag Archipelago, 227

Halder, Franz, General, 39, 210, 219
Halifax, Edward Wood, Viscount, 14, 34, 66,
    113
Hammerstein-Equord, Kurt Freiherr, Field
    Marshal, 158
Hand cypher, German, 53
Harriman, William Averell, 116, 131
Hart, Sir Basil Liddell, 39
Hartmann, Lt. General, 159
Heiho special service unit (tokumu kikan),
    159
Heinrici, Gotthard, General, 246
Heins, Colonel, 160
Henderson, Sir Nevile, 9
Herrenmenschentum, 234
Hess, Rudolf, 4, 5, 107
Hesse, Fritz, 9
Heydrich, Reinhard, 37
High Command, German Army (OKH), 45,
    46, 48, 54, 208, 210, 211
Hilfswillige, 240
Hilger, Gustav, 24
Hillgruber, Andreas, Professor, 137
Himmler, Heinrich, 138, 241
Hindenburg, Paul von, Field Marshal, 235
Hiranuma Cabinet, 15
Historikerstreit, 227
Hitler, Adolf, 3, 7, 8, 9, 10, 11, 17, 18, 19,
    20, 21, 22, 23, 25, 26, 27, 28, 34, 35, 41,
    43, 44, 45, 46, 47, 48, 50, 51, 54, 56, 58,
    60, 64, 66, 68, 70, 71, 76, 77, 81, 83, 84,
    85, 101, 104, 124, 126, 137, 140, 145,
    150, 152, 157, 159, 161, 163, 164, 165,
    167, 168, 170, 173, 174, 175, 176, 177,
    178, 179, 182, 207, 208, 209, 210, 211,
    213, 214, 215, 218, 219, 220, 221, 241,
    230, 232, 233
Hitler Youth, 233, 236
Hiwis, 269
Hoepner, Erich, General, 231
Hoffmann, Joachim, Dr, 239, 240
Holocaust, the, 227
Home Army (Poland), 169
Hoover, J. Edgar, 183
Hopkins, Harry, 113, 114, 116

Hoptner, Jacob B., 36, 37
Hossbach Conference, 8
Huber, Gestapo attache, 169
Hull, Cordell, US Sec. of State, 39
Hungary, 19
Hurricane, British fighter aircraft, 130

Imperial Conference 1941, Japanese, 177
Imperial General Staff, 53
Imperial Japanese Army, see Japanese Army
Independent Turkic Division, 269
India, 14, 23, 66, 102, 105, 118
International Military Tribunal, 38
Iran, 114, 118, 209
Iraq, 118, 209, 253
Italy, 10, 11, 13, 17, 19, 23, 24, 25

Jacobsen, Hans-Adolf, Professor, 136
Japan, 9, 10, 11, 13, 14, 15, 16, 17, 18, 19,
    21, 23, 24, 25, 28, 82, 137, 150–83, 204,
    209
Japanese Army, 152, 155, 172
Japanese Naval Mission (Shanghai), 170
Japanese Navy, 156, 163, 164, 166, 170, 173,
    174, 175, 178
Japanese war economy, 1941, 175
Jews, massacre of, 271
JIC, see Joint Intelligence Committee
Jodl, Alfred, Colonel General, 77, 221
Joint Intelligence Committee, 44, 47, 52, 59,
    61, 65, 66, 69, 70, 72, 101, 103, 178,
    180
Joint Planners (British), 70
Jomini, Antoine-Henri, Géneral, 134, 143,
    144, 146
Jukić, Ilija, Dr, 36

Kaganovich, Lazar Moisevich, 18
Kaifu, Japanese Prime Minister, 150
Kalmyk Cossack Corps, 269
Kamata, Senzō, General, 154
Kaminski, Bronislav, 243, 244, 245
Kaminski Brigade, 243, 245, 270
Kantōkuen, 176, 180
Kato Kikan, 153
Katyn incident, 140
Keine Kameraden, 230, 270
Keitel, Wilhelm, Field Marshal, 138, 232, 270
Kelley, Mr, US diplomat, 35
Kesselring, Albert, Field Marshal, 212
Khalkhin-Gol (NomonHan), 160
Kharlamov, N., Admiral, 115
Khrushchev, N. S., 129, 257
Kiev Special Military District, 80, 83, 85, 86
Kingcobra, US fighter aircraft, 130
Kirkpatrick, Ivone, Sir, 13
Kirponos, M. P., Colonel General, 85, 129
Klenov, P. S., Lt. General, 85, 87
Klich, N. A., Major General, 89

Klimovskikh, V. E., Major General, 85, 89,
    90
Klugman, James, 39
Kniga pamyati, Book of Remembrance,
    Russian, 274
Koestring, E. A., Major General, 82
Kommissar-Befehl (Commissar Order), 231,
    232
Komsomol, 261
Kondō, Admiral, 171
Konev, I. S., Marshal, 212
Konoe administration, 163
Kononov, I. N., Colonel, 242
KONR, see Committee for Liberation of the
    Peoples in Russia
Korobkov, A. A., 89, 90
Korolev, S. P., 125
Kostić, Petar, 37
Kozlov, V. I., Professor, 257
Krasnaya Zvezda, 261
Kravchuk, Leonid, President of the Ukraine,
    239
Kretschmer, Colonel, 169
Krivitsky, Walter, 154, 162
Krivosheyev, G. F., Colonel General, 259,
    260, 268, 269, 270, 271, 272
Kudryashov, Sergei, Dr, 3, 228
Kumanev, G. A., Professor, 141
Kurganov, I., Professor, 257
Kurile Islands, 171
Kurkin, Major General, 84
Kurusu, Saburo, 16
Kuznetsov, N. G., Admiral, 107, 127, 131
Kvasha, A. Ya., Professor, 258
Kwantung Army, 159, 160, 176

Lake Kawaguchi conference 1969, 150, 155
Lake Khasan (Changkufeng Hill), 160
Lake Yamanaka conference 1991, 150, 155
Lane, Arthur Bliss, US diplomat, 35
Latin America, 55
Lend-Lease, 130, 132, 171
Lend-Lease Bill, 56
Lenin, V. I., 134, 139
Leningrad, starvation in, 271
Leningrad Military District, 83, 86
Liberation Movement of the Peoples of Russia
    (ODNR), 238
Libya, 55, 209
Lietzmann, Joachim, Captain, 161, 163, 170
Lithuania, 19
Litvinov, M. M., 104, 131
Lockheed Scandal, 1972, 151
London Naval Conference, 162
Long March, China, 1935–6, 156
Loss ratios, Soviet–German, 266, 268, 269
Losses: German, 148, 216, 217, 218, 269,
    272; Soviet, 148, 256–8, 259, 260, 261,
    262, 263, 264–6, 267, 272, 273, 274

Lovell, John, US Captain, 37
Ludendorff, Erich, Field Marshal, 235
Luftflotten, see Fliegerkorps (German Air
    Corps)
Luftwaffe, see Fliegerkorps (German Air
    Corps)
Lyashchenko, N. G., General, 78

MacArthur, Douglas, General, 152, 153, 183
Mackensen, Eberhard, von, General, 18
Maeda, Tadashi, Captain, 181
Main Military Soviet, 86, 143
Maiskii, Ivan, 35, 58, 63, 69, 70, 104, 105,
    108, 113, 139
Malenkov, G. M., 88, 128
Malyshev, V. A., 131
Manstein, Erich von, Field Marshal, 231
Margesson, David, 112
Marita Operation, 26, 39, 40
Marshall, George, General, 113
Marshrutami narodnoi slavy, 271
Martin, David, 39
Marx, Karl, 134, 139
Mason-Macfarlane, Sir Noel, Lt. General,
    106, 107, 108, 109, 110
Matsuoka, Yosuke, 165, 166, 167, 169, 170,
    171, 173, 177
Matzky, Gerhard, General, 168, 169
Mein Kampf, 4
Meisinger, Gestapo attache, 169
Mekhlis, L. M., 89
Meretskov, K. A., Marshal, 82
Mertsalov, A. N., Professor, 98
MEW see Ministry of Economc Warfare
MI, see Military Intelligence
Mihajlović Draža, 39
Mikhalev, S. N., Lt. Colonel, 270
Mikoyan, A. I., 46, 123, 125, 130
Miles, Geoffrey, Admiral, 109
Military Bulletin (Moscow), 258
Military Intelligence, 44, 47, 48, 49, 50, 51,
    53, 54, 55, 58, 59, 60, 64, 71, 72: MI 5,
    163; MI 6, 163
Ministry of Economic Warfare, 60
Mitrofanova, A. V., Professor, 273
Mitsunobu, Tōyō, Captain, 176, 178
Miyazawa, Mr, 151
Moiseyev, M. A., General, 259, 260
Moldavia, 62, 67
Molotov, Viacheslav, 15, 19, 20, 21, 22, 24,
    25, 34, 44, 48, 50, 82, 86, 107, 128, 131,
    139, 140, 171
Moscow Air-Defence Command, 123, 130
Moskoff, V., historian, 144
Müller, Klaus-J., Dr, 228
Mussolini, Benito, 17, 18, 23, 25, 85

Narodnoe opolchenie, Soviet militia, 271
Naval Code A, German, 161

Naval Staff, Japanese, 163, 166, 170, 177,
    181
Navy Ministry, Japanese, 163, 177
Nedic, Milan, General, 38
Neue Züricher Zeitung, 49
New Order, Nazi, 65
Nicholas, Mr, 36
Nicolson, Harold, 111
Ninčić, Momcilo, Dr, 35
NKVD-NKGB (Soviet State Security), 252
Nomonhan, 16, 170
Nomura, Naokuni, Admiral, 162, 163, 170
Norway, 19, 45, 46, 49, 52, 67, 70
Nosenko, I. I., Shipbuilding Commissar, 84
NSPR, see People's Socialist Party of Russia

Occupation Headquarters, US (Japan), 155
Odessa Military District, 80, 83, 86
ODNR, see Liberation Movement of the
    Peoples of Russia
Office of Strategic Services (OSS), 37
Officer corps: German, 233–35; Soviet, 261,
    262, 263
Okamoto, Kiyomoto, General, 176
OKH, see High Command, German Army
Okuma, Shigenobu, 164
Oni ne propali bez vesti, 271
Onodera, Makoto, Major General, 154, 169
Order No. 227, Soviet, 1942, 147, 256
Ordnung Hilfspolizei, 240, 241
Ordnungdienst (Odi), 241
Organisation of Ukrainian Nationalists
    (OUN), 244
Organised crime, Japanese (boryokudan), 151
Orphans, Soviet, 273
Orsha conference, November 1941, 214, 215
Ōshima Hiroshi, Ambassador, 15, 16, 66, 70,
    150, 162, 164, 168, 173, 177, 178, 182
OSS, see Office of Strategic Services
Ostlegionen, 269, 241
Ostović, P. D., 39
Ott, Eugen, Colonel, 158, 159, 160, 168, 169,
    220
Ott, Mrs, 158, 159
OUN, see Organisation of Ukrainian
    Nationalists
Ozaki, Hotsumi, 181

Pabst, Willy, 37
Pacific Fleet, Soviet, 180
Pacific War (Taiheiyo Senso), 151
Pact of Steel, 1939, 11, 17
Palairet, Michael C., Sir, 36
Pan-Germanism, 234
Pan-Slavism, 234
Panzer-Verluste Ost, 268
Partisans, Soviet, 247, 270, 271
Paul, Prince Regent of Yugoslavia, 26, 34, 35,
    36, 58

Paulus, Friedrich von, Field Marshal, 39, 77
Pavlov, D. G., General, 89, 90, 145
Paxton, Bernard, US Colonel, 37
Pay scales, German occupied Russia, 250
Pearl Harbor, 179
People's Socialist Party of Russia (NSPR), 244, 245
Permanently operating factors, Stalinist doctrine, 144
Persia, 53
Persian Gulf, 23, 25
Pétain, Henri Philippe, Marshal, 22
Petrov, B. N., 146
Petrov, V., Soviet defector, 162
Plan for the Defence of the State Frontier, 1940, Soviet, 82
Ploesti oil fields, 23
Poland, 49, 62, 67, 157
Polish underground, 60, 72
Polyakov, L. E., 257, 258
Ponomarenko, P. K., 90
Poskrebyshev, A. N., Stalin's secretary, 85
Pound, Sir Dudley, Admiral of the Fleet, 110, 111, 112, 115
Pravda, 83
Prisoners of war, Soviet, 218, 230, 231, 232, 242, 260, 261, 270
Pronko, Colonel, 258

Radzievskii, A. I., General, 268
Raeder, Erich, Admiral, 48, 161
Railway Enigma, *see* Enigma decrypts
Ramsay Group, 160, 163, 181
Rapallo policy, 11
Raskol'nikov, F. F., 140
Ratnyi podvig zhenshchin, 273
Red Army, 78, 80, 82, 83, 86–7, 90–1, 124–5, 129, 141, 142, 143, 176, 210, 212, 256
Reichenau, Walther, Field Marshal, 231
Reinhardt, Klaus, Lt. General, 99
Reserve Army, German, 219
Rezun, V. B., 146
Ribbentrop, Joachim von, 7, 8, 9, 10, 11, 12, 13, 14, 15, 16, 17, 18, 19, 20, 21, 22, 23, 24, 25, 26, 27, 28, 37, 70, 84, 86, 138, 167, 168, 170, 171, 177, 178, 182
Rittberg, Hans, Count, 242
ROA, *see* Russian Liberation Army
Röling, Dutch judge, 153
Romania, 19, 21, 23, 24, 47
Rommel, Erwin, Field Marshal, 102
RONA, *see* Russian Liberation Peoples' Army
Roosevelt, Franklin Delano, US President, 113, 118, 169, 170, 179
Russian Corps (Serbia), 243
Russian Liberation Army (ROA), 228, 238, 269

Russian Liberation Peoples' Army (RONA), 238
Ryabyshev, D. I., Lt. General, 87, 88
Rychagov, P. V., Lt. General, 80

Sakhalin, 25, 171
Sakharov, Andrei, 227
Samoilovich, Major, 81
Scavenius, Danish minister, 220
Schenkendorf, General, 242
Schmidt, General, 231
Scholl, Erwin, Captain, 160
Schulenburg, Friedrich Verner, von der, Count, 27, 86
Schutzmannschaft (*Schuma*), 241
Schweppenburg, Geyr von, General, 234
Sealion (*Seelöwe*) Operation, 20, 44, 47, 54, 61, 62, 65, 82
Second Fleet, Japanese, 180
Second Front, 97, 108, 114, 115
Second Vienna Award, 30 August 1940, 19
Secret Intelligence Service (SIS), 45, 49, 52, 53, 54, 60, 63, 72
Security Service (SD), German, 182
Seeckt, Hans von, Colonel General, 160
Semyonov, K., 78
Sergeeva, A. V., 251
Seton-Watson, Hugh, Professor, 38
Shakhurin, A. I., 131
Sham, German radio deception, 68
Shaposhnikov, B. M., Marshal, 82, 98, 145, 263
Shigemitsu, Mamoru, 167
Shiratori, Toshio, 16, 154, 165, 167
Shirer, William, 39
Shomody, V. K., Major General, 271
Shone, Terence, Sir, 36
Siebel ferries, 67
Sigint, 45, 63, 64, 68, 72
Silver, Brian, Dr, 258
Simonov, Konstantin, 81
Simović, Dušan, General, 26, 35, 37, 38
Sino–Soviet Non-Aggression Pact, 1937, 170
SIS, *see* Secret Intelligence Service
Slovakia, 49
Smirnov, Ye. I., Colonel General, 266
Smuts, Jan Christian, Field Marshal, 43
Smyslovskii, B. A., 243
Sobennikov, P. P., Lt. General, 87
Sokolov, B. V., 259
Solzhenitsyn, Alexander, 227
Sorge, Richard, Dr, 159, 160, 161, 163, 169, 172, 181
Soviet of Workers and Peasants Defence, 128
Soviet–German Non-Aggression Treaty (Nazi–Soviet Pact 1939), 7, 83, 139, 140, 163, 124
Soviet–Japanese Neutrality Pact, 1941, 152

Soviet–Yugoslav Non-Aggression Pact, 5
    April 1941, 35
Spain, 47
Special Operations Executive, 106
Speer, Albert, 219
Spitfire, British fighter aircraft, 130
Spitsbergen, 112, 113, 114
Stalin, Josif, 4, 5, 13, 14, 15, 18, 19, 20, 21,
    23, 34, 43, 56, 57, 63, 66, 67, 76, 78, 79,
    81, 82, 83, 86, 87, 88, 90, 98, 101, 104,
    108, 110, 111, 112, 114, 117, 118, 125,
    126, 127, 128, 129, 134, 136, 138, 139,
    140, 141, 142, 143, 144, 145, 146, 147,
    152, 157, 163, 164, 165, 180, 213, 215,
    256, 263
Stalingrad, 77, 273
Stanhope, Lord, First Lord of Admiralty, 14
State Defence Committee, 123, 128, 130
State Department, secret documents of, 51
Stavka, 127, 143
Stoeckli, Fritz, Colonel, 263, 266
Straits Convention, 21
Streit, Christian, Dr, 270
Suez, 66, 209
Sugiyama, Gen, General, 171
Sweden, 24, 56
Syria, 43, 53, 54, 66, 102

Taifun, see Typhoon
Tankovyi udar, 268
Tanks, Soviet, 87, 268
Tatsumi, Eichi, Lt. General, 154
The Cost of the War to Russia, 255
The Peoples' Voice, 243, 245
The Tasks of the Political Propaganda in the
    Red Army in the Immediate Future,
    document, 1941, 79
Thomas, Georg, General, 215, 219
Thrace, 48
Timoshenko, S. K., Marshal, 79, 80, 81, 82,
    86, 88, 98, 126, 127, 129, 143, 145, 212
Todt, Fritz, Dr, 219
Tōjō, Hideki, General, 152, 154
Tokyo garrison, mutiny (ni-niroku jihen,
    1936), 155
Tokyo International War Crimes Tribunal,
    152, 153
Toyoda, Teijirō, Admiral, 172
Trans-Siberian Railway, 60
Transcaucasia, 209
Transit Agreement, Finnish–German, 1940,
    19
Treaty of Craiova, 7 September 1940, 19
Tripartite Pact (Germany, Italy, Japan), 27
    September 1940, 19, 167, 170, 172
Trusov, Major General, 77
Tsena pobedy, 257
Tukhachevskii, M. N., Marshal, 124
Tupikov, G. N., Lt. General, 36

Tupitsin, M. N., 90
Turkey, 22, 24, 47, 53, 55, 69, 137, 209
Typhoon, Operation, 144, 211–14

Ueda, Kankichi, General, 160
Ukraine, 44, 50, 59, 60, 63, 69
Ukranian Revolutionary Army (UPA), 269
Ultra, Intercepts, 101
United States of America, 21, 22, 113, 116,
    118, 154, 157, 163, 167, 171, 173, 174,
    175, 178, 179, 180, 181, 183, 208, 209,
    220, 221
Untermensch, 255
UPA, see Ukrainian Revolutionary Army
Urban life, German occupied Russia, 250, 251
US post-war strategy, Asia, 153
USA, see United States of America
Ushiba, Nobuhiko, 154

Vansittart, Sir Robert, 10, 13, 14
Varennikov, I. S., General, 87
Vashugin, N. I., Corp Commissar, 88
Vasil'chenko, K. F., Colonel, 147
Vasilevskii, A. M., Marshal, 82, 145
Vatutin, N. F., General, 127, 145
Vauhnik, Vladimir, Colonel, 36, 37
Vichy France, 21, 28
Viking (Vitiaz), as NSPR, 244, 245
Vivian, R. N., Captain, 162
Vlasov, A. A., Lt. General, 228, 239, 240,
    244, 245, 263
Voenno-istoricheskii zhurnal, 259
Voina i meditsina, 266
Volga Tartars, 241
Völkischer Beobachter, 213
Volkogonov, D., Colonel General, 3, 5, 143
Voretzsch, Ambassador, 159
Voronezh, 273
Voroshilov, K. E., Marshal, 131
Voskoboinikov, K. P., 243, 244, 245
Voznesenskii, N. A., 80, 128
Vyshinskii, A. Ya., 51, 57

Waffen-SS, 235
Waffenverband, SS, 269
Wang Ching-wei, 172
War bride cohort, Russian, 258
War Cabinet, British, 103, 115
War Department (US), 153
War Office, British, 46, 59, 111, 154
War-widow cohort, Russian, 258
Warsaw rising, 245
Wavell, Sir Archibold, Field Marshal, 102
Weekly intelligence summary, War Office, 59
Wegner, Bernd, 235
Wehrmachtabteilung, 158
Weizsäcker, Ernst, von, 10, 26, 27, 28, 86
Welles, Sumner, US, Under-Sec. of State, 34

Wenneker, Paul, Admiral, 160, 161, 162, 165, 171, 173, 177, 178, 181
Western Special Military District, 80, 83, 85, 86
Wetzell, General, 160
Whaley, Barton, 36
Wilhelm II, Kaiser, 28
Willoughby, Charles A., Major General, 183
Wiskemann, Elizabeth, 39
Wohlthat, Helmut, 171
Women, Soviet, at war, 261, 270
Woodward, Sir LLewellyn, historian, 34

Xian Incident, 156

Yakovlev, N. D., Marshal, 131

Yakovlev, A. N., 136
Yakovleva, A. K., 251
Yazov, D. T., Marshal, 98, 136
Yeltsin, B. N., 135, 150
Yoshida, Shigeru, 154
Yoshida administration, 153
Yugoslavia, 19, 24, 26, 55, 56, 57
Yugoslavia faces the future, 39

Zaporozhets, A. I., 79, 80
Zhdanov, A. A., 80
Zhilin, P. A., Lt. General, 142
Zhukov, G. K., Marshal, 80, 81, 82, 86, 88, 98, 126, 127, 129, 143, 145, 147, 213
Zigeunerbaron, anti-partisan operation, 271
Zinich, M. S., Professor, 273